HARRIET MA...

(1802–1876) was born in Nor... children in a strongly Unitarian family, and the da... of a successful cloth manufacturer. Her childhood was an unhappy one: she felt herself neglected and unloved. Suffering continually from ill-health, she was nevertheless well-educated, at a local Unitarian school and a boarding school in Bristol – though her education was interrupted by advancing deafness, requiring her to use an ear trumpet in later life.

Harriet Martineau's first article, 'Female Writers of Practical Divinity' was published when she was nineteen in a Unitarian magazine, *Monthly Repository*, to which she became a regular contributor. Her twenties were beset by misfortune: the death of her eldest brother was followed, in 1826, by that of her father. Then her fiancé died, and in 1829 the family business finally collapsed, leaving the Martineaus penniless. This was the turning point in Harriet's life.

Unable, because of her deafness, to become a governess like her sisters, she contributed to the family income through her writing: no longer made to put it aside in favour of more 'womanly' pursuits, she became the bread-winner of the family. With the enormous success of her twenty-four part series, *Illustrations of Political Economy*, she became a literary celebrity and moved to London. At the age of thirty-five, she was offered the editorship of a new economics periodical, but her adored brother James disapproved, and so she refused it. Instead she turned to fiction and wrote *Deerbrook* (also published by Virago). She then collapsed into bed where she was to remain for the next five years.

In 1855, thinking that she was about to die, she wrote her autobiography at break-neck speed – and lived for another twenty years. In those years, the happiest of her life, she wrote widely and prolifically on the enfranchise-ment of women, the abolition of slavery, education, travel and hypnotism. Harriet Martineau died at the age of seventy-four and was buried, by her own wishes, without religious rites.

*Harriet Martineau
1833*

HARRIET MARTINEAU'S
AUTOBIOGRAPHY

VOL. I.

With a New Introduction by Gaby Weiner

'Etiam capillus unus habet umbram suam'—PROVERB

'And this dear freedom hath begotten me this peace,
that I mourn not that end which must be,
nor spend one wish to have one minute added
to the uncertain date of my years'—BACON

Published by VIRAGO PRESS Limited 1983
41 William IV Street, London WC2N 4DB

First published in Great Britain in three volumes,
the first two containing the complete text of the
Autobiography, and the third including memorials
by Maria Weston Chapman, by Smith, Elder, & Co., 1877

Virago edition offset from Smith,
Elder, & Co., third edition 1877

Introduction copyright © Gaby Weiner 1983

British Library Cataloguing in Publication Data

Martineau, Harriet
    Autobiography of Harriet Martineau.
    Vol. 1.
    1. Martineau, Harriet 1802–1876—Biography
    2. Authors, English—19th century—Biography
    I. Title
    828′.809   PR4984.M5Z/
    ISBN 0-86068-425-3

The cover shows a detail from an illustration
of the house in which Harriet Martineau was
born and an early portrait, both reprinted in
the Smith, Elder, & Co., 1877 edition.

Printed in Finland by Werner Söderström Oy,
a member of Finnprint

CONTENTS

OF

THE FIRST VOLUME.

———◆◇◆———

PERIOD III.

TO THIRTY YEARS OLD.

PERIOD IV.

TO THIRTY-SEVEN YEARS OLD.

HOUSE IN WHICH HARRIET MARTINEAU WAS BORN

INTRODUCTION

> In the paths where Harriet Martineau trod at first
> almost all alone, many women are now following. Serious
> studies, political activity, a share in social reforms, an
> independent, self-supporting career, and freedom of
> thought and expression, are, by the conditions of our
> age, becoming open to thousands of women who would
> never have dared to claim them in the circumstances in
> which she first did so...
>
> More and more it will be customary for women to
> study such subjects as Harriet Martineau studied; more
> commonplace will it constantly become for women to
> use all their mental faculties and to exert everyone of
> their powers to the fullest extent in the highest freedom.[1]

So wrote one of Harriet Martineau's more youthful contemporaries eight years after the famous author's death
and at the beginning of the long struggle for political
equality which was to characterize the nineteenth
century women's movement. The achievements of this
eminent Victorian radical were many: she was an early
feminist, an international authority on the science of
political economy, a fervent advocate of the abolition
of slavery, a writer on numerous contemporary issues
and a brilliant and prolific journalist.

She became an acknowledged writer on politics and
economics at a time when it was virtually unknown for
a woman to enter these traditionally exclusive male
spheres, and wrote books and articles on the important

and popular issues of the day. Among the fifty or so books she wrote in her long career were volumes on travel, mesmerism (hypnotism), education, political reform, history, biography and religion.

She was an acute observer of the social scene, travelling widely in England and Scotland as well as overseas, and those chapters in the *Autobiography* which include descriptions of the political and intellectual élite of the day are amongst the most delightful and perceptive in the book.

She was also an outstanding writer of popular journalism (much of her work for the *Daily News* was undertaken after the period covered in the *Autobiography*), and a novelist of some repute.

In her main works, and also in her journalistic articles, she translated difficult and obscure themes for ordinary people and, given the didactic form of many of her works, was surprisingly popular with the Victorian reading public.

Harriet Martineau wrote her *Autobiography* in 1855 in three months, at breakneck speed, when she believed that death was imminent. She had thought seriously about it at two earlier stages of her life; in 1831 before she became famous, and during her first major illness, in the 1840s. She now felt, once more, that she should record her lifetime's experiences and her political and theological philosophies before her death, for two reasons; first, as a champion of truth and objectivity, she felt under an obligation to provide for posterity a true account of her life, and second, she believed she needed to explain her progression from Unitarianism to secular enlightenment: 'The most important part [of the *Autobiography*] is the true account of my conscious transition from the Xn [Christian] faith to my present philosophy.'[2]

She was convinced that she was dying; in fact she lived for a further twenty-one years. She did not alter or add to the *Autobiography*, however, but asked her close friend, Maria Weston Chapman, to write a third volume describing and commenting on the last years of her life. The two-volume *Autobiography* can be appreciated at several levels. It is an absorbing portrayal of the feelings, experiences and beliefs of an exceptional nineteenth-century woman, 'the first of the notable Englishwomen of the Nineteenth Century'.[3] It is a success story of the romantic kind – an unhappy childhood, an abortive love affair, fame at almost the first attempt, acceptance on a social level by the most important in the land, culminating in a long period of security and contentment. It can also be considered as a candid and dispassionate portrayal of early nineteenth-century middle-class culture and behaviour.

Many of the themes which were of central concern to the Victorian political and intellectual élite are to be found in her autobiography. Religious and philosophical considerations had a substantial place in the thoughts and ideas of the time, and even though, for Harriet Martineau, traditional religious creeds held little significance, she spent a great deal of time and energy defining and clarifying her own particular theological position. She used the *Autobiography* to explain her transition from Necessarian Unitarianism to secular rationalism, in the hope of confounding her critics.

Brought up as a Unitarian, she had been encouraged to regard the Scriptures as a historical, as well as a divine record and to believe that by the use of free and impartial reason, the Bible would clarify the 'natural' laws of science and society as well as giving guidance on faith and religious practice. Harriet Martineau further believed that if these 'natural' laws were learnt and understood, each social class and each section of society would come to accept that individual and social improvement could only be attained through mutual cooperation. Hence her concern to interpret complicated economic principles for the benefit of *all* sectors of the population.

In her early twenties she was converted to Necessarianism and its acceptance of the 'First Cause' as a universal and immutable law in which lay the origins of the spontaneous movements of society. Thus individuals had no choice but to act according to the laws of Nature. Only through education did she see a solution to the social problems of the day; people needed to be taught to understand and appreciate these 'natural' laws and then encouraged to plan for a better society.

After an extended visit to Palestine where she came to understand the relative moral frameworks of the different Eastern religions, she rejected the notion of a personal god and made the final transition to atheism and the belief in individual improvement through science, social reform and self-interest.

In parallel with her religious transformation and perhaps influenced by it, Harriet Martineau also underwent a total psychological metamorphosis. She described her unhappy childhood years as the winter of her life, the decades of achievement and fame in London as its stormy spring, and the productive and contented years at Ambleside as summer and autumn combined. She wrote: 'My life, as it has been seen, began with winter. Then followed a season of storm and sunshine.'[4]

The *Autobiography* gives a tantalizing glimpse of the rigours of an early nineteenth-century domestic household and the terrors it held for an anxious, frightened, withdrawn little girl who was afraid of the shadows and who was a constant irritant to a somewhat cool and unsympathetic family.

As she grew up and found the solution to some of her problems – financial insecurity, a need to achieve, emotional instability – in a literary career, and eventually attained recognition, prosperity and contentment, Harriet Martineau consistently displayed a belief in the ultimate perfectibility of the human race. 'Martineau's *Autobiography* is firmly organised as a progress away

from the isolated I-ness, a pilgrimage toward a nurturing
truth which would connect her to a larger whole.'[5]

Another issue of considerable concern to the early
Victorians was education; whether it should be extended to the masses and, if so, which form should it
take; if it should be offered to girls or whether study
might affect the reproductive functions of womanhood.
It will come as no surprise that Harriet Martineau was
one of the earliest and most insistent advocates of
education for all.

In the 1840s, she lobbied for a national system of
education, criticizing the system of parliamentary
grants on the basis that it offered support for existing
educational initiatives rather than expanding provision
for working-class children. In the next two decades she
turned her attention to the school curriculum, coming
to the conclusion that vocational as well as intellectual
training was vital.

> We still cling too much to the idea of books as the only
> education. Education still means books in the case of
> our nobles and gentry and, by a natural transference, in
> that of our young 'workies'. But we are growing wiser –
> learning to see that the grasp of realities, the cordial
> shaking of hands with nature, in industrial training, is
> as good for the intellect as books are for the expansion
> of the moral as well as the intellectual part of man.[6]

She was particularly concerned about extending educational opportunities for girls and women and regretted
the need for women to hide their intellectual efforts in
order to retain social acceptability.

> When I was young, it was not thought proper for young
> ladies to study very conspicuously; and especially with
> pen in hand. Young ladies (at least in provincial towns)
> were expected to sit down in the parlour to sew, – during
> which reading aloud was permitted, – or to practice
> their music; but so as to receive callers, without any
> signs of blue stockingism which could be reported
> abroad.[7]

She had derived enormous benefit and pleasure from her own broad education (exceptionally so for a girl growing up in the first two decades of the nineteenth century) and become a forceful advocate of female education, for two main reasons: first, as a means of expanding the intellect of women so that they would become better wives, mothers and daughters, and second, for employment and economic independence.

> So far from our country-women being all maintained as a matter of course by us, the breadwinners,* three million out of six adult Englishwomen work for sub-sistence; and two out of three for independence – we must improve and extend education to the utmost; and then open a fair field to the powers and energies we have educed. This will secure our welfare nationally and in our homes.[8]

Harriet Martineau's pre-occupation with the 'Woman Question' and her considerable commitment to extend-ing employment and political, as well as educational opportunities for women, has been noted but given little credit, by her biographers. Though she wrote prolifically on a wide range of subjects, there was almost always a section of each book devoted to an aspect of female injustice. The *Autobiography* is no exception and, in fact, gives a clear indication of her particular brand of feminism.

> Nobody can be further than I am from being satisfied with the condition of my own sex; under the law and custom of my own country. . . . Often as I am appealed to, to speak, or otherwise assist in the promotion of the cause of Woman, my answer is always the same: – that women, like men, can obtain whatever they show them-selves fit for. Let them be educated, – let their powers be cultivated to the extent for which the means are

---

* This article was written anonymously, as were many of her newspaper and journal articles. Harriet Martineau often implied that her articles had a male author (see above 'us, the breadwinners'), presumably to give them added weight.

already provided, and all that is wanted or ought to be desired will follow of course. Whatever a woman proves able to do, society will be thankful to see her do, – just as if she were a man. If she is scientific, science will welcome her, as it has welcomed every woman so qualified.[9]

Her feminism was a response to several powerful calls on her intellect; her outrage at any social prejudice or injustice (also characterized by her passionate stand against slavery); the impact of Necessarianism and its implied belief in human perfectibility regardless of sex; and her need, from a comparatively early age, to be economically independent.

Whilst she supported many women's initiatives in her lifetime and, in fact, articles written by her were instrumental in the establishment of two of the most influential feminist pressure groups of the nineteenth century, she never identified herself too closely with other feminists, possibly because she needed the approval of the literary establishment in order to earn her own living. Nevertheless the Society for Promoting the Employment of Women (the Langham Circle) took inspiration from an article entitled 'Female Industry' written in 1859, and the movement led by Josephine Butler for the repeal of the notorious Contagious Diseases Acts drew on a series of articles written in the *Daily News* in 1863.

Unitarianism played a considerable part in Harriet Martineau's life, not only because the Unitarian concepts of natural rights, freedom and toleration provided a firm foundation for her beliefs but also because of the literary and social connections which it offered. William James Fox, the Unitarian editor of the *Monthly Repository* for which she first wrote, was supportive of her earliest literary efforts and was instrumental in the publication of her best selling series, *Illustrations of Political Economy*. She wrote that it was at Fox's dining table that she witnessed the first meeting between John

Stuart Mill and his future wife, Harriet Taylor. The Unitarian connection enabled her to mix socially and correspond with Elizabeth Gaskell, Mary Carpenter, George Eliot, Mary Somerville, William Godwin (husband of Mary Wollstonecraft), the Brownings and Florence Nightingale among other eminent individuals.

Although not brought up as a Unitarian, Florence Nightingale received a sound Classical education from her Unitarian father, and was familiar with Unitarian thoughts and ideas. A similar education and shared interest in reform and social improvement led to a long and intimate correspondence between the two women. They both felt an immense need to exercise influence; Florence Nightingale focused her efforts on medical and army reform; Harriet Martineau concentrated on the abolition of slavery, economic change and the 'Woman Question'.

Florence Nightingale's memory of Harriet Martineau was as a fighter for justice – somewhat in the 'Nightingale' mould.

> She was born to be a destroyer of slavery, in whatever form, in whatever place, all over the world, wherever she saw or thought she saw it.
> The thought actually inspired her, whether in the degraded offspring of former English poor-law, of English serfdom forty years ago, – in any shape; whether in the fruits of any abuse, – social, legislative, or administrative, – or in actual slavery; or be it in the Contagious Diseases Acts, or no matter what, she rose to the occasion.[10]

It will come as no surprise that because she wrote authoritatively about subjects which many of her contemporaries reserved exclusively for men, Harriet Martineau became a target for considerable abuse during her lifetime, particularly at the time of the political economy series. Whilst few went as far as a Mr MacFarlain who described her as a 'rampant rationalist, a prophetess of mesmerism, an ill-favoured dogmatizing,

masculine spinster',[11] many of the criticisms made of
her were personal rather than professional. Some
focused on her appearance, 'compared with *her*, (Lord)
Brougham's face was charming';[12] others on her womanhood and unmarried, childless state.

The male press was particularly horrified when she
suggested that population control and celibacy could
provide a solution to overcrowding and unemployment.
The *Quarterly Review* wrote: 'But no; – such a character
is nothing to a female Malthusian. A woman who thinks
child-bearing is a crime against society. An unmarried
woman who declaims against marriage.'[13]

Fraser's Magazine was no less outraged: 'That is
indeed a wonder that such themes should occupy the
pen of any lady, old or young, without exciting a disgust
nearly approaching horror.'[14]

Harriet Martineau was remarkably stoical about at-
tacks on her femininity, preferring to ignore or forget the
statements of her most critical reviewers. Whilst she
never forgot or forgave the vitriolic of the *Quarterly
Review*, the *Autobiography* is highly selective in its
inclusion of reviewers' comments, inclining towards the
favourable rather than the hostile. One suspects that
this apparent distortion of the truth was the uninten-
tional consequence of a highly selective memory rather
than a deliberate manipulation of reality.

As she grew older, Harriet Martineau became dis-
missive of her earlier literary efforts and was modest to
the extreme about the quality and importance of her
life's work. In her own obituary, written by Harriet for
the *Daily News* some years before her death, she was
moderate in her appraisal:

> Her original power was nothing more than was due to
> earnestness and intellectual clearance within a certain
> range. With small imaginative and suggestive powers,
> and therefore nothing approaching genius, she could
> clearly see what she did see, and give a clear expression
> to what she had to say.[15]

Harriet Martineau is important and interesting for several reasons. Many of the topics on which she wrote have little relevance today; however, her work discloses the thoughts and pre-occupations of the early- and mid-nineteenth century from a viewpoint hitherto little known or understood. The candour and lack of sentimentality with which it is written is one refreshing aspect of her autobiography. However, the knowledge that Martineau's interpretation of middle-class intellectual life was deeply offensive to some of her contemporaries gives twentieth century readers an idea of the social conventions and concerns of the time. One reviewer greeted the *Autobiography* with these words:

> The tone in which she speaks of at least half of her London acquaintances, her sketches of friends and foe alike, the sovereign contempt in the one set of portraits, the rancorous animosity in the other, and the utter injustice and almost libellous character of many, are probably the features of the book which will leave the most painful impression.[16]

It is difficult to understand, today, why its publication was so controversial. Whilst she did have criticisms to make of her professional relationships with some individuals (she quarrelled with Dickens about his portrayal of women as, 'viz., to dress well and look pretty, as an adornment to the homes of men'), many of her portraits are affectionately drawn, although never sentimental.

Of Wordsworth, whom she lived near and knew personally, she wrote as a neighbour as well as a literary critic. After discussing his importance as a poet at some length, she wrote,

> In regard to politics, however, and even to religion, he grew more and more liberal in his latter years. It is in that view, and as a neighbour among the cottagers, that he is most genially remembered: and considering the course of flattery he was subjected to by his blue-stocking and clerical neighbours, who coaxed him into

a monologue, and then wrote down all he said for future
publication, it is wonderful that there is any thing so
genial to record.[17]

Her friendship with Charlotte Brontë is described at
some length although their period of familiarity was cut
short by Charlotte's premature death. Harriet had
greatly liked *Jane Eyre* and was certain that Currer
Bell was indeed a woman. 'I made up my mind...that
a certain passage in *Jane Eyre* about sewing on brass
rings, could have been written only by a woman or an
upholsterer.'[18]

Impressed by Harriet's first novel, *Deerbrook*, Charlotte sent her a copy of her own latest book, *Shirley*, 'in
acknowledgement of the pleasure and profit' she had
derived from Harriet's work. A meeting between the
two women was then arranged which Harriet described
with some tenderness.

When she was seated by me on the sofa, she cast up at
me such a look – so loving, so appealing, – that, in
connexion with her deep mourning dress, and the knowledge that she was the sole survivor of her family, I could
with the utmost difficulty return her smile, or keep my
composure. I should have been heartily glad to cry.[19]

Critical though some of the reviewers were of her
work, others were more admiring of Harriet Martineau's
skills and importance as a writer and autobiographer,
and were appreciative of those qualities which set her
apart from her fellow writers. One wrote:

In all her estimates of her powers, Harriet Martineau
rather undervalues herself than otherwise. She denies
herself genius, and using the word in its highest sense,
we must admit that the denial speaks only the truth.
But if there is such a thing as *interpretive genius*, she
was an extraordinary instance of it.[20]

The *Autobiography* may not be as truthful or objective as Harriet Martineau intended; it may indeed be
'less a confessional than a memoir and less an analysis

than a narrative'.[21] However, it is an immensely read-
able portrayal of the life of a then famous but now
nearly forgotten nineteenth century intellectual, commenting on the domestic and the personal, as well as
the social and the political.

Written by an exceptional journalist and trenchant
observer of the contemporary social scene, the re-issue
of this autobiography is a notable event.

Gaby Weiner, London 1982

NOTES

1. F. Fenwick-Miller, *Harriet Martineau*, (Eminent Women
   Series), W. H. Allen, London, 1889, pp. 221–2.
2. Harriet Martineau, letter to G. J. Holyoake, 15 February
   1855, British Museum.
3. W. H. Davenport, *Celebrated Englishwomen of the Victorian
   Era*, F. V. White & Co., London, 1884, p. 63.
4. Harriet Martineau, *Autobiography*, Smith, Elder, & Co.,
   London, 1877, Vol. 2, p. 205.
5. M. Myers, 'Harriet Martineau's Autobiography: The Making
   of a Female Philosopher' in *Women's Autobiography*, ed.
   Jelinek, E. C., Indiana University Press, 1980, p. 69.
6. Harriet Martineau, *Daily News*, 22 March 1853.
7. Martineau, *Autobiography*, op. cit., Vol. 1, p. 100.
8. Harriet Martineau, 'Female Industry' in *Edinburgh Review*,
   London, 1859, p. 336.
9. Martineau *Autobiography*, op. cit., Vol. 1, pp. 400–1.
10. M. Weston-Chapman, *Memorials*, letter from F. N., Smith,
    Elder, & Co., 1877, p. 479.
11. E. Boyle, *Biographical Essays 1790–1890*, Oxford Uni-
    versity Press, London, 1936, p. 182.
12. ibid., p. 182.
13. *Quarterly Review*, Chap. 7, No. XCVII, April 1833.
14. *Fraser's Magazine*, November 1833.
15. Harriet Martineau, 'Obituary' in *Daily News*, 29 June 1876.
16. W. R. Gregg, 'Harriet Martineau' in *Nineteenth Century*,
    ed. Knowles, J., Vol. Aug–Dec 1877, Henry S. King & Co.,
    London.
17. Martineau, *Autobiography*, op. cit., Vol. 2, p. 240.
18. ibid., Vol. 2, p. 324.
19. ibid., Vol. 2, p. 326.
20. H. S. Richardson, 'Harriet Martineau's Account of Herself'
    in *Contemporary Review*, London, 1877, Vol. 29, p. 112.
21. V. K. Pichanick, *Harriet Martineau: The Woman and Her
    Work*, University of Michigan, 1980, p. 201.

INTRODUCTION

HARRIET MARTINEAU'S AUTOBIOGRAPHY.

AMBLESIDE, March, 1855.

FROM MY YOUTH UPWARDS I have felt that it was one
of the duties of my life to write my autobiography
I have always enjoyed, and derived profit from, reading those of other persons, from the most meagre to
the fullest : and certain qualities of my own mind,—
a strong consciousness and a clear memory in regard
to my early feelings,—have seemed to indicate to
me the duty of recording my own experience. When
my life became evidently a somewhat remarkable
one, the obligation presented itself more strongly to
my conscience : and when I made up my mind to
interdict the publication of my private letters, the
duty became unquestionable. For thirteen or fourteen years it has been more or less a weight on
my mind that the thing was not done. Twice in my

VOL. I.   A

life I made a beginning; once in 1831, and again about ten years later, during my long illness at Tynemouth : but both attempts stopped short at an early period, answering no other purpose than preserving some facts of my childhood which I might otherwise have forgotten. Of late years, I have often said to my most intimate friends that I felt as if I could not die in peace till this work was done ; and there has been no lack of encouragement and instigation on their part : but, while I was in health, there was always so much to do that was immediately wanted, that, as usually happens in such cases, that which was not immediately necessary was deferred. At the beginning of this last winter, however, I had hopes of being able to unite my political work with this ; and on New Year's Day I said to myself that the year must not close without my having recorded the story of my life. I was probably strengthened in this purpose by having for some time past felt that my energies were declining, and that I had no longer a right to depend on being able to do whatever I chose. Two or three weeks more settled the business. Feeling very unwell, I went to London to obtain a medical opinion in regard to my health. Two able physicians informed me that I had a mortal disease, which might spare me some considerable space of life, but which might, as likely as not, destroy me at any moment. No doubt could remain after this as to what my next employment should be : and as soon after my return home as I had settled my business with my Executor, I began this autobiography. I thought it best to rewrite the early portion, that the whole might be offered from one point of view, and in a consistent spirit. Without any personal desire about living a few months or weeks more or less, I rather hope that I may be able to finish my story with my own hands. If not, it will be done by another, from materials of more or less value. But one part which ought to be done by myself is the statement of my reasons for so serious a step as forbidding the publication of my private correspondence; and I therefore stop at the Third Period of my Memoir, to write this Introduction, to the following passages of which I request the reader's earnest attention.

I admit, at the outset, that it is rather a piece of self-denial in me to interdict the publication of my letters. I have no solicitude about fame, and no fear of my reputation of any sort being injured by the publication of any thing I have ever put upon paper. My opinions and feelings have been remarkably open to the world; and my position has been such as to impose no reserves on a disposition naturally open and communicative; so that if any body might acquiesce in the publication of correspondence, it should be myself. Moreover, I am disposed to think that what my friends tell me is true ; that it would be rather an advantage to me than the contrary to be known by my private letters. All these considerations point out to me that I am therefore precisely the person to bear emphatic practical testimony on behalf of the principle of the privacy of epistolary intercourse; and therefore it is that I do hereby bear that testimony.

Epistolary correspondence is written speech; and the *onus* rests with those who publish it to show why the laws of honour which are uncontested in regard to conversation may be violated when the conversation is written instead of spoken. The plea is the utility of such material for biographical purposes; but who would admit that plea in regard to fireside conversation? The most valuable conversation, and that which best illustrates character, is that which passes between two friends, with their feet on the fender, on winter nights, or in a summer ramble : but what would be thought of the traitor who should supply such material for biographical or other purposes? How could human beings ever open their hearts and minds to each other, if there were no privacy guaranteed by principles and feelings of honour? Yet has this security lapsed from that half of human conversation which is written instead of spoken. Whether there is still time to restore it, I know not : but I have done my part towards an attempted restoration by a stringent provision in my Will against any public use whatever being made of my letters, unless I should myself authorize the publication of some, which will, in that case, be of some public interest, and not confidential letters. Most of my friends have burnt my letters,—partly because they knew my desire thus to enforce my assertion of the principle, and partly because it was less painful to destroy them while I was still among them than to escape the importunities of hunters of material after my death. Several eminent persons of this century have taken stringent precautions against the same mischief; and very many more, I fear, have taken the more painful precaution of writing no letters which any body would care to have. Seventy years ago, Dr. Johnson said in conversation 'It is now become so much the fashion to publish letters, that, in order to

avoid it, I put as little into mine as I can.' Nobody
will question the hardship and mischief of a practice
which acts upon epistolary correspondence as the spy
system under a despotism acts upon speech: and when
we find that a half a dozen of the greatest minds of
our time have deprived themselves and their friends of
their freedom of epistolary speech for the same reason,
it does seem to be time that those qualified to bear
testimony against such an infringement on personal
liberty should speak out.

'But,' say unscrupulous book-makers and readers,
'there are many eminent persons who are so far from
feeling as you do that they have themselves prepared
for the publication of their letters. There was Doddridge:—he left a copy of every letter and note that he
ever wrote, for this very purpose. There was Madame
D'Arblay:—on her death-bed, and in extreme old age,
she revised and had copies made of all the letters she
received and wrote when in the height of her fame as
Fanny Burney,—preparing for publication the smooth
compliments and monstrous flatteries written by hands
that had long become dust. There was Southey:—he
too kept copies, or left directions, by which he arranged
the method of making his private letters to his friends
property to his heirs. These, and many more, were of
a different way of thinking from you.'—They were
indeed : and my answer is,—what were the letters
worth, as letters, when these arrangements became
known ? What would fireside conversation be worth,
as confidential talk, if it was known that the speaker
meant to make it a newspaper article the next day ?
And when Doddridge's friends, and Southey's, heard
that what they had taken for conversational out-pour-

ing on paper was so much literary production, to appear hereafter in a book,—what was the worth of those much-prized letters then? Would the correspondents not as soon have received a page of a dissertation, or the proof of a review article? Surely the only word necessary as to this part of the question is a word of protest against every body, or every eminent person, being deprived of epistolary liberty because there have been some among their predecessors or contemporaries who did not know how to use it, or happen to value it.

We are recommended, again, to 'leave the matter to the discretion of survivors.' I, for my part, have too much regard for my Executors to bequeath to them any such troublesome office as withstanding the remonstrances of any number of persons who may have a mind to see my letters, or of asserting a principle which it is my business to assert for myself. If they were to publish my letters, they would do what I believe to be wrong: and if they refused to publish them, they might be subject to importunity or censure which I have no right to devolve upon them. And why are we to leave this particular piece of testamentary duty to the discretion of survivors, when we are abundantly exhorted, in the case of every other, to do our own testamentary duty ourselves,—betimes, carefully and conscientiously?

Then comes the profit argument,—the plea of how much the world would have lost without the publication of the letters of A. B. and C. This is true, in a way. The question is whether the world has not lost more by the injury to epistolary freedom than it has gained by reading the letters of nonconsenting letter-writers. There will always be plenty of consenting and willing letter-writers: let society have their letters. But there should be no others,—at least till privacy is altogether abolished as an unsocial privilege. This grossly utilitarian view does not yet prevail; and I do not think it ever will. Meantime, I claim the sanction of every principle of integrity, and every feeling of honour and delicacy, on behalf of my practice. I claim, over and above these, the sanction of the law.—Law reflects the principles of morals; and in this case the mirror presents a clear image of the right and the duty. The law vests the right of publication of private letters solely in the writer, no one else having any such right during the author's life, or after his death, except by his express permission. On the knowledge of this provision I have acted, in my arrangements about my own correspondence; and I trust that others, hitherto unaccustomed to the grave consideration of the subject, will feel, in justice to myself and others who act with me, that there can be no wrong, no moral inexpediency, in the exercise of a right thus expressly protected by the Law. If, by what I have done, I have fixed attention upon the morality of the case, this will be a greater social benefit than the publication of any letters written by me, or by persons far wiser and more accomplished than myself.

I have only to say further, in the way of introduction, a word or two as to my descent and parentage. On occasion of the Revocation of the Edict of Nantes, in 1688, a surgeon of the name of Martineau, and a family of the name of Pierre, crossed the Channel, and settled with other Huguenot refugees, in England. My ancestor married a young lady of the Pierre family, and settled in Norwich, where his descendants afforded a succession of surgeons up to my own day. My eminent uncle, Mr. Philip Meadows Martineau, and my eldest brother, who died before the age of thirty, were the last Norwich surgeons of the name.—My grandfather, who was one of the honourable series, died at the age of forty-two, of a fever caught among his poor patients. He left a large family, of whom my father was the youngest. When established as a Norwich manufacturer, my father married Elizabeth Rankin, the eldest daughter of a sugar-refiner at Newcastle upon Tyne. My father and mother had eight children, of whom I was the sixth: and I was born on the 12th of June, 1802.

HARRIET MARTINEAU'S AUTOBIOGRAPHY.

FIRST PERIOD.

TO EIGHT YEARS OLD.

SECTION I.

My first recollections are of some infantine impressions which were in abeyance for a long course of years, and then revived in an inexplicable way,—as by a flash of lightning over a far horizon in the night. There is no doubt of the genuineness of the remembrance, as the facts could not have been told me by any one else. I remember standing on the threshold of a cottage, holding fast by the doorpost, and putting my foot down, in repeated attempts to reach the ground. Having accomplished the step, I toddled (I remember the uncertain feeling) to a tree before the door, and tried to clasp and get round it; but the rough bark hurt my hands. At night of the same day, in bed, I was disconcerted by the coarse feel of the sheets,—so much less smooth and cold than those at home; and I was alarmed by the creaking of the bedstead when I moved. It was a turn-up bedstead in a cottage, or small farm-house at Carleton, where I

was sent for my health, being a delicate child. My
mother's account of things was that I was all but
starved to death in the first weeks of my life,—the
wetnurse being very poor, and holding on to her good
place after her milk was going or gone. The discovery
was made when I was three months old, and when I
was fast sinking under diarrhœa. My bad health
during my whole childhood and youth, and even my
deafness, was always ascribed by my mother to this.
However it might be about that, my health certainly
was very bad till I was nearer thirty than twenty
years of age; and never was poor mortal cursed with
a more beggarly nervous system. The long years of
indigestion by day and night-mare terrors are mournful to think of now.—Milk has radically disagreed
with me, all my life: but when I was a child, it was
a thing unheard of for children not to be fed on milk:
so, till I was old enough to have tea at breakfast, I
went on having a horrid lump at my throat for hours
of every morning, and the most terrific oppressions
in the night. Sometimes the dim light of the windows in the night seemed to advance till it pressed
upon my eyeballs, and then the windows would seem
to recede to an infinite distance. If I laid my hand
under my head on the pillow, the hand seemed to
vanish almost to a point, while the head grew as big as
a mountain. Sometimes I was panic struck at the
head of the stairs, and was sure I could never get
down; and I could never cross the yard to the garden
without flying and panting, and fearing to look
behind, because a wild beast was after me. The starlight sky was the worst; it was always coming down,
to stifle and crush me, and rest upon my head. I do

not remember any dread of thieves or ghosts in particular; but things as I actually saw them were
dreadful to me; and it now appears to me that I had
scarcely any respite from the terror. My fear of
persons was as great as any other. To the best of
my belief, the first person I was ever not afraid of
was Aunt Kentish, who won my heart and my confidence when I was sixteen. My heart was ready
enough to flow out; and it often did: but I always
repented of such expansion, the next time I dreaded to
meet a human face.—It now occurs to me, and it may
be worth while to note it,—what the extremest terror
of all was about. We were often sent to walk on the
Castle Hill at Norwich. In the wide area below, the
residents were wont to expose their feather-beds, and
to beat them with a stick. That sound,—a dull shock,
—used to make my heart stand still: and it was no
use my standing at the rails above, and seeing the
process. The striking of the blow and the arrival of
the sound did not correspond; and this made matters
worse. I hated that walk; and I believe for that
reason. My parents knew nothing of all this. It never
occurred to me to speak of any thing I felt most: and
I doubt whether they ever had the slightest idea of
my miseries. It seems to me now that a little closer
observation would have shown them the causes of the
bad health and fitful temper which gave them so much
anxiety on my account; and I am sure that a little
more of the cheerful tenderness which was in those
days thought bad for children, would have saved me
from my worst faults, and from a world of suffering.

My hostess and nurse at the above-mentioned cottage was a Mrs. Merton, who was, as was her husband,

a Methodist or melancholy Calvinist of some sort. The family story about me was that I came home the absurdest little preacher of my years (between two and three) that ever was. I used to nod my head emphatically, and say ' Never ky for. tyfles :' ' Dooty fust, and pleasure afterwards,' and so forth : and I sometimes got courage to edge up to strangers, and ask them to give me—' a maxim.' Almost before I could join letters, I got some sheets of paper, and folded them into a little square book, and wrote, in double lines, two or three in a page, my beloved maxims. I believe this was my first effort at book-making. It was probably what I picked up at Carleton that made me so intensely religious as I certainly was from a very early age. The religion was of a bad sort enough, as might be expected from the urgency of my needs ; but I doubt whether I could have got through without it. I pampered my vain-glorious propensities by dreams of divine favour, to make up for my utter deficiency of self-respect : and I got rid of otherwise incessant remorse by a most convenient confession and repentance, which relieved my nerves without at all, I suspect, improving my conduct.

To revert to my earliest recollections :—I certainly could hardly walk alone when our nursemaid took us, —including my sister Elizabeth, who was eight years older tban myself,—an unusual walk ; through a lane, (afterwards called by us the ' Spinner's Lane ') where some Miss Taskers, acquaintances of Elizabeth's and her seniors, were lodging, in a cottage which had a fir grove behind it. Somebody set me down at the foot of a fir, where I was distressed by the slight rising of the ground at the root, and by the long grass, which seemed a terrible entanglement. I looked up the tree, and was scared at its height, and at that of so many others. I was comforted with a fir-cone; and then one of the Miss Taskers caught me up in her arms and kissed me; and I was too frightened to cry till we got away.—I was not more than two years old when an impression of touch occurred to me which remains vivid to this day. It seems indeed as if impressions of touch were at that age more striking than those from the other senses. I say this from observation of others besides myself; for my own case is peculiar in that matter. Sight, hearing and touch were perfectly good in early childhood; but I never had the sense of smell; and that of taste was therefore exceedingly imperfect. —On the occasion I refer to, I was carried down a flight of steep back stairs, and Rachel (a year and half older than I) clung to the nursemaid's gown, and Elizabeth was going before, (still quite a little girl) when I put down my finger ends to feel a flat velvet button on the top of Rachel's bonnet. The rapture of the sensation was really monstrous, as I remember it now. Those were our mourning bonnets for a near relation; and this marks the date, proving me to have been only two years old.

I was under three when my brother James was born. That day was another of the distinct impressions which flashed upon me in after years. I found myself within the door of the best bedroom,—an impressive place from being seldom used, from its having a dark, polished floor, and from the awful large gay figures of the chintz bed hangings. That day the curtains were drawn, the window blinds were down, and an unknown old woman, in a mob cap, was at the fire, with a

bundle of flannel in her arms. She beckoned to me,
and I tried to go, though it seemed impossible to cross
the slippery floor. I seem to hear now the pattering
of my feet. When I arrived at her knee, the nurse
pushed out with her foot a tiny chair, used as a footstool, made me sit down on it, laid the bundle of flannel
across my knees, and opened it so that I saw the little
red face of the baby. I then found out that there was
somebody in the bed,—seeing a nightcap on the pillow.
This was on the 21st of April, 1805. I have a distinct
recollection of some incidents of that summer. My
mother did not recover well from her confinement, and
was sent to the sea, at Yarmouth. On our arrival
there, my father took me along the old jetty,—little
knowing what terror I suffered. I remember the strong
grasp of his large hand being some comfort ; but there
were holes in the planking of the jetty quite big enough
to let my foot through ; and they disclosed the horrible
sight of waves flowing and receding below, and great
tufts of green weeds swaying to and fro. I remember
the sitting-room at our lodgings, and my mother's
dress as she sat picking shrimps, and letting me try to
help her.—Of all my many fancies, perhaps none was
so terrible as a dream that I had at four years old.
The impression is as fresh as possible now ; but I cannot at all understand what the fright was about. I
know nothing more strange than this power of re-
entering, as it were, into the narrow mind of an infant,
so as to compare it with that of maturity ; and therefore it may be worth while to record that piece of
precious nonsense,—my dream at four years old. I
imagine I was learning my letters then from cards,
where each letter had its picture,—as a stag for S. I

dreamed that we children were taking our walk with
our nursemaid out of St. Austin's Gate (the nearest bit
of country to our house). Out of the public-house
there came a stag, with prodigious antlers. Passing
the pump, it crossed the road to us, and made a polite
bow, with its head on one side, and with a scrape of
one foot, after which it pointed with its foot to the
public-house, and spoke to me, inviting me in. The
maid declined, and turned to go home. Then came
the terrible part. By the time we were at our own
door, it was dusk, and we went up the steps in the
dark; but in the kitchen it was bright sunshine. My
mother was standing at the dresser, breaking sugar;
and she lifted me up, and set me in the sun, and gave
me a bit of sugar. Such was the dream which froze
me with horror! Who shall say why?—But my
panics were really unaccountable. They were a matter
of pure sensation, without any intellectual justification
whatever, even of the wildest kind. A magic-lantern
was exhibited to us on Christmas-day, and once or
twice in the year besides. I used to see it cleaned by
daylight, and to handle all its parts,—understanding
its whole structure; yet, such was my terror of the
white circle on the wall, and of the moving slides,
that, to speak the plain truth, the first apparition
always brought on bowel-complaint; and, at the age
of thirteen, when I was pretending to take care of
little children during the exhibition, I could never look
at it without having the back of a chair to grasp, or
hurting myself, to carry off the intolerable sensation.
My bitter shame may be conceived; but then, I was
always in a state of shame about something or other.
I was afraid to walk in the town, for some years, if I

remember right, for fear of meeting two people. One
was an unknown old lady who very properly rebuked
me one day for turning her off the very narrow pavement of London Lane, telling me, in an awful way,
that little people should make way for their elders.
The other was an unknown farmer, in whose field we
had been gleaning (among other trespassers) before the
shocks were carried. This man left the field after us,
and followed us into the city,—no doubt, as I thought,
to tell the Mayor, and send the constable after us. I
wonder how long it was before I left off expecting that
constable. There were certain little imps, however,
more alarming still. Our house was in a narrow
street; and all its windows, except two or three at the
back, looked eastwards. It had no sun in the front
rooms, except before breakfast in summer. One summer morning, I went into the drawing-room, which
was not much used in those days, and saw a sight
which made me hide my face in a chair, and scream
with terror. The drops of the lustres on the mantle-
piece, on which the sun was shining, were somehow
set in motion, and the prismatic colours danced vehemently on the walls. I thought they were alive,—
imps of some sort; and I never dared go into that
room alone in the morning, from that time forward.
I am afraid I must own that my heart has beat, all
my life long, at the dancing of prismatic colours on
the wall.

I was getting some comfort, however, from religion
by this time. The Sundays began to be marked days,
and pleasantly marked, on the whole. I do not know
why crocuses were particularly associated with Sunday
at that time; but probably my mother might have

walked in the garden with us, some early spring Sunday. My idea of Heaven was of a place gay with yellow and lilac crocuses. My love of gay colours was very strong. When I was sent with the keys to a certain bureau in my mother's room, to fetch miniatures of my father and grandfather, to be shown to visitors, I used to stay an unconscionable time, though dreading punishment for it, but utterly unable to resist the fascination of a certain watch-ribbon kept in a drawer there. This ribbon had a pattern in floss silk, gay and beautifully shaded; and I used to look at it till I was sent for, to be questioned as to what I had been about. The young wild parsley and other weeds in the hedges used to make me sick with their luscious green in spring. One crimson and purple sunrise I well remember, when James could hardly walk alone, and I could not therefore have been more than five. I awoke very early, that summer morning, and saw the maid sound asleep in her bed, and 'the baby' in his crib. The room was at the top of the house; and some rising ground beyond the city could be seen over the opposite roofs. I crept out of bed, saw James's pink toes showing themselves invitingly through the rails of his crib, and gently pinched them, to wake him. With a world of trouble I got him over the side, and helped him to the window, and upon a chair there. I wickedly opened the window, and the cool air blew in; and yet the maid did not wake. Our arms were smutted with the blacks on the window-sill, and our bare feet were corded with the impression of the rush-bottomed chair; but we were not found out. The sky was gorgeous, and I talked very religiously to the child.

I remember the mood, and the pleasure of expressing it, but nothing of what I said.

I must have been a remarkably religious child, for the only support and pleasure I remember having from a very early age was from that source. I was just seven when the grand event of my childhood took place,—a journey to Newcastle to spend the summer (my mother and four of her children) at my grandfather's; and I am certain that I cared more for religion before and during that summer than for anything else. It was after our return, when Ann Turner, daughter of the Unitarian Minister there, was with us, that my piety first took a practical character; but it was familiar to me as an indulgence long before. While I was afraid of everybody I saw, I was not in the least afraid of God. Being usually very unhappy, I was constantly longing for heaven, and seriously, and very frequently planning suicide in order to get there. I was sure that suicide would not stand in the way of my getting there. I knew it was considered a crime; but I did not feel it so. I had a devouring passion for justice;—justice, first to my own precious self, and then to other oppressed people. Justice was precisely what was least understood in our house, in regard to servants and children. Now and then I desperately poured out my complaints; but in general I brooded over my injuries, and those of others who dared not speak; and then the temptation to suicide was very strong. No doubt, there was much vindictiveness in it. I gloated over the thought that I would make somebody care about me in some sort of way at last: and, as to my reception in the other world, I felt sure that God could not be very angry with me for making haste to him when nobody else cared for me, and so many people plagued me. One day I went to the kitchen to get the great carving knife, to cut my throat; but the servants were at dinner; and this put it off for that time. By degrees, the design dwindled down into running away. I used to lean out of the window, and look up and down the street, and wonder how far I could go without being caught. I had no doubt at all that if I once got into a farm-house, and wore a woollen petticoat, and milked the cows, I should be safe, and that nobody would inquire about me any more.—It is evident enough that my temper must have been very bad. It seems to me now that it was downright devilish, except for a placability which used to annoy me sadly. My temper might have been early made a thoroughly good one, by the slightest indulgence shown to my natural affections, and any rational dealing with my faults : but I was almost the youngest of a large family, and subject, not only to the rule of severity to which all were liable, but also to the rough and contemptuous treatment of the elder children, who meant no harm, but injured me irreparably. I had no self-respect, and an unbounded need of approbation and affection. My capacity for jealousy was something frightful. When we were little more than infants, Mr. Thomas Watson, son of my father's partner, one day came into the yard, took Rachel up in his arms, gave her some grapes off the vine, and carried her home, across the street, to give her Gay's Fables, bound in red and gold. I stood with a bursting heart, beating my hoop, and hating every body in the world. I always hated Gay's Fables, and for long could not abide a red book.

Nobody dreamed of all this; and the 'taking down' system was pursued with me as with the rest, issuing in the assumed doggedness and wilfulness which made me desperately disagreeable during my youth, to every body at home. The least word or tone of kindness melted me instantly, in spite of the strongest predeterminations to be hard and offensive. Two occasions stand out especially in my memory, as indeed almost the only instances of the enjoyment of tenderness manifested to myself individually.

When I was four or five years old, we were taken to a lecture of Mr. Drummond's, for the sake, no doubt, of the pretty shows we were to see,—the chief of which was the Phantasmagoria of which we had heard, as a fine sort of magic-lantern. I did not like the darkness, to begin with; and when Minerva appeared, in a red dress, at first extremely small, and then approaching, till her owl seemed coming directly upon me, it was so like my nightmare dreams that I shrieked aloud. I remember my own shriek. A pretty lady who sat next us, took me on her lap, and let me hide my face in her bosom, and held me fast. How intensely I loved her, without at all knowing who she was! From that time we knew her, and she filled a large space in my life; and above forty years after, I had the honour of having her for my guest in my own house. She was Mrs. Lewis Cooper, then the very young mother of two girls of the ages of Rachel and myself, of whom I shall have to say more presently.— The other occasion was when I had a terrible ear-ache one Sunday. The rest went to chapel in the afternoon; and my pain grew worse. Instead of going into the kitchen to the cook, I wandered into a lumber

room at the top of the house. I laid my aching ear
against the cold iron screw of a bedstead, and howled
with pain; but nobody came to me. At last, I heard the
family come home from chapel. I heard them go into
the parlour, one after another, and I knew they were
sitting round the fire in the dusk. I stole down to the
door, and stood on the mat, and heard them talking and
laughing merrily. I stole in, thinking they would not
observe me, and got into a dark corner. Presently my
mother called to me, and asked what I was doing
there. Then I burst out,—that my ear ached so I did
not know *what* to do ! Then she and my father both
called me tenderly, and she took me on her lap, and
laid the ear on her warm bosom. I was afraid of
spoiling her starched muslin handkerchief with the
tears which *would* come; but I was very happy, and
wished that I need never move again. Then of course
came remorse for all my naughtiness; but I was always
suffering that, though never, I believe, in my whole
childhood, being known to own myself wrong. I must
have been an intolerable child : but I need not have
been so.

I was certainly fond of going to chapel before that
Newcastle era which divided my childhood into wo
equal portions : but my besetting troubles followed me
even there. My passion for justice was baulked there,
as much as any where. The duties preached were
those of inferiors to superiors, while the *per contra* was
not insisted on with any equality of treatment at all.
Parents were to bring up their children 'in the nurture
and admonition of the Lord,' and to pay servants due
wages; but not a word was ever preached about the justice due from the stronger to the weaker. I used to thirst

to hear some notice of the oppression which servants
and children had (as I supposed universally) to endure,
in regard to their feelings, while duly clothed, fed and
taught : but nothing of the sort ever came ; but instead, a doctrine of passive obedience which only made
me remorseful and miserable. I was abundantly obedient in act ; for I never dreamed of being otherwise ;
but the interior rebellion kept my conscience in a state
of perpetual torture. As far as I remember, my conscience was never of the least use to me; for I always
concluded myself wrong about every thing, while pretending entire complacency and assurance. My moral
discernment was almost wholly obscured by fear and
mortification.—Another misery at chapel was that I
could not attend to the service, nor refrain from indulging in the most absurd vain-glorious dreams,
which I was ashamed of, all the while. The Oc-
tagon Chapel at Norwich has some curious windows
in the roof ;—not skylights, but letting in light
indirectly. I used to sit staring up at those windows,
and looking for angels to come for me, and take me to
heaven, in sight of all the congregation,—the end of
the world being sure to happen while we were at
chapel. I was thinking of this, and of the hymns, the
whole of the time, it now seems to me. It was very
shocking to me that I could not pray at chapel. I believe that I never did in my life. I prayed abundantly
when I was alone; but it was impossible to me to do
it in any other way ; and the hypocrisy of appearing to
do so was a long and sore trouble to me.—All this is
very painful; but I really remember little that was not
painful at that time of my life.—To be sure, there was
Nurse Ayton, who used to come, one or two days in

the week, to sew. She was kind to me, and I was
fond of her. She told us long stories about her family;
and she taught me to sew. She certainly held the
family impression of my abilities,—that I was a dull,
unobservant, slow, awkward child. In teaching me to
sew, she used to say (and I quite acquiesced) that
' slow and sure' was the maxim for me, and ' quick
and well' was the maxim for Rachel. I was not
jealous about this,—it seemed to me so undeniable.
On one occasion only I thought Nurse Ayton unkind.
The back of a ricketty old nursing-chair came off when
I was a playing on it; and I was sure she could save me
from being scolded by sewing it on again. I insisted
that she could sew *anything.* This made my mother
laugh when she came up; and so I forgave nurse : and
I believe that was our only quarrel.

My first political interest was the death of Nelson.
I was then four years old. My father came in from
the counting-house at an unusual hour, and told my
mother, who cried heartily. I certainly had some conception of a battle, and of a great man being a public
loss. It always rent my heart-strings (to the last day
of her life,) to see and hear my mother cry; and in
this case it was clearly connected with the death of a
great man. I had my own notions of Bonaparte too.
One day, at dessert, when my father was talking
anxiously to my mother about the expected invasion,
for which preparations were made all along the Norfolk
coast, I saw them exchange a glance, because I was
standing staring, twitching my pinafore with terror.
My father called me to him, and took me on his knee,
and I said ' But, papa, what will you do if Boney
comes ?' 'What will I do?' said he, cheerfully,

'Why, I will ask him to take a glass of Port with
me,'—helping himself to a glass as he spoke. That
wise reply was of immense service to me. From the
moment I knew that 'Boney' was a creature who
could take a glass of wine, I dreaded him no more.
Such was my induction into the department of foreign
affairs. As to social matters,—my passion for justice
was cruelly crossed, from the earliest time I can remember, by the imposition of passive obedience and
silence on servants and tradespeople, who met with a
rather old-fashioned treatment in our house. We
children were enough in the kitchen to know how the
maids avenged themselves for scoldings in the parlour,
before the family and visitors, to which they must not
reply ; and for being forbidden to wear white gowns,
silk gowns, or any thing but what strict housewives
approved. One of my chief miseries was being sent
with insulting messages to the maids,—e.g., to 'bid
them not be so like cart-horses overhead,' and the
like. On the one hand, it was a fearful sin to alter a
message ; and, on the other, it was impossible to give
such an one as that : so I used to linger and delay to
the last moment, and then deliver something civil,
with all imaginable sheepishness, so that the maids
used to look at one another and laugh. Yet, one of
my most heartfelt sins was towards a servant who was
really a friend of my mother's, and infinitely respected,
and a good deal loved, by us children,—Susan Ormsby,
who came to live with us just before James was born,
and staid till that memorable Newcastle journey, above
four years afterwards. When she was waiting at dinner one day, I stuck my knife upright, in listening to
something, so that the point cut her arm. I saw her

afterwards washing it at the pump; and she shook her head at me in tender reproach. My heart was bursting; but I dared not tell her how sorry I was. I never got over it, or was happy with her again; and when we were to part, the night before our journey, and she was kissing us with tears, it was in dumb grief and indignation that I heard her tell my mother that children do not feel things as grown people do, and that they could not think of any thing else when they were going a journey.

One more fact takes its place before that journey,— the awakening of a love of money in me. I suspect I have had a very narrow escape of being an eminent miser. A little more, or a little less difficulty, or another mode of getting money would easily have made me a miser. The first step, as far as I remember, was when we played cards, one winter evening, at our uncle Martineau's, when I was told that I had won twopence. The pavement hardly seemed solid when we walked home,—so elated was I. I remember equal delight when Mrs. Meadows Taylor gave us children twopence when we expected only a halfpenny, to buy string for a top: but in this last case it was not the true *amor nummi*, as in the other. The same avarice was excited in the same way, a few years later, when I won eighteen-pence at cards, on a visit. The very sight of silver and copper was transporting to me, without any thought of its use. I stood and looked long at money, as it lay in my hand. Yet, I do not remember that this passion ever interfered with my giving away money, though it certainly did with my spending it otherwise. I certainly was very close, all my childhood and youth. I may as well mention here

that I made rules and kept them, in regard to my
expenditure, from the time I had an allowance. I
believe we gave away something out of our first allowance of a penny a week. When we had twopence, I
gave away half. The next advance was to half-a-
guinea a quarter, to buy gloves and sashes : then to
ten pounds a year (with help) for clothes ; then fifteen,
and finally twenty, without avowed help. I sewed in-
defatigably all those years,—being in truth excessively
fond of sewing, with the amusement of either gossip-
ping, or learning poetry by heart, from a book, lying
open under my work. I never had the slightest difficulty in learning any amount of verse ; and I knew
enough to have furnished me for a wandering reciter,
—if there had been such a calling in our time,—as I
used to wish there was. While thus busy, I made
literally all my clothes, as I grew up, except stays and
shoes. I platted bonnets at one time, knitted stockings as I read aloud, covered silk shoes for dances, and
made all my garments. Thus I squeezed something
out of the smaller allowance, and out of the fifteen
pounds, I never spent more than twelve in dress ; and
never more than fifteen pounds out of the twenty.
The rest I gave away, except a little which I spent in
books. The amount of time spent in sewing now
appears frightful ; but it was the way in those days,
among people like ourselves. There was some saving
in our practice of reading aloud, and in mine of learning poetry in such mass : but the censorious gossip
which was the bane of our youth drove prose and verse
out of the field, and wasted more of our precious youthful powers and dispositions than any repentance and
amendment in after life could repair. This sort of

occupation, the sewing however, was less unfitting than might now appear, considering that the fortunes of manufacturers, like my father, were placed in jeopardy by the war, and that there was barely a chance for my father ever being able to provide fortunes for his daughters. He and my mother exercised every kind of self-denial to bring us up qualified to take care of ourselves. They pinched themselves in luxuries to provide their girls, as well as their boys, with masters and schooling; and they brought us up to an industry like their own;—the boys in study and business, and the girls in study and household cares. Thus was I saved from being a literary lady who could not sew; and when, in after years, I have been insulted by admiration at not being helpless in regard to household employments, I have been wont to explain, for my mother's sake, that I could make shirts and puddings, and iron and mend, and get my bread by my needle, if necessary,—(as it once was necessary, for a few months,) before I won a better place and occupation with my pen.

SECTION II.

But it is time to set out on the second period of my childhood,—beginning with that memorable New-castle journey. That period was memorable, not only from the enlarging of a child's ideas which ensues upon a first long journey, but because I date from it my becoming what is commonly called 'a responsible being.' On my return home I began to take moral charge of myself. I had before, and from my earliest recollections, been subject to a haunting, wretched, useless remorse; but from the time of our return from Newcastle, bringing Ann Turner with us, I became practically religious with all my strength. Ann was, I think, fourteen when I was seven; and that she made herself my friend at all was a great thing for me; and it fell out all the more easily for her tendencies being exclusively re-ligious, while I was only waiting for some influence to determine my life in that direction.

Travelling was no easy matter in those days. My mother, our dear, pretty, gentle aunt Margaret, sister Elizabeth, aged fifteen, Rachel, myself, and little James, aged four, and in nankeen frocks, were all crammed into a post-chaise, for a journey of three or four days. Almost every incident of those days is

still fresh : but I will report only one, which is curious
from showing how little aware we children were of
our own value. I really think, if I had once conceived that any body cared for me, nearly all the sins
and sorrows of my anxious childhood would have been
spared me; and I remember well that it was Ann
Turner who first conveyed the cheering truth to me.
She asked me why my mother sat sewing so diligently
for us children, and sat up at night to mend my
stockings, if she did not care for me ; and I was
convinced at once ; —only too happy to believe it, and
being unable to resist such evidence as the stocking-
mending at night, when we children were asleep.
Well : on our second day's journey, we stopped at
Burleigh House, and the three elders of the party
went in, to see the picture gallery.—Children were
excluded ; so we three little ones were left to play
among the haymakers on the lawn. After what
seemed a long time, it suddenly struck us that the
elders must have forgotten us, and gone on to Newcastle without us. I, for my part, was entirely persuaded that we should never be missed, or remembered
more by any body ; and we set up a terrible lamentation. A good-natured haymaker, a sunburnt woman
whose dialect we could not understand, took us in
hand, and led us to the great door, where we were
soon comforted by my mother's appearance. I remember wondering why she and aunt Margaret
laughed aside when they led us back to the chaise.

Of course it was difficult to amuse little children
so cooped up for so long. There was a little quiet
romping, I remember, and a great deal of story telling
by dear aunty : but the finest device was setting us

to guess what we should find standing in the middle of grandpapa's garden. As it was something we had never seen or known about, there was no end to the guessing. When we arrived at the gates of the Forth, (my grandfather's house) the old folks and their daughters came out to meet us, all tearful and agitated : and I, loathing myself for the selfishness, *could not* wait, but called out,—' I want to see what that thing is in the garden.' After an enlightening hint, and without any rebuke, our youngest aunt took me by the hand, and led me to face the mystery. I could make nothing of it when I saw it. It was a large, heavy, stone sundial. That dial is worth this much mention, for it was of immeasurable value to me. I could see its face only by raising myself on tiptoe on its step : and there, with my eyes on a level with the plate, did I watch and ponder, day by day, painfully forming my first clear conceptions of Time, amidst a bright confusion of notions of day and night, and of the seasons, and of the weather. I loved that dial with a sort of superstition; and when, nearly forty years after, I built a house for myself at Ambleside, my strong wish was to have this very dial for the platform below the terrace : but it was not to be had. It had been once removed already,—when the railway cut through the old garden ; and the stone mass was too heavy, and far too much fractured and crumbled for a second removal. So a dear friend set up for me a beautiful new dial ; and I can only hope that it may possibly render as great a service to some child of a future generation as my grandfather's did for me.

It seems to me now that I seldom asked questions in those days. I went on for years together in a puzzle, for want of its ever occurring to me to ask questions. For instance, no accounts of a spring-gun answered to my conception of it;—that it was a pea-green musket, used only in spring! This absurdity at length lay by unnoticed in my mind till I was twenty! Even so! At that age, I was staying at Birmingham; and we were returning from a country walk in the dusk of the evening, when my host warned us not to cross a little wood, for fear of spring-guns; and he found and showed us the wire of one. I was truly confounded when the sense of the old mistake, dormant in my mind till now, came upon me. Thus it was with a piece of mystification imposed on me by my grandfather's barber in 1809. One morning, while the shaving-pot was heating, the barber took me on his knee, and pretended to tell me why he was late that morning. Had I ever heard of a falling star? Yes, I had. Well: a star had fallen in the night; and it fell in the Forth lane, which it completely blocked up, beside Mr. Somebody's orchard. It was quite round, and of the beautifullest and clearest crystal. 'Was it there still?' O yes,—or most of it: but some of the crystal was shivered off, and people were carrying it away when he arrived at the spot. He had to go round by Something Street; and it was that which made him late. 'Would there be any left by the time we went for our walk?' He hoped there might. I got through my lessons in a fever of eagerness that morning, and engaged the nurse maid to take us through that lane. There was the orchard, with the appletree stretching over the wall: but not a single spike of the crystal was left. I thought it odd; but it never occurred to me to doubt the story, or to speak to any body about it, except the barber. I lay in wait for him the next morning; and very sorry he professed to be ;—so sorry that he had not just picked up some crystals for me while there were so many; but no doubt I should come in the way of a fallen star myself, some day. We kept this up till October, when we bade him good bye : and my early notions of astronomy were cruelly bewildered by that man's rhodomontade. I dare not say how many years it was before I got quite clear of it.

There is little that is pleasant to say of the rest of that absence from home. There was a naughty boy staying at my grandfather's, who caused us to be insulted by imputations of stealing the green fruit, and to be shut out of the garden, where we had never dreamed of touching a gooseberry : and he led little James into mischief; and then canted and made his own part good. Our hearts swelled under the injuries he caused us. Then, we were injudiciously fed, and my nightmare miseries were intolerable. The best event was that my theological life began to take form. I had a prodigious awe of clergymen and ministers, and a strong yearning towards them for notice. No doubt there was much vanity in this ; but it was also one investment of the religious sentiment, as I know by my being at times conscious of a remnant of the feeling now, while radically convinced that the intellectual and moral judgment of priests of all persuasions is inferior to that of any other order of men. The first of the order who took any direct notice of me was, as far as I know, good Mr. Turner of Newcastle, my mother's pastor and friend before her marriage. At Newcastle, we usually went to tea at his house on

Sunday evenings; and it was then that we began the
excellent practice of writing recollections of one of the
sermons of the day.   When the minister preaches
what children can understand, this practice is of the
highest use in fixing their attention, and in disclosing
to their parents the character and imperfections of
their ideas on the most important class of subjects.
On occasion of our first attempt,—Rachel's and
mine,—I felt very triumphant before hand. I remembered the text; and it seemed to me that my
head was full of thoughts from the sermon. I
scrawled over the whole of a large slate, and was
not a little mortified when I found that all I had
written came into seven or eight lines of my mother's
handwriting. I made sure that I had not been
cheated, and then fell into discouragement at finding
that my grand 'sermon' came to nothing more.
However, my attempt was approved; I was allowed
to 'sit up to supper,' and the Sunday practice was
begun which continued till I grew too deaf to keep up
my attention successfully. For some years of that
long period, our success was small, because Mr.
Madge's, (our minister's) sermons conveyed few clear
ideas to children, though much sweet and solemn
impression. Dr. Carpenter's were the best I ever
listened to for the purpose:—so good that I have
known him carry a 'recollection' written by a cousin
of mine at the age of sixteen, to Mrs. Carpenter, as a
curiosity,—not a single sentence of his sermon being
altogether absent from the hearer's version of it.—
Another religious impression that we children brought
from Newcastle is very charming to me still. Cur
gentle, delicate aunt Mary, whom I remember so well

in her white gown, with her pink colour, thin silky brown hair, and tender manner towards us, used to get us round her knees as she sat in the window-seat at the Forth, where the westerly sun shone in, and teach us to sing Milton's hymn ' Let us with a gladsome mind.' It is the very hymn for children, set to its own simple tune ; and I always, to this day, hear aunt Mary's weak, earnest voice in it. That was the gentle hymn. The woe-breathing one was the German Evening Hymn. The heroic one, which never failed to rouse my whole being, was ' Awake, my soul; stretch every nerve,' sung to Artaxerxes.—In those days, we learned Mrs. Barbauld's Prose Hymns by heart ; and there were parts of them which I dearly loved : but other parts made me shiver with awe. I did not know what ' shaking bogs ' were, and was alarmed at that mysterious being ' Child of Mortality.' On the whole, however, religion was a great comfort and pleasure to me ; and I studied the New Testament very heartily and profitably, from the time that Ann Turner went south with us, and encouraged me to confession and morning and nightly prayer.

SECOND PERIOD.

TO THE AGE OF SEVENTEEN.

SECTION I.

I THINK it could not have been long after that time that I took up a project which was of extraordinary use to me. My mind, considered dull and unobservant and unwieldy by my family, was desperately methodical. Every thing must be made tabular that would at all admit of it. Thus, I adopted in an immense hurry Dr. Franklin's youthful and absurd plan of pricking down his day's virtues and vices under heads. I found at once the difficulty of mapping out moral qualities, and had to give it up,—as I presume he had too. But I tried after something quite as foolish, and with immense perseverance. I thought it would be a fine thing to distribute scripture instructions under the heads of the virtues and vices, so as to have encouragement or rebuke always ready at hand. So I made (as on so many other occasions) a paper book, ruled and duly headed. With the Old Testament, I got on very well; but I was amazed at the difficulty with the New. I knew it to be of so much more value and importance than the Old, that I could not account for the small number of cut and dry commands. I twisted meanings and wordings, and made figurative things into precepts, at an unconscionable rate, before I would give up: but, after rivalling any old puritan preacher in my free use of scripture, I was obliged to own that I could not construct the system I wanted. Thus it was that I made out that great step in the process of thought and knowledge,—that whereas Judaism was a preceptive religion, Christianity was mainly a religion of principles,—or assumed to be so.

For many years past, my amazement has been continually on the increase that Unitarians can conceive that they are giving their children a Christian education in making their religious training what it is. Our family certainly insisted very strongly, and quite sincerely, on being Christians, while despising and pitying the orthodox as much as they could be despised and pitied in return; while yet, it must have been from wonderful slovenliness of thought, as well as ignorance, that we could have taken Unitarianism to be Christianity, in any genuine sense,—in any sense which could justify separate Christian worship. In our particular case, family pride and affection were implicated in our dissent. It was not the dissent that was to be wondered at, but its having degenerated into Unitarianism. Our French name indicates our origin. The first Martineaus that we know of were expatriated Huguenots, who came over from Normandy on the Revocation of the Edict of Nantes. They were, of course, Calvinists,—so fully admitting the Christian religion to be a scheme of redemption as to deserve, without limitation or perversion, the title of Christians. But their descendants passed by degrees, with the congregations to which they belonged, out of Calvinism into the pseudo-Christianity of Arianism first, and then of Unitarianism, under the guidance of pastors whose natural sense revolted from the essential points of the Christian doctrine, while they had not learning enough, biblical, ecclesiastical, historical or philosophical, to discover that what they gave up was truly essential, and that the name of Christianity was a mere sham when applied to what they retained. One evening when I was a child, I entered the parlour when our Unitarian minister Mr. Madge, was convicting of error (and what he called idiotcy) an orthodox shoolmaster who happened to be our visitor. ' Look here,' said Mr. Madge, seizing three wine-glasses, and placing them in a row : ' here is the Father,—here's the Son,—and here's the Holy Ghost; do you mean to tell me that those three glasses can be in any case one ? 'Tis mere nonsense.' And so were we children taught that it was ' mere nonsense.' I certainly wondered exceedingly that so vast a majority of the people of Norwich could accept such nonsense, and so very few see through it as the Unitarians of the city : but there was no one to suggest to me that there might be more in the matter than we saw, or than even our minister was aware of. This was pernicious enough : but far worse was the practice, necessarily universal among Unitarians, of taking any liberties they please with the revelation they profess to receive. It is true, the Scriptures are very properly declared by them to be not the revelation itself, but the record of it : but it is only through the record that the revelation can be obtained—at least by Protestants : and any tamperings with the record are operations upon the revelation itself. To appreciate the full effect of such a procedure, it is only necessary to look at what the Unitarians were doing in the days of my youth. They were issuing an Improved Version, in which considerable portions were set aside (printed in a different type) as spurious. It is true, those portions flatly contradicted some other portions in regard to dates and other facts; but the shallow scholarship of the Unitarians made its own choice what to receive and what to reject, without perceiving that such a process was wholly incompatible with the conception of the Scriptures being the record of a divine revelation at all. Having begun to cut away and alter, there was no reason for stopping; and every Unitarian was at liberty to make the Scriptures mean what suited his own views. Mr. Belsham's Exposition of the Epistles is a remarkable phenomenon in this way. To get rid of some difficulties about heaven and hell, the end of the world, salvation and perdition, &c., he devised a set of figurative meanings which he applied with immense perseverance, and a poetical ingenuity remarkable in so thoroughly prosaic a man; and all the while, it never seems to have occurred to him that that could hardly be a revelation designed for the rescue of the human race from perdition, the explanation of which required all this ingenuity at the hand of a Belsham, after eighteen centuries. I was as deeply-interested a reader of those big volumes as any Unitarian in England; and their ingenuity gratified some of my faculties exceedingly; but there was throughout a haunting sense of unreality which made me uneasy,—a consciousness that this kind of solemn amusement was no fitting treatment of the burdensome troubles of conscience, and the moral irritations which made the misery of my life. This theological dissipation, and the music and poetry of psalms and hymns, charmed away my woes for the hour; but they were not the solid consolation I needed. So, to work I went in my own way, again and again studying the New Testament,—making 'Harmonies,' poring over the geography, greedily gathering up every thing I could find in the way of commentary and elucidation, and gladly working myself into an enthusiasm with the moral beauty and spiritual promises I found in the Sacred Writings. I certainly never believed, more or less, in the 'essential doctrines' of Christianity, which represent God as the predestinator of men to sin and perdition, and Christ as their rescuer from that doom. I never was more or less beguiled by the trickery of language by which the perdition of man is made out to be justice, and his redemption to be mercy. I never suffered more or less from fear of hell. The Unitarianism of my parents saved me from that. But nothing could save me from the perplexity of finding so much of indisputable statement of those doctrines in the New Testament, nor from a covert sense that it was taking a monstrous liberty with the Gospel to pick and choose what made me happy, and reject what I did not like or could not receive. When I now find myself wondering at Unitarians who do so,—who accept heaven and reject hell,—who get rid somehow of the reign of Christ and the apostles on earth, and derive somehow a sanction of their fancy of a heaven in the stars, peopled with old acquaintances, and furnished for favourite pursuits, I try to recal the long series of years during which I did the same thing, with far more, certainly, of complacency than of misgiving. I try to remember how late on in life I have said that I confidently reckoned on entering the train of Socrates in the next world, and getting some of his secrets out of Pythagoras, besides making friendship with all the Christian worthies I especially inclined to. When I now see the comrades of my early days comfortably appropriating all the Christian promises, without troubling themselves with the clearly-specified condition,—of faith in Christ as a Redeemer,—I remind myself that this is just what I did for more than the first half of my life. The marvel remains how they now, and I then, could possibly wonder at the stationary or declining fortunes of their sect,—so evidently as Unitarianism is a mere clinging, from association and habit, to the old privilege of faith in a divine revelation, under an actual forfeiture of all its essential conditions.

My religious belief, up to the age of twenty, was briefly this. I believed in a God, milder and more beneficent and passionless than the God of the orthodox, inasmuch as he would not doom any of his creatures to eternal torment. I did not at any time, I think, believe in the Devil, but understood the Scriptures to speak of Sin under that name, and of eternal detriment under the name of eternal punishment. I believed in inestimable and eternal rewards of holiness; but I am confident that I never in my life did a right thing, or abstained from a wrong one from any consideration of reward or punishment. To the best of my recollection, I always feared sin and remorse extremely, and punishment not at all ; but, on the contrary, desired punishment or any thing else that would give me the one good that I pined for in vain,—ease of conscience. The doctrine of forgiveness on repentance never availed me much, because forgiveness for the past was nothing without safety in the future; and my sins were not curable, I felt, by any single remission of their consequences,—if such remission were possible. If I prayed and wept, and might hope that I was pardoned at night, it was small comfort, because I knew I should be in a state of remorse again before the next noon. I do not remember the time when the forgiveness clause in the Lord's Prayer was not a perplexity and a stumbling-block to me. I did not care about being let off from penalty. I wanted to be at ease in conscience; and that could only be by growing good, whereas I hated and despised myself every day. My belief in Christ was that he was the purest of all beings, under God; and his sufferings for the sake of mankind made him as sublime in my view and my affections as any being could possibly be. The Holy Ghost was a mere fiction to me. I took all the miracles for facts, and contrived to worship the letter of the Scriptures long after I had, as desired, given up portions as 'spurious,' 'interpolations,' and so forth. I believed in a future life as a continuation of the present, and not as a new method of existence; and, from the time when I saw that the resurrection of the body and the immortality of the soul could not both be true, I adhered to the former,—after St. Paul. I was uncomfortably disturbed that Christianity had done so little for the redemption of the race : but the perplexity was not so serious as it would have been if I had believed in the perdition of the majority of men ; and, for the rest, I contrived to fix my view pretty exclusively on Christendom itself,—which Christians in general find a grand resource in their difficulties. In this way, and by the help of public worship, and of sacred music, and Milton, and the Pilgrim's Progress, I found religion my best resource, even in its first inconsistent and unsatisfactory form, till I wrought my way to something better, as I shall tell by and by.

When I was seven years old,—the winter after our return from Newcastle,—I was kept from chapel one Sunday afternoon by some ailment or other. When the house door closed behind the chapel-goers, I looked at the books on the table. The ugliest-looking of them was turned down open ; and my turning it up was one of the leading incidents of my life. That plain, clumsy, calf-bound volume was ' Paradise Lost ; ' and the common blueish paper, with its old-fashioned type, became as a scroll out of heaven to me. The first thing I saw was ' Argument,' which I took to mean a dispute, and supposed to be stupid enough : but there was something about Satan cleaving Chaos, which made me turn to the poetry ; and my mental destiny was fixed for the next seven years. That volume was henceforth never to be found but by asking me for it, till a young acquaintance made me a present of a little Milton of my own. In a few months, I believe there was hardly a line in Paradise Lost that I could not have instantly turned to. I sent myself to sleep by repeating it : and when my curtains were drawn back in the morning, descriptions of heavenly light rushed into my memory. I think this must have been my first experience of moral relief through intellectual resource. I am sure I must have been somewhat happier from that time forward; though one fact of which I am perfectly certain shows that the improvement must have been little enough. From the time when Ann Turner and her religious training of me put me, as it were, into my own moral charge, I was ashamed of my habit of misery,—and especially of crying. I tried for a long course of years,—I should think from about eight to fourteen,—to pass a single day without crying. I was a persevering child; and I know I tried hard: but I failed. I gave up at last; and during all those years, I never did pass a day without crying. Of course, my temper and habit of mind must have been excessively bad. I have no doubt I was an insufferable child for gloom, obstinacy and crossness. Still, when I remember my own placability,—my weakness of yielding every thing to the first word or tone of tenderness, I cannot but believe that there was grievous mistake in the case, and that even a little more sympathy and moral support would have spared me and others a hideous amount of fault and suffering.

How I found my way out we shall see hereafter: meantime, one small incident, which occurred when I was eleven years old, may foreshadow my release. Our eldest brother, Thomas, was seven years older than myself. He was silent and reserved generally, and somewhat strict to us younger ones, to whom he taught our Latin grammar. We revered and loved him intensely, in the midst of our awe of him: but once in my childhood I made him laugh against his will, by a pun in my Latin lesson (which was a great triumph) and once I ventured to confide to him a real difficulty,—without result. I found myself by his side during a summer evening walk, when something gave me courage to ask him—(the man of eighteen!) —the question which I had long been secretly revolving:—how, if God foreknew every thing, we could be blamed or rewarded for our conduct, which was thus absolutely settled for us beforehand. He considered for a moment, and then told me, in a kind voice, that this was a thing which I could not understand at present, nor for a long time to come. I dared not remonstrate ; but I was disappointed : and I felt that if I could feel the difficulty, I had a right to the solution. No doubt, this refusal of a reply helped to fix the question in my mind.

I have said that by this time I had begun to take moral or spiritual charge of myself. I did try hard to improve ; but I fear I made little progress. Every night, I reviewed the thoughts and actions of the day, and tried to repent ; but I could seldom comfort myself about any amendment. All the while, however, circumstances were doing for me what I could not do for myself,—as I have since found to be incessantly happening. The first great wholesome discipline of my life set in (unrecognised as such) when I was about eight years old. The kind lady who took me upon her lap at Mr. Drummond's lecture had two little girls, just the ages of Rachel and myself : and, after that incident, we children became acquainted, and very soon, (when the family came to live close beside us in Magdalen Street) as intimate as possible. I remember being at their house in the Market Place when I was seven years old ; and little

E. could not stand, nor even sit, to see the
magic-lantern, but was held in her papa's arms, because she was so very lame. Before the year was
out, she lost her leg. Being a quiet-tempered child,
and the limb being exceedingly wasted by disease,
she probably did not suffer very much under the
operation. However that might be, she met the
occasion with great courage, and went through it
with remarkable composure, so that she was the
talk of the whole city. I was naturally very deeply
impressed by the affair. It turned my imagination far too much on bodily suffering, and on the peculiar glory attending fortitude in that direction. I
am sure that my nervous system was seriously injured, and especially that my subsequent deafness was
partly occasioned by the exciting and vain-glorious
dreams that I indulged in for many years after my
friend E. lost her leg. All manner of deaths at the
stake and on the scaffold, I went through in imagination, in the low sense in which St. Theresa craved
martyrdom; and night after night, I lay bathed in
cold perspiration till I sank into the sleep of exhaustion. All this is detestable to think of now; but it
is a duty to relate the truth, because parents are apt
to know far too little of what is passing in their
children's imaginations, unless they win the confidence of the little creatures about that on which
they are shyest of all,—their aspirations. The good
side of this wretched extravagance of mine was that
it occasioned or strengthened a power of patience
under pain and privation which was not to be looked
for in a child so sensitive and irritable by nature.
Fortitude was in truth my favourite virtue: and the

power of bearing quietly a very unusual amount of
bodily pain in childhood was the poor recompense I
enjoyed for the enormous detriment I suffered from
the turn my imagination had taken.

This, however, is not the discipline I referred to as
arising from my companionship with E. In such a
case as hers, all the world acquiesces in the parents'
view and method of action: and in that case the
parents made a sad mistake. They enormously increased their daughter's suffering from her infirmity
by covering up the fact in an unnatural silence. E.'s
lameness was never mentioned, nor recognised in any
way, within my remembrance, till she, full late, did it
herself. It was taken for granted that she was like
other children; and the delusion was kept up in play-
hours at my expense. I might almost say that from
the time E. and I grew intimate, I never more had
any play. Now, I was fond of play,—given to
romp; and I really wonder now when I look back
upon the many long years during which I stood, with
cold feet and a longing mind, with E. leaning on my
arm, looking on while other children were at play.
It was a terrible uneasiness to me to go walks with
her,—shy child as I was,—fancying everybody in
the streets staring at us, on account of E.'s extreme
difficulty in walking. But the long self-denial which
I never thought of refusing or grumbling at, must
have been morally good for me, if I may judge by the
pain caused by two incidents;—pain which seems to
me now to swallow up all that issued from mere privation.—The fatigue of walking with E. was very
great, from her extreme need of support, and from its
being always on the same side. I was never very

strong; and when growing fast, I was found to be growing sadly crooked, from E.'s constant tugging at one arm. I cannot at all understand how my mother could put it upon me to tell E.'s mother that I must not walk with her, because it made me crooked: but this ungracious message I was compelled to carry; and it cost me more pain than long years of privation of play. The hint was instantly taken; but I suffered the shame and regret over again every time that I saw E. assigned to any one else; and I had infinitely rather have grown crooked than have escaped it by such a struggle.—The other incident was this. We children were to have a birthday party; and my father gave us the rare and precious liberty to play hide-and-seek in the warehouse, among the packing-cases and pigeon-holes where the bombasines were stored. For weeks I had counted the days and hours till this birthday and this play; but E. could not play hide-and-seek; and there we stood, looking at the rest,—I being cold and fidgetty, and at last uncontrollably worried at the thought that the hours were passing away, and I had not had one bit of play. I did the fatal thing which has been a thorn in my mind ever since. I asked E. if she would much mind having some one else with her for a minute while I hid once,—just once. O no,—she did not mind; so I sent somebody else to her, and ran off, with a feeling of self-detestation which is fresh at this day. I had no presence-of-mind for the game, —was caught in a minute; and came back to E. damaged in self-respect, for the whole remaining course of our friendship. However, I owe her a great deal; and she and her misfortune were among

the most favourable influences I had the benefit of
after taking myself in hand for self-government. I
have much pleasure in adding that nothing could be
finer than her temper in after life, when she had
taken her own case in hand, and put an end, as far as
it lay with her to do so, to the silence about her infirmity. After I wrote my ' Letter to the Deaf,' we
seemed to be brought nearer together by our companionship in infirmity. Years after that, when I
had written ' The Crofton Boys,' and was uneasy
lest my evident knowledge of such a case should jar
upon her feelings,—always so tenderly considered,—
I wrote her a confession of my uneasiness, and had in
reply a most charming letter,—free, cheerful, magnanimous ;—such a letter as has encouraged me to
write as I have now done.

The year 1811 was a marked one to me,—first, by
my being sent into the country for my health, for the
whole summer and autumn ; and next, for the birth of
the best-beloved member of my family,—my sister
Ellen.—It was not a genuine country life in a farm-
house, that summer, but a most constrained and conventional one, in the abode of a rich lawyer,—a
cousin of my father's, who sent a daughter of his to
our house for the advantage of city masters, in exchange for me, who went for health. I was not, on
the whole, happy there :—indeed, it is pretty clear
by this time that I was not happy anywhere. The
old fancy for running away came back strongly upon
me, and I was on the very point of attempting it
when a few words of concession and kindness upset
my purpose, as usual. I detested the governess,—
and with abundant reason. The very first day, she

shut me up and punished me because I, a town-bred
child, did not know what a copse was. 'Near yon-
der copse,' &c. She insisted that every body must
know what a copse is, and that therefore I was obstinate and a liar. After such a beginning, it will be
easily conceived that our relations could not be cordial
or profitable. She presently showed herself jealous of
my being in advance of her pupils in school-room
knowledge; and she daily outraged my sense of justice, expressly, and in the most purpose-like manner.
She was thoroughly vulgar; and in a few weeks she
was sent away.—One annoyance that I remember at
that place was (what now appears very strange) the
whispers I overheard about myself, as I sat on a little
stool in a corner of the dining-room, reading. My
hostess, who might have said anything in her ordinary voice without my attending to her, used to whis-
per to her morning visitors about my wonderful love
of reading,—that I never heard anything that was
said while I sat reading, and that I had written a
wonderful sermon. All the while, she pretended to
disguise it, winking and nudging, and saying '*We*
never hear any thing when we are reading.' '*We*
have written a sermon which is really quite wonderful
at *our* age,' &c. &c. I wished that sermon at Jericho
a hundred times; for in truth, I was heartily ashamed
of it. It was merely a narrative of St. Paul's adventures, out of the Acts; and I knew it was no more a
sermon than a string of parables out of the Gospels
would have been.

There were some sweet country pleasures that
summer. I never see chesnuts bursting from their
sheaths, and lying shining among the autumn leaves,

without remembering the old Manor-house where we children picked up chesnuts in the avenue, while my hostess made her call at the house. I have always loved orchards and apple-gatherings since, and blossomy lanes. The truth is, my remembrances of that summer may be found in 'Deerbrook,' though I now finally, (as often before,) declare that the characters are not real. More or less suggestion from real characters there certainly is; but there is not one, except the hero, (who is not English,) that any person is justified in pointing out as 'from the life.' Of the scenery too, there is more from Great Marlow than from that bleak Norfolk district; but the fresh country impressions are certainly derived from the latter. It was there that I had that precious morsel of experience which I have elsewhere detailed; *—the first putting my hand in among the operations of Nature, to modify them. After a morning walk, we children brought in some wild strawberry roots, to plant in our gardens. My plant was sadly withered by the time we got home; and it was then hot noon,—the soil of my garden was warm and parched, and there seemed no chance for my root. I planted it, grieved over its flabby leaves, watered it, got a little child's chair, which I put over it for shelter, and stopped up the holes in the chair with grass. When I went at sunset to look at it, the plant was perfectly fresh; and after that, it grew very well. My surprise and pleasure must have been very great, by my remembering such a trifle so long; and I am persuaded that I looked upon Nature with other eyes from the

* Household Education, p. 152.

moment that I found I had power to modify her
processes.

In November came the news which I had been
told to expect. My sister Rachel had been with us in
the country for a fortnight; and we knew that there
was to be a baby at home before we went back; and I
remember pressing so earnestly, by letter, to know the
baby's name as to get a rebuff. I was told to wait
till there was a baby. At last, the carrier brought
us a letter one evening which told us that we had a
little sister. I still longed to know the name, but
dared not ask again. Our host saw what was in my
mind. He went over to Norwich a day or two after,
and on his return told me that he hoped I should
like the baby's name now she had got one; —' Beer-
sheba.' I did not know whether to believe him or
not; and I had set my mind on ' Rose.' ' Ellen,'
however, satisfied me very well.—Homesick before,
I now grew downright ill with longing. I was sure
that all old troubles were wholly my fault, and fully
resolved that there should be no more. Now, as so
often afterwards, (as often as I left home) I was destined to disappointment. I scarcely felt myself at
home before the well-remembered bickerings began;
—not with me, but from the boys being troublesome,
James being naughty; and our eldest sister angry and
scolding. I then and there resolved that I would
look for my happiness to the new little sister, and
that she should never want for the tenderness which I
had never found. This resolution turned out more of
a prophecy than such decisions, born of a momentary
emotion, usually do. That child was henceforth a
new life to me. I did lavish love and tenderness on

her; and I could almost say that she has never caused
me a moment's pain but by her own sorrows. There
has been much suffering in her life; and in it I have
suffered with her: but such sympathetic pain is bliss
in comparison with such feelings as she has *not* excited in me during our close friendship of above forty
years. When I first saw her it was as she was lifted
out of her crib, at a fortnight old, asleep, to be shown
to my late hostess, who had brought Rachel and me
home. The passionate fondness I felt for her from
that moment has been unlike any thing else I have
felt in life,—though I have made idols of not a few
nephews and nieces. But she was a pursuit to me,
no less than an attachment. I remember telling a
young lady at the Gate-House Concert, (a weekly undress concert) the next night, that I should now see
the growth of a human mind from the very beginning. I told her this because I was very communicative to all who showed me sympathy in any degree.
Years after, I found that she was so struck by such a
speech from a child of nine that she had repeated it
till it had spread all over the city, and people said
somebody had put it into my head; but it was perfectly genuine. My curiosity *was* intense; and all
my spare minutes were spent in the nursery, watching,—literally watching,—the baby. This was a
great stimulus to me in my lessons, to which I gave
my whole power, in order to get leisure the sooner.
That was the time when I took it into my head to cut
up the Bible into a rule of life, as I have already told;
and it was in the nursery chiefly that I did it,—sitting on a stool opposite the nursemaid and baby, and
getting up from my notes to devour the child with

kisses.   There were bitter moments and hours,—as
when she was vaccinated or had her little illnesses.
My heart then felt bursting, and I went to my room,
and locked the door, and prayed long and desperately.
I knew then what the Puritans meant by ' wrestling
in prayer.'—One abiding anxiety which pressed upon
me for two years or more was lest this child should
be dumb : and if not, what an awful amount of
labour was before the little creature !   I had no
other idea than that she must learn to speak at all
as I had now to learn French,—each word by an express effort : and if I, at ten and eleven, found my
vocabulary so hard, how could this infant learn the
whole English language ?   The dread went off in
amazement when I found that she sported new words
every day, without much teaching at first, and then
without any.   I was as happy to see her spared the
labour as amused at her use of words in her pretty
prattle.

For nearly two years after our return from that
country visit, Rachel and I were taught at home.
Our eldest brother taught us Latin, and the next
brother, Henry, writing and arithmetic : and our
sister, French, reading and exercises.   We did not
get on well, except with the Latin.   Our sister expected too much from us, both morally and intellectually ; and she had not been herself carried on so far as
to have much resource as a teacher.   We owed to her
however a thorough grounding in our French grammar (especially the verbs) which was of excellent
service to us afterwards at school, as was a similar
grounding in the Latin grammar, obtained from our
brother.   As for Henry, he made our lessons in

arithmetic, &c. his funny time of day; and sorely did his practical jokes and ludicrous severity afflict us. He meant no harm; but he was too young to play schoolmaster; and we improved less than we should have done under less head-ache and heart-ache from his droll system of torture. I should say, on their behalf, that I, for one, must have seemed a most unpromising pupil,—my wits were so completely scattered by fear and shyness. I could never give a definition, for want of presence of mind. I lost my place in class for every thing but lessons that could be prepared beforehand. I was always saying what I did not mean. The worst waste of time, energy, money and expectation was about my music. Nature made me a musician in every sense. I was never known to sing out of tune. I believe all who knew me when I was twenty would give a good account of my playing. There was no music that I ever attempted that I did not understand, and that I could not execute,—under the one indispensable condition, that nobody heard me. Much money was spent in instruction; and I dislike thinking of the amount of time lost in copying music. My mother loved music, and, I know, looked to mè for much gratification in this way which she never had. My deafness put an end to all expectation of the kind at last; but long before that, my music was a misery to me,—while yet in another sense, my dearest pleasure. My master was Mr. Beckwith, organist of Norwich Cathedral;—an admirable musician; but of so irritable a temper as to be the worst of masters to a shy girl like me. It was known that he had been dismissed from one house or more for rapping his pupils' knuckles;

and that he had been compelled to apologize for
insufferable scolding. Neither of these things happened at our house; but really I wondered sometimes
that they did not,—so very badly did I play and sing
when he was at my elbow. My fingers stuck together
as in cramp, and my voice was as husky as if I had
had cotton-wool in my throat. Now and then he
complimented my ear; but he oftener told me that
I had no more mind than the music-book,—no more
feeling than the lid of the piano,—no more heart
than the chimney-piece; and that it was no manner
of use trying to teach me any thing. All this while,
if the room-door happened to be open without my observing it when I was singing Handel by myself, my
mother would be found dropping tears over her work,
and used myself, as I may now own, to feel fairly
transported. Heaven opened before me at the sound
of my own voice when I believed myself alone ;—
that voice which my singing-master assuredly never
heard. It was in his case that I first fully and suddenly learned the extent of the mischief caused by my
shyness. He came twice a week. On those days it
was an effort to rise in the morning,—to enter upon
a day of misery; and nothing could have carried me
through the morning but the thought of the evening,
when he would be gone,—out of my way for three
days, or even four. The hours grew heavier: my
heart fluttered more and more : I could not eat my
dinner; and his impatient loud knock was worse to
me than sitting down in the dentist's chair. Two
days per week of such feelings, strengthened by the
bliss of the evenings after he was gone, might account for the catastrophe, which however did not

shock me the less for that. Mr. Beckwith grew more and more cross, thinner and thinner, so that his hair and beard looked blacker and blacker, as the holidays approached, when he was wont to leave home for a week or two. One day when somebody was dining with us, and I sat beside my father at the bottom of the table, he said to my mother, ' By the way, my dear, there is a piece of news which will not surprise you much, I fancy. Poor John Beckwith is gone. He died yesterday.' Once more, that name made my heart jump into my mouth; but this time, it was with a dreadful joy. While the rest went on very quietly saying how ill he had looked for some time, and ' who would have thought he would never come back?'—and discussing how Mrs. B. and the children were provided for, and wondering who would be organist at the Cathedral, my spirits were dancing in secret rapture. The worst of my besetting terrors was over for ever! All days of the week would henceforth be alike, as far as that knock at the door was concerned. Of course, my remorse at this glee was great; and thus it was that I learned how morally injured I was by the debasing fear I was wholly unable to surmount.

Next to fear, laziness was my worst enemy. I was idle about brushing my hair,—late in the morning,—much afflicted to have to go down to the apple-closet in winter; and even about my lessons I was indolent. I learned any thing by heart very easily, and I therefore did it well : but I was shamefully lazy about using the dictionary, and went on, in full anticipation of rebuke, translating *la rosée* the rose, *tomber* to bury, and so on. This shows that there must have been plenty of provocation on my side, whatever mistakes there may have been on that of my teachers. I was sick and weary of the eternal 'Telemachus,' and could not go through the labours of the dictionary for a book I cared so little about. This difficulty soon came to an end; for in 1813 Rachel and I went to a good day-school for two years, where our time was thoroughly well spent; and there we enjoyed the acquisition of knowledge so much as not to care for the requisite toil.

Before entering on that grand new period, I may as well advert to a few noticeable points.—I was certainly familiar with the idea of death before that time. The death of Nelson, when I was four years old, was probably the earliest association in my mind of mournful feelings with death. When I was eight or nine, an aunt died whom I had been in the constant habit of seeing. She was old-fashioned in her dress, and peculiar in her manners. Her lean arms were visible between the elbow-ruffles and the long mits she wore; and she usually had an apron on, and a muslin handkerchief crossed on her bosom. She fell into absent-fits which puzzled and awed us children: but we heard her so highly praised (as she richly deserved) that she was a very impressive personage to us. One morning when I came down, I found the servants at breakfast unusually early: they looked very gloomy; bade me make no noise; but would not explain what it was all about. The shutters were half-closed; and when my mother came down, she looked so altered by her weeping that I hardly knew whether it was she. She called us to her, and told us that aunt Martineau had died very suddenly, of a disease of the heart. The whispers which were not meant for us somehow reached our ears all that week. We heard how my father and mother had been sent for in the middle of the night by the terrified servants, and how they had heard our poor uncle's voice of mourning before they had reached the house; and how she looked in her coffin, and all about the funeral: and we were old enough to be moved by the sermon in her praise at chapel, and especially by the anthem composed for the occasion, with the words from Job,—'When the ear heard her then it blessed her,' &c. My uncle's gloomy face and unpowdered hair were awful to us; and, during the single year of his widowhood, he occasionally took us children with him in the carriage, when he went to visit country patients. These drives came to an end with the year of widowhood; but he gave us something infinitely better than any other gift or pleasure in his second wife, whose only child was destined to fill a large space in our hearts and our lives.—Soon after that funeral, I somehow learned that our globe swims in space, and that there is sky all round it. I told this to James; and we made a grand scheme which we never for a moment doubted about executing. We had each a little garden, under the north wall of our garden. The soil was less than two feet deep; and below it was a mass of rubbish,—broken bricks, flints, pottery, &c. We did not know this; and our plan was to dig completely through the globe, till we came out at the other side. I fully expected to do this, and had an idea of an extremely deep hole, the darkness of which at the bottom would be lighted up by the passage of stars, slowly traversing the hole.

When we found our little spades would not dig through the globe, nor even through the brickbats, we altered our scheme. We lengthened the hole to our own length, having an extreme desire to know what dying was like. We lay down alternately in this grave, and shut our eyes, and fancied ourselves dead, and told one another our feelings when we came out again. As far as I can remember, we fully believed that we now knew all about it.

A prominent event of my childhood happened in 1812, when we went to Cromer for the sake of the baby's health. I had seen the sea, as I mentioned, when under three years old, as it swayed under the old jetty at Yarmouth : and I had seen it again at Tynemouth, when I was seven : but now it was like a wholly new spectacle ; and I doubt whether I ever received a stronger impression than when, from the rising ground above Cromer, we caught sight of the sparkling expanse. At Tynemouth, that singular incident took place which I have elsewhere narrated,* —that I was shown the sea, immediately below my feet, at the foot of the very slope on which I was standing, and could not see it. The rest of the party must have thought me crazy or telling a lie ; but the distress of being unable to see what I had so earnestly expected, was real enough ; and so was the amazement when I at last perceived the fluctuating tide. All this had gone out of my mind when we went to Cromer ; and the spectacle seemed a wholly new one. That was a marvellous month that the nursemaid and we children spent there. When we were not down

* Letters on the Laws of Man's Nature and Development, p. 161.

on the sands, or on the cliffs, I was always perched on
a bank in the garden whence I could see that straight
blue line, or those sparkles which had such a charm
for me.   It was much that I was happy for a whole
month; but I also obtained many new ideas, and
much development;—the last chiefly, I think, in a
religious direction.

In the preceding year another instance had occurred,—a most mortifying one to me,—of that
strange inability to see what one is looking for (no
doubt because one looks wrongly) of which the Tynemouth sea-gazing was a strong illustration.*   When
the great comet of 1811 was attracting all eyes, my
star-gazing was just as ineffectual.   Night after
night, the whole family of us went up to the long
windows at the top of my father's warehouse; and
the exclamations on all hands about the comet perfectly exasperated me,—because I could not see it!
' Why, there it is!'   ' It is as big as a saucer.'   ' It
is as big as a cheese-plate.'   ' Nonsense;—you might
as well pretend not to see the moon.'   Such were the
mortifying comments on my grudging admission that
I could not see the comet.   And I never did see it.
Such is the fact; and philosophers may make of it
what they may,—remembering that I was then nine
years old, and with remarkably good eyes.

* Letters on the Laws of Man's Nature and Development, p. 161.

SECTION II.

I WAS eleven when that delectable schooling began which I always recur to with clear satisfaction and pleasure. There was much talk in 1813 among the Norwich Unitarians of the conversion of an orthodox dissenting minister, the Rev. Isaac Perry, to Unitarianism. Mr. Perry had been minister of the Cherry Lane Chapel, and kept a large and flourishing boys' school. Of course, he lost his pulpit, and the chief part of his school. As a preacher he was wofully dull; and he was far too simple and gullible for a boys' schoolmaster. The wonder was that his school kept up so long, considering how completely he was at the mercy of naughty boys. But he was made to be a girls' schoolmaster. Gentlemanly, honourable, well provided for his work, and extremely fond of it, he was a true blessing to the children who were under him.—Rachel and I certainly had some preconception of our approaching change, when my father and mother were considering it; for we flew to an upper window one day to catch a sight of this Mr. Perry and our minister, Mr. Madge, before they turned the corner. That was my first sight of the black coat and grey pantaloons, and powdered hair, and pointing and see-sawing fore-finger, which I afterwards became so familiar with.

We were horribly nervous, the first day we went to school. It was a very large vaulted room, white-washed, and with a platform for the master and his desk; and below, rows of desks and benches, of wood painted red, and carved all over with idle boys' devices. Some good many boys remained for a time; but the girls had the front row of desks, and could see nothing of the boys but by looking behind them. The thorough way in which the boys did their lessons, however, spread its influence over us, and we worked as heartily as if we had worked together. I remember being somewhat oppressed by the length of the first morning,—from nine till twelve, and dreading a similar strain in the afternoon, and twice every day : but in a very few days, I got into all the pleasure of it; and a new state of happiness had fairly set in. I have never since felt more deeply and thoroughly the sense of progression than I now began to do. As far as I remember, we never failed in our lessons, more or less. Our making even a mistake was very rare ; and yet we got on fast. This shows how good the teaching must have been. We learned Latin from the old Eton grammar, which I therefore, and against all reason, cling to,—remembering the repetition-days (Saturdays) when we recited all that Latin, prose and verse, which occupied us four hours. Two other girls, besides Rachel and myself, formed the class; and we certainly attained a capability of enjoying some of the classics, even before the two years were over. Cicero, Virgil, and a little of Horace were our main reading then : and afterwards I took great de-

light in Tacitus. I believe it was a genuine understanding and pleasure, because I got into the habit
of thinking in Latin, and had something of the same
pleasure in sending myself to sleep with Latin as
with English poetry. Moreover, we stood the test
of verse-making, in which I do not remember that
we ever got any disgrace, while we certainly obtained,
now and then, considerable praise. When Mr. Perry
was gone, and we were put under Mr. Banfather, one
of the masters at the Grammar School, for Latin, Mr.
B. one day took a little book out of his pocket, and
translated from it a passage which he desired us to
turn into Latin verse. My version was precisely the
same as the original, except one word (*annosa* for
antiqua) and the passage was from the Eneid. Tests
like these seem to show that we really were well
taught, and that our attainment was sound, as far as
it went. Quite as much care was bestowed on our
French, the grammar of which we learned thoroughly,
while the pronunciation was scarcely so barbarous as
in most schools during the war, as there was a French
lady engaged for the greater part of the time. Mr.
Perry prided himself, I believe, on his process of composition being exceedingly methodical; and he enjoyed
above every thing initiating us into the mystery. The
method and mystery were more appropriate in our
lessons in school than in his sermons in chapel;—at
least, the sermons were fearfully dull; whereas the
lessons were highly interesting and profitable. The
only interest we could feel in his preaching was when
he first brought the familiar fore-finger into play, and
then built up his subject on the scaffolding which we
knew so well. There was the Proposition, to begin

with: then the Reason, and the Rule; then the
Example, ancient and modern; then the Confirmation; and finally, the Conclusion. This may be a
curious method, (not altogether apostolic) of preaching the gospel; but it was a capital way of introducing some order into the chaos of girls' thoughts.
One piece of our experience which I remember is
highly illustrative of this. In a fit of poetic fervour
one day we asked leave for once to choose our own
subject for a theme,—the whole class having agreed
before-hand what the subject should be. Of course,
leave was granted; and we blurted out that we
wanted to write ' on Music.' Mr. Perry pointed
out that this was not definite enough to be called a
subject. It might be on the Uses of Psalmody, or
on the effect of melody in certain situations, or of
martial music, or of patriotic songs, &c. &c.: but he
feared there would be some vagueness if so large a
subject were taken, without circumscription. However, we were bent on our own way, and he wisely let
us have it. The result may easily be foreseen. We
were all floating away on our own clouds, and what
a space we drifted over may be imagined. We came
up to Mr. P.'s desk all elate with the consciousness
of our sensibility and eloquence; and we left it prodigiously crest-fallen. As one theme after another was
read,—no two agreeing even so far as the Proposition, our folly became more and more apparent; and
the master's few, mild, respectful words at the end
were not necessary to impress the lesson we had
gained. Up went the fore-finger, with ' You perceive, ladies' . . . . and we saw it all; and thenceforth we were thankful to be guided, or dictated to,

in the choice of our topics. Composition was my favourite exercise; and I got credit by my themes, I believe. Mr. Perry told me so, in 1834, when I had just completed the publication of my Political Economy Tales, and when I had the pleasure of making my acknowledgments to him as my master in composition, and probably the cause of my mind being turned so decidedly in that direction. That was a gratifying meeting, after my old master and I had lost sight of one another for so many years. It was our last. If I remember right, we met on the eve of my sailing for America; and he was dead before my return.

Next to Composition, I think arithmetic was my favourite study. My pleasure in the working of numbers is something inexplicable to me,—as much as any pleasure of sensation. I used to spend my play hours in covering my slate with sums, washing them out, and covering the slate again. The fact is, however, that we had no lessons that were not pleasant. That was the season of my entrance upon an intellectual life. In an intellectual life I found then, as I have found since, refuge from moral suffering, and an always unexhausted spring of moral strength and enjoyment.

Even then, and in that happy school, I found the need of a refuge from trouble. Even there, under the care of our just and kind master, I found my passion for justice liable to disappointment as elsewhere. Some of our school-fellows brought a trumpery charge, out of school, against Rachel and me; and our dismay was great at finding that Mrs. Perry, and therefore, no doubt, Mr. Perry believed us capable of a dirty trick. We could not establish our innocence; and we had to bear the knowledge that we were considered guilty of the offence in the first place, and of telling a lie to conceal it in the next. How vehemently I used to determine that I would never, in all my life, believe people to be guilty of any offence, where disproof was impossible, and they asserted their innocence.—Another incident made a great impression on me. It happened before the boys took their final departure; and it helped to make me very glad when we girls (to the number of sixteen) were left to ourselves.

Mr. Perry was one day called out, to a visitor who was sure to detain him for some time. On such occasions, the school was left in charge of the usher, whose desk was at the farther end of the great room. On this particular day, the boys would not let the girls learn their lessons. Somehow, they got the most absurd masks within the sphere of our vision; and they said things that we could not help laughing at, and made soft bow-wows, cooings, bleatings, &c., like a juvenile House of Commons, but so as not to be heard by the distant usher. While we girls laughed, we were really angry, because we wanted to learn our lessons. It was proposed by somebody, and carried unanimously, that complaint should be made to the usher. I believe I was the youngest; and I know I was asked by the rest to convey the complaint. Quite innocently I did what I was asked. The consequence,—truly appalling to me,—was that coming up the school-room again was like running the gauntlet. O! that hiss! ' S-s-s—tell-tale—tell-tale! greeted me all the way up: but there was

worse at the end. The girls who had sent me said I
was served quite right, and they would have nothing
to do with a tell-tale. Even Rachel went against
me. And was I really that horrible thing called a
tell-tale ? I never meant it ; yet not the less was it
even so ! When Mr. Perry came back, the usher's
voice was heard from the lower regions—' Sir !' and
then came the whole story, with the names of all the
boys in the first class. Mr. Perry was generally the
mildest of men ; but when he went into a rage, he
did the thing thoroughly. He became as white as
his powdered hair, and the ominous fore-finger shook :
and never more than on this occasion. J. D., as
being usually ' correct,' was sentenced to learn only
thirty lines of Greek, after school. (He died not
long after, much beloved.) W. D., his brother, less
' correct ' in character, had fifty. Several more had
from thirty to fifty ; and R. S. (now, I believe, the
leading innkeeper in old Norwich)—' R. S., always
foremost in mischief, must now meet the consequences. R. S. shall learn SEVENTY lines of Greek
before he goes home.' How glad should I have been
to learn any thing within the compass of human
knowledge to buy off those boys ! They probably
thought I enjoyed seeing them punished. But I was
almost as horror-struck at their fate as at finding that
one could be a delinquent, all in a moment, with the
most harmless intentions.

An incident which occurred before Mr. Perry's
departure from Norwich startled me at the time, and
perhaps startles me even more now, as showing how
ineffectual the conscience becomes when the moral
nature of a child is too much depressed.—All was

going on perfectly well at school, as far as we knew, when Mr. Perry one day called, and requested a private interview with my father or mother. My mother and he were talking so long in the drawing-room, that dinner was delayed above half-an-hour, during which time I was growing sick with apprehension. I had no doubt whatever that we had done something wrong, and that Mr. Perry had come to complain of us. This was always my way,—so accustomed was I to censure, and to stiffen myself under it, right or wrong; so that all clear sense of right and wrong was lost. I believe that, at bottom, I always concluded myself wrong. In this case it made no difference that I had no conception what it was all about. When my mother appeared, she was very grave : the mood spread, and the dinner was silent and gloomy,—father, brothers and all. My mother had in her heart a little of the old-fashioned liking for scenes : and now we had one,—memorable enough to me ! ' My dear,' said she to my father, when the dessert was on the table, and the servant was gone, ' Mr. Perry has been here.' ' So I find, my love.' ' He had some very important things to say. He had something to say about—Rachel— and—Harriet.' I had been picking at the fringe of my doily ; and now my heart sank, and I felt quite faint. ' Ah ! here it comes,' thought I, expecting to hear of some grand delinquency. My mother went on, very solemnly. ' Mr. Perry says that he has never had a fault to find with Rachel and Harriet ; and that if he had a school full of such girls, he should be the happiest man alive.' The revulsion was tremendous. I cried desperately, I remember, amidst the rush of congratulations. But what a moral state it was, when my conscience was of no more use to me than this! The story carries its own moral.

What Mr. Perry came to say was, however, dismal enough. He was no man of the world; and his wife was no manager : and they were in debt and difficulty. Their friends paid their debts (my father taking a generous share) and they removed to Ipswich. It was the bitterest of my young griefs, I believe,— their departure. Our two years' schooling seemed like a lifetime to look back upon : and to this day it fills a disproportionate space in the retrospect of my existence,—so inestimable was its importance. When we had to bid our good master farewell, I was deputed to utter the thanks and good wishes of the pupil : but I could not get on for tears, and he accepted our grief as his best tribute. He went round, and shook hands with us all, with gracious and solemn words, and sent us home passionately mourning.— Though this seemed like the close of one period of my life, it was in fact the opening of its chief phase,— of that intellectual existence which my life has continued to be, more than any thing else, through its whole course.

After his departure, and before I was sent to Bristol, our mode of life was this. We had lessons in Latin and French, and I in music, from masters; and we read aloud in family a good deal of history, biography, and critical literature. The immense quantity of needlework and music-copying that I did remains a marvel to me; and so does the extraordinary bodily indolence. The difficulty I had in getting up in the morning, the detestation of the daily walk, and of all visiting, and of every break in the monotony that I have always loved, seem scarcely credible to me now,—active as my habits have since become. My health was bad, however, and my mind ill at ease. It was a depressed and wrangling life; and I have no doubt I was as disagreeable as possible. The great calamity of my deafness was now opening upon me; and that would have been quite enough for youthful fortitude, without the constant indigestion, languor and muscular weakness which made life a burden to me. My religion was a partial comfort to me; and books and music were a great resource: but they left a large margin over for wretchedness. My beloved hour of the day was when the cloth was drawn, and I stole away from the dessert, and read Shakspere by firelight in winter in the drawing-room. My mother was kind enough to allow this breach of good family manners; and again at a subsequent time when I took to newspaper reading very heartily. I have often thanked her for this forbearance since. I was conscious of my bad manners in keeping the newspaper on my chair all dinner-time, and stealing away with it as soon as grace was said; and of sticking to my Shakspere, happen what might, till the tea was poured out: but I could not forego those indulgences, and I went on to enjoy them uneasily. Our newspaper was the Globe, in its best days, when, without ever mentioning Political Economy, it taught it, and viewed public affairs in its light. This was not quite my first attraction to political economy (which I did not know by name till five, or six years later;) for I remember when at Mr. Perry's fastening upon the part of our geography book (I forget what it was)

which treated of the National Debt, and the various
departments of the Funds. This was fixed in my
memory by the unintelligible raillery of my brothers
and other companions, who would ask me with mock
deference to inform them of the state of the Debt, or
would set me, as a forfeit at Christmas Games, to
make every person present understand the operation
of the Sinking Fund. I now recal Mr. Malthus's
amusement, twenty years later, when I told him I
was sick of his name before I was fifteen. His work
was talked about then, as it has been ever since, very
eloquently and forcibly, by persons who never saw so
much as the outside of the book. It seems to me
that I heard and read an enormous deal against him
and his supposed doctrines ; whereas when, at a later
time, I came to inquire, I could never find any body
who had read his book. In a poor little struggling
Unitarian periodical, the Monthly Repository, in
which I made my first appearance in print, a youth,
named Thomas Noon Talfourd, was about this time
making *his* first attempts at authorship. Among his
earliest papers, I believe, was one ' On the System of
Malthus,' which had nothing in fact to do with the
real Malthus and his system, but was a sentimental
vindication of long engagements. It was prodigiously admired by very young people : not by me,
for it was rather too luscious for my taste,—but by
some of my family, who read it, and lived on it for
awhile : but it served to mislead me about Malthus,
and helped to sicken me of his name, as I told him
long afterwards. In spite of this, however, I
was all the while becoming a political economist
without knowing it, and, at the same time, a

sort of walking Concordance of Milton and Shakspere.

The first distinct recognition of my being deaf,
more or less, was when I was at Mr. Perry's,—when
I was about twelve years old. It was a very slight,
scarcely-perceptible hardness of hearing at that time;
and the recognition was merely this ;—that in that
great vaulted school-room before-mentioned, where
there was a large space between the class and the
master's desk or the fire, I was excused from taking
places in class, and desired to sit always at the top,
because it was somewhat nearer the master, whom I
could not always hear further off. When Mr. Perry
changed his abode, and we were in a smaller school-
room, I again took places with the rest. I remember
no other difficulty about hearing at that time. I certainly heard perfectly well at chapel, and all public
speaking (I remember Wilberforce in our vast St.
Andrew's Hall) and general conversation everywhere:
but before I was sixteen, it had become very noticeable, very inconvenient, and excessively painful to
myself. I did once think of writing down the whole
dreary story of the loss of a main sense, like hearing;
and I would not now shrink from inflicting the pain
of it on others, and on myself, if any adequate benefit
could be obtained by it. But, really, I do not see
that there could. It is true,—the sufferers rarely
receive the comfort of adequate, or even intelligent
sympathy: but there is no saying that an elaborate
account of the woe would create the sympathy, for
practical purposes. Perhaps what I have said in the
' Letter to the Deaf,' which I published in 1834,
will serve as well as anything I could say here to

those who are able to sympathise at all; and I will therefore offer no elaborate description of the daily and hourly trials which attend the gradual exclusion from the world of sound.

Some suggestions and conclusions, however, it is right to offer.—I have never seen a deaf child's education well managed at home, or at an ordinary school. It does not seem to be ever considered by parents and teachers how much more is learned by oral intercourse than in any other way; and, for want of this consideration, they find too late, and to their consternation, that the deaf pupil turns out deficient in sense, in manners, and in the knowledge of things so ordinary that they seem to be matters of instinct rather than of information. Too often, also, the deaf are sly and tricky, selfish and egotistical; and the dislike which attends them is the sin of the parent's ignorance visited upon the children. These worst cases are of those who are deaf from the outset, or from a very early age; and in as far as I was exempt from them, it was chiefly because my education was considerably advanced before my hearing began to go. In such a case as mine, the usual evil (far less serious) is that the sufferer is inquisitive,—*will* know every thing that is said, and becomes a bore to all the world. From this I was saved (or it helped to save me) by a kind word from my eldest brother. (From how much would a few more such words have saved me?) He had dined in company with an elderly single lady,—a sort of provincial blue-stocking in her time,—who was growing deaf, rapidly, and so sorely against her will that she tried to ignore the fact to the last possible moment. At that dinner-party, this lady sat next her old acquaintance, William Taylor of Norwich, who never knew very well how to deal with ladies (except, to his honour be it spoken, his blind mother;) and Miss N—— teased him to tell her all that every body said till he grew quite testy and rude. My brother told me, with tenderness in his voice, that he thought of me while blushing, as every body present did, for Miss N—— ; and that he hoped that if ever I should grow as deaf as she, I should never be seen making myself so irksome and absurd. This helped me to a resolution which I made and never broke,—never to ask what was said. Amidst remonstrance, kind and testy, and every sort of provocation, I have adhered to this resolution,—confident in its soundness. I think now, as I have thought always, that it is impossible for the deaf to divine what is worth asking for and what is not; and that one's friends may always be trusted, if left unmolested, to tell one whatever is essential, or really worth hearing.

One important truth about the case of persons deficient in a sense I have never seen noticed; and I much doubt whether it ever occurs to any but the sufferers under that deficiency. We sufferers meet with abundance of compassion for our privations: but the privation is, (judging by my own experience) a very inferior evil to the fatigue imposed by the obstruction. In my case, to be sure, the deficiency of three senses out of five renders the instance a very strong one: but the merely blind or deaf must feel something of the laboriousness of life which I have found it most difficult to deal with. People in general have only to sit still in the midst of Nature, to be amused and *diverted* (in the strict sense of the word,—*distracted*, in the French sense) so as to find ' change of work as good as rest :' but I have had, for the main part of my life, to go in search of impressions and influences, as the alternative from abstract or unrelieved thought, in an intellectual view, and from brooding, in a moral view. The fatigue belonging to either alternative may easily be conceived, when once suggested : and considerate persons will at once see what large allowance must in fairness be made for faults of temper, irritability or weakness of nerves, narrowness of mind, and imperfection of sympathy, in sufferers so worn with toil of body and mind as I, for one, have been. I have sustained, from this cause, fatigue which might spread over double my length of life; and in this I have met with no sympathy till I asked for it by an explanation of the case. From this labour there is, it must be remembered, no holiday, except in sleep. Life is a long, hard, unrelieved working-day to us, who hear, or see, only by express effort, or have to make other senses serve the turn of that which is lost. When three out of five are deficient, the difficulty of cheerful living is great, and the terms of life are truly hard.—-If I have made myself understood about this, I hope the explanation may secure sympathy for many who cannot be relieved from their burden, but may be cheered under it.

Another suggestion that I would make is that those who hear should not insist on managing the case of the deaf for them. As much sympathy as you please ; but no overbearing interference in a case which you cannot possibly judge of. The fact is,—

the family of a person who has a growing infirmity
are reluctant to face the truth ; and they are apt to
inflict frightful pain on the sufferer to relieve their
own weakness and uneasiness. I believe my family
would have made almost any sacrifice to save me from
my misfortune ; but not the less did they aggravate it
terribly by their way of treating it. First, and for
long, they insisted that it was all my own fault,—
that I was so absent,—that I never cared to attend
to any thing that was said,—that I ought to listen
this way, or that, or the other ; and even (while my
heart was breaking) they told me that 'none are so
deaf as those that won't hear.' When it became too
bad for this, they blamed me for not doing what I
was sorely tempted to do,—inquiring of them about
every thing that was said, and not managing in *their*
way, which would have made all right. This was
hard discipline ; but it was most useful to me in the
end. It showed me that I must take my case into
my own hands ; and with me, dependent as I was
upon the opinion of others, this was redemption from
probable destruction. Instead of drifting helplessly
as hitherto, I gathered myself up for a gallant breast-
ing of my destiny ; and in time I reached the rocks
where I could take a firm stand. I felt that here
was an enterprise ; and the spirit of enterprise was
roused in me ; animating me to sure success, with
many sinkings and much lapse by the way. While
about it, I took my temper in hand,—in this way. I
was young enough for vows,—was, indeed, at the very
age of vows ;—and I made a vow of patience about this
infirmity ;—that I would smile in every moment of
anguish from it ; and that I would never lose temper

at any consequences from it,—from losing public worship (then the greatest conceivable privation) to the spoiling of my cap-borders by the use of the trumpet I foresaw I must arrive at. With such a temper as mine was then, an infliction so worrying, so unintermitting, so mortifying, so isolating as loss of hearing must 'kill or cure.' In time, it acted with me as a cure, (in comparison with what my temper was in my youth:) but it took a long time to effect the cure; and it was so far from being evident, or even at all perceptible when I was fifteen, that my parents were determined by medical advice to send me from home for a considerable time, in hope of improving my health, nerves and temper by a complete and prolonged change of scene and objects.

Before entering upon that new chapter of my life, however, I must say another word about this matter of treatment of personal infirmity. We had a distant relation, in her young-womanhood when I was a child, who, living in the country, came into Norwich sometimes on market days, and occasionally called at our house. She had become deaf in infancy,—very very deaf; and her misfortune had been mismanaged. Truth to speak, she was far from agreeable: but it was less for that than on account of the trouble of her deafness that she was spoken of as I used to hear, long before I ever dreamed of being deaf myself. When it was announced by any child at the window that —— —— was passing, there was an exclamation of annoyance; and if she came up the steps, it grew into lamentation. 'What *shall* we do?' 'We shall be as hoarse as ravens all day.' 'We shall be completely worn out,' and so forth. Sometimes she was wished well at Jericho. When I was growing deaf, all this came back upon me ; and one of my self-questionings was—' Shall *I* put people to flight as ———— ———— does? Shall *I* be dreaded and disliked in that way all my life ? ' The lot did indeed seem at times too hard to be borne. Yet here am I now, on the borders of the grave, at the end of a busy life, confident that this same deafness is about the best thing that ever happened to me ;—the best, in a selfish view, as the grandest impulse to self-mastery ; and the best in a higher view, as my most peculiar opportunity of helping others, who suffer the same misfortune without equal stimulus to surmount the false shame, and other unspeakable miseries which attend it.

By this time, the battle of Waterloo had been fought. I suppose most children were politicians during the war. I was a great one. I remember Mr. Perry's extreme amusement at my breaking through my shyness, one day, and stopping him as he was leaving the school-room, to ask, with much agitation, whether he believed in the claims of one of the many Louis XVII.'s who have turned up in my time. It must be considered that my mother remembered the first French Revolution. Her sympathies were with the royal family ; and the poor little Dauphin was an object of romantic interest to all English children who knew anything of the story at all. The pretence that he was found set thousands of imaginations on fire, whenever it was raised ; and among many other wonderful effects, it emboldened me to speak to Mr. Perry about other things than lessons. Since the present war (of 1854) broke out,

it has amused me to find myself so like my old self
of forty years before, in regard to telling the servants
the news.   In the old days, I used to fly into the
kitchen, and tell my father's servants how sure
' Boney' was to be caught,—how impossible it was
that he should escape,—how his army was being
driven back through the Pyrenees,—or how he had
driven back the allies here or there.   Then, I wanted
sympathy, and liked the importance and the sensation
of carrying news.   Now, the way has been to summon
my own servants after the evening post, and bid
them get the map, or come with me to the globe, and
explain to them the state of the war, and give them
the latest news,—probably with some of the old associations lingering in my mind ; but certainly with
the dominant desire to give these intelligent girls an
interest in the interests of freedom, and a clear knowledge of the position and duties of England in regard
to the war.   I remember my father's bringing in
the news of some of the Peninsular victories, and
what his face was like when he told my mother of
the increase of the Income-tax to ten per cent., and
again, of the removal of the Income-tax.   I remember the proclamation of peace in 1814, and our all
going to see the illuminations ; those abominable
transparencies, among the rest, which represented
Bonaparte (always in green coat, white breeches and
boots) as carried to hell by devils, pitch-forked in the
fiery lake by the same attendants, or haunted by the
Duc d'Enghien.   I well remember the awful moment
when Mr. Drummond (of the chemical lectures)
looked in at the back door (on his way from the
counting-house) and telling my mother that ' Boney'

had escaped from Elba, and was actually in France.
This impressed me more than the subsequent hot
Midsummer morning when somebody (I forget
whether father or brother) burst in with the news
of the Waterloo slaughter. It was the slaughter
that was uppermost with us, I believe, though we
never had a relative, nor, as far as I know, even an
acquaintance, in either army or navy.

I was more impressed still with the disappointment
about the effects of the peace, at the end of the first
year of it. The country was overrun with disbanded
soldiers, and robbery and murder were frightfully frequent and desperate. The Workhouse Boards were
under a pressure of pauperism which they could not
have managed if the Guardians had been better informed than they were in those days ; and one of my
political panics (of which I underwent a constant succession) was that the country would become bankrupt
through its poor-law. Another panic was about revolution,—our idea of revolution being, of course, of
guillotines in the streets, and all that sort of thing.
Those were Cobbett's grand days, and the days of
Castlereagh and Sidmouth spy-systems and con-
spiracies. Our pastor was a great radical ; and he
used to show us the caricatures of the day (Hone's,
I think) in which Castlereagh was always flogging
Irishmen, and Canning spouting forth, and the
Regent insulting his wife, and the hungry, haggard
multitude praying for vengeance on the Court and
the Ministers ; and every Sunday night, after supper, when he and two or three other bachelor friends
were with us, the talk was of the absolute certainty
of a dire revolution. When, on my return from

Bristol in 1819, I ventured to say what my conscience bade me say, and what I had been led to see by a dear aunt, that it was wrong to catch up and believe and spread reports injurious to the royal family, who could not reply to slander like other people, I was met by a shout of derision first, and then by a serious reprimand for my immorality in making more allowance for royal sinners than for others. Between my dread of this worldliness, and my sense that they had a worse chance than other people, and my further feeling that respect should be shown them on account of their function first, and their defenceless position afterwards, I was in what the Americans would call 'a fix.' The conscientious uncertainty I was in was a real difficulty and trouble to me; and this probably helped to fix my attention upon the principles of politics and the characteristics of parties, with an earnestness not very common at that age. Still,—how astonished should I have been if any one had then foretold to me that, of all the people in England, I should be the one to write the ' History of the Peace!'

One important consequence of the peace was the interest with which foreigners were suddenly invested, in the homes of the middle classes, where the rising generation had seen no foreigners except old *émigrés*,—powdered old Frenchmen, and ladies with outlandish bonnets and high-heeled shoes. About this time there came to Norwich a foreigner who excited an unaccountable interest in our house,—considering what exceedingly proper people we were, and how sharp a look-out we kept on the morals of our neighbours. It was poor Polidori, well known afterwards as Lord

Byron's physician, as the author of 'the Vampire,'
and as having committed suicide under gambling
difficulties. When we knew him, he was a handsome, harum-scarum young man,—taken up by William Taylor as William Taylor did take up harum-
scarum young men,—and so introduced into the best
society the place afforded, while his being a Catholic,
or passing for such, ensured him a welcome in some
of the most aristocratic of the county houses. He was
a foolish rattle,—with no sense, scarcely any knowledge, and no principle; but we took for granted in
him much that he had not, and admired whatever he
had.   For his part, he was an avowed admirer of our
eldest sister, (who however escaped fancy-free;) and
he was for ever at our house. We younger ones ro-
manced amazingly about him,—drew his remarkable
profile on the backs of all our letters, dreamed of him,
listened to all his marvellous stories, and, when he got
a concussion of the brain by driving his gig against a
tree in Lord Stafford's park, were inconsolable. If he
had (happily) died then, he would have remained a hero
in our imaginations. The few following years, (which
were very possibly all the wilder for that concussion of
the brain) disabused every body of all expectation of
good from him; but yet when he died, frantic under
gaming debts, the shock was great, and the impression,
on my mind at least, deep and lasting.   My eldest
sister, then in a happy home of her own, was shocked
and concerned; but we younger ones felt it far more.
I was then in the height of my religious fanaticism;
and I remember putting away all doubts about the
theological propriety of what I was doing, for the sake
of the relief of praying for his soul.   Many times a
day, and with my whole heart, did I pray for his soul.

SECTION III.

As I have said, it was the state of my health and temper which caused me to be sent from home when I was in my sixteenth year. So many causes of unhappiness had arisen, and my temper was so thoroughly ajar, that nothing else would have done any effectual good. Every thing was a misery to me, and was therefore done with a bad grace; and hence had sprung up a habit of domestic criticism which ought never to have been allowed, in regard to any one member of the family, and least of all towards one of the youngest, and certainly the most suffering of all. My mother received and administered a check now and then, which did good for the time; but the family habit was strong; and it was a wise measure to institute an entire change. Two or three anecdotes will suffice to give an idea of what had to be surmounted.

I was too shy ever to ask to be taught any thing,— except, indeed, of good-natured strangers. I have mentioned that we were well practiced in some matters of domestic management. We could sew, iron, make sweets, gingerbread and pastry, and keep order generally throughout the house. But I did not

know,—what nobody can know without being taught,
—how to purchase stores, or to set out a table, or to
deal with the butcher and fishmonger. It is inconceivable what a trouble this was to me for many
years. I was always in terror at that great mountain of duty before me, and wondering what was to
become of me if my mother left home, or if I should
marry. Never once did it occur to me to go to my
mother, and ask to be taught: and it was not pride
but fear which so incapacitated me. I liked that
sort of occupation, and had great pleasure in doing
what I could do in that way; insomuch that I have
sometimes felt myself what General F. called his
wife,—' a good housemaid spoilt.' My ' Guides to
Service,' (' The Maid-of-all-Work,' ' Housemaid,'
' Lady's Maid' and ' Dress-maker,') written twenty
years afterwards, may show something of this.
Meantime, never was poor creature more dismally
awkward than I was when domestic eyes were upon
me : and this made me a most vexatious member of
the family. I remember once upsetting a basin of
moist sugar into a giblet pie. (I remember nothing
else quite so bad.) I never could find any thing I was
sent for, though I could lay my hands in the dark on
any thing I myself wanted. On one occasion, when a
workwoman was making mourning in the midst of us,
I was desired to take the keys, and fetch a set of cravats for marking, out of a certain drawer. My heart
sank at the order, and already the inevitable sentence
rung in my ears,—that I was more trouble than I
was worth ; which I sincerely believed. The drawer
was large, and crammed. I could not see one thing
from another ; and in no way could I see any cravats.

Slowly and fearfully I came back to say so. Of
course, I was sent again, and desired not to come
back without them. That time, and again the next,
I took every thing out of the drawer; and still found
no cravats. My eldest sister tried next; and great
was my consolation when she returned crest-fallen,—
having found no cravats. My mother snatched the
keys, under a strong sense of the hardship of having
to do every thing herself, when Rachel suggested
another place where they might have been put.
There they were found; and my heart was swelling
with vindictive pleasure when my mother, by a few
noble words, turned the tide of feeling completely.
In the presence of the workwoman, she laid her hand
on my arm, kissed me, and said, 'And now, my dear,
I have to beg *your* pardon.' I answered only by
tears; but the words supported me for long after.

I look back upon another scene with horror at
my own audacity, and wonder that my family could
endure me at all. At Mr. Perry's, one of our school-
fellows was a clever, mischievous girl,—so clever,
and so much older than myself as to have great influence over me when she chose to try her power,
though I disapproved her ways very heartily. She
one day asked me, in a corner, in a mysterious sort of
way, whether I did not perceive that Rachel was the
favourite at home, and treated with manifest partiality. Every body else, she said, observed it. This
had never distinctly occurred to me. Rachel was
handy and useful, and not paralysed by fear, as I
was; and, very naturally, our busy mother resorted
to her for help, and put trust in her about matters
of business, not noticing the growth of an equally

natural habit in Rachel of quizzing or snubbing me, as the elder ones did. From the day of this mischievous speech of my school-fellow, I was on the watch, and with the usual result to the jealous. Months,—perhaps a year or two—passed on while I was brooding over this, without a word to any one; and then came the explosion, one winter evening after tea, when my eldest sister was absent, and my mother, Rachel and I were sitting at work. Rachel criticised something that I said, in which I happened to be right. After once defending myself, I sat silent. My mother remarked on my ' obstinacy,' saying that I was ' not a bit convinced.' I replied that nothing convincing had been said. My mother declared that she agreed with Rachel, and that I ought to yield. Then I passed the verge, and got wrong. A sudden force of daring entering my mind, I said, in the most provoking way possible, that this was nothing new, as she always did agree with Rachel against me. My mother put down her work, and asked me what I meant by that. I looked her full in the face, and said that what I meant was that every thing that Rachel said and did was right, and every thing that I said and did was wrong. Rachel burst into an insulting laugh, and was sharply bidden to ' be quiet.' I saw by this that I had gained some ground; and this was made clearer by my mother sternly desiring me to practise my music. I saw that she wanted to gain time. The question now was how I should get through. My hands were clammy and tremulous: my fingers stuck to each other; my eyes were dim, and there was a roaring in my ears. I could easily have fainted; and it might have done n harm if I had. But I made a tremendous effort to appear calm. I opened the piano, lighted a candle with a steady hand, began, and derived strength from the first chords. I believe I never played better in my life. Then the question was—how was I ever to leave off? On I went for what seemed to me an immense time, till my mother sternly called to me to leave off and go to bed. With my candle in my hand, I said, 'Good night.' My mother laid down her work, and said, 'Harriet, I am more displeased with you to-night than ever I have been in your life.' Thought I, 'I don't care: I have got it out, and it is all true.' 'Go and say your prayers,' my mother continued; 'and ask God to forgive you for your conduct to-night; for I don't know that I can. Go to your prayers.' Thought I,—'No, I shan't.' And I did not: and that was the only night from my infancy to mature womanhood that I did not pray. I detected misgiving in my mother's forced manner; and I triumphed. If the right was on my side (as I entirely believed) the power was on hers; and what the next morning was to be I could not conceive. I slept little, and went down sick with dread. Not a word was said, however, then or ever, of the scene of the preceding night; but henceforth, a most scrupulous impartiality between Rachel and me was shown. If the occasion had been better used still,—if my mother had but bethought herself of saying to me, 'My child, I never dreamed that these terrible thoughts were in your mind. I am your mother. Why do you not tell me every thing that makes you unhappy?' I believe this would have wrought in a moment that cure which it took years to effect, amidst reserve and silence.

It has been a difficulty with me all my life (and its being a difficulty shows some deep-seated fault in me) how to reconcile sincerity with peace and good manners in such matters as other people's little mistakes of fact. As an example of what I mean,—a schoolfellow spelled Shakspere as I spell it here. Mr. Perry put in an *a*, observing that the name was never spelt in print without an *a*. I ventured to doubt this;\but he repeated his assertion. At afternoon school, I showed him a volume of the edition we had at home, which proved him wrong. He received the correction with so indifferent a grace that I was puzzled as to whether I had done right or wrong,—whether sincerity required me to set my master right before the face of his scholars. Of course, if I had been older, I should have done it more privately. But this is a specimen of the difficulties of that class that I have struggled with almost ever since. The difficulty was immensely increased by the family habit of requiring an answer from me, and calling me obstinate if the reply was not an unconditional yielding. I have always wondered to see the ease and success with which very good people humour and manage the aged, the sick and the weak, and sometimes every body about them. I could never attempt this; for it always seemed to me such contemptuous treatment of those whom I was at the moment respecting more than ever, on account of their weakness. But I was always quite in the opposite extreme ;—far too solemn, too rigid, and prone to exaggeration of differences and to obstinacy at the same time. It was actually not till I was near forty that I saw how the matter should really be,—saw it through a perfect

example of an union of absolute sincerity with all
possible cheerfulness, sweetness, modesty and deference for all, in proportion to their claims. I have
never attained righteous good-manners, to this day;
but I have understood what they are since the
beauties of J. S.'s character and manners were revealed to me under circumstances of remarkable
trial.

While organised, it seems to me, for sincerity, and
being generally truthful, except for the exaggeration
which is apt to beset persons of repressed faculties, I
feel compelled to state here (what belongs to this part
of my life) that towards one person I was habitually
untruthful, from fear. To my mother I would in my
childhood assert or deny any thing that would bring
me through most easily. I remember denying various
harmless things,—playing a game at battledore, for
one; and often without any apparent reason: and
this was so exclusively to one person that, though
there was remonstrance and punishment, I believe I
was never regarded as a liar in the family. It seems
now all very strange : but it was a temporary and
very brief phase. When I left home, all temptation
to untruth ceased, and there was henceforth nothing
more than the habit of exaggeration and strong
expression to struggle with.

Before I went to Bristol, I was the prey of three
griefs,—prominent among many. I cannot help
laughing while I write them. They were my bad
hand-writing, my deafness, and the state of my hair.
Such a trio of miseries! I was the first of my family
who failed in the matter of hand-writing; and why
I did remains unexplained. I am sure I tried hard;

but I wrote a vulgar, cramped, untidy scrawl till I was past twenty;—till authorship made me forget manner in matter, and gave freedom to my hand. After that, I did very well, being praised by compositors for legibleness first, and in course of time, for other qualities. But it was a severe mortification while it lasted; and many bitter tears I shed over the reflections that my awkward hand called forth. It was a terrible penance to me to write letters home from Bristol; and the day of the week when it was to be done was very like the Beckwith music-lesson days. If any one had told me then how many reams of paper I should cover in the course of my life, life would have seemed a sort of purgatory to me.—As to my deafness, I got no relief about that at Bristol. It was worse when I returned in weak health.—The third misery, which really plagued me seriously, was cured presently after I left home. I made my dear aunt Kentish the depositary of my confidence in all matters; and this, of course, among the rest. She induced me to consult a friend of hers, who had remarkably beautiful hair; and then it came out that I had been combing overmuch, and that there was nothing the matter with my hair, if I would be content with brushing it. So that grief was annihilated, and there was an end of one of those trifles which ' make up the sum of human things.'

And now the hour was at hand when I was to find, for the first time, a human being whom I was not afraid of. That blessed being was my dear aunt Kentish, who stands distinguished in my mind by that from all other persons whom I have ever known.

I did not understand the facts about my leaving home till I had been absent some months; and when I did, I was deeply and effectually moved by my mother's consideration for my feelings. We had somehow been brought up in a supreme contempt of boarding-schools: and I was therefore truly amazed when my mother sounded me, in the spring of 1817, about going for a year or two to a Miss Somebody's school at Yarmouth. She talked of the sea, of the pleasantness of change, and of how happy L. T——, an excessively silly girl of our acquaintance, was there: but I made such a joke of L. and her studies, and of the attainments of the young ladies, as we had heard of them, that my mother gave up the notion of a scheme which never could have answered. It would have been ruin to a temper like mine at that crisis to have sent me among silly and ignorant people, to have my ' manners formed,' after the most ordinary boarding-school fashion. My mother did much better in sending me among people so superior to myself as to improve me morally and intellectually, though the experiment failed in regard to health. A brother of my mother's had been unfortunate in business at Bristol, and had not health to retrieve his affairs; and his able and accomplished wife, and clever young daughters opened a school. Of the daughters, one was within a few weeks of my own age; and we have been intimate friends from that time (the beginning of 1818) till this hour. Another was two years younger; another, two years older; while the eldest had reached womanhood. Of these clever cousins we had heard much, for many years, without having seen any of them. At the opening of the year 1818, a letter arrived from my aunt to my mother, saying that it was time the young people should be becoming acquainted; that her girls were all occupied in the school, for the routine of which Rachel was somewhat too old; but that if Harriet would go, and spend some time with them, and take the run of the school, she would be a welcome guest, &c. &c. This pleased me much, and I heard with joy that I was to go when my father took his next journey to Bristol,—early in February. My notion was of a stay of a few weeks; and I was rather taken aback when my mother spoke of my absence as likely to last a year or more. It never entered my head that I was going to a boarding-school; and when I discovered, long after, that the Bristol family understood that I was, I was not (as I once might have been) angry at having been tricked into it, but profoundly contrite for the temper which made such management necessary, and touched by the trouble my mother took to spare my silly pride, and consider my troublesome feelings.

I was, on the whole, happy during the fifteen months I spent at Bristol, though home-sickness spoiled the last half of the time. My home affections seem to have been all the stronger for having been repressed and baulked. Certainly, I passionately loved my family, each and all, from the very hour that parted us; and I was physically ill with expectation when their letters became due; — letters which I could hardly read when they came, between my dread of something wrong, and the beating heart and swimming eyes with which I received letters in those days. There were some family anxieties during the latter

part of the time ; and there was one grand event,—
the engagement of my eldest sister, who had virtually
ceased to belong to us by the time I returned home.

I found my cousins even more wonderfully clever
than I had expected ; and they must have been somewhat surprised at my striking inferiority in knowledge, and in the power of acquiring it.   I still think
that I never met with a family to compare with theirs
for power of acquisition, or effective use of knowledge.
They would learn a new language at odd minutes ;
get through a tough philosophical book by taking
turns in the court for air ; write down an entire
lecture or sermon, without missing a sentence ; get
round the piano after a concert, and play and sing
over every new piece that had been performed.
Ability like this was a novel spectacle to me ; and
it gave me the pure pleasure of unmixed admiration ;
for I was certainly not conscious of any ability whatever at that time.   I had no great deal to do in the
school, being older than every girl there but one ;
and I believe I got no particular credit in such classes
as I did join.   For one thing, my deafness was now
bad enough to be a disadvantage ; but it was a worse
disqualification that my memory, always obedient to
my own command, was otherwise disobedient.   I could
remember whatever I had learned in my own way, but
was quite unable to answer in class, like far younger
girls, about any thing just communicated.   My
chief intellectual improvement during that important
period was derived from private study.   I read some
analytical books, on logic and rhetoric, with singular
satisfaction ; and I lost nothing afterwards that I
obtained in this way.   I read a good deal of History

too, and revelled in poetry,—a new world of which was opened to me by my cousins. The love of natural scenery was a good deal developed in me by the beauty around Bristol. One circumstance makes me think that I had become rather suddenly awakened to it not long before,—though my delight in the sea at Cromer dated some years earlier. Mr. Perry tried upon us the reading of L'Allegro and Il Penseroso; and it failed utterly. I did not feel any thing whatever, though I supposed I understood what I heard. Not long after he was gone, I read both pieces in the nursery, one day; and straightway went into a transport, as if I had discovered myself in possession of a new sense. Thus it was again now, when I was transferred from flat, bleak Norfolk to the fine scenery about Bristol. Even the humble beauty of our most frequent walk, by the Logwood Mills, was charming to me,—the clear running water, with its weedy channel, and the meadow walk on the brink: and about Leigh woods, Kingsweston, and the Downs, my rapture knew no bounds.

Far more important, however, was the growth of kindly affections in me at this time, caused by the free and full tenderness of my dear aunt Kentish, and of all my other relations then surrounding me. My heart warmed and opened, and my habitual fear began to melt away. I have since been told that, on the day of my arrival, when some of the school-girls asked my cousin M. what I was like, (as she came out of the parlour where I was) she said that I looked as if I was cross; but that she knew I was not; and that I looked unhappy. When I left Bristol, I was as pale as a ghost, and as thin as possible; and still very frowning

and repulsive-looking ; but yet with a comparatively
open countenance. The counteracting influence to
dear aunt Kentish's was one which visited me very
strongly at the same time,—that of a timid superstition. She was herself, then and always, very religious ; but she had a remarkable faculty of making
her religion suggest and sanction whatever she liked :
and, as she liked whatever was pure, amiable, unselfish
and unspoiling, this tendency did her no harm.
Matters were otherwise with me. My religion too
took the character of my mind ; and it was harsh,
severe and mournful accordingly. There was a great
furor among the Bristol Unitarians at that time about
Dr. Carpenter, who had recently become their pastor.
He was a very devoted Minister, and a very earnest
pietist : superficial in his knowledge, scanty in ability,
narrow in his conceptions, and thoroughly priestly in
his temper. He was exactly the dissenting minister
to be worshipped by his people, (and especially by the
young) and to be spoiled by that worship. He was worshipped by the young, and by none more than by me ;
and his power was unbounded while his pupils continued young : but, as his instructions and his scholars
were not bound together by any bond of essential
Christian doctrine, every thing fell to pieces as soon
as the merely personal influence was withdrawn. A
more extraordinary diversity of religious opinion than
existed among his pupils when they became men and
women could not be seen. They might be found at
the extremes of catholicism and atheism, and every
where between. As for me, his devout and devoted
Catechumen, he made me desperately superstitious,—
living wholly in and for religion, and fiercely fanatical

about it. I returned home raving about my pastor and teacher, remembering every word he had ever spoken to me,—with his instructions burnt in, as it were, upon my heart and conscience, and with an abominable spiritual rigidity and a truly respectable force of conscience curiously mingled together, so as to procure for me the no less curiously mingled ridicule and respect of my family. My little sister, then learning to sew on her stool at my mother's knee, has since told me what she perceived, with the penetrating eyes and heart of childhood. Whenever I left the room my mother and elder sisters used to begin to quiz my fanaticism,—which was indeed quizzical enough ; but the little one saw a sort of respect for me underlying the mockery, which gave her her first clear sense of moral obligation, and the nature of obedience to it.

The results of the Bristol experiment were thus good on the whole. My health was rather worse than better, through wear and tear of nerves,— home-sickness, religious emotions, overmuch study (so my aunt said, against my conviction) and medical mismanagement. I had learned a good deal, and had got into a good way of learning more. My domestic affections were regenerated ; and I had become sincerely and heartily religious, with some improvement in temper in consequence, and not a little in courage, hope and conscientiousness. The fanaticism was a stage which I should probably have had to pass through at any rate,—and by the same phase of pastor-worship,—whoever the pastor might have been.

THIRD PERIOD.

SECTION I.

I RETURNED home in April, 1819, and continued to reside in Norwich till November, 1832. These thirteen years, extending from my entering upon womanhood to my complete establishment in an independent position, as to occupation and the management of my own life, seem to form a marked period of themselves; and I shall treat them in that way.

My eldest sister's marriage in 1820 made young women at once of Rachel and myself. It was on all accounts a happy event, though we dreaded excessively the loss of her from home, which she eminently graced. But never did woman grow in grace more remarkably than she did by her marriage. When she had found her own heart, it proved a truly noble one; and the generosity, sweetness, and wisdom of her whole conduct towards her own children showed that her mistakes in her treatment of us were merely the crudities of inexperience. I may say, once for all, that her home at Newcastle was ever open to us, and that all possible kindness from her hospitable husband

and herself was always at our command, without
hindrance or difficulty, till my recovery from a hope-
less illness, in 1844, by Mesmerism, proved too much
for the natural prejudice of a surgeon and a surgeon's
wife, and caused, by the help of the ill-offices of
another relation, a family breach, as absurd as it was
lamentable. My sister was then under the early symptoms of her last illness; and matters might have ended
more happily if she had been in her usual state of
health and nerve, as they certainly would if advantage had not been taken of her natural irritation
against Mesmerism to gratify in another jealousies to
which she was herself far superior. My own certainty of this, and my grateful remembrance of the
long course of years during which I enjoyed her
friendship and generosity, and her cordial sympathy
in my aims and successes, incline me to pass over her
final alienation, and dwell upon the affectionate intercourse we enjoyed, at frequent intervals, for twenty
years from her marriage day.

Our revered and beloved eldest brother had, by this
time, settled in Norwich as a surgeon, in partnership
with our uncle, Mr. P. M. Martineau, the most eminent provincial surgeon of his day,—in some departments, if not altogether. My brother's health was
delicate, and we were to lose him by death in five
years. One of the sweetest recollections of my life is
that I had the honour and blessing of his intimate
friendship, which grew and deepened from my sister's
marriage to the time of his own death. My mother,
too, took me into her confidence more and more as
my mind opened, and, I may add, as my deafness increased, and bespoke for me her motherly sympathy.

For some years, indeed, there was a genuine and cordial friendship between my mother and me, which
was a benefit to me in all manner of ways; and, from
the time when I began to have literary enterprises,
(and quite as much before I obtained success as after)
I was sustained by her trustful, generous, self-denying
sympathy and maternal appreciation. After a time,
when she was fretted by cares and infirmities, I became as nervous in regard to her as ever, (even to the
entire breaking down of my health ;) but during the
whole period of which I am now treating,—(and it
is a very large space in my life)—there were no
limitations to our mutual confidence.

One other relation which reached its highest point,
and had begun to decline, during this period was one
which I must abstain from discussing. The briefest
possible notice will be the best method of treatment.
All who have ever known me are aware that the
strongest passion I have ever entertained was in regard to my youngest brother, who has certainly filled
the largest space in the life of my affections of any
person whatever. Now, the fact,—the painful fact,
—in the history of human affections is that, of all
natural relations, the least satisfactory is the fraternal.
Brothers are to sisters what sisters can never be to
brothers as objects of engrossing and devoted affection.
The law of their frames is answerable for this : and
that other law—of equity—which sisters are bound
to obey, requires that they should not render their
account of their disappointments where there can be
no fair reply. Under the same law, sisters are bound
to remember that they cannot be certain of their own
fitness to render an account of their own disappoint-

ments, or to form an estimate of the share of blame which may be due to themselves on the score of unreasonable expectations. These general considerations decide me to pass over one of the main relations and influences of my life in a few brief and unsatisfactory lines, though I might tell a very particular tale. If I could see a more truthful, just, and satisfactory method of treating the topic, I should most gladly adopt it.—As for the other members of our numerous family, I am thankful and rejoiced to bear testimony that they have given all possible encouragement to the labours of my life; and that they have been the foremost of all the world to appreciate and rejoice in my successes, and to respect that independence of judgment and action on my part which must often have given them pain, and which would have overpowered any generosity less deeply rooted in principle and affection than theirs.

When I was young, it was not thought proper for young ladies to study very conspicuously; and especially with pen in hand. Young ladies (at least in provincial towns) were expected to sit down in the parlour to sew,—during which reading aloud was permitted,—or to practice their music; but so as to be fit to receive callers, without any signs of bluestockingism which could be reported abroad. Jane Austen herself, the Queen of novelists, the immortal creator of Anne Elliott, Mr. Knightley, and a score of two more of unrivalled intimate friends of the whole public, was compelled by the feelings of her family to cover up her manuscripts with a large piece of muslin work, kept on the table for the purpose, whenever any genteel people came in. So it was with other young ladies, for some time after Jane Austen was in her grave ; and thus my first studies in philosophy were carried on with great care and reserve. I was at the work table regularly after breakfast,— making my own clothes, or the shirts of the household, or about some fancy work : I went out walking with the rest, —before dinner in winter, and after tea in summer : and if ever I shut myself into my own room for an hour of solitude, I knew it was at the risk of being sent for to join the sewing-circle, or to read aloud,— I being the reader, on account of my growing deafness. But I won time for what my heart was set upon, nevertheless,—either in the early morning, or late at night. I had a strange passion for translating, in those days ; and a good preparation it proved for the subsequent work of my life. Now, it was meeting James at seven in the morning to read Lowth's Prelections in the Latin, after having been busy since five about something else, in my own room. Now it was translating Tacitus, in order to try what was the utmost compression of style that I could attain. — About this I may mention an incident while it occurs. We had all grown up with a great reverence for Mrs. Barbauld (which she fully deserved from much wiser people than ourselves) and, reflectively, for Dr. Aikin, her brother,—also able in his way, and far more industrious, but without her genius. Among a multitude of other labours, Dr. Aikin had translated the Agricola of Tacitus. I went into such an enthusiasm over the original, and especially over the celebrated concluding passage, that I thought I would translate it, and correct it by Dr. Aikin's, which I could procure from our public library. I did

it, and found my own translation unquestionably the
best of the two. I had spent an infinity of pains over
it,—word by word; and I am confident I was not
wrong in my judgment. I stood pained and
mortified before my desk, I remember, thinking how
strange and small a matter was human achievement,
if Dr. Aikin's fame was to be taken as a testimony of
literary desert. I had beaten him whom I had
taken for my master. I need not point out that, in
the first place, Dr. Aikin's fame did not hang on this
particular work ; nor that, in the second place, I had
exaggerated his fame by our sectarian estimate of him.
I give the incident as a curious little piece of personal
experience, and one which helped to make me like
literary labour more for its own sake, and less for its
rewards, than I might otherwise have done.—Well :
to return to my translating propensities. Our cousin
J. M. L., then studying for his profession in Norwich,
used to read Italian with Rachel and me,—also
before breakfast. We made some considerable progress, through the usual course of prose authors and
poets ; and out of this grew a fit which Rachel and I
at one time took, in concert with our companions and
neighbours, the C.'s, to translate Petrarch. Nothing
could be better as an exercise in composition than
translating Petrarch's sonnets into English of the
same limits. It was putting ourselves under com-
pulsion to do with the Italian what I had set myself
voluntarily to do with the Latin author. I believe
we really succeeded pretty well ; and I am sure that
all these exercises were a singularly apt preparation
for my after work. At the same time, I went on
studying Blair's Rhetoric (for want of a better guide)

and inclining mightily to every kind of book or process which could improve my literary skill,—really
as if I had foreseen how I was to spend my life.

These were not, however, my most precious or
serious studies. I studied the Bible incessantly and
immensely; both by daily reading of chapters, after
the approved but mischievous method, and by getting
hold of all commentaries and works of elucidation that
I could lay my hands on. A work of Dr. Carpenter's,
begun but never finished, called ' Notes and Observations on the Gospel History,' which his catechumens
used in class, first put me on this track of study,—
the results of which appeared some years afterwards in
my ' Traditions of Palestine.' It was while reading
Mr. Kenrick's translation from the German of
' Helon's Pilgrimage to Jerusalem,' with which I
was thoroughly bewitched, that I conceived, and
communicated to James, the audacious idea of giving
a somewhat resembling account of the Jews and their
country, under the immediate expectation of the
Messiah, and even in his presence, while carefully
abstaining from permitting more than his shadow to
pass over the scene. This idea I cherished till I
found courage, under a new inspiration some years
after, to execute it: and so pleasant was the original
suggestion, and so congenial the subject altogether,
that even now, at the distance of a quarter of a
century, I regard that little volume with a stronger
affection than any other of my works but one;—that
one being ' Eastern Life.'

Dr. Carpenter was inclined also to the study of
philosophy, and wrote on it,—on mental and moral
philosophy; and this was enough, putting all predis-

position out of the question, to determine me to the
study.   He was of the Locke and Hartley school
altogether, as his articles on ' Mental and Moral
Philosophy,' in Rees's Cyclopedia, and his work on
' Systematic Education ' show.   He used to speak of
Hartley as one who had the intellectual qualities of
the seraphic order combined with the affections of the
cherubic ; and it was no wonder if Hartley became my
idol when I was mistress of my own course of study.
I must clear myself from all charge of having ever entertained his doctrine of Vibrations. I do not believe
that Dr. Carpenter himself could have prevailed with
me so far as that.   But neither did Hartley prevail
with Dr. Carpenter so far as that.   The edition of
Hartley that I used was Dr. Priestley's,—that which
gives the philosophy of Association, cleared from the
incumbrance of the Vibration theory.   That book I
studied with a fervour and perseverance which made it
perhaps the most important book in the world to me,
except the bible ; and there really is in it, amidst its
monstrous deficiencies and absurdities, so much that
is philosophically true, as well as holy, elevating and
charming, that its influence might very well spread
into all the events and experience of life, and chasten
the habits and feelings, as it did in my case during a
long series of years.   So far from feeling, as Dr.
Channing and other good men have done, that the
influence of that philosophy is necessarily, in all cases,
debasing, I am confident at this moment that the
spirit of the men, Locke and Hartley, redeems much
of the fault of their doctrine in its operation on young
minds ; and moreover, that the conscientious accuracy
with which they apply their doctrine to the moral

conduct of the smallest particulars of human life
(Hartley particularly) forms a far better discipline,
and produces a much more exalting effect on the
minds of students than the vague metaphysical
imaginations,—as various and irreconcilable as the
minds that give them forth, which Dr. Channing and
his spiritual school adopted (or believed that they
adopted) as a ' spiritual philosophy.' I know this,
—that while I read the Germans, Americans and
English who are the received exponents of that
philosophy with a general and extremely vague sense
of elevation and beauty as the highest emotion produced, I cannot at this hour look at the portrait of
Hartley prefixed to his work, or glance at his strange
Scholia,—which I could almost repeat, word for
word,—without a strong revival of the old mood of
earnest desire of self-discipline, and devotion to duty
which I derived from them in my youth. While the
one school has little advantage over the other in the
abstract department of their philosophy, the disciples
of Hartley have infinitely the advantage over the
dreaming school in their master's presentment of
the concrete department of fact and of action. Compelled as I have since been to relinquish both as
philosophy, I am bound to avow, (and enjoy the
avowal) that I owe to Hartley the strongest and best
stimulus and discipline of the highest affections and
most important habits that it is perhaps possible, (or
was possible for me) to derive from any book.—The
study of Priestley's character and works (natural to
me because he was the great apostle of Unitarianism)
necessarily led me to the study of the Scotch school
of philosophy, which I took the liberty to enjoy in its

own way, in spite of Priestley's contempt of it. I
never believed in it, because it was really inconceivable to me how anybody should ; and I was moreover
entirely wrong in not perceiving that the Scotch
philosophers had got hold of a fragment of sound
truth which the other school had missed,—in their
postulate of a fundamental complete faculty, which
could serve as a basis of the mind's operations,—
whereas Hartley lays down simply the principle of
association, and a capacity for pleasure and pain. I
ought to have perceived that the Scotch proposition of
Common Sense would answer much better for purposes of interpretation, if I had not yet knowledge
enough to show me that it was much nearer the fact
of the case. I did not perceive this, but talked as
flippantly as Priestley, with far less right to do so.
At the same time, I surrendered myself, to a considerable extent, to the charm of Dugald Stewart's
writings,—having no doubt that Priestley, if then
living, would have done so too. About Beattie and
Reid I was pert enough, from a genuine feeling of
the unsatisfactoriness of their writings ; but the truth
of detail scattered through Dugald Stewart's elegant
elucidations, the gentle and happy spirit, and the
beautiful style, charmed me so much that I must have
been among his most affectionate disciples, if I had
not been fortified against his seductions by my devotion to Hartley.

It appears to me now that, though my prevailing
weakness in study is excessive sympathy, intellectual
as well as moral, with my author, I even then felt
something of the need which long after became all-
powerful in me, of a clear distinction between the

knowable and the unknowable,— of some available indication of an indisputable point of view, whence one's contemplation of human nature, as of every thing else in the universe, should make its range. It may be that I am carrying back too far in my life this sense of need. When I consider how contentedly I went on, during the whole of this third period, floating and floundering among metaphysical imaginations, and giving forth inbred conceptions as truths of fact, I am disposed to think it probable that I am casting back the light of a later time among the mists of an earlier, and supposing myself sooner capable than I really was of practically distinguishing between a conception and a conviction. But there can be no mistake about the time and manner of my laying hold of a genuine conviction in a genuine manner, as I will presently tell. It would no doubt have been a fine thing for me,—an event which would have elevated my whole after-life,—if a teacher had been at hand to show me the boundary line between the knowable and the unknowable, as I see it now, and to indicate to me that the purely human view of the universe, derived solely from within, and proceeding on the supposition that Man and his affairs and his world are the centre and crown of the universe, could not possibly be the true one. But, in the absence of such a teacher,—in my inability to see the real scope and final operation of the discovery of Copernicus and Galileo,—and the ultimate connexion of physical and moral science,—it was the next best thing, perhaps, to obtain by my own forces, and for my own use, the grand conviction which henceforth gave to my life whatever it has had of steadiness, consistency, and progressiveness.

I have told how, when I was eleven years old, I put a question to my brother about the old difficulty of foreknowledge and freewill,—the reconciliation of God's power and benevolence, — and how I was baulked of an answer. That question had been in my mind ever since; and I was not driven from entertaining it by Milton's account of its being a favourite controversy in hell, nor even by a rebuke administered to one of our family by Mr. Turner of Newcastle, who disapproved inquiry into what he took for granted to be an unknowable thing. To me it seemed, turn it which way I would, to be certainly a knowable thing,—so closely as it presses on human morality,—to say nothing of man's religion and internal peace. Its being reconcilable with theology is quite another affair. I tried long to satisfy myself with the ordinary subterfuge ;—with declaring myself satisfied that good comes out of evil, and a kind of good which could accrue in no other way : but this would not do. I wrote religious poetry upon it, and wrought myself up to it in talk : but it would not do. This was no solution ; and it was unworthy of a rational being to pretend to think it so. I tried acquiesence and dismissal of the subject ; but that would not do, because it brought after it a clear admission of the failure of the scheme of creation in the first place, and of the Christian scheme in the next. The time I am now speaking of was, of course, prior to my study of Priestley and of Hartley, or I should have known that there was a recognised doctrine of Necessity.

One summer afternoon, when my brother James (then my oracle) was sitting with my mother and

me, telling us some of his experience after his first
session at the York College (the Unitarian college) I
seized upon some intimation that he dropped about
this same doctrine of Necessity. I uttered the difficulty which had lain in my mind for so many years;
and he just informed me that there was, or was held
to be, a solution in that direction, and advised me to
make it out for myself. I did so. From that time
the question possessed me. Now that I had got
leave, as it were, to apply the Necessarian solution, I
did it incessantly. I fairly laid hold of the conception
of general laws, while still far from being prepared to let
go the notion of a special Providence. Though at times
almost overwhelmed by the vastness of the view
opened to me, and by the prodigious change requisite
in my moral views and self-management, the revolution was safely gone through. My labouring
brain and beating heart grew quiet, and something
more like peace than I had ever yet known settled down
upon my anxious mind. Being aware of my weakness
of undue sympathy with authors whom I read with
any moral interest, I resolved to read nothing on this
question till I had thought it out; and I kept to my
resolve. When I was wholly satisfied, and could use
my new method of interpretation in all cases that
occurred with readiness and ease, I read every book
that I could hear of on the subject of the Will; and I
need not add that I derived confirmation from all I
read on both sides. I am bound to add that the
moral effect of this process was most salutary and
cheering. From the time when I became convinced
of the certainty of the action of laws, of the true importance of good influences and good habits, of the

firmness, in short, of the ground I was treading, and of the security of the results which I should take the right means to attain, a new vigour pervaded my whole life, a new light spread through my mind, and I began to experience a steady growth in self-command, courage, and consequent integrity and disinterestedness. I was feeble and selfish enough at best; but yet, I was like a new creature in the strength of a sound conviction. Life also was like something fresh and wonderfully interesting, now that I held in my hand this key whereby to interpret some of the most conspicuous of its mysteries.

That great event in my life seems very remote; and I have been hearing more or less of the free-will difficulty ever since; and yet it appears to me, now as then, that none but Necessarians at all understand the Necessarian doctrine. This is merely saying in other words that its truth is so irresistible that, when once understood, it is adopted as a matter of course. Some, no doubt, say of the doctrine that every body can prove it, but nobody believes it; an assertion so far from true as not to be worth contesting, if I may judge by my own intercourses. Certainly, all the best minds I know are among the Necessarians;—all indeed which are qualified to discuss the subject at all. Moreover, all the world is practically Necessarian. All human action proceeds on the supposition that all the workings of the universe are governed by laws which cannot be broken by human will. In fact, the mistake of the majority in this matter is usually in supposing an interference between the will and the action of Man. The very smallest amount of science is enough to enable any rational person to see that the constitution and action of the human faculty of Will are determined by influences beyond the control of the possessor of the faculty : and when this very plain fact is denied in words it is usually because the denier is thinking of something else,—not of the faculty of willing, but of executing the volition. It is not my business here to argue out a question which has been settled in my own mind for the greater part of my life ; but I have said thus much in explanation of the great importance of the conviction to me. For above thirty years I have seen more and more clearly how awful, and how irremediable except by the spread of a true philosophy, are the evils which arise from that monstrous remnant of old superstition,—the supposition of a self-determining power, independent of laws, in the human will ; and I can truly say that if I have had the blessing of any available strength under sorrow, perplexity, sickness and toil, during a life which has been any thing but easy, it is owing to my repose upon eternal and irreversible laws, working in every department of the universe, without any interference from any random will, human or divine.— As to the ordinary objection to the doctrine,—that it is good for endurance but bad for action,—besides the obvious reply that every doctrine is to be accepted or rejected for its truth or falsehood, and not because mere human beings fancy its tendency to be good or bad,—I am bound to reply from my own experience that the allegation is not true. My life has been (whatever else) a very busy one ; and this conviction, of the invariable action of fixed laws, has certainly been the main-spring of my activity. When it is considered that, according to the Necessarian doctrine, no action fails to produce effects, and no effort can be lost, there seems every reason for the conclusion which I have no doubt is the fact, that true Necessarians must be the most diligent and confident of all workers. The indolent dreamers whom I happen to know are those who find an excuse for their idleness in the doctrine of free-will, which certainly leaves but scanty encouragement to exertion of any sort : and at the same time, the noblest activity that I ever witness, the most cheerful and self-denying toil, is on the part of those who hold the Necessarian doctrine as a vital conviction.

As to the effect of that conviction on my religion, in those days of my fanaticism and afterwards, I had better give some account of it here, though it will lead me on to a date beyond the limits of this third period of my life.—In the first place, it appeared to me when I was twenty, as it appears to me now, that the New Testament proceeds on the ground of necessarian, rather than free-will doctrine. The prayer for daily bread is there, it is true ; but the Lord's prayer is compiled from very ancient materials of the theocratic age. The fatalistic element of the Essene doctrine strongly pervades the doctrine and morality of Christ and the apostles ; and its curious union with the doctrine of a special providence is possible only under the theocratic supposition which is the basis of the whole faith.—As for me, I seized upon the necessarian element with eagerness, as enabling me to hold to my cherished faith ; and I presently perceived, and took instant advantage of the discovery, that the practice of prayer, as prevailing throughout Christendom, is wholly unauthorised by the New Testament.

Christian prayer, as prevailing at this day, answers precisely to the description of that pharisaic prayer which Christ reprobated. His own method of praying, the prayer he gave to his disciples, and their practice, were all wholly unlike any thing now understood by Christian prayer, in protestant as well as catholic countries. I changed my method accordingly,—gradually, perhaps, but beginning immediately and decidedly. Not knowing what was good for me, and being sure that every external thing would come to pass just the same, whether I liked it or not, I ceased to desire, and therefore to pray for, any thing external, — whether ' daily bread,' or health, or life for myself or others, or any thing whatever but spiritual good. There I for a long time drew the line. Many years after I had outgrown the childishness of wishing for I knew not what,—of praying for what might be either good or evil,—I continued to pray for spiritual benefits. I can hardly say for spiritual aid ; for I took the necessarian view of even the higher form of prayer,—that it brought about, or might bring about, its own accomplishment by the spiritual dispositions which it excited and cherished. This view is so far from simple, and so irreconcilable with the notion of a revelation of a scheme of salvation, that it is clear that the one or the other view must soon give way. The process in my case was this. A long series of grave misfortunes brought me to the conviction that there is no saying beforehand what the external conditions of internal peace really are. I found myself now and then in the loftiest moods of cheerfulness when in the midst of circumstances which I had most dreaded, and the converse ; and thus I grew to be, generally speaking, really and truly careless as to what became of me. I had cast off the torment of fear, except in occasional weak moments. This experience presently extended to my spiritual affairs. I found myself best, according to all trustworthy tests of goodness, when I cared least about the matter. I continued my practice of nightly examination of my hourly conduct ; and the evidence grew wonderfully strong that moral advancement came out of good influences rather than self-management ; and that even so much self-reference as was involved in 'working out one's own salvation with fear and trembling' was demoralizing. Thus I arrived,—after long years, — at the same point of ease or resignation about my spiritual as my temporal affairs, and felt that (to use a broad expression uttered by somebody) it was better to take the chance of being damned than be always quacking one's self in the fear or it. (Not that I had any literal notion of being damned, — any more than any other born and bred Unitarian.) What I could not desire for myself, I could not think of stipulating for for others ; and thus, in regard to petition, my prayers became simply an aspiration,—' Thy will be done ! ' But still, the department of praise remained. I need hardly say that I soon drew back in shame from offering to a Divine being a homage which would be offensive to an earthly one : and when this practice was over, my devotions consisted in aspiration,—very frequent and heartfelt,—under all circumstances and influences, and much as I meditate now, almost hourly, on the mysteries of life and the universe, and the great science and art of human duty. In proportion as the taint of fear and desire and self-regard fell off, and the meditation had fact instead of passion for its subject, the aspiration became freer and sweeter, till at length, when the selfish superstition had wholly gone out of it, it spread its charm through every change of every waking hour,—and does now, when life itself is expiring.

As to the effect that all this had on my belief in Christianity,—it did not prevent my holding on in that pseudo-acceptance of it which my Unitarian breeding rendered easy. It was a grand discovery to me when I somewhere met with the indication, (since become a rather favourite topic with Unitarian preachers) that the fact of the miracles has nothing whatever to do with the quality of the doctrine. When miracles are appealed to by the Orthodox as a proof of, not only the supernatural origin, but the divine quality of the doctrine, the obvious answer is that devils may work miracles, and the doctrine may therefore be from hell. Such was the argument in Christ's time ; and such is it now among a good many protestants,— horrifying the Catholics and High-Churchmen of our time as much as it horrified the evangelists of old. The use to which it is turned by many who still call themselves Unitarians, and to which it was applied by me is,—the holding to Christianity in a manner as a revelation, after surrendering belief in the miracles. I suppose the majority of Unitarians still accept all the miracles (except the Miraculous Conception, of course)—even to the withering away of the fig-tree. Some hold to the resurrection, while giving up all the rest ; and not a few do as I did,—say that the interior evidence of a divine origin of that doctrine is enough, and that no amount of miracles could strengthen their faith. It is clear however that a Christianity which never was received as a scheme of salvation,—which never was regarded as essential to salvation,—which might be treated, in respect to its records, at the will and pleasure of each believer,— which is next declared to be independent of its external evidences, because those evidences are found to be untenable,—and which is finally subjected in its doctrines, as in its letter, to the interpretation of each individual,—must cease to be a faith, and become a matter of speculation, of spiritual convenience, and of intellectual and moral taste, till it declines to the rank of a mere fact in the history of mankind. These are the gradations through which I passed. It took many years to travel through them ; and I lingered long in the stages of speculation and taste, intellectual and moral. But at length I recognised the monstrous superstition in its true character of a great fact in the history of the race, and found myself, with the last link of my chain snapped,—a free rover on the broad, bright breezy common of the universe.

SECTION II.

At this time,—(I think it must have been in 1821,) was my first appearance in print. I had some early aspirations after authorship,—judging by an anecdote which hangs in my memory, though I believe I never thought about it, more or less, while undergoing that preparation which I have described in my account of my studies and translations. When I was assorting and tabulating scripture texts, in the way I described some way back, I one day told my mother, in a moment of confidence, that I hoped it might be printed, and make a book, and then I should be an authoress. My mother, pleased, I believe, with the aspiration, told my eldest sister; and she in an unfortunate moment of contempt, twitted me with my conceit in fancying I could be an authoress; whereupon I instantly resolved 'never to tell any body any thing again.' How this resolution was kept it is rather amusing now to consider, seeing that of all people in the world, I have perhaps the fewest reserves. The ambition seems to have disappeared from that time; and when I did attempt to write, it was at the suggestion of another, and against my own judgment and inclination. My brother James, then my idolized companion, discovered how

wretched I was when he left me for his college, after
the vacation ; and he told me that I must not permit
myself to be so miserable. He advised me to take
refuge, on each occasion, in a new pursuit ; and on
that particular occasion, in an attempt at authorship.
I said, as usual, that I would if he would : to which
he answered that it would never do for him, a young
student, to rush into print before the eyes of his
tutors ; but he desired me to write something that
was in my head, and try my chance with it in the
' Monthly Repository,' — the poor little Unitarian
periodical in which I have mentioned that Talfourd
tried his young powers. What James desired, I
always did, as of course ; and after he had left me to
my widowhood soon after six o'clock, one bright
September morning, I was at my desk before seven,
beginning a letter to the Editor of the ' Monthly
Repository,'—that editor being the formidable prime
minister of his sect,—Rev. Robert Aspland. I suppose I must tell what that first paper was, though I
had much rather not ; for I am so heartily ashamed of
the whole business as never to have looked at the
article since the first flutter of it went off. It was on
Female Writers on Practical Divinity. I wrote away,
in my abominable scrawl of those days, on foolscap
paper, feeling mightily like a fool all the time. I told
no one, and carried my expensive packet to the post-
office myself, to pay the postage. I took the letter V
for my signature,—I cannot at all remember why.
The time was very near the end of the month : I had
no definite expectation that I should ever hear any
thing of my paper ; and certainly did not suppose it
could be in the forthcoming number. That number

was sent in before service-time on a Sunday morning.
My heart may have been beating when I laid hands
on it; but it thumped prodigiously when I saw my
article there, and, in the Notices to Correspondents, a
request to hear more from V. of Norwich. There is
certainly something entirely peculiar in the sensation
of seeing one'sself in print for the first time :—the
lines burn themselves in upon the brain in a way of
which black ink is incapable, in any other mode. So
I felt that day, when I went about with my secret.—
I have said what my eldest brother was to us,—in
what reverence we held him. He was just married,
and he and his bride asked me to return from chapel
with them to tea. After tea he said, ' Come now, we
have had plenty of talk; I will read you something;'
and he held out his hand for the new ' Repository.'
After glancing at it, he exclaimed, ' They have got a
new hand here. Listen.' After a paragraph, he repeated, ' Ah ! this is a new hand; they have had
nothing so good as this for a long while.' (It would
be impossible to convey to any who do not know the
' Monthly Repository ' of that day, how very small a
compliment this was.) I was silent, of course. At the
end of the first column, he exclaimed about the style,
looking at me in some wonder at my being as still as
a mouse. Next (and well I remember his tone, and
thrill to it still) his words were—' What a fine sentence that is ! Why, do you not think so ? ' I
mumbled out, sillily enough, that it did not seem any
thing particular. ' Then,' said he, ' you were not
listening. I will read it again. There now ! ' As
he still got nothing out of me, he turned round upon
me, as we sat side by side on the sofa, with 'Harriet,

what is the matter with you? I never knew you so
slow to praise any thing before.' I replied, in utter
confusion,—'I never could baffle any body. The
truth is, that paper is mine.' He made no reply;
read on in silence, and spoke no more till I was on my
feet to come away. He then laid his hand on my
shoulder, and said gravely (calling me 'dear' for the
first time) 'Now, dear, leave it to other women to
make shirts and darn stockings; and do you devote
yourself to this.' I went home in a sort of dream, so
that the squares of the pavement seemed to float before my eyes. That evening made me an authoress.

It was not all so glorious, however. I immediately
after began to write my first work,—' Devotional
Exercises,' of which I now remember nothing. But
I remember my brother's anxious doubting looks, in
which I discerned some disappointment, as he read
the M.S. I remember his gentle hints about precision and arrangement of ideas, given with the utmost care not to discourage me; and I understood the
significance of his praise of the concluding essay (in a
letter from Madeira, where he was closing his precious life)—praise of the definiteness of object in that
essay, which, as he observed, furnished the key to his
doubts about the rest of the book, and which he conveyed only from an anxious desire that I should work
my way up to the high reputation which he felt I was
destined to attain. This just and gentle treatment,
contrasting with the early discouragements which had
confused my own judgment, affected me inexpressibly.
I took these hints to heart in trying my hand at a
sort of theologico-metaphysical novel, which I entered

upon with a notion of enlightening the world through the same kind of interest as was then excited by Mr. Ward's novel, 'Tremaine,' which was making a prodigious noise, and which perfectly enchanted me, except by its bad philosophy. I mightily enjoyed the prospect of this work, as did my mother; and I was flattered by finding that Rachel had higher expectations from it than even my own. But, at the end of half a volume, I became aware that it was excessively dull, and I stopped. Many years afterwards I burned it; and this is the only piece of my work but two (and a review) in my whole career that never was published.

Already I found that it would not do to copy what I wrote; and here (at the outset of this novel) I discontinued the practice for ever,—thus saving an immense amount of time which I humbly think is wasted by other authors. The prevalent doctrine about revision and copying, and especially Miss Edgeworth's account of her method of writing,—scribbling first, then submitting her manuscript to her father, and copying and altering many times over till, (if I remember right) no one paragraph of her 'Leonora' stood at last as it did at first, —made me suppose copying and alteration to be indispensable. But I immediately found that there was no use in copying if I did not alter; and that, if ever I did alter, I had to change back again; and I, once for all, committed myself to a single copy. I believe the only writings I ever copied were 'Devotional Exercises,' and my first tale;—a trumpery story called 'Christmas Day.' It seemed clear to me that distinctness and precision must be lost if alterations were

made in a different state of mind from that which
suggested the first utterance; and I was delighted
when, long afterwards, I met with Cobbett's advice;
—to know first what you want to say, and then say
it in the first words that occur to you. The excellence
of Cobbett's style, and the manifest falling off of
Miss Edgeworth's after her father's death (so frankly
avowed by herself) were strong confirmations of my
own experience. I have since, more than once,
weakly fallen into mannerism,—now metaphysically
elliptical,—now poetically amplified, and even, in one
instance, bordering on the Carlylish; but through all
this folly, as well as since having a style of my own,
—(that is, finding expression by words as easy as
breathing air)—I have always used the same method
in writing. I have always made sure of what I
meant to say, and then written it down without care
or anxiety,— glancing at it again only to see if any
words were omitted or repeated, and not altering a
single phrase in a whole work. I mention this because I think I perceive that great mischief arises
from the notion that botching in the second place
will compensate for carelessness in the first. I think
I perceive that confusion of thought, and cloudiness
or affectation in style are produced or aggravated by
faulty prepossessions in regard to the method of
writing for the press. The mere saving of time and
labour in my own case may be regarded as no incon-
siderable addition to my term of life.—Some modifications of this doctrine there must of course be in
accordance with the strength or weakness of the
natural faculty of expression by language: but I
speak as strongly as I have just done because I have

no reason to believe that the natural aptitude was particularly strong in myself. I believe that such facility as I have enjoyed has been mainly owing to my unconscious preparatory discipline ; and especially in the practice of translation from various languages, as above related. And, again, after seeing the manuscripts or proof-sheets of many of the chief authors of my own time, I am qualified to say that the most marked mannerists of their day are precisely those whose manuscripts show most erasures, and their proof-sheets most alterations.

SECTION III.

I HAVE said that it was through a long train of calamities that I learned some valuable truths and habits. Those calamities were now coming fast upon me. In 1820, my deafness was suddenly encreased by what might be called an accident, which I do not wish to describe. I ought undoubtedly to have begun at that time to use a trumpet; but no one pressed it upon me; and I do not know that, if urged, I should have yielded; for I had abundance of that false shame which hinders nine deaf people out of ten from doing their duty in that particular. The redeeming quality of personal infirmity is that it brings its special duty with it; but this privilege waits long to be recognised. The special duty of the deaf is, in the first place, to spare other people as much fatigue as possible; and, in the next, to preserve their own natural capacity for sound, and habit of receiving it, and true memory of it, as long as possible. It was long before I saw, or fully admitted this to myself; and it was ten years from this time before I began to use a trumpet. Thus, I have felt myself qualified to say more in the way of exhortation and remonstrance to deaf people than could be said by any one who had not only never been deaf, but had never shared the selfish and morbid feelings which are the ordinary attendant curses of suffering so absolutely peculiar as that of personal infirmity.

Next, our beloved brother, who had always shown a tendency to consumption, ruptured a blood-vessel in the lungs, and had to give up his practice and professional offices, and to go, first into Devonshire, and afterwards to Madeira, whence he never returned. He died at sea, on his way home.   I went with him and his wife into Devonshire, for the spring of 1823 ; and it was my office to read aloud for many hours of every day, which I did with great satisfaction, and with inestimable profit from his comments and unsurpassed conversation. Before breakfast, and while he enjoyed his classical reading on the sofa, I rambled about the neighbourhood of Torquay,—sometimes sketching, sometimes reading, sometimes studying the sea from the shelter of the caves, and, on the whole, learning to see nature, under those grave circumstances, with new eyes. Soon after our return, their child was born; and never was infant more beloved. It was my great solace during the dreary season of dismantling that home which we had had so much delight in forming, and sending those from us who were the joy of our lives. It was then that I learned the lesson I spoke of,—of our peace of mind being, at least in times of crisis, independent of external circumstances. Day by day, I had been silently growing more heart-sick at the prospect of the parting ; and I especially dreaded the night before ;—the going to bed, with the thoughtful night before me, after seeing every thing packed, and knowing that the task of the coming day was the parting. Yet that night was one of the happiest of my life. It is easy to conceive what the process of thought was, and what the character of the religious emotion which so elevated me. The lesson was a sound one, whatever might be the virtue of the thoughts and feelings involved. The next day, all was over at length. I was the last who held the dear baby,—even to the moment of his being put into the carriage. The voyage was injurious to him; and it was probably the cause of his death, which took place soon after reaching Madeira. There was something peaceful, and very salutary in the next winter, though it could not reasonably be called a very happy one. There was a close mutual reliance between my mother and myself,—my sister Rachel being absent, and our precious little Ellen, the family darling, at school. We kept up a close correspondence with our absent ones; and there were the beautiful Madeira letters always to look for. I remember reading Clarendon's Rebellion aloud to my mother in the evenings; and we took regular walks in all weathers. I had my own troubles and anxieties, however. A dream had passed before me since the visit of a student friend of my brother James's, which some words of my father's and mother's had strengthened into hope and trust. This hope was destined to be crushed for a time in two hearts by the evil offices of one who had much to answer for in what he did. This winter was part of the time of suspense. Under my somewhat heavy troubles my health had some time before begun to give way; and now I was suffering from digestive derangement which was not cured for four years after; and then only after severe and daily pain from chronic inflammation of the stomach. Still, with an ailing body, an anxious and often aching heart, and a mind which dreaded looking into the future, I regarded this winter of 1823-4 as a happy one;—the secret of which I believe to have been that I felt myself beloved at home, and enjoyed the keen relish of duties growing out of domestic love. At the end of the next June, my brother died. We were all prepared for the event, as far as preparation is ever possible; but my dear father, the most un-selfish of men, who never spoke of his own feelings, and always considered other people's, never, we think, recovered from this grief. He was very quiet at the time; but his health began to go wrong, and his countenance to alter; and during the two remain-ing years of his life, he sustained a succession of cares which might have broken down a frame less predisposed for disease than his had become. In our remembrance of him there is no pain on the ground of any thing in his character. Humble, simple, up-right, self-denying, affectionate to as many people as possible, and kindly to all, he gave no pain, and did all the good he could. He had not the advantage of an adequate education; but there was a natural shrewdness about him which partly compensated for the want. He was not the less, but the more, anxious to give his children the advantages which he had never received; and the whole family have always felt that they owe a boundless debt of gratitude to both their parents for the self-sacrificing efforts they made, through all the vicissitudes of the times, to fit their children in the best possible manner for independent action in life. My father's business, that of a Norwich manufacturer, was subject to the fluctuations to which all manufacture was liable during the war, and to others of its own ; and our parents' method was to have no reserves from their children, to let us know precisely the state of their affairs, and to hold out to us, in the light of this evidence, the probability that we might sooner or later have to work for our own living,—daughters as well as sons,—and that it was improbable that we should ever be rich. The time was approaching which was to prove the wisdom of their method. My father's business, never a very enriching one, had been for some time prosperous ; and this year (1824) he indulged my brother James and myself with a journey ;—a walking tour in Scotland, in the course of which we walked five hundred miles in a month. I am certainly of opinion now that that trip aggravated my stomach-complaint; and I only wonder it was no worse. I spent the next winter with my married sister, my sister-in-law, and other friends, and returned to Norwich in April, to undergo long months,—even years—of anxiety and grief.

In the reviews of my ' History of the Thirty Years' Peace,' one chapter is noticed more emphatically than all the rest ;—the chapter on the speculations, collapse, and crash of 1825 and 1826. If that chapter is written with some energy, it is no wonder; for our family fortunes were implicated in that desperate struggle, and its issue determined the whole course of life of the younger members of our family,—my own among the rest. One point on which my narrative in the History is emphatic is the hardship on the sober man of business of being involved in the destruction which overtook the speculator; and I had

family and personal reasons for saying this. My
father never speculated; but he was well nigh ruined
during that calamitous season by the deterioration in
value of his stock. His stock of manufactured goods
was larger, of course, than it would have been in a
time of less enterprise; and week by week its value
declined, till, in the middle of the winter, when the
banks were crashing down all over England, we began
to contemplate absolute ruin. My father was evidently a dying man;—not from anxiety of mind,
for his liver disease was found to be owing to obstruction caused by a prodigious gall-stone: but his illness
was no doubt aggravated and rendered more harassing by his cares for his family. In the spring he was
sent to Cheltenham, whence he returned after some
weeks with the impression of approaching death on
his face. He altered his Will, mournfully reducing
the portions left to his daughters to something which
could barely be called an independence. Then, three
weeks before his death, he wisely, and to our great relief, dismissed the whole subject. He told my brother
Henry, his partner in the business, that he had done
what he could while he could: that he was now a
dying man, and could be of no further use in the
struggle, and that he wished to keep his mind easy
for his few remaining days: so he desired to see no
more letters of business, and to hear no more details.
For a few more days, he sunned himself on the grassplat in the garden, in the warm June mornings: then
could not leave the house; then could not come down
stairs; and, towards the end of the month died
quietly, with all his family round his bed.—As for
my share in this family experience,—it was delight-

ful to me that he took an affectionate pleasure in my
poor little book,—of value to me now for that alone,
—' Addresses, Prayers and Hymns, for the use of
families and schools.' It was going through the
press at that time ; and great was my father's satisfaction ; and high were his hopes, I believe, of what I
should one day be and do. Otherwise, I have little
comfort in thinking of his last illness. The old habit
of fear came upon me, more irresistibly than ever, on
the assembling of the family; and I mourn to think
how I kept out of the way, whenever it was possible,
and how little I said to my father of what was in my
heart about him and my feelings towards him. The
more easily his humility was satisfied with whatever
share of good fell to him, the more richly he should
have been ministered to. By me he was not,—
owing to this unhappy shyness. My married sister,
who was an incomparable nurse, did the duty of
others besides her own ; and mine among the rest,
while I was sorrowing and bitterly chiding myself in
silence, and perhaps in apparent insensibility.

And now my own special trial was at hand. It is
not necessary to go into detail about it. The news
which got abroad that we had grown comparatively
poor,—and the evident certainty that we were never
likely to be rich, so wrought upon the mind of one
friend as to break down the mischief which I have referred to as caused by ill-offices. My friend had believed me rich, was generous about making me a poor
man's wife, and had been discouraged in more ways
than one. He now came to me, and we were soon
virtually engaged. I was at first very anxious and
unhappy. My veneration for his *morale* was such

that I felt that I dared not undertake the charge of
his happiness: and yet I dared not refuse, because I
saw it would be his death blow. I was ill,—I was
deaf,—I was in an entangled state of mind between
conflicting duties and some lower considerations; and
many a time did I wish, in my fear that I should fail,
that I had never seen him. I am far from wishing
that now; — now that the beauty of his goodness
remains to me, clear of all painful regrets. But there
was a fearful period to pass through. Just when I
was growing happy, surmounting my fears and doubts,
and enjoying his attachment, the consequences of his
long struggle and suspense overtook him. He became suddenly insane; and after months of illness of
body and mind, he died. The calamity was aggravated to me by the unaccountable insults I received
from his family, whom I had never seen. Years
afterwards, when his sister and I met, the mystery
was explained. His family had been given to understand, by cautious insinuations, that I was actually
engaged to another, while receiving my friend's
addresses ! There has never been any doubt in my
mind that, considering what I was in those days, it
was happiest for us both that our union was prevented
by any means. I am, in truth, very thankful for not
having married at all. I have never since been
tempted, nor have suffered any thing at all in relation
to that matter which is held to be all-important to
woman, — love and marriage. Nothing, I mean,
beyond occasional annoyance, presently disposed of.
Every literary woman, no doubt, has plenty of importunity of that sort to deal with; but freedom of
mind and coolness of manner dispose of it very easily:

and since the time I have been speaking of, my mind has been wholly free from all idea of love-affairs. My subsequent literary life in London was clear from all difficulty and embarrassment,—no doubt because I was evidently too busy, and too full of interest of other kinds to feel any awkwardness,—to say nothing of my being then thirty years of age; an age at which, if ever, a woman is certainly qualified to take care of herself. I can easily conceive how I might have been tempted,—how some deep springs in my nature might have been touched, then as earlier; but, as a matter of fact, they never were; and I consider the immunity a great blessing, under the liabilities of a moral condition such as mine was in the olden time. If I had had a husband dependent on me for his happiness, the responsibility would have made me wretched. I had not faith enough in myself to endure avoidable responsibility. If my husband had *not* depended on me for his happiness, I should have been jealous. So also with children. The care would have so overpowered the joy,—the love would have so exceeded the ordinary chances of life,—the fear on my part would have so impaired the freedom on theirs, that I rejoice not to have been involved in a relation for which I was, or believed myself unfit. The veneration in which I hold domestic life has always shown me that that life was not for those whose self-respect had been early broken down, or had never grown. Happily, the majority are free from this disability. Those who suffer under it had better be as I,—as my observation of married, as well as single life assures me. When I see what conjugal love is, in the extremely rare cases in wnich it is seen in its perfection,

I feel that there is a power of attachment in me
that has never been touched. When I am among
little children, it frightens me to think what my
idolatry of my own children would have been. But,
through it all, I have ever been thankful to be alone.
My strong will, combined with anxiety of conscience,
makes me fit only to live alone; and my taste and
liking are for living alone. The older I have grown,
the more serious and irremediable have seemed to
me the evils and disadvantages of married life, as it
exists among us at this time : and I am provided with
what it is the bane of single life in ordinary cases to
want—substantial, laborious and serious occupation.
My business in life has been to think and learn, and
to speak out with absolute freedom what I have
thought and learned. The freedom is itself a positive
and never-failing enjoyment to me, after the bondage
of my early life. My work and I have been fitted to
each other, as is proved by the success of my work
and my own happiness in it. The simplicity and independence of this vocation first suited my infirm and
ill-developed nature, and then sufficed for my needs,
together with family ties and domestic duties, such as
I have been blessed with, and as every woman's heart
requires. Thus, I am not only entirely satisfied with
my lot, but think it the very best for me,—under
my constitution and circumstances : and I long ago
came to the conclusion that, without meddling with
the case of the wives and mothers, I am probably the
happiest single woman in England. Who could have
believed, in that awful year 1826, that such would be
my conclusion a quarter of a century afterwards !

My health gave way, more and more; and my

suffering throughout the year 1827 from the pain
which came on every evening was such as it is disagreeable to think of now. For pain of body and
mind it was truly a terrible year, though it had its
satisfactions, one of the chief of which was a long
visit which I paid to my brother Robert and his wife
(always a dear friend of mine to this day) at their
home in Dudley. I remember our walks in the
grounds of Dudley Castle, and the organ-playing at
home, after my brother's business hours, and the in-
exhaustible charm of the baby, as gleams amidst the
darkness of that season. I found then the unequalled
benefit of long solitary walks in such a case as mine.
I had found it even at Norwich, in midwinter, when
all was bleak on that exposed level country ; and now,
amidst the beauty which surrounds Dudley, there was
no end of my walks or of my relish for them ; and I
always came home with a cheered and lightened heart.
Such poetry as I wrote (I can't bear to think of it)
I wrote in those days. The mournful pieces, and
those which assume *not* to be mournful, which may be
found in my ' Miscellanies' (published in America)
may be referred to that period. And so may some
dull and doleful prose writings, published by the
solemn old Calvinistic publisher, Houlston, of Wellington in Shropshire. An acquaintance of mine had
some time before put me in the way of correspondence
with Houlston ; and he had accepted the first two
little eightpenny stories I sent him. I remember the
amusement and embarrassment of the first piece of
pecuniary success. As soon as it was known in the
house that the letter from Wellington contained five
pounds, everybody wanted, and continued to want all

day, to borrow five pounds of me. After a pause, Houlston wrote to ask for another story of somewhat more substance and bulk. My 'Globe' newspaper readings suggested to me the subject of Machine-breaking as a good one,—some recent outrages of that sort having taken place : but I had not the remotest idea that I was meditating writing on Political Economy, the very name of which was then either unknown to me, or conveyed no meaning. I wrote the little story called 'The Rioters ; ' and its success was such that some hosiers and lace-makers of Derby and Nottingham sent me a request to write a tale on the subject of Wages, which I did, calling it ' The Turn Out.' The success of both was such as to dispose Mr. Houlston to further dealings; and I wrote for him a good many tracts, which he sold for a penny, and for which he gave me a sovereign apiece. This seems to be the place in which to tell a fact or two about the use made of those early writings of mine by the old man's sons and successors. Old Houlston died not very long afterwards, leaving among his papers, (I now remember,) a manuscript story of mine which I suppose lies there still ;—about a good governess, called, I think, ' Caroline Shirley.' I mention this that, if that story should come out with my name after my death, it may be known to have been written somewhere about this time,—1827. Old Houlston died, on perfectly good terms with me, as far as I remember. The next thing I heard was (and I heard it from various quarters) that those little tracts of mine, and some of my larger tales, were selling and circulating as Mrs. Sherwood's—Houlston being her publisher. This was amusing ; and I had no other objection to it than that it was not true. Next, certain friends and relations of my own who went to the Houlstons' shop in Paternoster Row, and asked for any works by me, had foisted upon them any rubbish that was convenient, under pretence of its being mine. A dear old aunt was very mysterious and complimentary to me, one day, on her return from London, about ' Judith Potts ; ' and was puzzled to find all her allusions lost upon me. At length, she produced a little story so entitled, which had been sold to her as mine over the Houlstons' counter, and, as she believed, by Mr. Houlston himself. This was rather too bad; for ' Judith Potts ' was not altogether a work that one would wish to build one's fame on : but there was worse to come. Long years after, when such reputation as I have had was at its height, (when I was ill at Tynemouth, about 1842,) there had been some machine-breaking ; and Messrs. Houlston and Stoneman (as the firm then stood) brought out afresh my poor little early story of ' The Rioters,' with my name in the title-page for the first time, and not only with every external appearance of being fresh, but with interpolations and alterations which made it seem really so. For instance, ' His Majesty ' was altered to ' Her Majesty.' By advice of my friends, I made known the trick far and wide ; and I wrote to Messrs. Houlston and Stoneman, to inform them that I was aware of their fraudulent transaction, and that it was actionable. These caterers for the pious needs of the religious world replied with insults, having nothing better to offer. They pleaded my original permission to their father to use my name or not ; which was a fact, but no excuse for the present use of it : and to

the gravest part of the whole charge,—that of il-
legal alterations for the fraudulent purpose of concealing the date of the book, they made no reply whatever. I had reason to believe, however, that by the
exertions of my friends, the trick was effectually exposed. As far as I remember, this is almost the only
serious complaint I have had to make of any publisher, during my whole career.

Meantime, in 1827 I was on excellent terms with
old Houlston, and writing for him a longer tale than
I had yet tried my hand on. It was called ' Principle and Practice;' and it succeeded well enough to
induce us to put forth a ' Sequel to Principle and
Practice' three or four years after. These were all
that I wrote for Houlston, as far as I remember, except a little book whose appearance made me stand
aghast. A most excellent young servant of ours, who
had become quite a friend of the household, went out
to Madeira with my brother and his family, and confirmed our attachment to her by her invaluable services to them. Her history was a rather remarkable,
and a very interesting one ; and I wrote it in the form
of four of Houlston's penny tracts. He threw them
together, and made a little book of them ; and the
heroine, who would never have heard of them as
tracts, was speedily put in possession of her Memoirs
in the form of the little book called ' My Servant
Rachel.' An aunt of mine, calling on her one day,
found her standing in the middle of the floor, and her
husband reading the book over her shoulder. She
was hurt at one anecdote,—which was certainly true,
but which she had forgotten : but, as a whole, it
could not but have been most gratifying to her. She

ever after treated me with extreme kindness, and even
tenderness; and we are hearty friends still, whenever
we meet.—And here ends the chapter of my
authorship in which Houlston, my first patron, was
concerned.

It was in the autumn of 1827, I think, that a
neighbour lent my sister Mrs. Marcet's 'Conversations on Political Economy.' I took up the book,
chiefly to see what Political Economy precisely was;
and great was my surprise to find that I had been
teaching it unawares, in my stories about Machinery
and Wages. It struck me at once that the principles
of the whole science might be advantageously conveyed in the same way,—not by'being smothered up
in a story, but by being exhibited in their natural
workings in selected passages of social life. It has
always appeared very strange to me that so few people
seem to have understood this. Students of all manner of physical sciences afterwards wanted me to
'illustrate' things of which social life (and therefore
fiction) can afford no illustration. I used to say till
I was tired that none but moral and political science
admitted of the method at all; and I doubt whether
many of those who talk about it understand the
matter, to this day. In the 'Edinburgh Review' of
my Political Economy series,—a review otherwise as
weak as it is kind,—there is the best appreciation of
the principle of the work that I have seen anywhere;
—a page or so[1] of perfect understanding of my view
and purpose. That view and purpose date from my
reading of Mrs. Marcet's Conversations. During

[1] *Edinburgh Review.* Vol. lvii., pp. 6 and 7.

that reading, groups of personages rose up from the pages, and a procession of action glided through its arguments, as afterwards from the pages of Adam Smith, and all the other Economists. I mentioned my notion, I remember, when we were sitting at work, one bright afternoon at home. Brother James nodded assent : my mother said 'do it;' and we went to tea, unconscious what a great thing we had done since dinner.

There was meantime much fiddle-faddling to be gone through, with such work as 'Principle and Practice' and the like. But a new educational period was about to open.—My complaint grew so serious, and was so unbearably painful, and, in truth, medically mismanaged at Norwich, that my family sent me to Newcastle, to my sister's, where her husband treated me successfully, and put me in the way of entire cure. It was a long and painful business ; but the method succeeded ; and, in the course of time, and by the unremitting care of my host and hostess, I was sent home in a condition to manage myself. It was some years before the stomach entirely recovered its tone ; but it was thoroughly healthy from that time forward.

While I was at Newcastle, a spirited advertisement from the new editor of the 'Monthly Repository,' Mr. Fox, met my eye, appealing for literary aid to those who were interested in its objects. I could not resist sending a practical reply ; and I was gratified to learn, long afterwards, that when my name was mentioned to Mr. Fox, before he issued his appeal, he had said that he wished for my assistance from the moment when he, as editor, discovered from the office books

that I was the writer of certain papers which had
fixed his attention : but that he could not specially invite my contributions while he had no funds which
could enable him to offer due remuneration. His
reply to my first letter was so cordial that I was
animated to offer him extensive assistance; and if he
had then no money to send me, he paid me in something more valuable—in a course of frank and
generous criticism which was of the utmost benefit to
me. His editorial correspondence with me was unquestionably the occasion, and in great measure the
cause, of the greatest intellectual progress I ever made
before the age of thirty. I sent him Essays, Reviews,
and poetry (or what I called such)—the best speci-
mens of which may be found in the ' Miscellanies,'
before mentioned.—The Diffusion Society was at that
time the last novelty. A member of the Committee
who overrated his own influence, invited me to write
a Life of Howard the Philanthropist, which I did,
with great satisfaction, and under the positive promise
of thirty pounds for it. From time to time, tidings
were sent to me of its being approved, and at length
of its being actually in type. In the approaching
crisis of my fortunes, when I humbly asked when I
might expect any part of the payment, I could
obtain no clear answer : and the end of the matter
was that it was found that half-a-dozen or more Lives
of Howard had been ordered in a similar manner, by
different members of the Committee ; that my manuscript was found, after several years, at the bottom of
a chest,—not only dirty, but marked and snipped, —
its contents having been abundantly used without any
acknowledgment,—as was afterwards admitted to me

by some of the members who were especially interested in the prison question. I am far from re-
gretting the issue now, because new materials have
turned up which would have shamed that biography
out of existence : but the case is worth mentioning, as
an illustration of the way in which literary business
is managed by corporate directories. I believe most
people who ever had any connexion with the Diffusion
Society have some similar story to tell.

While I was at Newcastle, a change, which turned
out a very happy one, was made in our domestic arrangements. My cousin, James Martineau Lee, who
had succeeded my brother as a surgeon at Norwich,
having died that year, his aged mother,—(my
father's only surviving sister),—came to live with us ;
and with us she remained till her death in 1840.
She was hardly settled with us when the last of our
series of family misfortunes occurred. I call it a misfortune, because in common parlance it would be so
treated ; but I believe that my mother and all her
other daughters would have joined heartily, if asked,
in my conviction that it was one of the best things
that ever happened to us. My mother and her
daughters lost, at a stroke, nearly all they had in the
world by the failure of the house,—the old manu-
factory,—in which their money was placed. We
never recovered more than the merest pittance ; and
at the time, I, for one, was left destitute ;—that is to
say, with precisely one shilling in my purse. The
effect upon me of this new 'calamity,' as people
called it, was like that of a blister upon a dull, weary
pain, or series of pains. I rather enjoyed it, even at
the time ; for there was scope for action ; whereas, in

the long, dreary series of preceding trials, there was nothing possible but endurance. In a very short time, my two sisters at home and I began to feel the blessing of a wholly new freedom. I, who had been obliged to write before breakfast, or in some private way, had henceforth liberty to do my own work in my own way; for we had lost our gentility. Many and many a time since have we said that, but for that loss of money, we might have lived on in the ordinary provincial method of ladies with small means, sewing, and economizing, and growing narrower every year; whereas, by being thrown, while it was yet time, on our own resources, we have worked hard and usefully, won friends, reputation and independence, seen the world abundantly, abroad and at home, and, in short, have truly lived instead of vegetated.

It was in June, 1829, that the old Norwich house failed. I had been spending a couple of days at a country town, where the meeting of the provincial Unitarian Association took place. Some of the members knew, on the last day, what had happened to us; but I heard it first in the streets of Norwich on my way to our own house. As well as I can remember, a pretty faithful account of the event is given in one of my Political Economy tales,—' Berkeley the Banker;' mixed up, however, with a good many facts about other persons and times. I need not give the story over again here, nor any part of it but what is concerned in the history of my own mind and my own work.—It was presently settled that my mother, my dear old aunt and I should live on in the family house. One sister went forth to earn the indepen- hence which she achieved after busy and honourable

years of successful exertion. The youngest was busy
teaching and training the children, chiefly, of the
family, till her marriage.

The question was—what was *I* to do, with my
deafness precluding both music and governessing. I
devised a plan for guiding the studies of young people
by correspondence, and sent out written proposals :
but, while everybody professed to approve the scheme,
no pupil ever offered. I was ere long very glad of
this ; for the toil of the pen would have been great,
with small results of any kind, in comparison to those
which accrued from what I did write.—In the first
place, I inquired about my 'Life of Howard,' and
found, to my interior consternation, that there was no
prospect in that quarter. Nobody knew that I was
left with only one shilling, insomuch that I dreaded
the arrival of a thirteenpenny letter, in those days of
dear postage. The family supposed me to be well-
supplied, through Houlston's recent payment for one
of my little books : but that money had gone where
all the rest was. The sale of a ball-dress brought me
three pounds. That was something. I hoped, and
not without reason, that my needle would bring me
enough for my small expenses, for a time ; and I did
earn a good many pounds by fancy-work, in the
course of the next year,—after which it ceased to be
necessary. For two years, I lived on fifty pounds a
year. My mother, always generous in money matters, would not hear of my paying my home expenses
till she saw that I should be the happier for her allow-
ing it : and then she assured me, and proved to me,
that, as she had to keep house at all events, and as
my habits were exceedingly frugal (taking no wine,

&c.), thirty pounds a year would repay her for my residence. Twenty pounds more sufficed for clothes, postage and sundries : and thus did I live, as long as it was necessary, on fifty pounds a year.—I must mention here a gift which dropped in upon me at that time which gave me more pleasure than any money-gift that I ever received. Our rich relations made bountiful presents to my sisters, for their outfit on leaving home : but they supposed me in possession of the money they knew I had earned, and besides concluded that I could not want much, as I was to stay at home. My application about the Howard manuscript, however, came to the knowledge of a cousin of mine,—then and ever since, to this hour, a faithful friend to me ; and he, divining the case, sent me ten pounds, in a manner so beautiful that his few lines filled me with joy. That happened on a Sunday morning ; and I well remember what a happy morning it was. I had become too deaf now for public worship ; and I went every fair Sunday morning over the wildest bit of country near Norwich,—a part of Mousehold, which was a sweet breezy common, over-looking the old city in its most picturesque aspect. There I went that Sunday morning ; and I remember well the freshness of the turf and the beauty of the tormentilla which bestarred it, in the light and warmth of that good cousin's kindness.

I now wrote to Mr. Fox, telling him of my changed circumstances, which would compel me to render less gratuitous service than hitherto to the ' Repository.' Mr. Fox replied by apologetically placing at my disposal the only sum at his command at that time,—fifteen pounds a year, for which I was to do as much reviewing as I thought proper. With this letter arrived a parcel of nine books for review or notice. Overwhelming as this was, few letters that I had ever received had given me more pleasure than this. Here was, in the first place, work ; in the next, continued literary discipline under Mr. Fox; and lastly, this money would buy my clothes. So to work I went, with needle and pen. I had before begun to study German ; and now, that study was my recreation ; and I found a new inspiration in the world of German literature, which was just opening, widely and brightly, before my eager and awakened mind. It was truly *life* that I lived during those days of strong intellectual and moral effort.

After I had received about a dozen books, Mr. Fox asked me to send him two or three tales, such as his ' best readers ' would not pass by. I was flattered by this request; but I had no idea that I could fulfil his wish, any more than I could refuse to try. Now was the time to carry out the notion I had formed on reading ' Helon's Pilgrimage to Jerusalem,'—as I related above. I wrote ' The Hope of the Hebrew ' (the first of the ' Traditions of Palestine,') and two others, as unlike it and each other as I could make them : — viz, 'Solitude and Society,' and ' The Early Sowing,'—the Unitarian City Mission being at that time under deliberation.

I carried these stories to London myself, and put them into Mr. Fox's own hands,—being kindly invited for a long stay at the house of an uncle, in pursuit of my own objects. The Hebrew tale was put forth first ; and the day after its appearance, such inquiries were made of Mr. Fox at a public dinner in

regard to the authorship that I was at once determined to make a volume of them; and the 'Traditions of Palestine' appeared accordingly, in the
next spring. Except that first story, the whole
volume was written in a fortnight. By this little
volume was my name first made known in literature.
I still love the memory of the time when it was
written, though there was little other encouragement
than my own pleasure in writing, and in the literary
discipline which I continued to enjoy under Mr. Fox's
editorship. With him I always succeeded; but I
failed in all other directions during that laborious
winter and spring. I had no literary acquaintance or
connection whatever; and I could not get any thing
that I wrote even looked at; so that every thing went
into the 'Repository' at last. I do not mean that
any amount of literary connexion would necessarily
have been of any service to me; for I do not believe
that 'patronage,' 'introductions' and the like are
of any avail, in a general way. I know this;—that
I have always been anxious to extend to young or
struggling authors the sort of aid which would have
been so precious to me in that winter of 1829–1830,
and that, in above twenty years, I have never succeeded but once. I obtained the publication of 'The
Two Old Men's Tales,'—the first of Mrs. Marsh's
novels: but, from the time of my own success to this
hour, every other attempt, of the scores I have made,
to get a hearing for young or new aspirants has failed.
My own heart was often very near sinking,—as were
my bodily forces; and with reason. During the daylight hours of that winter, I was poring over fine
fancy-work, by which alone I earned any money; and

after tea, I went upstairs to my room, for my day's
literary labour. The quantity I wrote, at prodigious
expenditure of nerve, surprises me now,—after my
long breaking-in to hard work. Every night that
winter, I believe, I was writing till two, or even three
in the morning,—obeying always the rule of the
house,—of being present at the breakfast table as the
clock struck eight. Many a. time I was in such a
state of nervous exhaustion and distress that I was
obliged to walk to and fro in the room before I could
put on paper the last line of a page, or the last half
sentence of an essay or review. Yet was I very
happy. The deep-felt sense of progress and expansion was delightful ; and so was the exertion of all
my faculties ; and, not least, that of will to overcome
my obstructions, and force my way to that power of
public speech of which I believed myself more or less
worthy. The worst apprehension I felt,—far worse
than that of disappointment,mortification and poverty,
—was from the intense action of my mind. Such
excitement as I was then sustaining and enjoying
could not always last ; and I dreaded the reaction, or
the effects of its mere cessation. I was beginning,
however, to learn that the future,—our intellectual
and moral future,—had better be left to take care of
itself, as long as the present is made the best use of ;
and I found, in due course, that each period of the
mind's training has its own excitements, and that the
less its condition is quacked, or made the subject of
anticipation at all, the better for the mind's health.
But my habit of anxiety was not yet broken. It was
scarcely weakened. I have since found that persons
who knew me only then, do not recognize me or my

portraits now,—or at any time within the last twenty years. The frown of those old days, the rigid face, the sulky mouth, the forbidding countenance, which looked as if it had never had a smile upon it, told a melancholy story which came to an end long ago : but it was so far from its end then that it amazes me now to think what liberality and forbearance were requisite in the treatment of me by Mr. Fox and the friends I met at his house, and how capable they were of that liberality. My Sabbatarian strictness, and my prejudices on a hundred subjects must have been absurd and disagreeable enough to them : but their gentleness, respect and courtesy were such as I now remember with gratitude and pleasure. They saw that I was outgrowing my shell, and they had patience with me till I had rent it and cast it off; and if they were not equally ready with their sympathy when I had found freedom, but disposed to turn from me, in proportion as I was able to take care of myself, to do the same office for other incipient or struggling beings, this does not lessen my sense of obligation to them for the help and support they gave me in my season of intellectual and moral need.

My griefs deepened towards the close of that London visit. While failing in all my attempts to get my articles even looked at, proposals were made to me to remain in town, and undertake proof-correcting and other literary drudgery, on a salary which would, with my frugal habits, have supported me, while leaving time for literary effort on my own account. I rejoiced unspeakably in this opening, and wrote home in high satisfaction at the offer which would enable my young sister,—then only eighteen,—to re-

main at home, pursuing her studies in companionship
with a beloved cousin of nearly her own age, and
gaining something like maturity and self-reliance
before going out into the cold dark sphere of
governessing. But, to my disappointment,— I
might almost say, horror,—my mother sent me
peremptory orders to go home, and fill the place
which my poor young sister was to vacate. I rather
wonder that, being seven and twenty years old, I did
not assert my independence, and refuse to return,—
so clear as was, in my eyes, the injustice of remanding
me to a position of helplessness and dependence, when
a career of action and independence was opening before me. If I had known what my young sister was
thinking and feeling, I believe I should have taken
my own way, for her sake : but I did not know all :
the instinct and habit of old obedience prevailed, and
I went home, with some resentment, but far more
grief and desolation in my heart. My mother afterwards looked back with surprise upon the peremptori-
ness with which she had assumed the direction of my
affairs ; and she told me, (what I had suspected before) that my well-meaning hostess, who knew nothing of literature, and was always perplexing me
with questions as to 'how much I should get' by
each night's work, had advised my return home, to
pursue,—not literature but needlework, by which,
she wrote, I had proved that I could earn money,
and in which career I should always have the encouragement and support of herself and her family.
(Nothing could be more gracious than the acknowledgment of their mistake volunteered by this family
at a subsequent time.) My mother was wont to be

guided by them, whenever they offered their counsel ;
and this time it cost me very dear.   I went down to
Norwich, without prospect,—without any apparent
chance of independence; but as fully resolved against
being dependent as at any time before or after.

My mother received me very tenderly.   She had
no other idea at the moment than that she had been
doing her best for my good; and I, for my part,
could not trust myself to utter a word of what was
swelling in my heart.   I arrived worn and weary
with a night journey ; and my mother was so uneasy
at my looks that she made me lie down on her bed
after breakfast, and, as I could not sleep, came and
sat by me for a talk.—My news was that the Central
Unitarian Association had advertized for prize Essays,
by which Unitarianism was to be presented to the
notice of Catholics, Jews, and Mohammedans.   The
Catholic was one to be adjudicated on at the end of
September (1830) and the other two in the following
March.   Three sub-committees were appointed for
the examination of the manuscripts sent in, and for
decision on them ; and these sub-committees were
composed of different members, to bar all suspicion of
partiality.   The essays were to be superscribed with a
motto ; and the motto was to be repeated on a sealed
envelope, containing the writer's name, which was
not to be looked at till the prize was awarded ; and
then only in the case of the successful candidate.
The prizes were ten guineas for the Catholic, fifteen
for the Jewish, and twenty for the Mohammedan
essay.   I told my mother, as she sat by the bedside,
of this gleam of a prospect for me ; and she replied
that she thought it might be as well to try for one

prize. My reply was ' If I try at all, it shall be for all.' The money reward was trifling, even in the eyes of one so poor and prospectless as I was; but I felt an earnest desire to ascertain whether I could write, as Mr. Fox and other personal friends said I could. I saw that it was a capital opportunity for a fair trial of my competency in comparison with others; and I believe it was no small consideration to me that I should thus, at all events, tide over many months before I need admit despair. My mother thought this rather desperate work; but she gave me her sympathy and encouragement during the whole period of suspense,—as did the dear old aunt who lived with us. No one else was to know; and my secret was perfectly kept. The day after my return, I began to collect my materials; and before the week was done, I had drawn out the scheme of my Essay, and had begun it. It was done within a month; and then it had to be copied, lest any member of the sub-committee should know my hand. I discovered a poor school-boy who wrote a good hand; and I paid him a sovereign which I could ill spare for his work. The parcel was sent in a circuitous way to the office in London: and then, while waiting in suspense, I wrote the Tale called ' Five Years of Youth,' which I have never looked at since, and have certainly no inclination to read. Messrs. Darton and Harvey gave me twenty pounds for this; and most welcome was such a sum at that time. It set me forward through the toil of the Mohammedan Essay, which I began in October, I think. The 'Monthly Repository' for October contained a notification that the sub-committee sitting on the first of the three occasions had

adjudged the prize for the Catholic Essay to me; and
the money was presently forwarded. That announcement arrived on a Sunday morning; and again I had
a charming walk over Mousehold, as in the year before, among the heather and the bright tormentilla.

Next day, I went to the Public Library, and
brought home Sale's Koran. A friend whom I met
said 'What do you bore yourself with that book for?
You will never get through it.' He little guessed
what I meant to get out of it, and out of Sale's preliminary Essay. It occurred to me that the apologue
form would suit the subject best; and I ventured
upon it, though fearing that such daring might be
fatal. One of the sub-committee, an eminent scholar,
told me afterwards that it was this which mainly influenced his suffrage in my favour. In five weeks,
the work was done: but my tribulation about its preparation lasted much longer; for the careless young
usher who undertook the copying was not only idle
but saucy; and it was doubtful to the last day
whether the parcel could be in London by the first
of March. Some severe threatening availed however;
and that and the Jewish Essay, sent round by different hands (the hands of strangers to the whole
scheme) done up in different shapes, and in different
kinds of paper, and sealed with different wax and
seals, were deposited at the office on the last day of
February. The Jewish Essay was beautifully copied
by a poor woman who wrote a clerk-like hand. The
titles of the three Essays were—
'The Essential Faith of the Universal Church'
  (to Catholics).

'The Faith as Unfolded by Many Prophets' (to Mohammedans).

'The Faith as Manifested through Israel' (to Jews).

The last of these was grounded on Lessing's 'Hundred Thoughts on the Education of the Human Race,' which had taken my fancy amazingly, in the course of my German studies,—fancy then being the faculty most concerned in my religious views. Though my mind was already largely prepared for this piece of work by study, and by having treated the theory in the 'Monthly Repository,' and though I enjoyed the task in a certain sense, it became very onerous before it was done. I was by that time nearly as thin as possible; and I dreamed of the destruction of Jerusalem, and saw the burning of the Temple, almost every night. I might well be exhausted by that great and portentous first of March; for the year had been one of tremendous labour. I think it was in that year that a prize was offered by some Unitarian authority or other for an Essay on Baptism, for which I competed, but came in only third. If that was the year, my work stood thus :— my literary work, I mean ; for, in that season of poverty, I made and mended everything I wore,— knitting stockings while reading aloud to my mother and aunt, and never sitting idle a minute. I may add that I made considerable progress in the study of German that year. My writings within the twelve months were as follows :—

'Traditions of Palestine' (except the first tale).

'Five Years of Youth.'

Seven tracts for Houlston.

Essay on Baptism.

Three Theological Essays for prizes, and
Fifty-two articles for the ' Monthly Repository.'

By this time my mother was becoming aware of
the necessity of my being a good deal in London, if I
was to have any chance in the field of literature ; and
she consented to spare me for three months in the spring
of every year. An arrangement was made for my
boarding at the house of a cousin for three months
from the first of March ; and up I went, little dreaming what would be happening, and how life would be
opening before me, by that day twelvemonths. One
of my objects in the first instance was improving myself in German. An admirable master brought me
forward very rapidly, on extremely low terms, in consideration of my helping him with his English pre-
faces to some of his works. After a few weeks of
hard work, writing and studying, I accepted an invitation to spend a few days with some old friends in
Kent. There I refreshed myself among pretty
scenery, fresh air, and pleasant drives with hospitable
friends, and with the study of Faust at night, till a
certain day, early in May, which was to prove very
eventful to me. I returned on the outside of the
coach, and got down, with my heavy bag, at my
German master's door, where I took a lesson. It
was very hot ; and I dragged myself and my bag
home, in great fatigue, and very hungry. Dinner
was ordered up again by my hostess, and I sat an
hour, eating my dinner, resting and talking. Then
I was leaving the room, bonnet in hand, when a
daughter of my hostess seemed to recollect something,
and called after me to say, ' O, I forgot ! I suppose '
(she was a very slow and hesitating speaker)—' I

suppose.......you know.......you know about.......those
prizes.......those prize essays, you know.'

'No.......not I! What do you mean?'

'O! well, we thought.........we thought you
knew......'

'Well,—but what?'

'O? you have.......why.......you have got all the
prizes.'

'Why J! why did you not tell me so before?'

'Oh! I thought......I thought you might know.'

'How should I,—just up from the country? But
what do *you* know?'

'Why only......only the Secretary of the Unitarian Association has been here,—with a message,
—with the news from the Committee.'—It was
even so.

The next day was the Unitarian May Meeting;
and I had come up from Kent to attend it. I was
shocked to hear, after the morning service, that, in
reading the Report in the evening, the whole story of
the Essays must be told, with the announcement of
the result. I had reckoned for weeks on that meeting, at which Rammohun Roy was to be present, and
where the speaking was expected to be particularly
interesting; and I neither liked to stay away nor to
encounter the telling of my story. Mr. and Mrs. Fox
promised to put me into a quiet pew if I would go as
soon as the gates were opened. I did so; but the
Secretary came, among others, to be introduced, and
to congratulate; and I knew when the dreaded
moment was coming, amidst his reading of the
Report, by a glance which he sent in my direction,
to see if his wife, who sat next me, was keeping up

my attention.   I thought the story of all the measures
and all the precautions taken by the various Committees the longest I had ever sat under, and the
silence with which it was listened to the very deadest.
I heard little indeed but the beating of my own heart.
Then came the catastrophe, and the clapping and the
'Hear! Hear!' I knew that many of my family
connexions must be present, who would be surprised
and gratified.   But there was one person more than
I expected.   I slipped out before the meeting was
over, and in the vestibule was met by my young
sister with open arms, and with an offer to go home
with me for the night.   She was in the midst of an
uncomfortable brief experiment of governessing, a few
miles from town, and had been kindly indulged with
a permission to go to this meeting, too late to let me
know.   She had arrived late, and got into the gallery; and before she had been seated many minutes,
heard my news, so strangely told!   She went home
with me; and, after we had written my mother the
account of the day, we talked away nearly all the rest
of that May night.—It was truly a great event to
me,—the greatest since my brother's reception of my
first attempt in print.   I had now found that I could
write, and I might rationally believe that authorship
was my legitimate career.

Of course, I had no conception at that time of the
thorough weakness and falseness of the views I had
been conveying with so much pains and so much
complacency.   This last act in connexion with the
Unitarian body was a *bonâ fide* one; but all was prepared for that which ensued,—a withdrawal from
the body through those regions of metaphysical fog in

which most deserters from Unitarianism abide for the rest of their time. The Catholic essay was ignorant and metaphysical, if my recollection of it is at all correct : and the other two mere fancy pieces : and I can only say that if either Mohammedans or Jews have ever been converted by them, such converts can hardly be rational enough to be worth having. I had now plunged fairly into the spirit of my time, that of self-analysis, pathetic self-pity, typical interpretation of objective matters, and scheme-making in the name of God and Man. That such was the stage then reached by my mind, in its struggles upward and onward, there is outstanding proof in that series of papers called ' Sabbath Musings ' which may be found in the ' Monthly Repository ' of 1831. There are the papers : and I hereby declare that I considered them my best production, and expected they would outlive every thing else I had written or should write. I was, in truth, satisfied that they were very fine writing, and believed it for long after,—little aware that the time could ever come when I should write them down, as I do now, to be morbid, fantastical, and therefore unphilosophical and untrue. I cannot wonder that it did not occur to the Unitarians (as far as they thought of me at all) that I was really not of them, at the time that I had picked up their gauntlet, and assumed their championship. If it did not occur to me, no wonder it did not to them. But the clear-sighted among them might and should have seen, by the evidence of those essays themselves, that I was one of those merely nominal Christians who refuse whatever they see to be impossible, absurd or immoral in the scheme or the records of Christianity, and pick

out and appropriate what they like, or interpolate it
with views, desires and imaginations of their own.
I had already ceased to be an Unitarian in the tech-
nical sense. I was now one in the dreamy way of
metaphysical accommodation, and on the ground of
dissent from every other form of Christianity : the
time was approaching when, if I called myself so at
all, it was only in the free-thinking sense. Then
came a few years during which I remonstrated with
Unitarians in vain against being claimed by them,
which I considered even more injurious to them than
to me. They were unwilling, as they said, and as I
saw, to recognize the complete severance of the theological bond between us : and I was careful to assert,
in every practicable way, that it was no doing of mine
if they were taunted by the orthodox with their
sectarian fellowship with the writer of 'Eastern
Life.' At length, I hope and believe my old co-
religionists understand and admit that I disclaim
their theology *in toto*, and that by no twisting of
language or darkening of its meanings can I be made
out to have any thing whatever in common with
them about religious matters. I perceive that they
do not at all understand my views or the grounds of
them, or the road to them; but they will not deny
that I understand theirs,— chosen expositor as I
was of them in the year 1831; and they must take
my word for it that there is nothing in common between their theology and my philosophy. Our stand-
point is different; and all our views and estimates
are different accordingly. Of course, I consider my
stand-point the truer one; and my views and estimates the higher, wider, and more accurate, as I

shall have occasion to show. I consider myself the best qualified of the two parties to judge of the relative value of the views of either, because I have the experience of both, while I see that they have no comprehension of mine: but the point on which we may and ought to agree is that my severance from their faith was complete and necessarily final when I wrote 'Eastern Life,' though many of them could not be brought to admit it, nor some (whom I asked) to assert it at the time. While I saw that many Unitarians resented as a slander the popular imputation that their sect is 'a harbourage for infidels,' I did not choose that they should have that said of them in my case: and it is clear that if they were unwilling to exchange a disownment with me, they could have no right to quarrel with that imputation in future.

SECTION IV.

My prize-money enabled me to go to Dublin, to visit my brother James and his wife; and I stayed there till September,—writing all the time, and pondering the scheme of my Political Economy Series. I sketched out my plan in a very small blue book which was afterwards begged of me as a relic by a friend who was much with me at that time. My own idea was that my stories should appear quarterly. My brother and the publishers urged their being monthly. The idea was overwhelming at first: and there were times when truly I was scared at other parts of the scheme than that. The whole business was the strongest act of will that I ever committed myself to; and my will was always a pretty strong one. I could never have even started my project but for my thorough, well-considered, steady conviction that the work was wanted,—was even craved by the popular mind. As the event proved me right, there is no occasion to go into the evidence which determined my judgment. I now believed that for two years I must support an almost unequalled amount of literary labour: that, owing to the nature of some of the subjects to be treated, my effort would probably be fatal to my reputation : that the chances of failure in a scheme of such extent, begun without money or interest, were most formidable ; and that failure would be ruin. I staked my all upon this project, in fact, and with the belief that long, weary months must pass before I could even discern the probabilities of the issue ; for the mere preparations must occupy months. In the first place,—in that autumn of 1831,—I strengthened myself in certain resolutions, from which I promised myself that no power on earth should draw me away. I was resolved that, in the first place, the thing should be done. The people wanted the book ; and they should have it. Next, I resolved to sustain my health under the suspense, if possible, by keeping up a mood of steady determination, and unfaltering hope. Next, I resolved never to lose my temper, in the whole course of the business. I knew I was right ; and people who are aware that they are in the right need never lose temper. Lastly, I resolved to refuse, under any temptation whatever, to accept any loan from my kind mother and aunt. I felt that I could never get over causing them any pecuniary loss,—my mother having really nothing to spare, and my aunt having been abundantly generous to the family already. My own small remnant of property (which came to nothing after all) I determined to risk ; and, when the scheme began to take form, I accepted small loans from two opulent friends, whom I was able presently to repay. They knew the risks as well as I ; and they were men of business ; and there was no reason for declining the timely aid, so freely and kindly granted. What those months of suspense were like, it is necessary now to tell.

I wrote to two or three publishers from Dublin, opening my scheme; but one after another declined having any thing to do with it, on the ground of the disturbed state of the public mind, which afforded no encouragement to put out new books. The bishops had recently thrown out the Reform Bill; and every body was watching the progress of the Cholera,— then regarded with as much horror as a plague of the middle ages. The terrifying Order in Council which froze men's hearts by its doleful commands and recommendations, was issued just at the same time with my poor proposals; and no wonder that I met only refusals. Messrs. Baldwin and Cradock, however, requested me to take London on my way back to Norwich, that we might discuss the subject. I did so; and I took with me as a witness a laywer cousin who told me long afterwards what an amusing scene it was to him. Messrs. Baldwin and Cradock sat superb in their arm-chairs, in their brown wigs, looking as cautious as possible, but relaxing visibly under the influence of my confidence. My cousin said that, in their place, he should have felt my confidence a sufficient guarantee,—so fully as I assigned the grounds of it: and Messrs. Baldwin and Cradock seemed to be nearly of the same mind, though they brought out a long string of objections, beginning with my proposed title, and ending with the Reform Bill and the Cholera. They wanted to suppress the words Political Economy altogether; but I knew that science could not be smuggled in anonymously. I gave up the point for the time, feeling assured that they would find their smuggling scheme impracticable. 'Live and let live' was *their* title and its inadequacy was vexatious enough, as showing their imperfect conception of the plan : but it was necessary to let them have their own way in the matter of preliminary advertising. They put out a sort of feeler in the form of an advertisement in some of the Diffusion Society's publications; but an intimation so vague and obscure attracted no notice. This melancholy fact Messrs. Baldwin and Cradock duly and dolefully announced to me. Still, they did not let go for some time ; and I afterwards heard that they were so near becoming my publishers that they had actually engaged a stitcher for my monthly numbers. Fortunately for me, as it turned out, but most discouragingly at the time, they withdrew, after a hesitation of many weeks. They had read and approved of a part of the manuscript of ' Life in the Wilds,'—my first number : but they went on doubting; and at last wrote to me that, considering the public excitement about the Reform Bill and the Cholera, they dared not venture.

Here was the whole work to begin again. I stifled my sighs, and swallowed my tears, and wrote to one publisher after another, receiving instant refusals from all, except Messrs. Whittaker. They kept up the negotiation for a few posts, but at length joined the general chorus about the Reform Bill and the Cholera. They offered however to do their best for the work as mere publishers, on the usual terms of commission. My mother and aunt re-urged my accepting a loan from them of money which they were willing to risk in such a cause : but of course I would not hear of this. Mr. Fox appeared at that time earnest in the project ; and a letter from him came by the same post

with Messrs. Whittakers' last, saying that booksellers
might be found to share the risk; and he named one
(who, like Baldwin and Cradock, afterwards failed)
who would be likely to go halves with me in risk and
profit. I did not much relish either the plan or the
proposed publisher; but I was in no condition to refuse suggestions. I said to my mother, ' You know
what a man of business would do in my case.' —
' What?'—' Go up to town by the next mail, and
see what is to be done.'—' My dear, you would not
think of doing such a thing, alone, and in this
weather!' — ' I wish it.' — ' Well, then, let us
show Henry the letters after dinner, and see what he
will say.'—As soon as the cloth was removed, and
we had drawn round the fire, I showed my brother
Henry the letters, with the same remark I had made
to my mother. He sat looking into the fire for
several minutes, while nobody spoke : and then he
turned to me, and said oracularly ' Go!'—I sprang
up,—sent to have my place taken by the early morning coach, tied up and dispatched borrowed books,
and then ran to my room to pack. There I found a
fire, and my trunk airing before it. All was finished
an hour before tea time; and I was at leisure to read
to my old ladies for the rest of the evening. On my
mother observing that she could not have done it, my
aunt patted me on the shoulder, and said that, at least,
the back was fitted to the burden. This domestic
sympathy was most supporting to me; but, at the
same time, it rendered success more stringently necessary.

My scheme of going to London was not at all a
wild one, unless the speed of the movement, and the

state of the weather made it so. It was the beginning of December, foggy and sleety. I was always sure of a home in London, with or without notice; and without notice I presented myself at my cousin's door that dreary December Saturday night. It was a great Brewery house, always kept open, and cooking daily going on, for the use of the partners. My kind cousin and his family were to leave home the next morning for three weeks: but, as he observed, this would rather aid than hinder my purposes, as I went for work. I was really glad to be alone during those three eventful weeks,—feeling myself no intruder, all the while, and being under the care of attentive servants.

My first step on Monday was seeing the publisher mentioned by Mr. Fox. He shook his head; his wife smiled; and he begged to see the opening chapters, promising to return them, with a reply, in twenty-four hours. His reply was what was already burnt in upon my brain. He had ' no doubt of the excellence,—wished it success,—but feared that the excitement of the public mind about the Reform Bill and the Cholera would afford it no chance,' &c., &c. I was growing as sick of the Reform Bill as poor King William himself. I need not detail, even if I could remember, the many applications I made in the course of the next few days. Suffice it that they were all unsuccessful, and for the same alleged reasons. Day after day, I came home weary with disappointment, and with trudging many miles through the clay of the streets, and the fog of the gloomiest December I ever saw. I came home only to work; for I must be ready with two first numbers in case of a publisher turning up any day. All the while, too, I was as determined as ever that my scheme should be fulfilled. Night after night, the Brewery clock struck twelve, while the pen was still pushing on in my trembling hand. I had promised to take one day's rest, and dine and sleep at the Foxes'. Then, for the first time, I gave way, in spite of all my efforts. Some trifle having touched my feelings before saying ' Good-night,' the sluices burst open, and I cried all night. In the morning, Mr. Fox looked at me with great concern, stepped into the next room, and brought a folded paper to the breakfast table, saying ' Don't read this now. I can't bear it. These are what may be called terms from my brother.' (A young bookseller who did not pretend to have any business, at that time.) ' I do not ask you even to consider them ; but they will enable you to tell publishers that you hold in your hand terms offered by a publisher : and this may at least procure attention to your scheme.' These were, to the subsequent regret of half a score of publishers, the terms on which my work was issued at last.

I immediately returned to town, and went straight to Whittakers'. Mr. Whittaker looked bored, fidgeted, yawned, and then said, with extreme rudeness, ' I have told you already that these are not times for new enterprises.' ' Then,' said I, rising, ' it is now time for me to consider the terms from another publisher which I hold in my hand.' ' O, indeed,— really, Ma'am ? ' said he, reviving. ' Do me the favour to give me a short time for consideration. Only twenty-four hours, Ma'am.' I refreshed his memory about the particulars, and endeavoured to

make him see why the times were not unseasonable
for this special work, though they might be for light
literature.

It was next necessary to look at the paper I had
been carrying. I read it with dismay. The very
first stipulation was that the work should be published
by subscription : and, moreover, the subscription must
be for five hundred copies before the work began.
Subscribers were to be provided by both parties ; and
Charles Fox was to have half the profits, besides the
usual bookseller's commission and privileges. The
agreement was to cease at the end of any five numbers, at the wish of either party. As Charles Fox
had neither money nor connexion, I felt that the
whole risk was thrown upon me ; and that I should
have all the peril, as well as the toil, while Charles
Fox would enjoy the greater part of the proceeds, in
case of success, and be just where he was before, in
case of failure. In fact, he never procured a single
subscriber ; and he told me afterwards that he knew
from the beginning that he never should. After pondering this heart-sickening Memorandum, I looked
with no small anxiety for Whittakers' final reply. I
seemed to see the dreaded words through the envelope ; and there they were within. Mr. Whittaker
expressed his 'regrets that the public mind being so
engrossed with the Reform Bill and the approach of
the Cholera,' &c., &c. The same story to the end!
Even now, in this low depth of disappointment, there
were lower depths to be explored. The fiercest trial
was now at hand.

I remonstrated strongly with Mr. Fox about the
subscription stipulation ; but in vain. The mortifica-

tion to my pride was not the worst part of it, though
that was severe enough.   I told him that I could not
stoop to that method, if any other means were left ; to
which he replied ' You will stoop to conquer.' But
he had no consolation to offer under the far more
serious anxiety which I strove to impress on his mind
as my main objection to the scheme.   Those persons
from whom I might hope for pecuniary support were
precisely those to whom I despaired of conveying any
conception of my aim, or of the object and scope of
my work.   Those who would, I believed, support it
were, precisely, persons who had never seen or heard
of me, and whose support could not be solicited.   My
view was the true one, as I might prove by many
pages of anecdote.   Suffice it that, at the very time
when certain members of parliament were eagerly inquiring about the announced work, the wife of one of
them, a rich lady of my acquaintance, to whom a prospectus had been sent, returned it, telling me that
she ' knew too well what she was about to buy a pig
in a poke :' and the husband of a cousin of mine, a
literary man in his way, sent me, in return for the
prospectus, a letter, enclosing two sovereigns, and a
lecture against my rashness and presumption in supposing that I was adequate to such a work as authorship, and offering the enclosed sum as his mite
towards the subscription ; but recommending rather a
family subscription which might eke out my earnings
by my needle.   I returned the two sovereigns, with
a declaration that I wished for no subscribers but
those who expected full value for their payment, and
that I would depend upon my needle and upon charity
when I found I could not do better, and not before.

This gentleman apologised handsomely afterwards. The lady never did. It should be remembered that it is easy enough to laugh at these incidents now ; but that it was a very different matter then, when success seemed to be growing more and more questionable and difficult every day. I had no resource, however, but to try the method I heartily disapproved and abhorred. I drew up a Prospectus, in which I avoided all mention of a subscription, in the hope that it might soon be dispensed with, but fully explanatory of the nature and object of the work. To this I added in my own handwriting an urgent appeal to all whom I could ask to be subscribers. I went to Mr. Fox's, one foggy morning, to show him one of these, and the advertisement intended for the next day's papers, announcing the first of February as the day of publication : (for it was now too late to open with the year). I found Mr. Fox in a mood as gloomy as the day. He had seen Mr. James Mill, who had assured him that my method of exemplification,—(the grand principle of the whole scheme) could not possibly succeed ; and Mr. Fox now required of me to change my plan entirely, and issue my Political Economy in a didactic form! Of course, I refused. He started a multitude of objections,— feared every thing, and hoped nothing. I saw, with anguish and no little resentment, my last poor chance slipping from me. I commanded myself while in his presence. The occasion was too serious to be misused. I said to him, ' I see you have taken fright. If you wish that your brother should draw back, say so *now*. Here is the advertisement. Make up your mind before it goes to press.' He replied, ' I do not

wish altogether to draw back.' 'Yes, you do,' said
I: ' and I had rather you would say so at once. But
I tell you this:—the people want this book, and they
shall have it.' 'I know that is your intention,' he
replied: ' but I own I do not see how it is to come to
pass.' 'Nor I: but it *shall*. So, say that you
have done with it, and I will find other means.' ' I
tell you, I do not wish altogether to draw out of it;
but I cannot think of my brother going on without
decisive success at the outset.' ' What do you mean,
precisely?' 'I mean that he withdraws at the end
of two numbers, unless the success of the work is secured in a fortnight.' ' What do you mean by success being secured?' ' You must sell a thousand in
a fortnight.' ' In a fortnight! That *is* unreason-
nable!' 'Is this your ultimatum?' 'Yes.' 'We
shall not sell a thousand in the first fortnight : nevertheless, the work shall not stop at two numbers. It
shall go on to five, with or without your brother.'
' So I perceive you say.' ' What is to be done with
this advertisement?' I inquired. 'Shall I send it,
—yes or no?' ' Yes: but remember Charles gives
up at the end of two numbers, unless you sell a
thousand in the first fortnight.'

I set out to walk the four miles and a half to the
Brewery. I could not afford to ride, more or less ;
but, weary already, I now felt almost too ill to walk
at all. On the road, not far from Shoreditch, I became too giddy to stand without support; and I
leaned over some dirty palings, pretending to look at
a cabbage bed, but saying to myself, as I stood with
closed eyes, ' My book will do yet.' I moved on as
soon as I could, apprehending that the passers-by

took me to be drunk : but the pavement swam before
my eyes so that I was glad enough to get to the
Brewery. I tried to eat some dinner; but the vast
rooms, the plate and the liveried servant were too
touching a contrast to my present condition; and I
was glad to go to work, to drown my disappointment
in a flow of ideas. Perhaps the piece of work that I
did may show that I succeeded. I wrote the Preface
to my 'Illustrations of Political Economy' that
evening ; and I hardly think that any one would discover from it.that I had that day sunk to the lowest
point of discouragement about my scheme.—At
eleven o'clock, I sent the servants to bed. I finished
the Preface just after the Brewery clock had struck
two. I was chilly and hungry : the lamp burned low,
and the fire was small. I knew it would not do to go
to bed, to dream over again the bitter disappointment
of the morning. I began now, at last, to doubt
whether my work would ever see the light. I
thought of the multitudes who needed it,—and
especially of the poor,—to assist them in managing
their own welfare. I thought too of my own conscious power of doing this very thing. Here was the
thing wanting to be done, and I wanting to do it;
and the one person who had seemed to best understand the whole affair now urged me to give up
either the whole scheme, or, what was worse, its main
principle ! It was an inferior consideration, but still,
no small matter to me, that I had no hope or prospect
of usefulness or independence if this project failed :
and I did not feel that night that I could put my
heart into any that might arise. As the fire
crumbled, I put it together till nothing but dust and

ashes remained; and when the lamp went out, I
lighted the chamber candle; but at last it was necessary to go to bed; and at four o'clock I went, after
crying for two hours with my feet on the fender.   I
cried in bed till six, when I fell asleep; but I was at
the breakfast table by half-past eight, and ready for
the work of the day.

The work of the day was to prepare and send out
my Circulars.   After preparing enough for my family,
I took into my confidence the before-mentioned
cousin,—my benefactor and my host at that time.
He was regarded by the whole clan as a prudent and
experienced man of business; and I knew that his
countenance would be of great value to me.   That
countenance he gave me, and some good suggestions,
and no discouragement.—It was very disagreeable to
have to appeal to monied relations whose very confidence and generosity would be a burden on my mind
till I had redeemed my virtual pledges; while the
slightest indulgence of a critical spirit by any of them
must be exceedingly injurious to my enterprise.   It
was indeed not very long before I had warnings from
various quarters that some of my relations were doing
me 'more harm by their tongues than they could
ever do good by their guineas.'   This was true,
as the censors themselves have since spontaneously
and handsomely told me.   I could not blame them
much for saying what they thought of my rashness
and conceit, while I cordially honour the candour of
their subsequent confession : but their sayings were so
much added to the enormous obstructions of the case.
From my first act of appeal to my monied relations,
however, I derived such singular solace that every in-

cident remains fresh in my mind, and I may fairly indulge in going over it once more.

My oldest surviving uncle and his large family, living near Clapham, had always been ready and kind in their sympathy ; and I was now to find the worth of it more than ever in connexion with the greatest of my enterprises. On the next Sunday, I returned with them when they went home from Chapel. While at luncheon, my uncle told me that he understood I had some new plan, and he was anxious to know what it was. His daughters proposed that I should explain it after dinner, when their brothers would be present. After dinner, accordingly, I was called upon for my explanation, which I gave in a very detailed way. All were silent, waiting for my uncle to make his remark, the very words of which I distinctly remember, at the distance of nearly a quarter of a century. In his gentle and gracious manner he said, 'You are a better judge, my dear, than we of this scheme ; but we know that your industry and energy are the pride of us all, and ought to have our support.' When we ladies went to the drawing-room, I knew there would be a consultation between my uncle and his sons : and so there was. At the close of the pleasant evening, he beckoned to me, and made me sit beside him on the sofa, and told me of the confidence of his family and himself that what I was doing would be very useful : that his daughters wished for each a copy of the Series, his sons two each ; and that he himself must have five. 'And,' he concluded, 'as you will like to pay your printer immediately, you shall not wait for our money.' So saying, he slipped a packet of bank

notes and gold into my hand, to the amount of payment for fourteen copies of the whole series! To
complete the grace of his hospitality, he told me that
he should go to town late the next morning, and
would escort me ; and he desired me to sleep as late as
I liked. And I did sleep,—the whole night through,
and awoke a new creature. Other members of the
family did what they thought proper, in the course of
the week ; and then I had only to go home, and await
the result.

I was rather afraid to show myself to my mother,
—thin as I was, and yellow, and coughing with
every breath ; and she was panic-struck at the evident
symptoms of liver-complaint which the first half-hour
disclosed. I was indeed in wretched health ; and
during the month of April following, when I was
writing 'Demerara,' I was particularly ill. I do
not think I was ever well again till, at the close of
1833, I was entirely laid aside, and confined to my
bed for a month, by inflammation of the liver. I am
confident that that serious illness began with the toils
and anxieties, and long walks in fog and mud, of two
years before. My mother took my health in hand
anxiously and most tenderly. In spite of my entreaties, she would never allow me to be wakened in
the morning ; and on Sundays, the day when Charles
Fox's dispatches came by manufacturer's parcel, my
breakfast was sent up to me, and I was not allowed
to rise till the middle of the day. For several weeks
I dreaded the arrival of the publisher's weekly letter.
He always wrote gloomily, and sometimes rudely.
The subscription proceeded very little better than I
had anticipated. From first to last, about three

hundred copies were subscribed for : and before that number had been reached, the success of the work was such as to make the subscription a mere burden. It was a thoroughly vexatious part of the business altogether,—that subscription. A clever suggestion of my mother's, at this time, had, I believe, much to do with the immediate success of the book. By her advice, I sent, by post, a copy of my Prospectus (without a word about subscription in it) to almost every member of both Houses of Parliament. There was nothing of puffery in this,—nothing that I had the least objection to do. It was merely informing our legislators that a book was coming out on their particular class of subjects.

I may as well mention in this place, that I had offered (I cannot at all remember when) one of my tales,—the one which now stands as ' Brooke and Brooke Farm,'—to the Diffusion Society, whence it had been returned. Absurd as were some of the stories afterwards set afloat about this transaction, there was thus much foundation for them. Mr. Knight, then the publisher of the Society, sent me a note of cordial and generous encouragement; but a sub-committee, to whose judgment the manuscript was consigned, thought it ' dull,' and pronounced against its reception accordingly. I knew nothing about this sub-committee, or about the method employed, and had in fact forgotten, among so many failures, that particular one, when, long after, I found to my regret and surprise, that the gentlemen concerned had been supposing me offended and angry all the while, and somehow an accomplice in Lord Brougham's mockery of their decision. In vain I told them that I now thought them perfectly right to form and express their own judgment, and that I had never before heard who had been my judges. I fear the soreness remains in their minds to this day, though there never was any in mine. Lord Brougham's words travelled far and wide, and were certainly anything but comfortable to the sub-committee. He said he should revive the torture for their sakes, as hanging was too good for them. He tore his hair over the tales, he added, unable to endure that the whole Society, ' instituted for the very purpose, should be driven out of the field by a little deaf woman at Norwich.'—As I have said, I cannot remember at what time I made my application; but I imagine it must have been during that eventful year 1831,—in which case the writing of that story must come into the estimate of the work of that year.

A cheering incident occurred during the interval of awaiting the effects of the Circular. Every body knows that the Gurneys are the great bankers of Norwich. Richard Hanbury Gurney, at that time one of the Members for Norfolk, was in the firm; and he was considered to be one of the best-informed men in England on the subject of Currency. The head officer of the bank, Mr. Simon Martin, deserved the same reputation, and had it, among all who knew him. He sent for my brother Henry, who found him with my Circular before him. He said that he had a message to communicate to me from the firm: and the message was duly delivered, when Mr. Martin had satisfied himself that my brother conscientiously believed me adequate to my enterprise. Messrs. Gurney considered the scheme an important one, promising public benefit: they doubted whether it would be immediately appreciated: they knew that I could not afford to go on at a loss, but thought it a pity that a beneficial enterprise should fall to the ground for want of immediate support; and they therefore requested that, in case of discouragement in regard to the sale, I should apply to them before giving up. 'Before she gives up, let her come to us,' were their words: words which were as pleasant to me in the midst of my success as they could have been if I had needed the support so generously offered.

Meantime the weekly letter grew worse and worse. But on the Sunday preceding the day of publication came a bit of encouragement in the shape of a sentence in these, or nearly these words. 'I see no chance of the work succeeding unless the trade take it up better. We have only one considerable booksellers' order,—from A and B for a hundred copies.' 'Why, there,' said my mother, 'is a hundred towards your thousand!' 'Ah, but,' said I, 'where are the other nine hundred to come from, in a fortnight? The edition consisted of fifteen hundred.

To the best of my recollection I waited ten days from the day of publication, before I had another line from the publisher. My mother, judging from his ill-humour, inferred that he had good news to tell; whereas I supposed the contrary. My mother was right; and I could now be amused at his last attempts to be discouraging in the midst of splendid success. At the end of those ten days, he sent with his letter a copy of my first number, desiring me to make with all speed any corrections I might wish to make, as he

had scarcely any copies left.   He added that the demand led him to propose that we should now print
two thousand.   A postscript informed me that since
he wrote the above he had found that we should want
three thousand.   A second postscript proposed four
thousand, and a third five thousand.   The letter was
worth having, now it had come.   There was immense
relief in this ; but I remember nothing like intoxica-
tion ;—like any painful reaction whatever.   I remember walking up and down the grassplat in the
garden (I think it was on the tenth of February)
feeling that my cares were over.   And so they were.
From that hour I have never had any other anxiety
about employment than what to choose, nor any real
care about money.   Eight or nine years after I found
myself entirely cut off by illness from the power of
working, and then my relations and friends aided me
in ways so generous as to make it easy for me to
accept the assistance.   But even then, I was never
actually pinched for money ; and, from the time that
the power of working was restored, I was at once as
prosperous as ever, and became more and more so till
now, when illness has finally visited me in a condition
of independence.   I think I may date my release
from pecuniary care from that tenth of February,
1832.

The entire periodical press, daily, weekly, and, as
soon as possible, monthly, came out in my favour ;
and I was overwhelmed with newspapers and letters,
containing every sort of flattery.   The Diffusion
Society wanted to have the Series now ; and Mr.
Hume offered, on behalf of a new society of which
he was the head, any price I would name for the pur-

chase of the whole. I cannot precisely answer for the date of these and other applications ; but, as far as I remember, there was, from the middle of February onwards, no remission of such applications, the meanest of which I should have clutched at a few weeks before. Members of Parliament sent down blue books through the post-office, to the astonishment of the postmaster, who one day sent word that I must send for my own share of the mail, for it could not be carried without a barrow ;—an announcement which, spreading in the town, caused me to be stared at in the streets. Thus began *that* sort of experience. Half the hobbies of the House of Commons, and numberless notions of individuals, anonymous and other, were commended to me for treatment in my Series, with which some of them had no more to do than geometry or the atomic theory. I had not calculated on this additional labour, in the form of correspondence ; and very weary I often was of it, in the midst of the amusement. One necessity arose out of it which soon became very clear,—that I must reside in London, for the sake of the extensive and varied information which I now found was at my service there, and which the public encouragement of my work made it my duty to avail myself of.

It seemed hard upon my kind mother and aunt that the first consequence of the success they buoyed me up in hoping for should be to take me to London, after all : but the events of the summer showed them the necessity of the removal. We treated it as for a time ; and I felt that my mother would not endure a permanent separation. The matter ended in their joining me in a small house in London, before many

months were over ; and meantime, my mother stipu-
lated for my being in the house of some family well
known to her.   I obtained lodgings in the house of a
tailor in Conduit Street, whose excellent wife had
been an acquaintance of ours from her childhood to
her marriage.   There I arrived in November 1832 ;
and there I lodged till the following September, when
I went, with my mother and aunt, into a house
(No. 17) in Fludyer Street, Westminster, where I
resided till the breakdown of my health (which
took place in 1839) removed me from London altogether.

Here I stop, thinking that the third period of my
life may be considered as closing with the conquest of
all difficulty about getting a hearing from the public
for what I felt I had to say.   Each period of my life
has had its trials and heart-wearing difficulties,—except (as will be seen) the last; but in none had the
pains and penalties of life a more intimate connexion
with the formation of character than in the one which
closes here.   And now the summer of my life was
bursting forth without any interval of spring.   My
life began with winter, burst suddenly into summer,
and is now ending with autumn,—mild and sunny.
I have had no spring ; but that cannot be helped now.
It was a moral disadvantage, as well as a great loss of
happiness ; but we all have our moral disadvantages to
make the best of, and 'happiness' is *not*, as the poet
says, ' our being's end and aim,' but the result of one
faculty among many, which must be occasionally over-
borne by others, if there is to be any effectual exercise
of the whole being.   So I am satisfied in a higher
sense than that in which the Necessarian is always

satisfied. I cannot but know that in my life there has been a great waste of precious time and material; but I had now, by thirty years of age, ascertained my career, found occupation, and achieved independence; and thus the rest of my life was provided with its duties and its interests. Any one to whom that happens by thirty years of age may be satisfied; and I was so.

FOURTH PERIOD.

SECTION I.

IT was a dark, foggy November morning when I arrived in London. My lodgings were up two pair of stairs; for I did not yet feel secure of my permanent success, and had no conception of what awaited me in regard to society. A respectable sitting room to the front, and a clean, small bedroom behind, seemed to me all that could possibly be desired,— seeing that I was to have them all to myself. To be sure, they did look very dark, that first morning of yellow fog; but it was seldom so dark again; and when the spring came on, and I moved down into the handsomer rooms on the first floor, I thought my lodgings really pleasant. In the summer mornings, when I made my coffee at seven o'clock, and sat down to my work, with the large windows open, the sun-blinds down, the street fresh watered, and the flower-girls' baskets visible from my seat, I wished for nothing better. The evening walks in the Parks, when London began to grow 'empty,' were one of my chief pleasures; and truly I know few things

better than Kensington Gardens and the Serpentine
in the evenings of August and September. I had
lived in a narrow street all my life, except during
occasional visits ; and I therefore did not now object
to Conduit Street, though it *was* sometimes too noisy,
or too foggy, or too plashy, or too hot. It is well
that I did not then know the charms of a country
residence ; or, knowing them, never thought of them
as attainable by me. I have long felt that nothing
but the strongest call of duty could make me now
live in a street ; and if I allowed myself to give way
to distress at the mysteries of human life, one of my
greatest perplexities would be at so many people
being obliged so to live. Now that I have dwelt for
nine years in a field, where there is never any dust,
never any smoke, never any noise ; where my visitors
laugh at the idea of the house ever being cleaned,
because it never gets dirty ; where there is beauty to
be seen from every window, and in bad weather it is
a treat to stand in the porch and see it rain, I cannot but wonder at my former contentment. I have
visited and gone over our old house in Magdalen
Street, at Norwich, within a few years ; and I could
not but wonder how my romantic days could ever
have come on in such a place. There it stands,—a
handsome, plain brick house, in a narrow street,—
Norwich having nothing but narrow streets. There
it is,—roomy and good-looking enough ; but prosaic
to the last degree. Except the vine on its back gable
there is not an element of naturalness or poetry about
it. Yet there were my dreamy years passed. In my
London lodging, a splendid vision was to open upon
me ;—one which I am glad to have enjoyed, because

it *was* enjoyment; and because a diversified experience
is good ; and because I really gained much knowledge
of human life and character from it.   I became the
fashion, and I might have been the 'lion' of several
seasons, if I had chosen to permit it.   I detested the
idea, and absolutely put down the practice in my own
case : but I saw as much of a very varied society as if
I had allowed myself to be lionised, and with a more
open mind than if I had not insisted on being treated
simply as a lady or let alone.   The change from my
life in Norwich to my life in London was certainly
prodigious, and such as I did not dream of when I
exchanged the one for the other.   Before we lost our
money, and when I was a young lady 'just introduced,' my mother insisted on taking me to balls and
parties, though that sort of visiting was the misery of
my life.   My deafness was terribly in the way, both
because it made me shy, and because underbred people,
like the card-players and dancers of a provincial town,
are awkward in such a case.   Very few people spoke
to me ; and I dare say I looked as if I did not wish to
be spoken to.   From the time when I went to London, all that was changed.   People began with me as
with a deaf person ; and there was little more awkwardness about hearing, when they had once reconciled themselves to my trumpet.   They came to me
in good will, or they would not have come at all.
They and I were not jumbled together by mere pro-
pinquity ; we met purposely ; and, if we continued our
intercourse, it was through some sort of affinity.   I
now found what the real pleasures of social intercourse
are, and was deeply sensible of its benefits : but it
really does not appear to me that I was intoxicated

with the pleasure, or that I over-rated the benefit. I
think so because I always preferred my work to this
sort of play. I think so because some sober friends,
—two or three whom I could trust,—said, first, that
I might and probably should say and do some foolish
things, but that I should ' prove ultimately unspoil-
able ; ' and afterwards that I was not spoiled. I
think so because I altered no plan or aim in life on
account of any social distinction; and I think so,
finally, because, while vividly remembering the seven
years from 1832 to 1839, and feeling as gratefully
and complacently as ever the kindness and attachment
of friends, and the good-will of a multitude of acquaintances, I had no inclination to return to literary
life in London after my recovery at Tynemouth, and
have for ten years rejoiced, without pause or doubt, in
my seclusion and repose in my quiet valley. There is
an article of mine on ' Literary Lionism ' in the
London and Westminster Review of April, 1839,
which was written when the subject was fresh in my
thoughts and feelings. In consideration of this, and
of my strong repugnance to detailing the incidents of
my own reception in society, on entering the London
world, while such an experience cannot be wholly
passed over in an account of my life, I think the best
way will be to cite that article,—omitting those
passages only which are of a reviewing character. By
this method, it will appear what my impressions were
while in conflict with the practice of literary lionism ;
and I shall be spared the disgusting task of detailing
old absurdities and dwelling on old flatteries, which
had myself for their subject. Many of the stories
which I could tell are comic enough ; and a few are

exceedingly interesting : but they would be all spoiled, to myself and every body else, by their relating to myself. The result on my own convictions and feelings is all that it is necessary to give ; and that result can be given in no form so trustworthy as in the record penned at the time. It must be remembered that the article appeared in an anonymous form, or some appearance of conceit and bad taste may hang about even that form of disclosure.—The statement and treatment of the subject will however lead forward so far into my London life that I must fill up an intermediate space. I must give some account of my work before I proceed to treat of my play hours.

In meditating on my course of life at that time, and gathering together the evidences of what I was learning and doing, I am less disposed than I used to be to be impatient with my friends for their incessant rebukes and remonstrances about over-work. From the age of fifteen to the moment in which I am writing, I have been scolded in one form or another, for working too hard ; and I wonder my friends did not find out thirty years ago that there is no use in their fault-finding. I am heartily sick of it, I own ; and there may be some little malice in the satisfaction with which I find myself dying, after all, of a disease which nobody can possibly attribute to over-work. Though knowing all along that my friends were mistaken as to what was moderate and what immoderate work, in other cases than their own (and I have always left *them* free to judge and act for themselves) I have never denied that less toil and more leisure would be wholesome and agreeable to me. My pleas have been that I have had no power of choice, and

that my critics misjudged the particular case. Almost
every one of them has proceeded on the supposition
that the labour of authorship involved immense
'excitement;' and I, who am the quietest of quiet
bodies, when let alone in my business, have been
warned against 'excitement' till I am fairly sick of
the word. One comfort has always been that those
who were witnesses of my work-a-day life always
came round to an agreement with me that literary
labour is not necessarily more hurtfully exciting than
any other serious occupation. My mother, alarmed
at a distance, and always expecting to hear of a brain
fever, used to say, amidst the whirl of our London
spring days, 'My dear, I envy your calmness.' And
a very intimate friend, one of the strongest remon-
strants, told me spontaneously, when I had got
through a vast pressure of work in her country house,
that she should never trouble me more on that head,
as she saw that my authorship was the fulfilment of a
natural function,—conducive to health of body and
mind, instead of injurious to either. It would have
saved me from much annoyance (kindly intended) if
others had observed with the same good sense, and
admitted conviction with equal candour. Authorship
has never been with me a matter of choice. I have
not done it for amusement, or for money, or for fame,
or for any reason but because I could not help it.
Things were pressing to be said; and there was more
or less evidence that I was the person to say them.
In such a case, it was always impossible to decline the
duty for such reasons as that I should like more
leisure, or more amusement, or more sleep, or more of
any thing whatever. If my life *had* depended on

more leisure and holiday, I could not have taken it. What wanted to be said must be said, for the sake of the many, whatever might be the consequences to the one worker concerned. Nor could the immediate task be put aside, from the remote consideration, for ever pressed upon me, of lengthening my life. The work called for to-day must not be refused for the possible sake of next month or next year. While feeling far less injured by toil than my friends took for granted I must be, I yet was always aware of the strong probability that my life would end as the lives of hard literary workers usually end,—in paralysis, with months or years of imbecility. Every one must recoil from the prospect of being thus burdensome to friends and attendants ; and it certainly was a matter of keen satisfaction to me, when my present fatal disease was ascertained, that I was released from that liability, and should die of something else, far less formidable to witnesses and nurses. Yet, the contemplation of such a probability in the future was no reason for declining the duty of the time ; and I could not have written a volume the less if I had foreknown that, at a certain future day and hour, I should be struck down like Scott and Southey, and many another faithful labourer in the field of literature.

One deep and steady conviction, obtained from my own experience and observation, largely qualified any apprehensions I might have, and was earnestly impressed by me upon my remonstrating friends ; that enormous loss of strength, energy and time is occasioned by the way in which people go to work in literature, as if its labours were in all respects different from any other kind of toil. I am confident that in-

tellectual industry and intellectual punctuality are as
practicable as industry and punctuality in any other
direction. I have seen vast misery of conscience and
temper arise from the irresolution and delay caused by
waiting for congenial moods, favourable circumstances,
and so forth. I can speak, after long experience,
without any doubt on this matter. I have suffered,
like other writers, from indolence, irresolution, dis-
taste to my work, absence of 'inspiration,' and all
that : but I have also found that sitting down, however reluctantly, with the pen in my hand, I have
never worked for one quarter of an hour without finding myself in full train ; so that all the quarter hours,
arguings, doubtings, and hesitation as to whether I
should work or not which I gave way to in my inexperience, I now regard as so much waste, not only of
time but, far worse, of energy. To the best of my
belief, I never but once in my life left my work because I could not do it : and that single occasion was
on the opening day of an illness. When once experience had taught me that I could work when I chose,
and within a quarter of an hour of my determining to
do so, I was relieved, in a great measure, from those
embarrassments and depressions which I see afflicting
many an author who waits for a mood instead of sum-
moning it, and is the sport, instead of the master, of
his own impressions and ideas. As far as the grosser
physical influences are concerned, an author has his
lot pretty much in his own hands, because it is in his
power to shape his habits in accordance with the laws
of nature : and an author who does not do this has
no business with the lofty vocation. I am very far
indeed from desiring to set up my own practices as an

example for others ; and I do not pretend that they are wholly rational, or the best possible; but, as the facts are clear,—that I have, without particular advantages of health and strength, done an unusual amount of work without fatal, perhaps without injurious consequences, and without the need of pernicious stimulants and peculiar habits,—it may be as well to explain what my methods were, that others may test them experimentally, if they choose.

As for my hours,—it has always been my practice to devote my best strength to my work ; and the morning hours have therefore been sacred to it, from the beginning. I really do not know what it is to take any thing but the pen in hand, the first thing after breakfast, except, of course, in travelling. I never pass a day without writing ; and the writing is always done in the morning. There have been times when I have been obliged to 'work double tides,' and therefore to work at night : but it has never been a practice ; and I have seldom written any thing more serious than letters by candlelight. In London, I boiled my coffee at seven or half-past, and went to work immediately till two, when it was necessary to be at liberty for visitors till four o'clock. It was impossible for me to make calls. I had an immense acquaintance, no carriage, and no time; and I therefore remained at home always from two till four, to receive all who came, and I called on nobody. I knew that I should be quizzed or blamed for giving myself airs : but I could not help that. I had engaged before I came to London to write a number of my Series every month for two years ; and I could not have fulfilled my engagement and made morning visits too. Sydney Smith was one of the quizzers. He thought I might have managed the thing better, by ' sending round an inferior authoress in a carriage to drop the cards.'

When my last visitor departed, I ran out for an hour's walk, returning in time to dress and read the newspaper, before the carriage came,— somebody's carriage being always sent,—to take me out to dinner. An evening visit or two closed the day's engagements. I tried my best to get home by twelve or half-past, in order to answer the notes I was sure to find on my table, or to get a little reading before going to rest between one and two. A very refreshing kind of visit was (and it happened pretty often) when I walked to the country, or semi-country house of an intimate friend, and slept there,—returning before breakfast, or in time to sit down to my morning's work. After my mother and aunt joined me in London, I refused Sunday visiting altogether, and devoted that evening to my old ladies. So much for the times of working.

I was deeply impressed by something which an excellent clergyman told me one day, when there was nobody by to bring mischief on the head of the relater. This clergyman knew the literary world of his time so thoroughly that there was probably no author of any mark then living in England, with whom he was not more or less acquainted. It must be remembered that a new generation has now grown up. He told me that he had reason to believe that there was no author or authoress who was free from the habit of taking some pernicious stimulant; either strong green tea, or strong coffee at night, or wine or spirits or laudanum. The amount of opium taken, to relieve the wear and tear of authorship, was, he said, greater than most people had any conception of: and *all* literary workers took something. 'Why, I do not,' said I. 'Fresh air and cold water are my stimulants.'—'I believe you,' he replied. 'But you work in the morning; and there is much in that.' I then remembered that when, for a short time, I had to work at night (probably on one of the Poor-law tales, while my regular work occupied the mornings) a physician who called on me observed that I must not allow myself to be exhausted at the end of the day. He would not advise any alcoholic wine; but any light wine that I liked might do me good. 'You have a cupboard there at your right hand,' said he. 'Keep a bottle of hock and a wine-glass there, and help yourself when you feel you want it.' 'No, thank you,' said I. 'If I took wine, it should not be when alone; nor would I help myself to a glass. I might take a little more and a little more, till my solitary glass might become a regular tippling habit. I shall avoid the temptation altogether.' Physicians should consider well before they give such advice to brain-worn workers.

As for the method, in regard to the Political Economy Tales, I am not sorry to have an opportunity of putting it on record. When I began, I furnished myself with all the standard works on the subject of what I then took to be a science. I had made a skeleton plan of the course, comprehending the four divisions, Production, Distribution, Exchange and Consumption: and, in order to save my nerves from being overwhelmed with the thought of what I had undertaken, I resolved not to look beyond the department on which I was engaged. The subdivisions arranged themselves as naturally as the primary ones ; and when any subject was episodical (as Slave Labour) I announced it as such. Having noted my own leading ideas on the topic before me, I took down my books, and read the treatment of that particular subject in each of them, making notes of reference on a separate sheet for each book, and restraining myself from glancing even in thought towards the scene and nature of my story till it should be suggested by my collective didactic materials. It was about a morning's work to gather hints by this reading. The next process, occupying an evening, when I had one to spare, or the next morning, was making the Summary of Principles which is found at the end of each number. This was the most laborious part of the work, and that which I certainly considered the most valuable. By this time, I perceived in what part of the world, and among what sort of people, the principles of my number appeared to operate the most manifestly. Such a scene I chose, be it where it might.

The next process was to embody each leading principle in a character : and the mutual operation of these embodied principles supplied the action of the story. It was necessary to have some accessories,—some out-works to the scientific erection ; but I limited these as much as possible ; and I believe that in every instance, they really were rendered subordinate. An hour or two sufficed for the outline of my story. If the scene was foreign, or in any part of England with which I was not familiar, I sent to the library for books of travel or topography : and the collecting and

noting down hints from these finished the second
day's work. The third day's toil was the severest.
I reduced my materials to chapters, making a copious
table of contents for each chapter on a separate sheet,
on which I noted down, not only the action of the
personages and the features of the scene, but all the
political economy which it was their business to convey, whether by exemplification or conversation,—so
as to absorb all the materials provided. This was not
always completed at one sitting, and it made me
sometimes sick with fatigue : but it was usually done
in one day.   After that, all the rest was easy.   I
paged my paper ; and then the story went off like a
letter. I never could decide whether I most enjoyed
writing the descriptions, the narrative, or the argu-
mentative or expository conversations. I liked each
best while I was about it.

As to the actual writing,—I did it as I write letters, and as I am writing this Memoir,—never altering the expression as it came fresh from my brain.
On an average I wrote twelve pages a day,—on large
letter paper (quarto, I believe it is called), the page
containing thirty-three lines. In spite of all precautions, interruptions occurred very often. The
proof-correcting occupied some time ; and so did sitting for five portraits in the year and half before I
went to America. The correspondence threatened to
become infinite. Many letters, particularly anonymous ones, required or deserved no answer : but there
were others from operatives, young persons, and others
which could be answered without much expenditure of
thought, and wear and tear of interest : and I could
not find in my heart to resist such clients.   Till my

mother joined me, I never failed to send her a bulky packet weekly; as much for my own satisfaction as for hers,—needing as I did to speak freely to some one of the wonderful scenes which life was now opening to me. Having no maid, I had a good deal of the business of common life upon my hands. On the conclusion of a number, I sometimes took two days' respite; employing it in visiting some country house for the day and night, and indulging in eight hours' sleep, instead of the five, or five and a half, with which I was otherwise obliged to be satisfied: but it happened more than once that I finished one number at two in the morning, and was at work upon another by nine. During the whole period of the writing of the three Series,—the Political Economy, Taxation, and Poor-laws—I never remember but once sitting down to read whatever I pleased. That was a summer evening, when I was at home and my old ladies were out, and I had two hours to do what I liked with. I was about to go to the United States; and I sat down to study the geography and relations of the States of the American Union; and extremely interesting I found it,—so soon as I was hoping to travel through them.

The mode of scheming and constructing my stories having been explained, it remains to be seen whence the materials were drawn. A review of the sources of my material will involve some anecdotes which may be worth telling, if I may judge by my own interest, and that which I witness in others, in the history of the composition of any well-known work.

If I remember right, I was busy about the twelfth number,—' French Wines and Politics,'—when I

went to London, in November, 1832. That is, I had
done with the department of Production, and was
finishing that of Distribution. The first three numbers were written before the stir of success began :
and the scenery was furnished by books of travel
obtained from the Public Library, and of farming by
the late Dr. Rigby of Norwich,—a friend of the late
Lord Leicester, (when Mr. Coke). The books of
travel were Lichtenstein's South Africa for 'Life in
the Wilds:' Edwards's (and others') 'West Indies'
for 'Demerara;' and McCulloch's 'Highlands and
Islands of Scotland' for the two Garveloch stories.
Mr. Cropper of Liverpool heard of the Series early
enough to furnish me with some statistics of Slavery
for 'Demerara;' and Mr. Hume in time to send me
Blue Books on the Fisheries, for 'Ella of Garveloch.'
—My correspondence with Mr. Cropper deserves
mention, in honour of that excellent and devoted
man. About the time that the success of my scheme
began to be apparent, there arrived in Norwich a person who presented himself as an anti-slavery agent.
It was the well-known Elliott Cresson, associated
with the American Colonization scheme, which he
hoped to pass upon us innocent provincial Britons as
the same thing as anti-slavery. Many even of the
Quakers were taken in ; and indeed there were none
but experienced abolitionists, like the Croppers, who
were qualified even to suspect,—much less to detect,
—this agent of the slaveholders and his false pre-
tences. Kind-hearted people, hearing from Mr.
Cresson that a slave could be bought and settled
blissfully in Liberia for seven pounds ten shillings,
raised the ransom in their own families and among

their neighbours, and thought all was right. Mr. Cresson obtained an introduction to my mother and me, and came to tea, and described what certainly interested us very much, and offered to furnish me with plenty of evidence of the productiveness of Liberia, and the capabilities of the scheme, with a view to my making it the scene and subject of one of my tales. I was willing, thinking it would make an admirable framework for one of my pieces of doctrine ; and I promised, not to write a story, but to consider of it when the evidence should have arrived. The papers arrived ; and my conclusion was,—not to write about Liberia. Some time after, I had a letter from Mr. Cropper, who was a perfect stranger to me, saying that Elliott Cresson was announcing everywhere from the platform in his public lectures that I had promised him to make the colony of Liberia one of my Illustrations of Political Economy : and it was the fact that the announcement was made in many places. Mr. Cropper offered to prove to me the unreliableness of Cresson's representations, and the true scope and aim of the Colonization scheme. He appealed to me not to publish in its favour till I had heard the other side ; and offered to bear the expense of suppressing the whole edition, if the story was already printed. I had the pleasure of telling him by return of post that I had given no such promise to Mr. Cresson, and that I had not written, nor intended to write, any story about Liberia or American Colonization. Before I went to the United States, this agent of the slaveholders had exposed his true character by lecturing, all over England, in a libellous tone, against Garrison and the true abolitionists of America. When I had begun to see into the character and policy of the enterprise, and before I had met a single abolitionist in America, I encountered Mr. Cresson, face to face, ir the Senate Chamber at Washington. He was very obsequious; but I would have nothing to say to him. He was, I believe, the only acquaintance whom I ever 'cut.' It was out of this incident that grew the correspondence with Mr. Cropper which ended in his furnishing me with material for an object precisely the reverse of Elliott Cresson's.

On five occasions in my life I have found myself obliged to write and publish what I entirely believed would be ruinous to my reputation and prosperity. In no one of the five cases has the result been what I anticipated. I find myself at the close of my life prosperous in name and fame, in my friendships and in my affairs. But it may be considered to have been a narrow escape in the first instance; for every thing was done that low-minded recklessness and malice could do to destroy my credit and influence by gross appeals to the prudery, timidity, and ignorance of the middle classes of England. My own innocence of intention, and my refusal to conceal what I thought and meant, carried me through: but there is no doubt that the circulation of my works was much and long restricted by the prejudices indecently and maliciously raised against me by Mr. Croker and Mr. Lockhart, in the Quarterly Review. I mention these two names, because Messrs. Croker and Lockhart openly assumed the honour of the wit which they (if nobody else) saw in the deed; and there is no occasion to suppose any one else concerned in it. As there is, I believe, some lingering feeling still,—some doubt about my being once held in horror as a 'Malthusian,' I had better tell simply all I know of the matter.

When the course of my exposition brought me to the Population subject, I, with my youthful and provincial mode of thought and feeling,—brought up too amidst the prudery which is found in its great force in our middle class,—could not but be sensible that I risked much in writing and publishing on a subject which was not universally treated in the pure, benevolent, and scientific spirit of Malthus himself. I felt that the subject was one of science, and therefore perfectly easy to treat in itself; but I was aware that some evil associations had gathered about it,— though I did not know what they were. While writing 'Weal and Woe in Garveloch,' the perspiration many a time streamed down my face, though I knew there was not a line in it which might not be read aloud in any family. The misery arose from my seeing how the simplest statements and reasonings might and probably would be perverted. I said nothing to any body; and, when the number was finished, I read it aloud to my mother and aunt. If there had been any opening whatever for doubt or dread, I was sure that these two ladies would have given me abundant warning and exhortation,—both from their very keen sense of propriety and their anxious affection for me. But they were as complacent and easy as they had been interested and attentive. I saw that all ought to be safe. But it was evidently very doubtful whether all would be safe. A few words in a letter from Mr. Fox put me on my guard. In the course of some remarks on the sequence of my topics, he wrote, ' As for the Population

question, let no one interfere with you. Go straight
through it, *or you'll catch it.*' I did go straight
through it; and happily I had nearly done when a
letter arrived from a literary woman, who had the
impertinence to write to me now that I was growing
famous, after having scarcely noticed me before, and
(of all subjects) on this, though she tried to make her
letter decent by putting in a few little matters besides.
I will call her Mrs. Z. as I have no desire to point out
to notice one for whom I never had any respect or
regard. She expressed, on the part of herself and
others, an anxious desire to know how I should deal
with the Population question; said that they did not
know what to wish about my treating or omitting it;
—desiring it for the sake of society, but dreading it
for me; and she finished by informing me that a
Member of Parliament, who was a perfect stranger to
me, had assured her that I already felt my difficulty;
and that he and she awaited my decision with anxiety.
Without seeing at the moment the whole drift of this
letter, I was abundantly disgusted by it, and fully
sensible of the importance of its being answered immediately, and in a way which should admit of no
mistake. I knew my reply was wanted for show;
and I sent one by return of post which was shown to
some purpose. It stopped speculation in one danger-
ous quarter. I showed my letter to my mother and
brother; and they emphatically approved it, though it
was rather sharp. They thought, as I did, that some
sharpness was well directed towards a lady who professed to have talked over difficulties of this nature,
on my behalf, with an unknown Member of Parliament
by her own fireside. My answer was this. I believe

I am giving the very words; for the business impressed itself deeply on my mind. 'As for the questions you put about the principles of my Series, —if you believe the Population question to be, as you say, the most serious now agitating society, you can hardly suppose that I shall omit it, or that I can have been heedless of it in forming my plan. I consider it, as treated by Malthus, a strictly philosophical question. So treating it, I find no difficulty in it; and there can be no difficulty in it for those who approach it with a single mind. To such I address myself. If any others should come whispering to me what I need not listen to, I shall shift my trumpet, and take up my knitting.' I afterwards became acquainted with the Member of Parliament whom my undesired correspondent quoted; and I feel confident that his name was used, very unwarrantably, for the convenience of the lady's prurient curiosity.—I also saw her. She called on me at my lodgings (to catch a couple of franks from a Member of Parliament) and she mentioned my letter,—obtaining no response from me. She was then a near neighbour and an acquaintance of an intimate friend of mine. One winter morning, I was surprised by a note from this friend, sent three miles by a special messenger, to say, 'Mrs. Z. purposes to visit you this morning. I conjure you to take my advice. On the subject which she will certainly introduce, be deaf, dumb, blind and stupid. I will explain hereafter.' The morning was so stormy that no Mrs. Anybody could come. My friend's explanation to me was this. Mrs. Z. had declared her anxiety to her, in a morning call, to obtain from me, for her own satisfaction and other

people's, an avowal which might be reported as to the
degree of my knowledge of the controversies which
secretly agitated society on the true bearings of the
Population question.   All this was no concern of
mine; and much of it was beyond my comprehension.
The whole interference of Mrs. Z. and her friends (if
indeed there was anybody concerned in it but herself)
was odious and impertinent nonsense in my eyes; and
the fussy lady ever found me, as well as my friend,
ready to be as ' deaf, dumb, blind and stupid ' as
occasion might require.   I rather suspect that Mrs.
Z. herself was made a tool of for the purposes of Mr.
Lockhart, who employed his then existing intimacy
with her to get materials for turning her into ridicule
afterwards.   The connexion of Mr. Lockhart with
this business presently appeared.

In an evening party in the course of the winter, I
was introduced to a lady whose name and connexions
I had heard a good deal of.   Instead of being so civil
as might be anticipated from her eagerness for an
introduction, she was singularly rude and violent, so
as to make my hostess very uncomfortable.   She
called me ' cruel ' and ' brutal,' and scolded me for
my story ' Cousin Marshall.'   I saw that she was
talking at random, and asked her whether she had
read the story.   She had not.   I good-humouredly,
but decidedly, told her that when she had read it, we
would discuss it, if she pleased; and that meantime
we would drop it.   She declared she would not read
it for the world; but she presently followed me about,
was kind and courteous, and finished by begging to
be allowed to set me down at my lodgings.   When I
alighted, she requested leave to call.   She did so.

when my mother was with me for two or three weeks, and invited us to dine at her house in the country, on the first disengaged day. She called for us, and told us during our drive that she had resisted the strongest entreaties from Mr. Lockhart to be allowed to meet me that day. She had some misgiving, it appeared, which made her steadily refuse; but she invited Lady G——, a relative of Lockhart's, and an intimate friend of her own. Lady G. was as unwilling as Lockhart was eager to come; and very surly she looked when introduced. She sat within hearing of my host and me at dinner; and as soon as we returned to the drawing-room, she took her seat by me, with a totally changed manner, and conversed kindly and agreeably. I was wholly unaware what lay under all this: but the fact soon came out that the atrocious article in the Quarterly Review which was avowedly intended to 'destroy Miss Martineau,' was at that time actually printed; and Mr. Lockhart wanted to seize an opportunity which might be the last for meeting me,—all unsuspecting as I was, and trusting to his being a gentleman, on the strength of meeting him in that house. I was long afterwards informed that Lady G. went to him early the next day, (which was Sunday) and told him that he would repent of the article, if it was what he had represented to her; and I know from the printers that Mr. Lockhart went down at once to the office, and cut out 'all the worst passages of the review,' at great inconvenience and expense. What he could have cut out that was worse than what stands, it is not easy to conceive.

While all this was going on without my knowledge, warnings came to me from two quarters that some-

thing prodigious was about to happen. Mr. Croker
had declared at a dinner party that he expected a
revolution under the Whigs, and to lose his pension ;
and that he intended to lay by his pension while he
could get it, and maintain himself by his pen ; and
that he had ' begun by tomahawking Miss Martineau
in the Quarterly.' An old gentleman present, Mr.
Whishaw, was disgusted at the announcement and at
the manner of it, and, after consulting with a friend
or two, called to tell me of this, and put me on my
guard. On the same day, another friend called to
tell me that my printers (who also printed the
Quarterly) thought I ought to know that ' the
filthiest thing that had passed through the press for
a quarter of a century ' was coming out against me
in the Quarterly. I could not conceive what all this
meant ; and I do not half understand it now : but it
was enough to perceive that the design was to discredit me by some sort of evil imputation. I saw at
once what to do. I wrote to my brothers, telling
them what I had heard, and earnestly desiring that
they would not read the next Quarterly. I told them
that the inevitable consequence of my brothers taking
up my quarrels would be to close my career. I had
entered upon it independently, and I would pursue
it alone. From the moment that any of them stirred
about my affairs, I would throw away my pen ; for I
would not be answerable for any mischief or trouble
to them. I made it my particular request that we
might all be able to say that they had not read the
article. I believe I am, in fact, the only member of
the family who ever read it.—The day before publication, which happened to be Good Friday, a friend

called on me,—a clergyman who occasionally wrote for the Quarterly,—and produced the forthcoming number from under his cloak. ' Now,' said he, ' I am going to leave this with you. Do not tell me a word of what you think of it; but just mark all the lies in the margin : and I will call at the door for it, on my way home in the afternoon.' I did it; sat down to my work again (secure from visitors on a Good Friday) and then went out, walking and by omnibus, to dine in the country. I remember thinking in the omnibus that the feelings called forth by such usage are, after all, more pleasurable than painful ; and again, when I went to bed, that the day had been a very happy one. The testing of one's power of endurance is pleasurable ; and the testing of one's power of forgiveness is yet sweeter : and it is no small benefit to learn something more of one's faults and weaknesses than friends and sympathisers either will or can tell. The compassion that I felt on this occasion for the low-minded and foul-mouthed creatures who could use their education and position as gentlemen to ' destroy' a woman whom they knew to be innocent of even comprehending their imputations, was very painful : but, on the other hand, my first trial in the shape of hostile reviewing was over, and I stood unharmed, and somewhat enlightened and strengthened. I mentioned the review to nobody : and therefore nobody mentioned it to me. I heard, some years after, that one or two literary ladies had said that they, in my place, would have gone into the mountains or to the antipodes, and never have shown their faces again ; and that there were inquiries in abundance of my friends how I stood it. But I gave no sign.

The reply always was that I looked very well and
happy,—just as usual.—The sequel of the story is
that the writer of the original article, Mr. Poulett
Scrope, requested a mutual friend to tell me that he
was ready to acknowledge the political economy of
the article to be his; but that he hoped he was too
much of a gentleman to have stooped to ribaldry, or
even jest; and that I must understand that he was
not more or less responsible for any thing in the
article which we could not discuss face to face with
satisfaction. Messrs. Lockhart and Croker made no
secret of the ribaldry being theirs. When the indignation of the literary world was strong in regard
to this and other offences of the same kind, and Mr.
Lockhart found he had gone too far in my case, he
spared no entreaties to the lady who made Lady G.
meet me to invite him,—professing great admiration
and good-will, and declaring that I must know his
insults to be mere joking. She was won upon at last,
and came one day with her husband, to persuade me
to go over to dinner to meet Mr. Lockhart. When I
persisted in my refusal, she said, in some vexation,—
‘ But what am I to say to Lockhart?—because I
promised him.’ I replied, ‘ I have nothing to do
with what you say to Mr. Lockhart : but I will tell
you that I will never knowingly meet Mr. Lockhart;
and that, if I find myself in the same house with him,
I will go out at one door of the drawing-room when
ne comes in at the other.’ Her husband, hitherto
silent, said, ‘ You are quite right. I would on no
account allow you to be drawn into an acquaintance
with Lockhart at our house : and the only excuse I
can offer for my wife’s rashness is that she has never

read that Quarterly article.' From other quarters I had friendly warnings that Lockhart had set his mind on making my acquaintance, in order to be able to say that I did not mind what he had done. He was the only person but two whose acquaintance I ever refused. I never saw him but once; and that was twenty years afterwards, when he wore a gloomy and painful expression of countenance, and walked listlessly along the street and the square, near his own house, swinging his cane. My companion told me who he was; and we walked along the other side of the street, having a good and unobserved view of him till he reached his own house. The sorrows of his later years had then closed down upon him, and he was sinking under them : but the pity which I felt for him then was not more hearty, I believe, than that which filled my mind on that Good Friday, 1833, when he believed he had ' destroyed ' me.

As for destroying me,—it was too late, for one thing. I had won my public before Croker took up his ' tomahawk.' The simple fact, in regard to the circulation of my Series, was that the sale increased largely after the appearance of the Quarterly review of it, and diminished markedly and immediately on the publication of the flattering article on it in the Edinburgh Review. The Whigs were then falling into disrepute among the great body of the people ; and every token of favour from Whig quarters was damaging to me, for a time. In the long run, there is no doubt that the Quarterly injured me seriously. For ten years there was seldom a number which had not some indecent jest about me,—some insulting introduction of my name. The wonder is what could be gained that was worth the trouble : but it certainly seems to me that this course of imputation originated some obscure dread of me and my works among timid and superficial readers. For one instance among many :—a lady, calling on a friend of mine, wondered at seeing books of mine on the table, within the children's reach ;—they being ' improper books,' she had been told,—declared to be so by the Quarterly Review. My friend said, ' Though I don't agree with you, I know what you are thinking of. You must carry this home, and read it,'—taking down from the shelf the volume which contained the Garveloch stories. The visitor hesitated, but yielded, and a few days after, brought back the book, saying that this could not be the one, for it was so harmless that her husband had read it aloud to the young people in the evening. ' Well,' said my friend, ' try another.' The lady and her husband read the whole series through in this way, and never could find out the ' improper book.'

And what was all this for ? I do not at all know. All that I know is that a more simple-minded, virtuous man, full of domestic affections, than Mr. Malthus, could not be found in all England ; and that the desire of his heart and the aim of his work were that domestic virtue and happiness should be placed within the reach of all, as Nature intended them to be. He found, in his day, that a portion of the people were underfed ; and that one consequence of this was a fearful mortality among infants ; and another consequence, the growth of a recklessness among the destitute which caused infanticide, corruption of morals, and, at best, marriage between

pauper boys and girls, while multitudes of respectable
men and women, who paid rates instead of consuming
them, were unmarried at forty, or never married at all.
Prudence as to the time of marriage, and to making
due provision for it was, one would think, a harmless
recommendation enough, under the circumstances.
Such is the moral aspect of Malthus's work. As to its
mathematical basis, there is no one, as I have heard
Mr. Hallam say, who could question it that might
not as well dispute the multiplication table. As for
whether Mr. Malthus's doctrine, while mathematically
indisputable, and therefore assailable in itself only by
ribaldry and corrupt misrepresentation, may not be
attacking a difficulty at the wrong end,—that is a fair
matter of opinion. In my opinion, recent experience
shows that it does attack a difficulty at the wrong end.
The repeal of the corn-laws, with the consequent improvement in agriculture, and the prodigious increase
of emigration have extinguished all present apprehension and talk of ' surplus population,'—that great
difficulty of forty or fifty years ago. And it should
be remembered, as far as I am concerned in the controversy, that I advocated in my Series a free trade
in corn, and exhibited the certainty of agricultural
improvement, as a consequence ; and urged a carefully conducted emigration ; and, above all, education
without limit. It was my business, in illustrating
Political Economy, to exemplify Malthus's doctrine
among the rest. It was that doctrine ' pure and
simple,' as it came from his virtuous and benevolent
mind, that I presented ; and the presentment was
accompanied by an earnest advocacy of the remedies
which the great natural laws of Society put into our

power,—freedom for bringing food to men, and freedom for men to go where food is plentiful; and enlightenment for all, that they may provide for themselves under the guidance of the best intelligence. Mr. Malthus, who did more for social ease and virtue than perhaps any other man of his time, was the ' best-abused man ' of the age. I was aware of this; and I saw in him, when I afterwards knew him, one of the serenest and most cheerful men that society can produce. When I became intimate enough with the family to talk over such matters, I asked Mr. Malthus one day whether he had suffered in spirits from the abuse lavished on him. ' Only just at first,' he answered.—' I wonder whether it ever kept you awake a minute.'—' Never after the first fortnight,' was his reply. The spectacle of the good man in his daily life, in contrast with the representations of him in the periodical literature of the time, impressed upon me, more forcibly than any thing in my own experience, the everlasting fact that the reformers of morality, personal and social, are always subject at the outset to the imputation of immorality from those interested in the continuance of corruption.—I need only add that all suspicious speculation, in regard to my social doctrines, seems to have died out long ago. I was not ruined by this first risk, any more than by any subsequent enterprises; but I was probably never so near it as when my path of duty led me among the snares and pitfalls prepared for the innocent and defenceless by Messrs. Croker and Lockhart, behind the screen of the Quarterly Review.

The behaviour of the Edinburgh was widely different. From the time of my becoming acquainted

o 2

with the literary Whigs who were paramount at that time, I had heard the name of William Empson on all hands: and it once or twice crossed my mind that it was odd that I never saw him. Once he left the room as I entered it unexpectedly : and another time, he ran in among us at dessert, at a dinner party, to deliver a message to the hostess, and was gone, without an introduction to me,—the only stranger in company. When his review of my Series in the Edinburgh was out, and he had ascertained that I had read it, he caused me to be informed that he had declined an introduction to me hitherto, because he wished to render impossible all allegations that I had been favourably reviewed by a personal friend : but that he was now only awaiting my permission to pay his respects to me. The review was, to be sure, extraordinarily laudatory ; but the praise did not seem to me to be very rational and sound ; while the nature of the criticism showed that all accordance between Mr. Empson and me on some important principles of social morals was wholly out of the question. His objection to the supposition that society could exist without capital punishment is one instance of what I mean ; and his view of the morality or immorality of opinions (apart from the process of forming them) is another. But there was some literary criticism which I was thankful for ; and there was such kindliness and generosity in the whole character of the man's mind ; —his deeds of delicate goodness came to my knowledge so abundantly ; and he bore so well certain mortifications about the review with which he had taken his best pains, that I was as ready as himself to be friends. And friends we were, for several years.

We were never otherwise than perfectly friendly, though I could not help feeling that every year, and every experience, separated us more widely in regard to intellectual and moral sympathy. He was not, from the character of his mind, capable of having opinions; and he was, as is usual in such cases, disposed to be afraid of those who had. He was in a perpetual course of being swayed about by the companions of the day, on all matters but politics. There he was safe; for he was hedged in on every side by the dogmatic Whigs, who made him their chief dogmatist. He was full of literary knowledge;—an omnivorous reader with a weak intellectual digestion. He was not personally the wiser for his reading; but the profusion that he could pour out gave a certain charm to his conversation, and even to his articles, which had no other merit, except indeed that of a general kindliness of spirit. During my intercourse with him and his set, he married the only child of his old friend, Lord Jeffrey : and after the death of Mr. Napier, who succeeded Jeffrey in the editorship of the Edinburgh Review, Mr. Empson accepted the offer of it,—rather to the consternation of some of his best friends. He had been wont to shake his head over the misfortunes of the review in Napier's time, saying that that gentleman had no literary faculty or cultivation whatever. When he himself assumed the management, people said we should now have nothing but literature. Both he and his predecessor, however, inserted (it was understood) as a matter of course, all articles sent by Whig Ministers, or by their underlings, however those articles might contradict each other even in the same number. All hope of real

editorship, of political and moral consistency, was now
over; and an unlooked-for failure in modesty and
manners in good Mr. Empson spoiled the literary
prospect; so that the review lost character and reputation quarter by quarter, while under his charge.
His health had so far, and so fatally, failed before he
became Editor, that he ought not to have gone into
the enterprise; and so his oldest and best friends told
him. But the temptation was strong; and, unfortunately, he could not resist it. Unfortunately, if
indeed it is desirable that the Edinburgh Review
should live,—which may be a question. It is a
great evil for such a publication to change its politics
radically; and this must be done if the Edinburgh is
to live; for Whiggism has become mere death in life,
—a mere transitional state, now nearly worn out.
When Mr. Empson's review of me appeared, however,
the Whigs were new in office, Jeffrey's parliamentary
career was an object of high hope to his party, and
the Edinburgh was more regarded than the younger
generation can now easily believe. Mr. Empson's
work was therefore of some consequence to him, to
me, and to the public. As I have said, the sale of
my Series declined immediately,—under the popular
notion that I was to be a pet of the Whigs. As for
ourselves, we met very pleasantly at dinner, at his old
friend, Lady S.'s, where nobody else was invited.
Thence we all went together to an evening party;
and I seldom entered a drawing-room afterwards
without meeting my kind-hearted reviewer. —Such
were the opposite histories of my first appearance in
the Edinburgh and Quarterly Reviews.—I may as
well add that I speak under no bias, in either case, of

contributor or candidate interest : for I never wrote or
desired to write for either review.   I do not remember that I was ever asked; and I certainly never
offered.   I think I may trust my memory so far as to
say this confidently.

To return to the subject of the materials furnished
to me as I proceeded in my work.   There were still
three more numbers written in Norwich, besides
those which I have mentioned.   The Manchester
operatives were eager to interest me in their controversies about Machinery and Wages ; and it was
from them that I received the bundles of documents
which qualified me to write 'A Manchester Strike.'

It was while I was about this number that the
crisis of the Reform Bill happened.   One May morning, I remember, the people of Norwich went out, by
hundreds and thousands, to meet the mail.   At that
time, little Willie B——, the son of the Unitarian
Minister at Norwich, used to come every morning to
say certain lessons to my mother, with whom he was
a great favourite.   On that morning, after breakfast,
in came Willie, looking solemn and business-like, and
stood before my mother with his arms by his sides, as
if about to say a lesson, and said, ' Ma'am, papa sends
you his regards, and the Ministry has resigned.'
' Well, Willie, what does that mean ? '   ' I don't
know, Ma'am.'   We, however, knew so well that,
for once, and I believe for the only time in those busy
years, I could not work.   When my mother came in
from ordering dinner, she found me sitting beside
Willie, mending stockings.   She expressed her amazement : and I told her, what pleased her highly, that
I really could not write about twopenny galloons, the

topic of the morning, after hearing of Lord Grey's resignation. We went out early into the town, where the people were all in the streets, and the church bells were muffled and tolling. I do not remember a more exciting day. My publisher wrote a day or two afterwards, that the London booksellers need not have been afraid of the Reform Bill, any more than the Cholera, for that during this crisis, he had sold more of my books than ever. Every thing indeed justified my determination not to defer a work which was the more wanted the more critical became the affairs of the nation.

In spite of all I could say, the men of Manchester persisted that *my* hero was *their* hero, whose name however I had never heard. It gratified me to find that my doctrinĕ was well received, and, I may say, cordially agreed in, even at that time, by the leaders of the genuine Manchester operatives; and they, for their part, were gratified by their great topics of interest being discussed by one whom they supposed to have ' spent all her life in a cotton-mill,' as one of their favourite Members of Parliament told me they did.—It occurs to me that my life ought indeed to be written by myself or some one else who can speak to its facts; for, if the reports afloat about me from time to time were to find their way into print after my death, it would appear the strangest life in the world. I have been assigned a humbler life than that of the Cotton-mill. A friend of mine heard a passenger in a stage-coach tell another that I was ' of very low origin,—having been a maid-of-all-work.' This was after the publication of my model number of the ' Guide to Service,' done at the request of the

Poor-law Commissioners. My reply to the request
was that I would try, if the Maid-of-all-work might
be my subject. I considered it a compliment, when I
found I was supposed to have been relating my own
experience. One aunt of mine heard my Series ex-
tolled (also in a coach) as wonderful for a young
creature, seventeen and no more on her last birthday;
and another aunt heard the same praise, in the same
way, but on the opposite ground that I was wonderfully energetic for eighty-four! So many people
heard that I was dreadfully conceited, and that my
head was turned with success, that I began to think,
in spite of very sober feelings and of abundant self-
distrust, that the account must be true. A shopman
at a printseller's was heard by a cousin of mine, after
the publication of ' Vanderput and Snoek,' giving an
impressive account of my residence in Holland : and
long after, Mr. Laing made inquiries of a relation
about how long I had lived in Norway,—of which
' Feats on the Fiord' were supposed to be an
evidence : but I had visited neither country when I
wrote of them, and shall die without seeing Norway
now. Every body believed at one time that I had
sought Lord Brougham's patronage;—and this report I did not like at all. Another,—that he had
written the chief part of the books,—was merely
amusing. Another gave me some little trouble in
the midst of the amusement;—that I had been
married for two years before the Series was finished,
and that I concealed the fact for convenience. More
than one of my own relations required the most express and serious assurance from me that this was not
true before they would acquit me of an act of trickery

so unlike me,—who never had any secrets. The husband thus assigned to me was a gentleman whom I had then never heard of, and whom I never saw till some years afterwards, when he had long been a married man. After my Eastern journey in 1846, it was widely reported, and believed in Paris, that my party and I had quarrelled, as soon as we landed in France; and that I had gone on by myself, and travelled through those eastern countries entirely alone. I could not conceive what could be the meaning of the compliments I received on my 'wonderful courage,' till I found how unwilling people were to credit that I had been well taken care of. My 'Eastern Life' disabused all believers in this nonsense; and I hope this Memoir will discredit all the absurd reports which may yet be connected with my station and my doings in life, in the minds of those who know me only from rumour.

'Cousin Marshall,' which treats of the Poor-laws, was written and at press before Lord Brougham had devised his scheme of engaging me to illustrate the operation of the Poor-laws. I obtained my material, as to details, from a brother who was a Guardian, and from a lady who took an interest in workhouse management. For 'Ireland' and 'Homes Abroad,' I obtained facts from Blue-books on Ireland and Colonization which were among the many by this time sent me by people who had 'hobbies.' These were all that I wrote at Norwich.

Five of my numbers had appeared before Lord Brougham saw any of them, or knew anything about them. He was at Brougham in June, 1832, when Mr. Drummond,—the Thomas Drummond of sacred

memory in Ireland,—sent him my numbers, up to
' Ella of Garveloch' (inclusive). A friend of both
was at that time at Norwich, canvassing for the
representation : and Lord Brougham wrote to him,
with his customary vehemence, extolling me and my
work, and desiring him to engage me to illustrate the
Poor-laws in aid of the Commission then appointed to
the work of Poor-law inquiry. It was hardly right in
me to listen to any invitation to further work. That
I should have done so for any considerations of fame
or money can never have been believed by any who
knew what proposals and solicitations from all manner of editors and publishers I refused. It was the
extreme need and difficulty of Poor-law reform that
won me to the additional task. I had for many years
been in a state of despair about national affairs, on
account of this ' gangrene of the state,' as the
French Commissioners had reported it, ' which it
was equally impossible to remove and to let alone.'
When Lord Brougham wrote to his friend an account
of the evidence which was actually obtained, and
which would be placed at my disposal ; and when he
added that there was an apparent possibility of cure,
declaring that his ' hopes would be doubled' if I
could be induced to help the scheme, the temptation
to over-work was irresistible. When I met Lord
Brougham in town, he urged me strongly to promise
six numbers within a year. I was steady in refusing
to do more than four altogether : and truly that was
quite enough, in addition to the thirty numbers of my
own Series, (including the ' Illustrations of Taxation'). These thirty-four little volumes were produced in two years and a half,—the greater part of

the time being one unceasing whirl of business and
social excitement. After my settlement in London,
Lord Brougham called on me to arrange the plan.
He informed me that the evidence would be all placed
in my hands; and that my Illustrations would be
published by the Diffusion Society. He then requested me to name my terms. I declined. He
proceeded to assign the grounds of the estimate he
was about to propose, telling me what his Society
and others had given for various works, and why he
considered mine worth more than some to which I
likened it. Finally he told me I ought not to have
less than one hundred pounds apiece for my four
numbers. He said that the Society would pay me
seventy-five pounds on the day of publication of each;
and that he then and there guaranteed to me the remaining twenty-five pounds for each. If I did not
receive it from the Society, I should from him. He
afterwards told the Secretary of the Society and two
personal friends of his and mine that these were the
terms he had offered, and meant to see fulfilled. I
supplied the works which, he declared, fully answered
his expectations; and indeed he sent me earnest and
repeated thanks for them. The Society fulfilled its
engagements completely and punctually : but Lord
Brougham did not fulfil his own, more or less. I
never saw or heard any thing of the four times
twenty-five pounds I was to receive to make up my
four hundred pounds. I believe that he was reminded of his engagement, while I was in America,
by those to whom he had avowed it: but I have
never received any part of the money to this day. I
never made direct application to him for it; partly

because I never esteemed or liked him, oɪ relished being implicated in business with him, after the first flutter was over, and I could judge of him for myself; and partly because such an amount of unfulfilled promises lay at his door, at the time of his enforɔed retirement from power, that I felt that my application would be, like other people's applications, as fruitless as it would be disagreeable. I do not repent doing those tales, because I hope and believe they were useful at a special crisis: but they never suc-ceeded to any thing like the extent of my own Series; and it certainly appeared that all connexion with the Diffusion Society, and Lord Brougham, and the Whig government, was so much mere detriment to my usefulness and my influence.

I had better relate here all that I have to say about that bâtch of Tales. Lord Brougham sent me all the evidence as it was delivered in by the Commissioners of Inquiry into the operation of the Poor-laws. There can be no stronger proof of the strength of this evidence than the uniformity of the suggestions to which it gave rise in all the minds which were then intent on finding the remedy. I was requested to furnish my share of conclusions and suggestions. I did so, in the form of a programme of doctrine for my illustrations, some of which expose the evils of the old system, while others pourtray the features of its proposed successor. My document actually crossed in the street one sent me by a Member of the government detailing the heads of the new Bill. I sat down to read it with no little emotion, and some apprehension; and the moment when, arriving at the end, I found that the government scheme and my own were

identical, point by point, was not one to be easily forgotten. I never wrote anything with more glee
than 'The Hamlets,'—the number in which the
proposed reform is exemplified : and the spirit of the
work carried me through the great effort of writing that
number and 'Cinnamon and Pearls' in one month,—
during a country visit in glorious summer weather.

Soon after my Poor-law Tales began to appear, I
received a message from Mr. Barnes, Editor-in-chief
of the 'Times,' intimating that the 'Times' was
prepared to support my work, which would be a
valuable auxiliary of the proposed reform. I returned
no answer, not seeing that any was required from an
author who had never had any thing to do with her
reviewers, or made any interest in reviews. I said
this to the friend who delivered the message, expressing at the same time my satisfaction that the government measure was to have the all-powerful support
of the 'Times.' The Ministers were assured of the
same support by the same potentate. How the other
newspapers would go there was no saying, because
the proposed reform was not a party measure ; but
with the 'Times' on our side we felt pretty safe.
It was on the seventeenth of April, 1834, that Lord
Althorp introduced the Bill. His speech, full of
facts, earnest and deeply impressive, produced a
strong effect on the House; and the Ministers went
home to bed with easy minds,—little imagining
what awaited them at the breakfast table. It was
no small vexation to me, on opening the 'Times' at
breakfast on the eighteenth, to find a vehement and
total condemnation of the New Poor-law. Every
body in London was asking how it happened. I do

not know, except in as far as I was told by some
people who knew more of the management of the
paper than the world in general. Their account was
that the intention had really been, up to the preceding day, to support the measure; but that such reports
arrived of the hostility of the country-justices,—a
most important class of customers,—that a meeting
of proprietors was held in the evening, when the
question of supporting or opposing the measure was
put to the vote. The policy of humouring the
country-justices was carried by one vote. So went
the story. Another anecdote, less openly spoken of,
I believe to have been true. Lord Brougham wrote
a note, I was told, to Lord Althorp, the same morning, urging him to timely attendance at the Cabinet
Council, as it must be immediately decided whether
Barnes, (who was not very favourably described,) and
the ' Times' should be propitiated or defied. A
letter or message arriving from Lord Althorp which
rendered the sending the note unnecessary, Lord
Brougham tore it up, and threw it into the waste-
basket under the table. The fragments were by
somebody or other abstracted from the basket, pasted
together, and sent to Mr. Barnes, whose personal
susceptibility was extreme. From that day began
the baiting of Lord Brougham in the ' Times' which
set every body inquiring what so fierce a persecution
could mean ; and the wonder ceased only when the
undisciplined politician finally fell from his rank as a
statesman, and forfeited the remains of his reputation
within two years afterwards. A searching domestic
inquiry was instituted; but, up to the time of my being
told the story, no discovery had been made of the mis-

chief-maker who had picked up the scraps of the note.

After talking over the debate and the comment on it with my mother and aunt, that April morning, I went up to my study to work, and was presently interrupted by a note which surprised me so much that I carried it to my mother. It was from a lady with whom I had only a very slight acquaintance,—the wife of a Member of Parliament of high consideration. This lady invited me to take a drive with her that morning, and mentioned that she was going to buy plants at a nursery. My mother advised me to leave my work early, for once, and go, for the fresh air and the pleasure. My correspondent called for me, and, before we were off the stones, out came the reason of the invitation. Her husband was aghast at the course of the ' Times,' and had been into the City to buy the 'Morning Chronicle,'—then a far superior paper to what it has been since. He and a friend were now the proprietors of the ' Chronicle,' and no time was to be lost in finding writers who could and would support the New Poor-law. I was the first to be invited, because I was known to have been acquainted with the principles and provisions of the measure from the beginning. The invitation to me was to write ' leaders ' on the New Poor-law, as long as such support should be wanted. I asked why the proprietor did not do it himself, and found that he was really so engaged in parliamentary committees as to be already over-worked. I declared myself over-worked too ; but I was entreated to take a few hours for consideration. An answer was to be sent for at five o'clock. My mother and I talked the matter over. The inducements were very strong ; for I could

not but see that I was the person for the work : but
my mother said it would kill me,—busy as I was at
present. I believed that it would injure my own
Series ; and I therefore declined.—For many months
afterwards, even for years, it was a distasteful task
to read the ' Times ' on the New Poor-law,—so
venomous, so unscrupulous, so pertinacious, so mischievous in intention, and so vicious in principle was
its opposition to a reform which has saved the state.
But, as the reform was strong enough to stand, this
hostility has been eventually a very great benefit.
Bad as was the spirit of the opposition, it assumed
the name of humanity, and did some of the work of
humanity. Every weak point of the measure was
exposed and every extravagance chastised.   Its
righteousness and principled humanity were ignored ;
and every accidental pressure or inconvenience was
made the most of.   The faults of the old law were
represented (as by Mr. Dickens in ' Oliver Twist ')
as those of the new, and every effort was made to
protract the exercise of irresponsible power by the
country justices : but the measure was working, all
the while, for the extinction of the law-made vices
and miseries of the old system ; and the process was
aided by the stimulating vigilance of the ' Times,'
which evoked at once the watchfulness and activity of
officials and the spirit of humanity in society,—both
essential conditions of the true working of the new
law.—My share in the punishment I could never
understand.   Neither my mother nor I mentioued to
any person whatever the transaction of that morning :
but in a few days appeared a venomous attack on
the member of parliament who had bought the

'Chronicle,' in the course of which he was taunted with going to a young lady in Fludyer Street for direction in his political conduct. After that, there were many such allusions:—my friends were appealed to to check my propensity to write about all things whatsoever,—the world having by this time quite books enough of mine : and the explanation given of the ill success and bad working of the Whig measures was that the Ministers came to me for them. This sort of treatment gave me no pain, because I was not acquainted with any body belonging to the ' Times,' and I was safe enough with the public by this time : but I thought it rather too much when Mr. Sterling, ' the Thunderer of the " Times," ' and at that period editor-in-chief, obtained an invitation to meet me, after the publication of my books on America, alleging that he himself had never written a disrespectful word of me. My reply was that he was responsible, as editor, and that I used the only method of self-defence possible to a woman under a course of insult like that, in declining his acquaintance. Not long afterwards, when I was at Tynemouth, hopelessly ill, poor and helpless, the ' Times ' abused and insulted me for privately refusing a pension. Again Mr. Sterling made a push for my acquaintance ; and I repeated what I had said before : whereupon he declared that ' it cut him to the heart ' that I should impute to him the ribaldry and coarse insults of scoundrels and ruffians who treated me as I had been treated in the ' Times.' I dare say what he said of his own feelings was true enough ; but it will never do for responsible editors, like Sterling and Lockhart, to shirk their natural retribution for the sins of their publications by laying the blame on some impalpable offender who, on his part, has very properly relied on their responsibility. It appears to me that social honesty and good faith can be preserved only by thus enforcing integrity in the matter of editorial responsibility.

A curious incident occurred, much to the delight of my Edinburgh reviewer, in connexion with that story,—'The Hamlets,'—which, as I have said, I enjoyed writing exceedingly. While I was preparing its doctrine and main facts, I went early one summer morning, with a sister, to the Exhibition at Somerset House, (as it was in those days). I stopped before a picture by Collins,—'Children at the Haunts of the Sea-fowl;' and, after a good study of it, I told my sister that I had before thought of laying the scene by the sea-side, and that this bewitching picture decided me. The girl in the corner, in the red petticoat, was irresistible; and she should be my heroine. There should be a heroine,—a girl and a boy, instead of two boys. I did this, and, incited by old associations, described myself and a brother (in regard to character) in these two personages. Soon after, at a music-party, my hostess begged to introduce to me Mr. Collins the artist, who wished to make his acknowledgments for some special obligation he was under to me. This seemed odd, when I was hailing the opportunity for precisely the same reason. Mr. Collins begged to shake hands with me because I had helped him to his great success at the Academy that year. He explained that Mrs. Marcet had paid him a visit when he had fully sketched, and actually begun his picture, and had said to him, 'Before you go on with this, you ought to read Miss Martineau's description in " Ella of Garveloch " of destroying the eagle's nest.' Mr. Collins did so, and in consequence altered his picture in almost every part; and now, in telling me the incident, he said that his chief discontent with his work was not having effaced the figure of the girl in the corner. He was reconciled to her, however, when I told him that the girl in the red petticoat was the heroine of the story I was then writing. This incident strikes me as a curious illustration of the way in which minds play into one another when their faculties of conception and suggestion are kindred, whatever may be their several modes of expression. One of my chief social pleasures was meeting Wilkie, and planning pictures with him, after his old manner, though alas! he was now painting in his new. He had returned from Spain, with his portfolios filled with sketches of Spanish ladies, peasants and children; and he enjoyed showing these treasures of his, I remember, to my mother and me one day when we went by invitation to Kensington, to see them. But his heart was, I am sure, in his old style. He used to watch his opportunity,—being very shy,—to get a bit of talk with me unheard, about what illustrations of my stories should be, saying that nothing would make him so happy, if he were but able, as to spend the rest of his painting-life in making a gallery from my Series. He told me which group or action he should select from each number, as far as then published, and dwelt particularly, I remember, on the one in ' Ireland,' which was Dora letting down her petticoat from her shoulders as she entered the cabin. I write this in full recollection of Wilkie's countenance, voice and

words, but in total forgetfulness of my own story,
Dora, and the cabin. I have not the book at hand
for reference, but I am sure I am reporting Wilkie
truly. He told me that he thought the resemblance
of our respective mind's-eyes was perfectly singular;
and that, for aught he saw, each of us might, as well
as not, have done the other's work, as far as the
pictorial faculties were concerned.

I have one more little anecdote to tell about the
heroine of ' The Hamlets.' I was closely questioned
by Miss Berry, one day when dining there, about the
sources of my draughts of character,—especially of
children,—and above all, of Harriet and Ben in
' The Hamlets.' I acknowledged that these last were
more like myself and my brother than any body else.
Whereupon the lively old lady exclaimed, loud enough
to be heard by the whole party, ' My God! did you
go out shrimping?' ' No,' I replied; ' nor were we
workhouse children. What you asked me about was
the characters.'

While these Poor-law tales were appearing, I received a letter from Mrs. Fry, requesting an interview
for purposes of importance, at any time and place I
might appoint. I appointed a meeting in Newgate,
at the hour on Tuesday morning when Mrs. Fry
was usually at that post of sublime duty. Wishing
for a witness, as our interview was to be one of
business, I took with me a clerical friend of mine as
an appropriate person. After the usual services, Mrs.
Fry led the way into the Matron's room, where we
three sat down for our conference. Mrs. Fry's objects
were two. The inferior one was to engage me to interest the government in her newly planned District

Societies. The higher one was connected with the Poor-law reform then in preparation. She told me that her brother, J. J. Gurney, and other members of her family had become convinced by reading ' Cousin Marshall' and others of my tales that they had been for a long course of years unsuspectingly doing mischief where they meant to do good; that they were now convinced that the true way of benefiting the poor was to reform the Poor-law system; and that they were fully sensible of the importance of the measure to be brought forward, some months hence, in parliament. Understanding that I was in the confidence of the government as to this measure, they desired to know whether I could honourably give them an insight into the principles on which it was to be founded. Their object in this request was good. They desired that their section of the House of Commons should have time and opportunity to consider the subject, which might not be attainable in the hurry of a busy session. On consideration, I had no scruple in communicating the principles, without, of course, any disclosure of the measures. Mrs. Fry noted them down, with cheerful thanks, and assurances that they would not be thrown away. They were not thrown away. That section of Members came well prepared for the hearing of the measure, and one and all unflinchingly supported it.

From the time of my settlement in London, there was no fear of any dearth of information on any subject which I wished to treat. Every party, and every body who desired to push any object, forwarded to me all the information they held. It was, in fact, rather ridiculous to see the onset on my acquaintances made

by riders of hobbies. One acquaintance of mine told
me, as I was going to his house to dinner, that three
gentlemen had been at his office that morning;—one
beseeching him to get me to write a number on the
navigable rivers of Ireland ; a second on (I think) the
Hamiltonian (or other) system of Education ; and a
third, who was confident that the welfare of the
nation depended on it, on the encouragement of flax-
growing in the interior of Guiana. Among such
applicants, the Socialists were sure to be found ; and
Mr. Owen was presently at my ear, laying down the
law in the way which he calls ' proof,' and really interesting me by the candour and cheerfulness, the
benevolence and charming manners which would
make him the most popular man in England if he
could but distinguish between assertion and argument,
and abstain from wearying his friends with his mono-
tonous doctrine. If I remember right, it was after
my anti-socialist story, ' For Each and for All,' that
I became acquainted with Mr. Owen himself ; but the
material was supplied by his disciples, — for the
chance of what use I might make of it: so that I was
perfectly free to come out as their opponent. Mr.
Owen was not at all offended at my doing so.
Having still strong hopes of Prince Metternich for
a convert, he might well have hopes of me : and, believing Metternich to be, if the truth were known, a
disciple of his, it is no wonder if I also was given out
as being so. For many months my pleasant visitor
had that hope of me ; and when he was obliged to
give it up, it was with a kindly sigh. He was sure
that I desired to perceive the truth ; but I had got
unfortunately bewildered. I was like the traveller

who could not see the wood, for the trees. I cannot recal the story, more or less; ('For Each and for All;') but I know it must have contained the stereotyped doctrine of the Economists of that day. What I witnessed in America considerably modified my views on the subject of Property; and from that time forward I saw social modifications taking place which have already altered the tone of leading Economists, and opened a prospect of further changes which will probably work out in time a totally new social state. If that should ever happen, it ought to be remembered that Robert Owen was the sole apostle of the principle in England at the beginning of our century. Now that the Economy of Association is a fact acknowledged by some of our most important recent institutions,—as the London Clubs, our Model Lodging-houses, and dozens of new methods of Assurance, every one would willingly assign his due share of honour to Robert Owen, but for his unfortunate persistency in his other characteristic doctrine,—that Man is the creature of circumstances,—his notion of 'circumstances' being literally *surroundings*, no allowance, or a wholly insufficient allowance, being made for constitutional structure and differences. His certainty that we might make life a heaven, and his hallucination that we are going to do so immediately, under his guidance, have caused his wisdom to be overlooked in his absurdity, and his services to be too nearly forgotten in vexation and fatigue at his eccentricity. I own I became weary of him, while ashamed, every time I witnessed his fine temper and manners, of having felt so. One compact that we made, three parts in earnest, seems to me, at this distance of time, excessively ludicrous.

I saw that he was often wide of the mark, in his
strictures on the religious world, through his ignorance of the Bible ; and I told him so. He said he
knew the Bible so well as to have been heartily sick
of it in his early youth. He owned that he had
never read it since. He promised to read the four
Gospels carefully, if I would read ' Hamlet,' with a
running commentary of Necessarian doctrine in my
own mind. My share was the easier, inasmuch as I
was as thoroughgoing a Necessarian as he could
desire. I fulfilled my engagement, internally laughing all the while at what Shakspere would be thinking, if he could know what I was about. No doubt,
Mr. Owen did his part too, like an honourable man ;
and no doubt with as much effect produced on him by
this book as by every other, as a blind man in the
presence of the sunrise, or a deaf one of an oratorio.
Robert Owen is not the man to think differently of a
book for having read it ; and this from no want of
candour, but simply from more than the usual human
inability to see any thing but what he has made up
his mind to see.

I cannot remember what put the scene and story
of my twelfth number, ' French Wines and Politics,'
into my head : but I recal some circumstances about
that and the following number, ' The Charmed Sea,'
which amused me extremely at the time. Among
the very first of my visitors at my lodgings was Mrs.
Marcet, whose ' Conversations ' had revealed to me
the curious fact that, in my earlier tales about Wages
and Machinery, I had been writing Political Economy
without knowing it. Nothing could be more kindly
and generous than her acknowledgment and enjoy-

ment of what she called my 'honours.' The best of
it was, she could never see the generosity on which
her old friends complimented her, because, by her own
account, there was no sort of rivalship between us.
She had a great opinion of great people ;—of people
great by any distinction,—ability, office, birth and
what not: and she innocently supposed her own taste
to be universal.   Her great pleasure in regard to me
was to climb the two flights of stairs at my lodgings
(asthma notwithstanding) to tell me of great people
who were admiring, or at least reading, my Series.
She brought me 'hommages' and all that sort of
thing, from French savans, foreign ambassadors, and
others; and, above all the rest was her satisfaction in
telling me that the then new and popular sovereign,
Louis Philippe, had ordered a copy of my Series for
each member of his family, and had desired M. Guizot
to introduce a translation of it into the national
schools.   This was confirmed, in due time, by the
translator, who wrote to me for some particulars of
my personal history, and announced a very large order
for the work from M. Guizot.   Before I received this
letter, my twelfth number was written, and I think
in the press.   About the same time, I heard from
some other quarter, (I forget what) that the Emperor
of Russia had ordered a copy of the Series for every
member of *his* family; and my French translator
wrote to me, some time afterwards, that a great number of copies had been bought, by the Czar's order,
for his schools in Russia.   While my twelfth number
was printing, I was writing the thirteenth, 'The
Charmed Sea,'—that sea being the Baikal Lake,
the scenery Siberian, and the personages exiled Poles.

The Edinburgh Review charged me with relaxing my
Political Economy for the sake of the fiction, in this
case,—the reviewer having kept his article open for
the appearance of the latest number obtainable before
the publication of the review. There was some little
mistake about this; the fact being that the bit of
doctrine I had to deal with,—the origin of currency,
—hardly admitted of any exemplification at all.
Wherever the scene had been laid, the doctrine would
have been equally impracticable in action, and must
have been conveyed mainly by express explanation or
colloquial commentary. If any action were practicable
at all, it must be in some scene where the people were
at the first remove from a state of barter: and the
Poles in Siberia, among Mongolian neighbours, were
perhaps as good for my purpose as any other personages. Marco Polo's account of the stamped leather
currency he met with in his travels determined me in
regard to Asiatic scenery, in the first place; and the
poet Campbell's appeals to me in behalf of the Poles,
before I left Norwich, and the visits of the venerable
Niemcewicz, and other Poles and their friends, when
I went to London, made me write of the Charmed
Sea of Siberia. My reviewer was right as to the
want of the due subordination of other interests to
that of the science; but he failed to perceive that that
particular bit of science was abstract and uninterest-
ing. I took the hint, however; and from that time
I was on my guard against making my Series a
vehicle for any of the 'causes' of the time. I saw
that if my Edinburgh reviewer could not perceive that
some portions of doctrine were more susceptible of
exemplification than others, such discrimination was

not to be expected of the whole public ; and I must
afford no occasion for being supposed to be forsaking
my main object for such temporary interests as came
in my way. — Meantime, the incidents occurred
which amused my friends and myself so much, in
connexion with these two numbers. On the day of
publication of the twelfth, Mrs. Marcet climbed my
staircase, and appeared, more breathless than ever, at
a somewhat early hour,—as soon as my door was
open to visitors. She was in a state of distress and
vexation. ' I thought I had told you,' said she, in
the midst of her panting,—' but I suppose you did
not hear me :—I thought I had told you that the
King of the French read all your stories, and made
all his family read them : and now you have been
writing about Egalité ; and they will never read you
again.' I told her I had heard her very well ; but it
was not convenient to me to alter my story, for no
better reason than that. It was from history, and
not from private communication, that I drew my
materials ; and I had no doubt that Louis Philippe
and his family thought of his father very much as I
did. My good friend could not see how I could hope
to be presented at the Tuileries after this : and I could
only say that it had never entered my head to wish it.
I tried to turn the conversation to account by im-
pressing on my anxious friend the hopelessness of all
attempts to induce me to alter my stories from such
considerations as she urged. I wrote with a view to
the people, and especially the most suffering of them ;
and the crowned heads must, for once, take their
chance for their feelings. A month after, I was subjected to similar reproaches about the Emperor of

Russia. He was, in truth, highly offended. He ordered every copy of my Series to be delivered up, and then burnt or deported; and I was immediately forbidden the empire. His example was followed in Austria; and thus, I was personally excluded, before my Series was half done, from two of the three greatest countries in Europe, and in disfavour with the third,—supposing I wished to go there. My friends, Mr. and Mrs. F——, invited me to go to the south of Europe with them on the conclusion of my work: and our plan was nearly settled when reasons appeared for my going to America instead. My friends went south when I went west. Being detained by inundation on the borders of Austrian Italy, they were weary of their dull hotel. All other amusement being exhausted, Mr. F—— sauntered round the open part of the house, reading whatever was hung against the walls. One document contained the names and description of persons who were not to be allowed to pass the frontier; and mine was among them. If I had been with my friends, our predicament would have been disagreeable. They could not have deserted me; and I must have deprived them of the best part of their journey.

In planning my next story, ' Berkeley the Banker,' I submitted myself to my reviewer's warning, and spared no pains in thoroughly incorporating the doctrine and the tale. I remember that, for two days, I sat over my materials from seven in the morning till two the next morning, with an interval of only twenty minutes for dinner. At the end of my plotting, I found that, after all, I had contrived little but relationships, and that I must trust to the uprising of new involutions in the course of my narrative. I had believed before, and I went on during my whole career of fiction-writing to be more and more thoroughly convinced, that the creating a plot is a task above human faculties. It is indeed evidently the same power as that of prophecy : that is, if all human action is (as we know it to be) the inevitable result of antecedents, all the antecedents must be thoroughly comprehended in order to discover the inevitable catastrophe. A mind which can do this must be, in the nature of things, a prophetic mind, in the strictest sense ; and no human mind is that. The only thing to be done, therefore, is to derive the plot from actual life, where the work is achieved for us : and, accordingly, it seems that every perfect plot in fiction is taken bodily from real life. The best we know are so derived. Shakspere's are so : Scott's one perfect plot (the ' Bride of Lammermoor ') is so ; and if we could know where Boccaccio and other old narrators got theirs, we should certainly find that they took them from their predecessors, or from the life before their eyes. I say this from no mortification at my own utter inability to make a plot. I should say the same, (after equal study of the subject) if I had never tried to write a tale. I see the inequality of this kind of power in contemporary writers ; an inequality wholly independent of their merits in other respects; and I see that the writers (often inferior ones) who have the power of making the best plots do it by their greater facility in forming analogous narratives with those of actual experience. They may be, and often are, so inferior as writers of fiction to others who cannot make plots that one is tempted to wish that they and their superiors could be rolled into one, so as to make a perfect novelist or dramatist. For instance, Dickens cannot make a plot,—nor Bulwer,—nor Douglas Jerrold, nor perhaps Thackeray; while Fanny Kemble's forgotten ' Francis the First,' written in her teens, contains mines of plot, sufficient to furnish a groundwork for a score of fine fictions. As for me, my incapacity in this direction is so absolute that I always worked under a sense of despair about it. In the ' Hour and the Man,' for instance, there are prominent personages who have no necessary connexion whatever with the story; and the personages fall out of sight, till at last, my hero is alone in his dungeon, and the story ends with his solitary death. I was not careless, nor unconscious of my inability. It was inability, ' pure and simple.' My only resource therefore was taking suggestion from facts, witnessed by myself, or gathered in any way I could. That tale of ' Berkeley the Banker ' owed its remarkable success, not to my hard work of those two days; but to my taking some facts from the crisis of 1825-6 for the basis of my story. The toil of those two days was not thrown away, because the amalgamation of doctrine and narrative was more complete than it would otherwise have been: but no protraction of the effort would have brought out a really good plot, any more than the most prodigious amount of labour in practising would bring out good music from a performer unendowed with musical faculty.

The story was, in a great degree, as I have already said, our own family history of four years before. The most amusing thing to me was that the relative

(not one of my nearest relations) who was presented
as Berkeley,—(by no means exactly, but in the main
characteristics and in some conspicuous speeches) was
particularly delighted with that story. He seized it
eagerly, as being about banking, and expressed his
admiration, far and wide, of the character of the
banker, as being so extremely natural! His unconscious pleasure was a great relief to me: for, while I
could not resist the temptation his salient points
offered me, I dreaded the consequences of my free use
of them.

About the next number, ' Vanderput and Snoek,'
I have a curious confession to make. It was necessary to advertise on the cover of each tale the title
of the next. There had never been any difficulty
thus far,—it being my practice, as I have said, to
sit down to the study of a new number within a day
or two, or a few hours, of finishing its predecessor.
My banking story was, however, an arduous affair ;
and I had to write the first of my Poor-law series. I
was thus driven so close that when urged by the
printer for the title of my next number, I was wholly
unprepared. All I knew was that my subject was to
be Bills of Exchange. The choice of scene lay between Holland and South America, where Bills of
Exchange are, or then were, either more numerous
or more important than any where else. I thought
Holland on the whole the more convenient of the
two ; so I dipped into some book about that country
(Sir William Temple, I believe it was), picked out the
two ugliest Dutch names I could find, made them
into a firm, and boldly advertised them. Next, I had
to consider how to work up to my title : and in this I

met with most welcome assistance from my friends, Mr. and Mrs. F——, of Highbury. They were well acquainted with the late British Consul at Rotterdam, then residing in their neighbourhood. They had previously proposed to introduce me to this gentleman, for the sake of the information he could give me about Dutch affairs : and I now hastened to avail myself of the opportunity. The ex-consul was made fully aware of my object, and was delighted to be of use. We met at Mr. F.'s breakfast table ; and in the course of the morning he gave me all imaginable information about the aspect and habits of the country and people. When I called on his lady, some time afterwards, I was struck by the pretty picture presented by his twin daughters, who were more exactly alike than any other twins I have ever seen. They sat beside a work-table, at precisely the same angle with it : each had a foot on a footstool, for the sake of her netting. They drew their silk through precisely at the same instant, and really conveyed a perplexing impression of a mirror where mirror there was none. The Dromios could not be more puzzling. The temptation to put these girls into a story was too strong to be resisted : but, as I knew the family were interested in my Series at the moment, I waited a while. After a decent interval, they appeared in ' The Park and the Paddock ; ' and then only in regard to externals ; for I knew nothing more of them whatever.

When I had to treat of Free Trade, I took advantage, of course, of the picturesque scenery and incidents connected with smuggling. The only question was what part of the coast I should choose for my seventeenth and eighteenth numbers, 'The Loom and the Lugger.' I questioned all my relations and friends who had frequented Eastbourne and that neighbourhood about the particulars of the locality and scenery. It struck me as curious that, of all the many whom I asked, no one could tell me whether there was a lighthouse at Beachy Head. A cousin told me that she was acquainted with a farmer's family living close by Beachy Head, and in the very midst of the haunts of the smugglers. This farmer was under some obligation to my uncle, and would be delighted at the opportunity of rendering a service to any of the name. My publisher was willing to set down the trip to the account of the expenses of the Series; and I went down, with a letter of introduction in my hand, to see and learn all I could in the course of a couple of days. My time was limited, not only by the exigencies of my work, but by an engagement to meet my Edinburgh reviewer for the first time,—as I have mentioned above,—and to another very especial party for the same evening. On a fine May evening, therefore, I presented myself at the farm-house door, with my letter in my hand. I was received with surpassing grace by two young girls,—their father and elder sister being absent at market. Tea was ready presently; and then, one of the girls proposed to walk to 'the Head' before dark. When we returned, every thing was arranged; and the guest chamber looked most tempting to an over-worked Londoner. The farmer and one daughter devoted the whole of the next day to me. We set forth, carrying a new loaf and a bottle of beer, that we might not be hurried in

our explorations. I then and there learned all that
appears in 'The Loom and the Lugger' about loca-
lities and the doings of smugglers. Early the following morning I went to see Pevensey Castle, and
in the forenoon was in the coach on my way back
to town. I was so cruelly pressed for time that,
finding myself alone in the coach, I wrote on my
knees all the way to London, in spite of the
jolting. At my lodging, I was in consternation
at seeing my large round table heaped with the
letters and parcels which had arrived during those
two days. I dispatched fourteen notes, dressed, and
was at Lady S.'s by the time the clock struck six.
The quiet, friendly dinner was a pure refreshment;
but the evening party was a singular trial. I had
been compelled to name the day for this party, as I
had always been engaged when invited by my hostess.
I thought it odd that my name was shouted by the
servants, in preference to that of Lady C——, with
whom I entered the room: and the way in which my
hostess took possession of me, and began to parade
me before her noble and learned guests, showed me
that I must at once take my part, if I desired to
escape the doom of 'lionising.' The lady, having
two drawing-rooms open, had provided a 'lion' for
each. Rammohun Roy was stationed in the very
middle of one, meek and perspiring; and I was intended for the same place in the other. I saw it just
in time. I took my stand with two or three acquaintances behind the folding-doors, and maintained
my retirement till the carriage was announced. If
this was bad manners, it was the only alternative
to worse. I owe to that incident a friendship

which has lasted my life. That friend, till that evening known to me only by name, had been behind the scenes, and had witnessed all the preparations; and very curious she was to see what I should do. If I had permitted the lionising, she would not have been introduced to me. When I got behind the door, she joined our trio; and we have been intimate friends to this day. Long years after, she gave me her account of that memorable evening. What a day it was! When Lady S. set me down at midnight, and I began to undress, and feel how weary I was, it seemed incredible that it was that very morning that I had seen Pevensey Castle, and heard the dash of the sea, and listened to the larks on the down. The concluding thought, I believe, before I fell into the deep sleep I needed, was that I would never visit a second time at any house where I was 'lionised.'

The Anti-corn-law tale, 'Sowers not Reapers,' cost me great labour,—clear as was the doctrine, and familiar to me for many a year past. I believe it is one of the most successful for the incorporation of the doctrine with the narrative: and the story of the Kays is true, except that, in real life, the personages were gentry. I had been touched by that story when told it, some years before; and now it seemed to fit in well with my other materials. Two years afterwards I met with a bit of strong evidence of the monstrous vice and absurdity of our corn-laws in the eyes of Americans. This story, 'Sowers not Reapers,' was republished in America while I was there; and Judge Story, who knew more about English laws, manners and customs, condition, literature, and even topography than any other man in the

United States, told me that I need not expect his countrymen in general to understand the book, as even he, after all his preparedness, was obliged to read it twice,—first to familiarise himself with the conception, and then to study the doctrine. Thus incredible was it that so proud and eminent a nation as ours should persist in so insane and suicidal a policy as that of protection, in regard to the most indispensable article of food.

Among the multitude of letters of suggestion which had by this time been sent me, was an anonymous one from Oxford, which gave me the novel information that the East India Company constituted a great monopoly. While thinking that, instead of being one, it was a nest of monopolies (in 1833) I speculated on which of them I might best take for an illustration of my anti-monopoly doctrine. I feared an opium story might prove immoral, and I did not choose to be answerable for the fate of any Opium-eaters. Salt was too thirsty a subject for a July number. Cinnamon was fragrant, and pearls pretty and cool: and these, of course, led me to Ceylon for my scenery. I gathered what I could from books, but really feared being obliged to give up a singularly good illustrative scene for want of the commonest facts concerning the social life of the Cingalese. I found scarcely any thing even in Maria Graham and Heber. At this precise time, a friend happened to bring to my lodging, for a call, the person who could be most useful to me,—Sir Alexander Johnstone, who had just returned from governing Ceylon, where he had abolished Slavery, established Trial by Jury, and become more thoroughly acquainted with the

Cingalese than perhaps any other man then in England.   It was a remarkable chance; and we made the
most of it; for Sir Alexander Johnstone was as well
pleased to have the cause of the Cingalese pleaded as
I was to become qualified to do it.   Before we had
known one another half an hour, I confided to him
my difficulty.   He started off, promising to return
presently; and he was soon at the door again, with
his carriage full of books, prints and other illustrations, affording information not to be found in any
ordinarily accessible books.   Among the volumes he
left with me was a Colombo almanack, which furnished me with names, notices of customs, and other
valuable matters.   The friend who had brought us
together was highly delighted with the success of the
introduction, and bestirred himself to see what else
he could do.   He invited me to dinner the next day
(aware that there was no time to lose;) and at his
table I met as many persons as he could pick up who
had recently been in Ceylon.   Besides Sir Alexander
Johnstone, there was Holman, the blind traveller,
and Captain Mangles, and two or three more; and a
curiously oriental day we had of it, in regard to conversation and train of thought.   I remember learning
a lesson that day on other than Cingalese matters.
Poor Holman boasted of his achievements in climbing
mountains, and of his always reaching the top quicker
than his comrades; and he threw out some sarcasms
against the folly of climbing mountains at all, as
waste of time, because there were no people to be
found there, and there was generally rain and cold.
It evidently never occurred to him that people with
eyes climb mountains for another purpose than a race

against time; and that his comrades were pausing to
look about them when he outstripped them.   It was
a hint to me never to be critical in like manner about
the pleasures of the ear.—After I had become a
traveller, Sydney Smith amused himself about my
acquaintance with Holman; and I believe it was
reading what I said in the preface to my American
book which put his harmless jokes into his head.   In
that preface I explained the extent to which my deafness was a disqualification for travel, and for reporting
of it: and I did it because I knew that, if I did not,
the slaveholders would make my deafness a pretext
for setting aside any part of my testimony which
they did not like.   Soon after this preface appeared,
and when he had heard from me of my previous
meeting with Holman, Sydney Smith undertook to
answer a question asked by somebody at a dinner
party, what I was at that time about.   'She is writing
a book,' said Sydney Smith, 'to prove that the only
travellers who are fit to write books must be both
blind and deaf.'

My number on the monopolies in cinnamon and
pearls went off pleasantly after my auspicious beginning.   Sir A. Johnstone watched over its progress,
and seriously assured me afterwards, in a call made
for the purpose, that there was, to the best of his
belief, not a single error in the tale.   There was much
wrath about it in Ceylon, however; and one man
published a book to show that every statement of
mine, on every point, from the highest scientific to
the lowest descriptive, was absolutely the opposite of
the truth.   This personage was an Englishman, interested in the monopoly: and the violence of his
opposition was of service to the right side.

Soon after I went to my London lodgings, my mother came up, and spent two or three weeks with me. I saw at once that she would never settle comfortably at Norwich again; and I had great difficulty in dissuading her from at once taking a house which was very far beyond any means that I considered it right to reckon on. For the moment, and on occasion of her finding the particular house she had set her mind on quite out of the question, I prevailed on her to wait. I could not wonder at her desire to come up and enjoy such society as she found me in the midst of; and I thought it, on the whole, a fortunate arrangement when, under the sanction of two of my brothers, she took the small house in Fludyer Street, Westminster, where the rest of my London life was passed. That small house had, for a wonder, three sitting-rooms; and we three ladies needed this. The house had no nuisances, and was as airy as a house in Fludyer Street could well be : and its being on the verge of St. James's Park was a prodigious advantage for us all,—the Park being to us, in fact, like our own garden. We were in the midst of the offices, people and books which it was most desirable for me to have at hand; and the house was exactly the right size for us; and of the right cost,—now that I was able to pay the same amount as my aunt towards the expenses of our household. My mother's little income, with these additions, just sufficed;—allowance being made for the generosity which she loved to exercise. I may as well finish at once what I have to say about this matter. For a time, as I anticipated, all went well. My mother's delight in her new social sphere was extreme. But, as I had also anticipated, troubles arose. For one of two great troubles, meddlers and mischief-makers were mainly answerable. The other could not be helped. It was, (to pass it over as lightly as possible) that my mother, who loved power and had always been in the habit of exercising it, was hurt at confidence being reposed in me; and distinctions shown, and visits paid to me; and I, with every desire to be passive, and being in fact wholly passive in the matter, was kept in a state of constant agitation at the influx of distinctions which I never sought, and which it was impossible to impart. What the meddlers and mischief-makers did was to render my old ladies, and especially my mother, discontented with the lowliness of our home. They were for ever suggesting that I ought to live in some sort of style, —to have a larger house in a better street, and lay out our mode of living for the society in which I was moving. Of course they were not my own earned friends who made such suggestions. Their officiousness proved their vulgarity; and my mother saw and said this. Yet every word told upon her heart; and thence every word helped to pull down my health and strength. No change could be made but by my providing the money; and I could not conscientiously engage to do it. It was my fixed resolution never to mortgage my brains. Scott's recent death impressed upon me an awful lesson about that. Such an effort as that of producing my Series, was one which could never be repeated. Such a strain was quite enough for one lifetime. I did not receive any thing like what I ought for the Series, owing to the hard terms under which it was pub-

lished. I had found much to do with my first gains
from it; and I was bound in conscience to lay by for
a time of sickness or adversity, and for means of recreation, when my task should be done. I therefore
steadily refused to countenance any scheme of ambition, or to alter a plan of life which had been settled
with deliberation and with the sanction of the family.
To all remonstrances about my own dignity my reply
was that if my acquaintance cared for me they would
come and see me in a small house and a narrow
street: and all who objected to the smallness of either
might stay away. I could not expose myself to the
temptation to write in a money-getting spirit; nor
yet to the terrible anxieties of assuming a position
which could be maintained only by excessive toil. It
was necessary to preserve my independence of thought
and speech, and my power of resting, if necessary;—
to have, in short, the world under my feet instead of
hanging round my neck: and therefore did I refuse
all entreaty and remonstrance about our house and
mode of living. I was supported, very cordially, by
the good cousin who managed my affairs for me: but
an appeal to my brothers became necessary, at last.
They simply elicited by questions the facts that the
circumstances were unchanged;—that the house was
exactly what we had expected; that our expenses had
been accurately calculated; and that my mother's income was the same as when she had considered the
house a proper one for our purposes: in short, that
there was no one good reason for a change. The
controversy was thus closed; but not before the train
was laid for its being closed in another manner. The
anxieties of my home were too much for me, and I

was by that time wearing down fast. The illness
which laid me low for nearly six years at length
ensued; and when it did, there could be no doubt in
any mind of its being most fortunate that I had con-
tracted no responsibilities which I could not fulfil.
It was a great fault in me, (and I always knew that
it was) that I could not take these things more
lightly. I did strive to be superior to them: but I
began life, as I have said, with a most beggarly set
of nerves; I had gone through such an amount of
suffering and vicissitude as had weakened my *physique*,
if it had strengthened my *morale*; and now, I was
under a pressure of toil which left me no resource
wherewith to meet any constant troubling of the
affections. I held my purpose, because it was clearly
right: but I could not hold my health and nerve.
They gave way; and all questions about London
residence were settled a few years after by our leaving
London altogether. Soon after my illness laid me
low, my dear old aunt died; and my mother removed
to Liverpool to be taken care of by three of her
children who were settled there.

I was entering upon the first stage of this career of
anxiety when I was writing my twenty-first number,
—' A Tale of the Tyne.' The preparation of it was
terribly laborious, for I had to superintend at that
time the removal into the Fludyer Street house. The
weather was hot, and the unsettlement extreme. I
had to hire and initiate the servants; to receive and
unpack the furniture; and to sit down at night, when
all this was done, to write my number. At that
time, of all seasons, arose a very serious trouble, which
not only added to my fatigue of correspondence in the

day, but kept me awake at night by very painful feelings of indignation, grief and disappointment. It was thought desirable, by myself as well as by others, that my plan of Illustration of Political Economy should be rendered complete by some numbers on modes of Taxation. The friends with whom I discussed the plan reminded me that I must make fresh terms with Charles Fox, the publisher. They were of opinion that I had already done more than enough for him by continuing the original terms through the whole Series thus far, the agreement being dissoluble at the end of every five numbers, and he having never fulfilled, more or less, the original condition of obtaining subscribers. He had never obtained one. I accordingly wrote to Mr. Charles Fox, to inquire whether he was willing to publish five additional numbers on the usual terms of booksellers' commission. The reply was from his brother; and it was long before I got over the astonishment and pain that it caused. He claimed, for Charles, half the profits of the Series, to whatever length it might extend. He supported the claim by a statement of eight reasons, so manifestly unsound that I was equally ashamed for myself and for him that he should have ventured to try them upon me. In my reply, I said that there was no foundation in law or equity for such a claim. As Mr. Charles Fox wrote boastfully of the legal advice he should proceed upon, I gladly placed the affair in the hands of a sound lawyer,—under the advice of my counsellors in the business. I put all the documents,—the original agreement and the whole correspondence,—into my lawyer's hands; and his decision was that my publisher, in making this

claim, had 'not a leg to stand upon.' I was very
sure of this; but the pain was not lessened thereby.
I could not but feel that I had thrown away my consideration and my money upon a man who made this
consideration the ground of an attempt to extort
more. The whole invention and production of the
work had been mine; and the entire sale was, by his
own admission, owing to me. The publisher, holding
himself free to back out of a losing bargain if I had
not instantly succeeded, had complacently pocketed
his commission of thirty per cent. (on the whole) and
half the profits, for simply selling the book to the
public whom I sent to his shop: and now he was
threatening to go to law with me for a prolongation
of his unparalleled bargain. I sent him my lawyer's
decision, and added that, as I disliked squabbles
between acquaintances on money matters, I should
obviate all pretence of a claim on his part by making
the new numbers a supplement, with a new title,—
calling them 'Illustrations of Taxation.' I did not
take the work out of his hands, from considerations of
convenience to all parties : but I made no secret of his
having lost me for a client thenceforth. He owed to
me such fortune as he had; and he had now precluded
himself from all chance of further connexion. He
published the Supplement, on the ordinary terms of
commission : and there was an end. I remember
nothing of that story,—' A Tale of the Tyne;' and I
should be rather surprised if I did under the circumstances. The only incident that I recal about it is
that Mr. Malthus called on purpose to thank me for
a passage, or a chapter, (which has left no trace in
my memory) on the glory and beauty of love and the

blessedness of domestic life ; and that others, called stern Benthamites, sent round messages to me to the same effect. They said, as Mr. Malthus did, that they had met with a faithful expositor at last.

In ' Briery Creek,' I indulged my life-long sentiment of admiration and love of Dr. Priestley, by making him, under a thin disguise, the hero of my tale. I was staying at Lambton Castle when that number appeared ; and I was extremely surprised by being asked by Lady Durham who Dr. Priestley was, and all that I could tell her about him. She had seen in the newspapers that my hero was the Doctor ; and I found that she, the daughter of the Prime Minister, had never heard of the Birmingham riots ! I was struck by this evidence of what fearful things may take place in a country, unknown to the families of the chief men in it.

Of number twenty-three, ' The Three Ages,' I remember scarcely any thing. The impression remaining is that I mightily enjoyed the portraiture of Wolsey and More, and especially a soliloquy or speech of Sir Thomas More's. What it is about I have no recollection whatever : and I need not say that I have never looked at the story from the day of publication till now : but I have a strong impression that I should condemn it, if I were to read it now. I have become convinced that it is a mistake of serious importance to attempt to put one's mind of the nineteenth century into the thought of the sixteenth ; and wrong, as a matter of taste, to fall into a sort of slang style, or mannerism, under the notion of talking old English. The temptation is strong to young people whose historical associations are vivid, while their intellectual sympathy is least discriminating; and young writers of a quarter of a century ago may claim special allowance from the fact that Scott's historical novels were then at the height of their popularity: but I believe that, all allowance being made, I should feel strong disgust at the affectations which not only made me very complacent at the time, but brought to me not a few urgent requests that I would write historical novels. Somewhere in that number there is a passage which Lord John Russell declared to be treason, saying that it would undoubtedly bear a prosecution. The publisher smirked at this, and heartily wished somebody would prosecute. We could not make out what passage his Lordship meant; but we supposed it was probably that part which expresses pity for the Royal Family in regard to the mode in which their subsistence is provided;—such of them, I mean, as have not official duties. If it be that passage, I can only say that every man and every woman who is conscious of the blessing of living either by personal exertion or on hereditary property is thus declared guilty of treason in thought, whenever the contrast of a pensioned or eleemosynary condition and an independent one presents itself, in connexion with the Royal Family, as it was in the last generation. It might be in some other passage, however, that the liability lurked. I did not look very closely; for I cannot say that I should have at all relished the prosecution,—the idea of which was so exhilarating to my publisher.

Number twenty-four, ' The Farrers of Budge Row,' seems on the whole to be considered the best story of the Series. I have been repeatedly exhorted to reproduce the character of Jane in a novel. This Jane was so far a personal acquaintance of mine that I had seen her, two or three times; on her stool behind the books, at the shop where we bought our cheese, in the neighbourhood of Fludyer Street. Her old father's pride then was in his cheeses,—which deserved his devotion as much as cheeses can : but my mother and I were aware that his pride had once a very different object ; and it was this knowledge which made me go to the shop, to get a sight of the father and daughter. There had been a younger brother of that quiet woman, who had been sent to college, and educated for one of the learned professions ; but his father had changed his mind, and insisted so cruelly and so long on the young man being his shopman, that the poor fellow died broken-hearted. This anecdote, and an observation that I heard on the closeness with which the daughter was confined to the desk, originated the whole story.

I wrote the chief part of the concluding number, ' The Moral of Many Fables,' during the journey to the north which I took to see my old grandmother before my departure for America, and to visit my eldest sister at Newcastle, and Lord and Lady Durham at Lambton Castle. The fatigue was excessive ; and when at Lambton, I went down a coalpit, in order to see some things which I wanted to know. The heats and draughts of the pit, combined with the fatigue of an unbroken journey by mail from Newcastle to London, in December, caused me a severe attack of inflammation of the liver, and compelled the omission of a month in the appearance of my numbers. The toil and anxiety incurred to ob-

tain the publication of the work had, as I have
related, disordered my liver, two years before. I
believe I had never been quite well, during those two
years; and the toils and domestic anxieties of the
autumn of 1833 had prepared me for overthrow by
the first accident.—After struggling for ten days to
rise from my bed, I was compelled to send word to
printer and publisher that I must stop for a month.
Mr. Fox (the elder) sent a cheering and consolatory
note which enabled me to give myself up to the
pleasure of being ill, and lying still, (as still as the
pain would let me) without doubt or remorse. There
was something to be done first, however; for the
printer's note was not quite such a holiday matter as
Mr. Fox's. It civilly explained that sixteen guineas'
worth of paper had been wetted, which would be
utterly spoiled, if not worked off immediately. It
was absolutely necessary to correct two proofs, which,
as it happened, required more attention than any
which had ever passed under my eye, from their
containing arithmetical statements. Several literary
friends had offered to correct my proofs; but these
were not of a kind to be so disposed of. So, I set to
work with dizzy eyes, and a quivering brain; propped
up with pillows, and my mother and the maid alternately sitting by me with sal volatile, when I believed
I could work a little. I was amused to hear, long
afterwards, that it was reported to be my practice to
work in this delightful style,—' when exhausted, to
be supported in bed by her mother and her maid.
These absurd representations about myself and my
ways taught me some caution in receiving such as
were offered me about other authors.

It was no small matter, by this time, to have a month's respite from the fluctuations of mind which I underwent about every number of my work. These fluctuations were as regular as the tides; but I did not recognise this fact till my mother pointed it out in a laughing way which did me a world of good. When I told her, as she declared I did once a month, that the story I was writing would prove an utter failure, she was uneasy for the first few months, but afterwards amused: and her amusement was a great support to me. The process was indeed a pretty regular one. I was fired with the first conception, and believed that I had found a treasure. Then, while at work, I alternately admired and despised what I wrote. When finished, I was in absolute despair; and then, when I saw it in print, I was surprised to see how well it looked. After an interval of above twenty years, I have not courage to look at a single number,—convinced that I should be disgusted by bad taste and metaphysics in almost every page. Long before I had arrived at this closing number, my mother and aunt had got into the way of smiling at each other, and at me, whenever I bade them prepare for disgrace; and they asked me how often I had addressed the same exhortation to them before.—There was another misery of a few hours, long which we had to bear once a month: and that was the sending the manuscript to the printing-office. This panic was the tax I have always paid for making no copy of anything I write. I sent the parcel by a trusty messenger, who waited for a receipt. One day, the messenger did not return for several hours —the official being absent whose duty it was to re-

ceive such packets. My mother said, 'I tell you
what, Harriet; I can't bear this. . . . . .' 'Nor I
either,' I replied. 'We must carry it ourselves next
time.' 'So I would every time; but I doubt our
being the safest messengers,' I was replying, when
the note of acknowledgment was brought in. Now,
at this new year 1834, I had a whole month of respite
from all such cares, and could lie in bed without
grudging the hours as they passed. It was indeed a
significant yielding when, in 1831, I gave way to
solicitations to produce a number a month. I did
give way, (though with a trembling heart) because I
knew that when I had once plunged into an enterprise, I always got through it, at whatever cost. I
could not have asked any body to go into such an
undertaking; and the cost was severe: but I got
through; and,—if my twenty-fourth number was
really the best, as people said,—without disgrace.

I was not through it yet, however. The 'Illustrations of Taxation' had still to be written. I had
designed six; and I forget when and why I determined there should be only five: but I rather think it
was when I found the first series must have an additional number. All I am sure of is that it was a
prodigious relief, which sent my spirits up sky high,
when I resolved to spare myself a month's work.
Rest and leisure had now become far more important
to me than fame and money. Nothing struck me so
much, or left so deep and abiding an impression after
the close of this arduous work, as my new sense of the
value of time. A month had never before appeared
to me what it now became; and I remember the
real joy of finding in February, 1832, that it was

leap year, and that I had a day more at my command
than I had calculated. The abiding effect has perhaps not been altogether good. No doubt I have
done more than I should without such an experience :
but I think it has narrowed my mind. When I consider how some who knew me well have represented
me as ' industrious in my pleasures ; ' and how some
of my American friends had a scheme at Niagara to
see whether I could pass a day without asking or
telling what o'clock it was, I feel convinced that my
respect for ' time and the hour' has been too much
of a superstition and a bigotry. I say this now
(1855) while finding that I *can* be idle; while, in
fact, feeling myself free to do what I please,— that is,
what illness admits of my doing, for above half of
every day. I find, in the last stage of life, that I *can*
play and be idle; and that I enjoy it. But I still
think that the conflict between constitutional indolence and an overwrought sense of the value of
time has done me some harm in the midst of some
important good.

The Taxation numbers had, as I have said, still to
be done; and, I think, the last of the Poor-law tales.
I was aware that, of all the many weak points of
the Grey administration, the weakest was Finance.
Lord Althorp, then Chancellor of the Exchequer,
complained of the hardship of being put into that
office, when Nature had made him a grazier. It
struck me that some good might be done, and no
harm, if my Illustrations proceeded *pari passu* with
the financial reforms expected from the Whig government; and I spoke on the subject to Lieutenant
Drummond, who had just become private secretary to

Lord Althorp.   I was well acquainted with Mr. Drummond ; and it occurred very naturally that I told him that if he knew of any meditated measure which would be aided by illustration, I would help, in all silence and discretion,—provided always that I approved of the scheme.   About this time the London shopkeepers were raising a selfish outcry against the House-tax, one of the very best on the list of imposts.   It was understood on all hands that the clamour was not raised by the house-owners, but by their tenants, whose rents had been fixed in consideration of their payment of the tax.   If they could get rid of the tax, the tenants would pocket the amount during the remaining term of their leases. . Large and noisy deputations besieged the Treasury ; and many feared that the good-natured Lord Althorp would yield.   Just at this time, Mr. Drummond called on me, with a private message from Lords Grey and Althorp, to ask whether it would suit my purpose to treat of Tithes at once, instead of later,—the reason for such inquiry being quite at my service. As the principles of Taxation involve no inexorable order, like those of Political Economy at large, I had no objection to take any topic first which might be most useful.   When I had said so, Mr. Drummond explained that a tithe measure was prepared by the Cabinet which Ministers would like to have introduced to the people by my Number on that subject, before they themselves introduced it in parliament. Of course, this proceeded on the supposition that the measure would be approved by me.   Mr. Drummond said he would bring the document, on my promising that no eye but my own should see it, and that I

would not speak of the affair till it was settled ;
and, especially, not to any member of any of the
Royal Commissions, then so fashionable. It was a
thing unheard of, Mr. Drummond said, to commit
any Cabinet measure to the knowledge of any body
out of the Cabinet before it was offered to parliament.
Finally, the Secretary intimated that Lord Althorp
would be obliged by any suggestion in regard to
principles and methods of Taxation.

Mr. Drummond had not been gone five minutes
before the Chairman of the Excise Commission called,
to ask, in the name of the Commissioners, whether it
would suit my purpose to write immediately on the
Excise, offering, on the part of Lord Congleton (then
Sir Henry Parnell) and others, to supply me with the
most extraordinary materials, by my exhibition of
which the people might be enlightened and prepared
on the subject before it should be brought forward in
parliament. The Chairman, Mr. Henry Wickham,
required a promise that no eye but my own should see
the evidence ; and that the secret should be kept with
especial care from the Chancellor of the Exchequer
and his secretary, as it was a thing unheard of that
any party unconcerned should be made acquainted
with this evidence before it reached the Chancellor of
the Exchequer. I could hardly help laughing in his
face ; and wondered what would have happened if he
and Mr. Drummond had met on the steps, as they
very nearly did. Of course, I was glad of the information offered ; but I took leave to make my own
choice among the materials lent. A few days afterwards I met Mr. Wickham before the Horse Guards,
and thought he would not know me,—so deep was

he in reverie. Before I was quite past, however, he started, and stopped me with eagerness, saying intensely, ' O! Miss Martineau, Starch! Starch!' And he related the wonderful, the amazing evidence that had reached the Commissioners on the mischievousness of the duty on starch. I was obliged, however, to consider some other matters than the force of the evidence, and I declined expatiating on starch, finding the subject of green glass bottles, soap and sweets answer my purpose better. These two last, especially, yielded a very strong case.

At the end of a note to Mr. Drummond on Tithes that evening, I expressed myself plainly about the House-tax and the shopkeepers, avowing my dread that Lord Althorp might yield to the clamour. Mr. Drummond called next day with the promised tithe document; and he told me that he had handed my note to Lord Althorp, who had said ' Tell her that I may be altogether of her mind; but that if she was here, in my place, with hundreds of shopkeepers yelling about the doors, she would yield, as I must do.' ' Never,' was my message back, ' so long as the House-tax is admitted to be the best on the list.' And I fairly told him that the Whig government was perilling the public safety by yielding every thing to clamour, and nothing without it.

I liked the Tithe measure, and willingly propounded it in my tale ' The Tenth Haycock.' It was discussed that session, but deferred ; and it passed, with some modifications, a session or two later.—Mr. Drummond next came to open to me, on the same confidential conditions, Lord Althorp's scheme for the Budget, then due in six weeks. His object was to learn what I thought of certain intended alterations of existing taxes. With some pomp and preface, he announced that a change was contemplated which Lord Althorp hoped would be agreeable to me as a dissenter,—a change which Lord Althorp anticipated would be received as a boon by the dissenters. He proposed to take off the tax upon saddle-horses, in the case of the clergy and dissenting Ministers. 'What shall I tell Lord Althorp that you think of this?' inquired the Secretary. 'Tell him I think the dissenting Ministers would like it very much if they had any saddle-horses,' I replied.—'What! do you mean that they will not take it as a boon?'—'If you offer it as a boon, they will be apt to take it as an insult. How should dissenting Ministers have saddle-horses, unless they happen to have private fortunes?' He questioned me closely about the dissenting Ministers I knew; and we found that I could actually point out only two among the Unitarians who kept saddle-horses, and they were men of property.

'What, then, would you substitute?' was the next question. 'I would begin upon the Excise; set free the smallest articles first, which least repay the expense of collection, and go on to the greatest.'— 'The Excise! Ah! Lord Althorp bade me tell you that the Commission on Excise have collected the most extraordinary evidence, which he will take care that you shall have, as soon as he gets it himself.' (It was at that moment in the closet, within two feet of my visitor.) I replied that the evils of the Excise system were well known to be such as to afford employment to any Chancellor of the Exchequer for a course of years; and I should venture to send Lord

Althorp my statement of them, hoping that he would glance at it before he brought out his Budget. I worked away at the two Excise stories ('The Jerseymen Meeting' and 'The Jerseymen Parting,') making out a strong case, among others, about Green Glass Bottles and Sweets, more as illustrative examples than as individual cases. I sent the first copy I could get to the Chancellor of the Exchequer, a day and a half before he brought out his Budget. When I opened the 'Times,' the morning after, I was highly amused at seeing that he had made a curious alteration in his intentions about the saddle-horse duty, applying the remission to those clergymen and ministers only whose income was under two hundred pounds a year,—having evidently no idea of the cost of keeping a horse. Not less amusing was it to see that he had taken off the duty from green glass bottles and sweets. He was in fact open to suggestion and correction from any quarter,—being consciously, as I have mentioned that he said, one of Nature's graziers, and a merely man-made Chancellor of the Exchequer.

By this time, the summer of 1834 was far advanced, and I was much exhausted with fatigue and hot weather, and the hurry of preparation for my trip to America. I was drooping in idea over my last number, 'The Scholars of Arneside,' when a cordial friend of mine said, 'You will go with great spirit through your last number,—the final task of such an enterprise.' This prophecy wrought its own accomplishment. I did go through it with spirit; and I found myself, after making my calls, with one day left for packing and preparation. Many interruptions

occurred during the last few days which deferred my
conclusion till I felt and saw that my mother was so
anxious that I must myself keep down worry of
nerves. On the Friday before I was to leave home
for above two years, my mother said, with anxious
kindness, ' My dear, have you done?' 'No,
mother.' On Saturday night, she put her head in
at my study door, with ' My dear, have you done?'
'Indeed I have not.' Sunday came,—my place
taken by mail for Tuesday, no packing done, and
my number unfinished! The case seemed desperate.
My mother staid at home and took every precaution
against my being disturbed : but some one came on
indispensable business, and did not release me till
our early Sunday dinner hour. My mother looked
anxiously in my face; and I could only shake my
head. After dinner, she in a manner mounted guard
over my study door. At five o'clock I flew down
stairs with the last sheet, with the ink still wet, in
my hand. My sister Ellen was with us, and at the
moment writing to some Derbyshire friends. By a
sudden impulse, I seized her paper, and with the wet
pen with which I had just written 'The End,' I
announced the conclusion of my work. My mother
could say little but ' After all we have gone through
about this work, to think how it has ended!' I flew
up stairs again to tie up parcels and manuscripts, and
put away all my apparatus; and I had just finished
this when I was called to tea. After tea I went into
St. James's Park for the first thoroughly holiday
walk I had taken for two years and a half. It felt
very like flying. The grass under foot, the sky overhead, the trees round about, were wholly different

from what they had ever appeared before. My business was not, however, entirely closed. There were the proof-sheets of the last Number to be looked over. They followed me to Birmingham, where Ellen and I travelled together, in childish spirits, on the Tuesday.

My mother had reason for her somewhat pathetic exultation on the conclusion of my Series. Its success was unprecedented, I believe. I am told that its circulation had reached ten thousand in England before my return from America. Mr. Babbage calling on me one day, when he was in high spirits about the popularity of his own work, ‘Machinery and Manufactures,’ said, ‘Now there is nobody here to call us vain, we may tell each other that you and I are the only people in the market. I find no books are selling but yours and mine.’ (It was a time of political agitation.) I replied, ‘I find no books are selling but yours and mine.’ ‘Well!’ said he, ‘what I came to say is that we may as well advertise each other. Will you advertise mine if I advertise yours, &c., &c?’ And this was the work which had struggled into existence with such extreme difficulty! Under the hard circumstances of the case, it had not made me rich. I have at this time received only a little more than two thousand pounds for the whole work. But I got a hearing,—which was the thing I wanted. The barrier was down, and the course clear; and the money was a small matter in comparison. It was pleasant, too, to feel the ease of having money, after my straitened way of life for some years. My first indulgence was buying a good watch,—the same which is before my eyes as I write. I did not trouble myself with close economies while

working to such advantage ; and I now first learned
the bliss of helping the needy effectually. I was able
to justify my mother in removing to London, and to
refresh myself by travel, at the end of my task. My
American journey cost me four hundred pounds, in
addition to one hundred which I made when there.
I had left at home my usual payment to my mother;
but she refused to take it, as she had a boarder in my
place. Soon after my return, when my first American
book was published, I found myself able to lay by
one thousand pounds, in the purchase of a deferred
annuity, of which I am now enjoying the benefit in
the receipt of one hundred pounds a year. I may
finish off the subject of money by saying that I lately
calculated that I have earned altogether by my books
somewhere about ten thousand pounds. I have had
to live on it, of course, for five-and-twenty years ; and
I have found plenty to do with it : but I have enough,
and I am satisfied. I believe I might easily have
doubled the amount, if it had been my object to get
money ; or even, if an international copyright law had
secured to me the proceeds of the sale of my works in
foreign countries. But such a law was non-existent
in my busy time, and still is in regard to America.
There is nothing in money that could pay me for the
pain of the slightest deflexion from my own convictions, or the most trifling restraint on my freedom
of thought and speech. I have therefore obtained the
ease and freedom, and let slip the money. I do not
speak as one who has resisted temptation, for there
has really been none. I have never been at a loss for
means, or really suffering from poverty, since the publication of my Series. I explain the case simply that

there may be no mystery about my not being rich after such singular success as I so soon met with.

One more explanation will bring this long section to a close. I make it the more readily because it is possible that an absurd report which I encountered in America may be still in existence. It was said that I travelled, not on my own resources, but on means supplied by Lord Brougham and his relative Lord Henley, to fulfil certain objects of theirs. Nobody acquainted with me would listen to such nonsense; but I may as well explain what Lord Henley had to do with my going to America. Lord Brougham had no concern with it whatever, beyond giving me two or three letters of introduction. The story is simply this. One evening, in a party, Lady Mary Shepherd told me that she was commissioned to bring about an interview between myself and her nephew, Lord Henley, who had something of importance to say to me : and she fixed me to meet Lord Henley at her house at luncheon a day or two after. She told me meantime the thing he chiefly wanted, which was to know how, if I had three hundred pounds a year to spend in charity, I should employ it. When we met, I was struck by his excessive agitation, which his subsequent derangement might account for. His chief interest was in philanthropic subjects ; and he told me, with extreme emotion, (what so many others have told me) that he believed he had been doing mischief for many years where he most meant to do good, by his methods of alms-giving. Since reading ' Cousin Marshall ' and others of my Numbers, he had dropped his subscriptions to some hurtful charities, and had devoted his funds to Education, Benefit

Societies and Emigration. Upon his afterwards asking whether I received visitors, and being surprised to
find that I could afford the time, some remarks were
made about the extent and pressure of my work ; and
then Lord Henley asked whether I did not mean to
travel when my Series was done. Upon my replying
that I did, he apologised for the liberty he took in
asking where I thought of going. I said I had not
thought much about it ; but that I supposed it would
be the usual route, to Switzerland and Italy. ' O ! do
not go over that beaten track,' he exclaimed. ' Why
should you ? Will you not go to America ? ' I replied, ' Give me a good reason, and perhaps I will.'
His answer was, ' Whatever else may or may not be
true about the Americans, it is certain that they have
got at principles of justice and mercy in their treatment of the least happy classes of society which we
should do well to understand. Will you not go, and
tell us what they are ? ' This, after some meditation,
determined me to cross the Atlantic. Before my return, Lord Henley had disappeared from society ; and
he soon after died. I never saw him, I believe, but
that once.

After short visits, with my sister Ellen, at Birmingham, in Derbyshire and at Liverpool, I sailed
(for there were no steamers on the Atlantic in those
days) early in August, 1834.

SECTION II.

According to my promise,* I reprint the bulk of
an article on 'Literary Lionism,' written in 1837,
which will show, better than anything which I can now
relate, how I regarded the flatteries of a drawing-room
while living in the midst of them. It makes me
laugh as I read it to have recalled to my memory
the absurd incidents which were occurring every day,
and which drove me to write this article as a relief to
feelings of disgust and annoyance. There is not a
stroke that is not from the life. The works reviewed
are 'The Lion of a Party,' from a publication of that
time, 'Heads of the People;' and an oration of
Emerson's on the Life of the Scholar. Omitting only
the review part and the extracts, I give the whole.

'This "Lion" is indeed one of the meanest of his
tribe ; but he is one of a tribe which has included, and
does now include, some who are worthy of a higher
classification. Byron was an "interesting creature,"
and received blushing thanks for his last "divine poem."
Scott lost various little articles which would answer
for laying up in lavender ; and Madame de Stael was

exhibited almost as ostensibly at the British Gallery as
any of the pictures on the walls, on the evening when
the old Marquis of A—— obtained an introduction
to her, and accosted her with " Come now. Madame
de Stael, you must talk English to me." As she
scornfully turned from him, and continued her discourse
in her own way, the discomfited Marquis seemed to
think himself extremely ill used in being deprived of
the entertainment he expected from the *prima donna*
of the company. In as far as such personages as these
last acquiesce in the modern practice of " Lionism,"
they may be considered to be implicated in whatever
reproach attaches to it ; but the truth seems to be
that, however disgusting and injurious the system, and
however guilty some few individuals may be in avail-
ing themselves of it for their small, selfish, immediate
purposes, the practice, with its slang term, is the birth
of events, and is a sign of the times,—like newspaper
puffery, which is an evidence of over-population, or
like joint-stock companies and club-houses, which indicate that society has obtained a glimpse of that great
principle of the economy of association, by which it
will probably, in some future age, reconstitute itself.

' The practice of " Lionism " originates in some
feelings which are very good,—in veneration for intellectual superiority, and gratitude for intellectual gifts ;
and its form and prevalence are determined by the fact,
that literature has reached a larger class, and interested a different order of people from any who formerly
shared its advantages. A wise man might, at the time
of the invention of printing, have foreseen the age of
literary "Lionism," and would probably have smiled at
it as a temporary extravagance. The whole course of

literary achievement has prophesied its transient reign.
The voluntary, self-complacent, literary "Lion" might,
in fact, be better called the mouse issuing from the
labouring mountain, which has yet to give birth to
the volcano.

'There was a time when literature was cultivated
only in the seclusion of monasteries. There sat the
author of old, alone in his cell,—alone through days,
and months, and years. The echoes of the world
have died away ; the voice of praise could not reach
him there, and his grave yawned within the very
inclosure whence he should never depart. He might
look abroad from the hill-side, or the pinnacle of
rock where his monastery stood, on

> " the rich leas,
> The turfy mountains where lived nibbling sheep,
> And flat meads thatch'd with stover them to keep :
> ———————————— the broom groves,
> Whose shadow the dismissed bachelor loves,
> Being lass-lorn : the pole-clipt vineyard,
> And the sea-marge, sterile and rocky hard."

On these he might look abroad, but never on the
assemblages of men. Literary achievement in such
circumstances might be, to a certain degree, encouraged
by visions of future usefulness and extended fame, but
the strongest stimulus must have been the pleasure
of intellectual exercise. The toil of composition must
there have been its own reward, and we may even now
witness with the mind's eye the delight of it painted
upon the face under the cowl. One may see the
student hastening from the refectory to the cell, drawn
thither by the strong desire of solving a problem, of
elucidating a fact, of indulging the imagination with

heavenly delights, and contemplating the wealth stored
in his memory. One may see him coming down with
radiant countenance from the heights of speculation,
to cast into the worship of the chapel the devotion he
had there gained. One may see the glow upon his
cheek as he sits alone beside his lamp, noting his
discoveries, or elaborating the expression of his ideas.
There are many who think that no one ever wrote a
line, even in the most private diary, without the belief,
or the hope, that it would be read. It might be so
with the monastic author; but in his case there could
rarely be the appendage of praise to the fact of its
being read; and the prospect of influence and applause
was too remote to actuate a life of literary toil. It is
probable that if an echo of fame came to him on any
of the four winds, it was well, and he heartily enjoyed
the music of the breeze; but that in some instances
he would have passed his days in the same manner,
cultivating literature for its own sake, if he had known
that his parchments would be buried with him.

‘ The homage paid to such men when they did come
forth into the world was, on the part of the many, on
the ground of their superiority alone. A handful of
students might feel thankfulness towards them for
definite services, but the crowd gazed at them in
vague admiration, as being holier or wiser than other
people. As the blessings of literature spread, strong
personal gratitude mingled with the homage,—gratitude not only for increase of fame and honour to the
country and nation to which the author belonged, but
for the good which each worshipper derived from the
quickening of his sympathies, the enlargement of his
views, the elevation of his intellectual being. To each

of the crowd the author had opened up a spring of
fresh ideas, furnished a solution of some doubt, a gratification of the fancy or the reason. When, on a certain memorable Easter day in the fourteenth century,
Petrarch mounted the stairs of the Capitol, crowned
with laurel, and preceded by twelve noble youths, re-
citing passages of his poetry, the praise was of the
noblest kind that it has been the lot of authorship to
receive. It was composed of reverence and gratitude,
pure from cold selfishness and from sentimental passion,
which is cold selfishness in a flame-coloured disguise.
When, more than four centuries later, Voltaire was
overpowered with acclamations in the theatre at Paris,
and conveyed home in triumph, crying feebly, ' You
suffocate me with roses,' the homage, though inferior
in character to that which greeted Petrarch, was honourable, and of better origin than popular selfishness.
The applauding crowd had been kept ignorant by the
superstition which had in other ways so afflicted them,
that they were unboundedly grateful to a man of power
who promised to relieve them from the yoke. Voltaire
had said, ' I am tired of hearing it repeated that twelve
men were sufficient to found Christianity: I will show
the world that one is sufficient to destroy it;' and he
was believed.   He was mistaken in his boast, and his
adorers in confiding in it; but this proves only that
they were ignorant of Christianity, and not that their
homage of one whom they believed to have exploded
error and disarmed superstition, and whom they knew
to have honoured and served them by his literary
labours, was otherwise than natural and creditable
to their hearts.

   ' The worship of popular authors at the present

time is an expression of the same thoughts and
feelings as were indicated by the crowning of Petrarch
and the greeting of Voltaire in the theatre, but with
alterations and additions according to the change in
the times. Literary "lions" have become a class,—an
inconceivable idea to the unreflecting in the time of
Petrarch, and even of Voltaire. This testifies to the
vast spread of literature among our people. How
great a number of readers is required to support, by
purchase and by praise, a standing class of original
writers! It testifies to the deterioration of literature
as a whole. If, at any one time, there is a *class* of
persons to whom the public are grateful for intellectual
excitement, how *médiocre* must be the quality of the
intellectual production! It by no means follows that
works of merit, equal to any which have yet blessed
mankind, are not still in reserve ; but it is clear that
the great body of literature has entirely changed its
character,—that books are no longer the scarce fruit
of solemn and protracted thought, but rather, as they
have been called, "letters to all whom they may concern." That literary " lions " now constitute a class,
testifies to the frequency of literary success,—to the
extension of the number of minds from which a superficial and transient sympathy may be anticipated.
But the newest feature of all is the class of "lionisers,"
—new, not because sordid selfishness is new,—not because social vanity is new,—not because an inhuman
disregard of the feelings of the sensitive, the foibles of
the vain, the privileges of the endowed, is new : but
because it is somewhat new to see the place of cards,
music, masks, my lord's fool, and my lady's monkey,
supplied by authors in virtue of their authorship.

'It is, to be sure, quite to be expected that low-minded persons should take advantage of any prevalent feeling, however respectable, to answer their own purposes; but the effect, in this instance, would be odd to a resuscitated gentleman of the fifteenth century. If he happened to be present at one of the meetings of the British Association for the Advancement of Science, he would there see the popular veneration for intellectual achievement under a pretty fair aspect. There is no harm, and some good, in seeing a group waiting for Sir John Herschel to come out into the street, or a rush in the rooms to catch a sight of Faraday,—or ladies sketching Babbage, and Buckland, and Back,—or a train of gazers following at the heels of Whewell or Sedgwick, or any popular artist or author who might be present among the men of science. In all this there is no reproach, and some honour, to both parties, though of a slight and transient kind. The sordid characteristics of the modern system appear when the eminent person becomes a guest in a private house. If the resuscitated gentleman of the fifteenth century were to walk into a country house in England in company with a lady of literary distinction, he might see at once what is in the mind of the host and hostess. All the books of the house are lying about, —all the gentry in the neighbourhood are collected; the young men peep and stare from the corners of the room; the young ladies crowd together, even sitting five upon three chairs, to avoid the risk of being addressed by the stranger. The lady of the house devotes herself to "drawing out" the guest, asks for her opinion of this, that, and the other book, and intercedes for her young friends, trembling on their three

chairs, that each may be favoured with " just one line
for her album." The children are kept in the nursery,
as being unworthy the notice of a literary person, or
brought up severally into the presence, "that they may
have it to say all their lives that they had been introduced," &c., &c. Some youth in a corner is meantime
sketching the guest, and another is noting what she
says,—probably something about black and green tea,
or the state of the roads, or the age of the moon.
Such a scene, very common now in English country
houses, must present an unfavourable picture of our
manners to strangers from another country or another
age. The prominent features are the sufferings of one
person, and the selfishness of all the rest. They are
too much engrossed with the excitement of their
own vanity and curiosity to heed the pain they
are inflicting on one who, if she happens to have
more feeling and less vanity than they, can hardly
enjoy being told that children cannot be interesting
to her, and that young people do not wish to speak
to her.

'In a country town it is yet worse. There may
be seen a coterie of " superior people " of the place,
gathered together to make the most of a literary
foreigner who may be passing through. Though he
speaks perfect English, the ladies persist in uttering
themselves, after hems and haws, in French that he
can make nothing of,—French as it was taught in
our boarding schools during the war. The children
giggle in a corner at what the boys call "the jabber;"
and the maid who hands the tea strives to keep the
corners of her mouth in order. In vain the guest
speaks to the children, and any old person who may
be present, in English almost as good as their own ;

he is annoyed to the last by the " superior people," who intend that it should get abroad through the town that they had enjoyed a vast deal of conversation in French with the illustrious stranger.

'Bad as all this is, the case is worse in London,— more disgusting, if it is impossible to be more ridiculous. There, ladies of rank made their profit of the woes of the Italian and Polish refugees, the most eagerly in the days of the deepest unhappiness of the exiles, when the novelty was strongest. These exiles were collected in the name of hospitality, but for purposes of attraction, within the doors of fashionable saloons; there they were stared out of countenance amidst the sentimental sighs of the gazers; and if any one of them, —any interesting Count or melancholy-looking Prince, happened unfortunately to be the author of a " sweet poem," or a " charming tragedy," he was called out from among the rest to be flattered by the ladies, and secured for fresh services. It was not uncommon, during the days of the novelty of the Italian refugees, while they were yet unprovided with employments by which they might live, (and for aught we know, it may not be uncommon still,) for ladies to secure the appearance of one or two of these first-rate "lions" with them the next evening at the theatre or opera, and to forget to pay. Till these gentlemen had learned by experience to estimate the friendship of the ladies to whom they were so interesting, they often paid away at public places the money which was to furnish them with bread for the week. We have witnessed the grief and indignation with which some of them have announced their discovery that their woes and their accomplishments were hired with champagne, coffee, and fine words, to amuse a party of languid fine people.

'These gentlemen, however, are no worse treated than many natives. A new poet, if he innocently accepts a promising invitation, is liable to find out afterwards that his name has been inserted in the summonses to the rest of the company, or sent round from mouth to mouth to secure the rooms being full. If a woman who has written a successful play or novel attends the soirée of a "lionising" lady, she hears her name so announced on the stairs as to make it certain that the servants have had their instructions; she finds herself seized upon at the door by the hostess, and carried about to lord, lady, philosopher, gossip, and dandy, each being assured that she cannot be spared to each for more than ten seconds. She sees a "lion" placed in the centre of each of the two first rooms she passes through,—a navigator from the North Pole in the one, a dusky Egyptian bey or Hindoo rajah in another; and it flashes upon her that she is to be the centre of attraction in a third apartment. If she is vain enough to like the position, the blame of ministering to a pitiable and destructive weakness remains with the hostess, and she is answerable for some of the failure of power which will be manifest in the next play or novel of her victim. If the guest be meek and modest, there is nothing for it but getting behind a door, or surrounding herself with her friends in a corner. If she be strong enough to assert herself, she will return at once to her carriage, and take care how she enters that house again. A few instances of what may be seen in London during any one season, if brought together, yield but a sorry exhibition of the manners of persons who give parties to gratify their own vanity instead of enjoying the society and the pleasure of their

friends.   In one crowded room are three "lions,"—
a new musical composer, an eminent divine who pub-
lishes, and a lady poet.   These three stand in three
corners of the room, faced by a gaping crowd.   Weary
at length of their position, they all happen to move
towards the centre table at the same moment.   They
find it covered with the composer's music, the divine's
sermons, and the lady's last new poem; they laugh in
each other's faces, and go back to their corners.   A
gentleman from the top of Mont Blanc, or from the
North Pole, is introduced to a lady who is dying to be
able to say that she knows him, but who finds at the
critical moment that she has nothing to say to him.
In the midst of a triple circle of listeners, she asks him
whether he is not surprised at his own preservation;
whether it does not prove that Providence is everywhere, but more particularly in barren places?   If a
sigh or a syllable of remonstrance escapes from any
victim, there is one phrase always at hand for use, a
phrase which, if it ever contained any truth, or exerted
any consolatory influence, has been long worn out, and
become mere words,—" This is a tax you must pay
for your eminence."   There may, perhaps, be as much
assumption with regard to the necessity of this tax as
of some others.   Every tax has been called absolutely
necessary in its day; and the time may arrive when
some shall dispute whether it be really needful that an
accomplished actor should be pestered with the flattery
of his art; that authors should be favoured with more
general conversation only that any opinions they may
drop may be gathered up to be reported; and that
women, whom the hardest treatment awaits if their
heads should be turned, should be compelled to hear

what the prime minister, or the Russian ambassador, or the poet laureate, or the " lion " of the last season, has said of them. Those on whom the tax is levied would like to have the means of protest, if they should not see its necessity quite so clearly as others do. They would like to know why they are to be unresistingly pillaged of their time by importunity about albums, and despoiled of the privacy of correspondence with their friends by the rage for autographs, so that if they scribble a joke to an acquaintance in the next street, they may hear of its existence five years after in a far corner of Yorkshire, or in a book of curiosities at Hobart Town. They would like to know why they must be civil when a stranger, introduced by an acquaintance at a morning call, makes her curtsey, raises her glass, borrows paper and pencil of the victim, draws a likeness, puts it into her reticule, and departs. They would like to know why they are expected to be gratified when eight or nine third-rate painters beg them to sit for their portraits, to be hung out as signs to entice visitors to the artist's rooms.'

*   *   *   *   *   *

'Authors would like to know why they must receive flattery as if it were welcome, and be made subject to fine speeches, which presuppose a disgusting degree of vanity in the listener. They would like to know whether it is absolutely necessary that they should be accused of pride and ingratitude if they decline honours of such spurious origin as most of these, and of absurd vanity if they do not repel them. They would like to know whether it is quite necessary, in generous and Christian England, that any class should

submit to have its most besetting sin, its peculiar
weakness, fostered and aggravated for the purposes of
persons whose aim it is to have brilliant parties and a
celebrated acquaintance. The being honoured through
the broad land, while the soul is sinking under its sense
of ignorance and weakness at home, is a tax which a
popular author must pay ; and so is the being cen-
sured for what may prove the best deeds of his life,
and the highest thoughts of his mind. He may be
obliged to submit to be gazed at in public, and to be
annoyed with handfuls of anonymous letters in his
study, where he would fain occupy himself with something far higher and better than himself and his
doings. These things may be a tax which he must
pay ; but it may be questionable whether it is equally
necessary for him to acquiesce in being the show
and attraction of an assemblage to which he is invited
as a guest, if not as a friend.

'This matter is not worth losing one's temper
about,—just because nothing is worth it. There
is another reason, too, why indignation would be
absurd,—that no individuals or classes are answerable for the system. It is the birth of the times,
as we said before, and those may laugh who can,
and those who must suffer had better suffer good-
humouredly ; but not the less is the system a great
mischief, and therefore to be exposed and resisted by
those who have the power. If its effects were merely
to ensure and hasten the ruin of youthful poets, who
are satisfied to bask in compliments and the lamp-light
of saloons, to complete the resemblance to pet animals
of beings who never were men, the world would lose
little, and this species of coxcombry, like every other,

might be left to have its day. But this is far from
being all that is done. There is a grievous waste of
time of a higher order of beings than the rhyming
dandy—waste of the precious time of those who have
only too few years in which to think and to live.
There is an intrusion into the independence of their
observation of life. If their modesty is not most painfully outraged, their idea of the literary life is depraved.
The one or the other must be the case, and we generally witness both in the literary pets of saloons.

'Some plead that the evil is usually so temporary,
that it cannot do much mischief to any one who really
has an intellect, and is therefore of consequence to the
world. But the mischief is not over with praise and
publicity. The reverse which ensues may be salutary.
As Carlyle says, "Truly, if Death did not intervene;
or, still more happily, if Life and the Public were not
a blockhead, and sudden unreasonable oblivion were
not to follow that sudden unreasonable glory, and
beneficently, though most painfully, damp it down,
one sees not where many a poor glorious man, still
more, many a poor glorious woman (for it falls harder
on the distinguished female), could terminate, far short
of Bedlam." Such reverse may be the best thing to
be hoped; but it does not leave things as they were
before the season of flattery set in. The safe feeling
of equality is gone; habits of industry are impaired;
the delicacy of modesty is exhaled; and it is a great
wonder if the temper is not spoiled. The sense of
elevation is followed by a consciousness of depression:
those who have been the idols of society feel, when de-
posed, like its slaves; and the natural consequence is
contempt and repining. Hear Dryden at the end of

a long course of mutual flatteries between himself and
his patrons, and of authorship to please others, often
to the severe mortification of his better nature :—" It
will continue to be the ingratitude of mankind, that
they who teach wisdom by the surest means shall
generally live poor and unregarded, as if they were
born only for the public, and had no interest in their
own well-being, but were to be lighted up like tapers,
and waste themselves for the benefit of others." '

*   *   *   *   *   *

' The crowning evil which arises from the system of
" lionism " is, that it cuts off the retreat of literary
persons into the great body of human beings. They
are marked out as a class, and can no longer take
refuge from their toils and their publicity in ordinary
life. This is a hardship shared by authors who are far
above being directly injured by the prevalent practice.
There are men who continue to enter society for the
sake of the good it yields, enjoying intercourse, despising homage, smiling at the vanities of those who must
needs be vain, and overlooking the selfishness of such
as are capable of no higher ambition than of being
noted for their brilliant parties,—there are men thus
superior to being " lions " who yet find themselves
injured by " lionism." The more they venerate their
own vocation, and the more humbly they estimate the
influence of their own labours on human affairs, the
more distinctly do they perceive the mischief of their
separation from others who live and think ; of their
being isolated as a class. The cabinet-maker is of a
different class from the hosier, because one makes furniture and the other stockings. The lawyer is of a
different class from the physician, because the science

of law is quite a different thing from the science of medicine. But the author has to do with those two things precisely which are common to the whole race, —with living and thinking. He is devoted to no exclusive department of science ; and the art which he practises,—the writing what he thinks,—is quite a subordinate part of his business. The very first necessity of his vocation is to live as others live, in order to see and feel, and to sympathise in human thought. In proportion as this sympathy is impaired, will his views be partial, his understanding, both of men and books, be imperfect, and his power be weakened accordingly. A man aware of all this will sigh, however good-naturedly he may smile, at such lamentations as may often be overheard in " brilliant parties." " How do you like Mrs. ——, now you have got an introduction to her ? " " O, I am *so* disappointed! I don't find that she has anything in her." " Nothing in her ! Nothing, with all her science !" "O, I should never have found out who she was, if I had not been told ; and she did not say a thing that one could carry away." Hence,—from people not finding out who she was without being told,—came Mrs. ——'s great wisdom; and of this advantage was all the world trying to deprive her.'

*   *   *   *   *   *

' Amidst the " lower observances " of life, even the pedantry of literary coteries, the frivolities of the drawing-room, and the sentimentalities of " lion " worship, there is for the self-relying, " tuition in the serene and beautiful laws" of human existence. But the tuition is for the self-relying alone,—for those who, in the deep interest of their vocation of thought, work

from far other considerations than the desire of applause. None but a man who can do without praise
can come out safe from the process of being "lionised:"
and no one who cannot do without praise is likely to
achieve any thing better than he has already done.
The newspapers may tell of his " expanding intellect,"
and his publisher may prophesy of the rich fruits of
his coming years: but he has done his best. Having
gained much applause by a particular quality of his
writing, he will be always trying to get more applause
by a stronger exhibition of the quality, till it grows
into pure extravagance. If he has energy, it will grow
into bombast in the hot-house of drawing-room favour.
If he is suggestive, and excels in implication, he will
probably end in a Lord Burleigh's shake of the head.
He deprives himself of the repose and independence of
thought, amid which he might become aware of his
own tendencies, and nourish his weaker powers into an
equality with the stronger. Fashion, with all its
lights, its music, its incense, is to him a sepulchre,—
the cold deep grave in which his powers and his ambition must rot into nothingness. We have often wondered, while witnessing the ministering of the poison
to the unwary, the weak and the vain, whether their
course began with the same kind of aspiration, felt as
early, as that which the greatest of the world's thinkers
have confessed. It seems as if any who have risen so
far into success as to attract the admiration (and therefore the sympathy) of numbers, must have had a long
training in habits of thought, feeling, and expression ;
must have early felt admiration of intellectual achievement, and the consciousness of kindred with the
masters of intellect ; must have early known the stir-

rings of literary ambition, the pleasure of thinking, the luxury of expressing thought, and the heroic longing to create or arouse somewhat in other minds. It is difficult to believe that any one who has succeeded has not gone through brave toils, virtuous struggles of modesty, and a noble glow of confidence : that he has not obtained glimpses of realities unseen by the outward eye, and been animated by a sense of the glory of his vocation: that, up to the precincts of the empire of fashion, he has been, in all essential respects, on an equality with any of God's peerage. If so, what a sight of ruin is here : aspirations chained down by the fetters of complaisance! desires blown away by the breath of popularity, or the wind of ladies' fans ! confidence pampered into conceit; modesty depraved into misgiving and dependence ; and the music of the spheres exchanged for opera airs and the rhymes of an album ! Instead of " the scholar beloved of earth and heaven," we have the mincing dandy courted by the foolish and the vain. Instead of the son of wisdom, standing serene before the world to justify the ways of his parent, we have the spoiled child of fortune, ready to complain, on the first neglect, that all the universe goes wrong because the darkness is settling down upon him after he has used up his little day. What a catastrophe of a mind which must have had promise in its dawn !

" Even where the case is not so mournful as this, the drawing-room is still the grave of literary promise. There are some who on the heath, or in the shadow of the wood, whispered to themselves, with beating hearts, while communing with some master-mind, " I am also a poet." In those days they could

not hear the very name of Chaucer or Shakspere
without a glow of personal interest, arising out of a
sense of kindred. Now, lounging on sofas, and, quaff-
ing coffee and praise, they are satisfied with mediocrity, gratified enough that one fair creature has shut
herself up with their works at noon-day, and that another has pored over them at midnight. They now speak
of Chaucer and Shakspere with the same kind of
admiration with which they themselves are addressed
by others. The consciousness, the heart-felt emotion,
the feeling of brotherhood,—all that is noble is gone,
and is succeeded by a low and precarious self-compla-
cency, a sceptical preference of mediocrity to excellence. They underrate their vocation, and are lost.'

*   *   *   *   *   *   *   *

' When we think how few writers in a century live
for centuries, it is astonishing to perceive how many
in every year dismiss all doubt of their own greatness,
and strut about in the belief that men's minds are full
of them, and will be full of them when a new age has
arisen, and they and their flatterers have long been
gone to learn elsewhere, perhaps, the littleness of all
our knowledge. Any degree of delight, any excess of
glee may be llowed for, and even respected, in one
actually in the intense enjoyment of authorship, when
all comparison with others is out of the question for the
hour, and the charm of his own conceptions eclipses
all other beauty, the fervour of his own persuasions
excludes the influence of all other minds ; but if a man
not immediately subject to the inspiration of his art,
deliberately believes that his thoughts are so far beyond
his age, or his feelings so universal and so felicitously
expressed as that he is even now addressing a remote

posterity, no further proof of his ignorance and error is needed. The prophecy forbids its own accomplishment. There is probably no London season when some author is not told by some foolish person that he or she is equal to Shakspere; and it is but too probable that some have believed what they have been told, and in consequence stopped short of what, by patient and humble study and labour, they might have achieved ; while it is almost certain, if such could but see it, that whenever Shakspere's equal shall arise, it will be in some unanticipated form, and in such a mode that the parity of glory shall be a secret to himself, and to the world, till he is gone from it.

'Another almost unavoidable effect of literary "lionism" is to make an author overrate his vocation ; which is, perhaps, as fatal an error as underrating it. All people interested in their work are liable to overrate their vocation. There may be makers of dolls' eyes who wonder how society would go on without them. But almost all men, but popular authors, leave behind them their business and the ideas which belong to it when they go out to recreate themselves. The literary "lion," however, hears of little but books, and the kind of books he is interested in. He sees them lining the walls and strewing the tables wherever he goes: all the ideas he hears are from books ; all the news is about books, till it is no wonder if he fancies that books govern the affairs of the world. If this fancy once gets fixed in his brain there is an end of his achievements. His sagacity about human interests, and his sympathy with human feelings, are gone. If he had not been enchanted, held captive within the magic circle of fashion, he might have stepped abroad

to see how the world really goes on. He might have
found there philosophers who foresee the imperishable
nature of certain books ; who would say to him, " Cast
forth thy word into the everliving, everworking universe ; it is a seed grain that cannot die ; unnoticed
to-day, it will be found flourishing as a banyan-grove
(perhaps, alas ! as a hemlock forest) after a thousand
years : " * all this, however, supposing vital perfection
in the seed, and a fitting soil for it to sink into. He
might have found some who will say with Fenelon,
with all earnestness, " If the riches of both Indies, if
the crowns of all the kingdoms of Europe were laid at
my feet, in exchange for my love of reading, I would
spurn them all." But even among these, the reading
and thinking class, he would be wise to observe how
much more important are many things than books ;
how little literature can compete in influence with the
winds of heaven, with impulses from within, with the
possession of land and game, with professional occu-
pations, with the news of the day, with the ideas and
affections belonging to home and family. All these
rank, as they ought to do, before books in their operation upon minds. If he could have gone out of the
circle of the highly cultivated, he would have found
the merchant on 'change, the shopkeeper at his ledger,
mothers in their nurseries, boys and girls serving their
apprenticeships or earning their bread, with little
though of books. It is true that in this class may
be found those who are, perhaps, the most wrought
upon by books,—those to whom literature is a luxury ;
but to such, two or three books are the mental food of

* Sartor Resartus, p. 38.

a whole youth, while two or three more may sustain
their mature years. These are they to whom the vocation of the author, in the abstract, is beyond comparison for nobleness, but to whom the vocation of this
particular author is of less importance than that of the
monkey that grimaces on Bruin's back, as he paces
along Whitechapel or Cheapside. If he could have
gone further still, he would have heard little children
talking to their haggard mothers of some happy possibility of bacon to their potatoes on some future day ;
he would have seen whole societies where no book is
heard of but the " Newgate Calendar." How do books
act upon the hundreds of thousands of domestic servants,—upon the millions of artisans who cannot sever
the sentences they speak into the words which compose
them,—upon the multitude who work on the soil, the
bean-setters in spring, the mowers in summer, the
reapers in autumn, who cover the broad land ? How
do books act upon the tribe who traverse the seas, obtaining guidance from the stars, and gathering knowledge from every strand ? There is scarcely anything
which does not act more powerfully upon them,—not
a word spoken in their homes, not an act of their
handicraft, not a rumour of the town, not a glimpse
of the green fields. The time will doubtless come
when books will influence the life of such ; but then
this influence will be only one among many, and the
books which will give it forth will hardly be of the
class in which the literary " lion " has an interest.
Meantime, unless he goes abroad, in imagination at
least, from the enchanted circle of which he is, for the
time, the centre, he is in imminent peril, while relaxing in his intellectual toil, of overrating his vocation.

' This, however, is sometimes a preparation for being ashamed of the vocation. Some of the anxiety which popular authors have shown, towards the end of their career, to be considered as gentlemen rather than as authors, is no doubt owing to the desire, in aristocratic England, to be on a par with their admirers in the qualifications which most distinguish *them* : and much also to the universal tendency to depreciate what we possess in longing for something else,—the tendency which inclines so many men of rank to distinguish themselves as authors, statesmen, or even sportsmen, while authors and legislators are struggling for rank. But there can be no doubt that the subsidence of enthusiasm, which must sooner or later follow the excitement caused by popular authorship, the mortifications which succeed the transports of popularity, have a large share in producing the desire of aristocratic station, the shame of their vocation, by which some favourites of the drawing-room cast a shadow over their own fame. Johnson says of Congreve—" But he treated the muses with ingratitude ; for, having long conversed familiarly with the great, he wished to be considered rather as a man of fashion than of wit ; and when he received a visit from Voltaire, disgusted him by the despicable foppery of desiring to be considered, not as an author, but a gentleman : to which the Frenchman replied, ' that if he had been only a gentleman, he should not have come to visit him.' "

' He must be a strong man who escapes all the pitfalls into this tomb of ambition and of powers. He must have not only great force of intellect to advance amidst such hindrances, but a fine moral vigour to

hold the purpose of his life amidst the voices which
are crying to him all the way up the mountain of his
toil ; syren voices, in which he must have an accurate
ear to discover that there is little of the sympathy he
needs, however much of the blandishment that he
cannot but distrust.

' To any one strong enough to stand it, however,
the experience of literary " lionism " yields much that
is worth having. If authorship be the accomplishment of early and steady aspiration ; if the author
feels that it is the business of his life to think and say
what he thinks, while he is far from supposing it the
business of other people's lives to read what he says:
if he holds to his aim, regarding the patronage of
fashion and the flattery of the crowd only as a piece
of his life, like a journey abroad, or a fit of sickness,
or a legacy, or any thing which makes him feel for the
time, without having any immediate connexion with
the chief interest of his existence, he is likely to profit
rather than suffer by his drawing-room reputation.
Some essential conditions must be observed. It is
essential that his mind should not be spent and dissi-
pated amidst a crowd of pleasures ; that his social engagements should not interfere with his labours of the
study. He must keep his morning hours (and they
must be many) not only free but bright. He must
have ready for them a clear head and a light heart.
His solitude must be true solitude while it lasts, un-
profaned by the intrusions of vanities, (which are
cares in masquerade) and undisturbed by the echoes
of applause. It is essential that he should be active
in some common business of life, not dividing the
whole of his time between the study and the drawing-

room, and so confining himself to the narrow world of
books and readers.'

*   *   *   *   *   *   *   *

' A man so seriously devoted to an object is not
likely to find himself the guest of the coarsest perpe-
trators of " lionism." He is not likely to accept the
hospitality on condition of being made a show; but he
need not part with his good humour. Those who give
feasts, and hire the talents of their neighbours to
make those feasts agreeable, are fulfilling their little
part,—are doing what they are fit for, and what might
be expected of them, as the dispensers of intellectual
feasts are doing *their* part in bringing together beauty
and attraction from the starry skies, and the green
earth, and the acts and thoughts of men. When once
it is discerned that it is useless to look for the grapes
and figs of these last among the thorns and thistles of
the first, the whole matter is settled. Literary " lionism " is a sign of the times ; and it is the function of
certain small people to exhibit it ; and there is an end.
Neither it nor they are to be quarrelled with for what
cannot be helped.

' It will be hard upon the author faithful to his
vocation, and it will be strange, if some valuable
friendships do not arise out of the intercourses of
the drawing-room where his probation goes forward.
This is one of the advantages which his popularity,
however temporary, is likely to leave behind. He is
likely, moreover, to shake off a few prejudices, educational, or engendered in the study. He can hardly
fail to learn something of the ways of thinking and
feeling of new classes of persons, or orders of minds
before unknown. He is pretty sure, also, to hear

much that is said in his own dispraise that would never have reached him in retirement; and this kind of information has great weight, if not great virtue, with every one; not only because there is almost invariably some truth involved in every censure, but because most people agree with Racine in his experience, that an adverse criticism gives ·more pain than the extremest applause can afford pleasure. These things constitute altogether a great sum of advantages, in addition to the enjoyments of relaxation and kindly intercourse which are supposed to be the attributes of all social assemblages. If many small wits and feeble thinkers have been extinguished by the system of literary "lionism," it may be hoped that some few have taken what is good and left what is bad in it, deriving from their exposure to it an improved self-reliance and fresh intellectual resources.

' Many are the thousands who have let the man die within them from cowardly care about meat and drink, and a warm corner in the great asylum of safety, whose gates have ever been thronged by the multitude who cannot appreciate the free air and open heaven. And many are the hundreds who have let the poet die within them that their complacency may be fed, their vanity intoxicated, and themselves securely harboured in the praise of their immediate neighbours. Few, very few are they who, "noble in reason," and conscious of being "infinite in faculties," have faith to look before and after,—faith to go on to " reverence the dreams of their youth,"—faith to appeal to the godlike human mind yet unborn,—the mind which the series of coming centuries is to reveal. Among the millions who are now thinking and feeling on our own soil, is it likely that there is not one who might take up the song of Homer,—not one who might talk the night away with Socrates,—not one who might be the Shakspere of an age when our volcanoes shall have become regions of green pasture and still waters, and new islands shall send forth human speech from the midst of the sea? What are such men about? If one is pining in want, rusting in ignorance, or turning from angel to devil under oppression, it is too probable that another may be undergoing extinction in the drawing-rooms,—surrendering his divine faculties to wither in lamp-light, and be wafted away in perfume and praise. As surely as the human thought has power to fly abroad over the expanse of a thousand years, it has need to rest on that far shore, and meditate, " Where now are the flatteries, and vanities, and competitions, which seemed so important in their day? Where are the ephemeral reputations, the glow-worm ideas, the gossamer sentiments, which the impertinent voice of Fashion pronounced immortal and divine? The deluge of oblivion has swept over them all, while the minds which were really immortal and divine are still there, ' for ever singing as they shine' in the firmament of thought, and mirrored in the deep of ages out of which they rose." ' *

Among the traits from the life is that paragraph of the foregoing extracts about the pedantry of the 'superior people' of a provincial town. Norwich, which has now no claims to social superiority at all, was in my childhood a rival of Lichfield itself, in the

* London and Westminster Review, No. LXIII. April, 1839.

time of the Sewards, for literary pretension and the vulgarity of pedantry. William Taylor was then at his best; when there was something like fulfilment of his early promise, when his exemplary filial duty was a fine spectacle to the whole city, and before the vice which destroyed him had coarsened his *morale,* and drowned his intellect. During the war, it was a great distinction to know any thing of German literature; and in Mr. Taylor's case it proved a ruinous distinction. He was completely spoiled by the flatteries of shallow men, pedantic women, and conceited lads. We girls had the advantage. We could listen and amuse ourselves, without being called upon to take any part; and heartily amused we often were, after the example of our mother. When she went to Norwich, a bonny young bride, with plenty of sense and observation, and a satirical turn, and more knowledge, even of books, than the book people gave her credit for, she used to carry home her own intense amusement from the supper-tables of the time, and keep her good stories alive till we were old enough to enjoy them. We took our cue from her; and the blue-stocking ladies who crammed themselves from reviews and publishers' lists in the morning to cut a figure in the evening, as conversant with all the literature of the day, were little aware how we children were noting all their vanities and egotisms, to act them to-morrow in our play. The lady who cleared her throat to obtain a hearing for her question whether Mr. William Taylor had read the charming anecdote of the Chinese Emperor Chim-Cham-Chow, was a capital subject for us: and so was another who brought out her literary observations amidst an incessant complacent purring: and so was

another who sported youthful vivacity, and political
enthusiasm with her scanty skirts and uncovered head
to past seventy. These and many more barely condescended to notice my mother, (who, in genuine
ability, was worth them all,) except in her quality
of hostess. The gentlemen took wine with her, and
the ladies ate her fricassees and custards; but they
talked vile French in her presence, knowing that she
did not understand it, and that the foreigner they had
caught could speak English very well. This sort of
display, and the contrast which struck us whenever we
chanced to meet with genuine superiority, was no doubt
of service to us, as a preparation for the higher kind
of life which we were afterwards to work out for ourselves. It enabled me, for one, to see, twenty years
later, that there is no essential difference between
the extreme case of a cathedral city and that of literary
London, or any other place, where dissipation takes
the turn of book talk instead of dancing or masquer-
ading.

Among the mere pedants were some who were
qualified for something better. Such women as Mrs.
Opie and Mrs. John Taylor ought to have been
superior to the nonsense and vanity in which they
participated. I do not remember Dr. Sayers; and I
believe he died before I could possibly remember him;
but I always heard of him as a genuine scholar; and I
have no doubt he was superior to his neighbours in
modesty and manners. Dr. Enfield, a feeble and
superficial man of letters, was gone also from these
literary supper-tables before my time. There was Sir
James Smith, the botanist,—made much of, and
really not pedantic and vulgar, like the rest, but weak

and irritable. There was Dr. Alderson, Mrs. Opie's
father, solemn and sententious and eccentric in manner,
but not an able man in any way. William Taylor
was managed by a regular process,—first, of feeding,
then of wine-bibbing, and immediately after of poking
to make him talk : and then came his sayings, de-
voured by the gentlemen, and making ladies and
children aghast ;—defences of suicide, avowals that
snuff alone had rescued him from it : information given
as certain, that ' God save the King ' was sung by
Jeremiah in the temple of Solomon,—that Christ
was watched on the day of his supposed ascension,
and observed to hide himself till dusk, and then to
make his way down the other side of the mountain; and
other such plagiarisms from the German Rationalists.
When William Taylor began with ' I firmly believe,'
we knew that something particularly incredible was
coming. We escaped without injury from hearing
such things half a dozen times in a year ; and from a
man who was often seen to have taken too much wine:
and we knew, too, that he came to our house because
he had been my father's schoolfellow, and because
there had always been a friendship between his excellent mother and our clan. His virtues as a son were
before our eyes when we witnessed his endurance of
his father's brutality of temper and manners, and his
watchfulness in ministering to the old man's comfort
in his infirmities. When we saw, on a Sunday morning, William Taylor guiding his blind mother to
chapel, and getting her there with her shoes as clean
as if she had crossed no gutters in those flint-paved
streets, we could forgive any thing that had shocked
or disgusted us at the dinner-table. But matters grew
worse in his old age, when his habits of intemperance

kept him out of the sight of ladies, and he got round
him a set of ignorant and conceited young men, who
thought they could set the world right by their
destructive propensities.   One of his chief favourites
was George Borrow, as George Borrow has himself
given the world to understand.   When this polyglot
gentleman appeared before the public as a devout
agent of the Bible Society in foreign parts, there was
one burst of laughter from all who remembered the
old Norwich days.   At intervals, Southey came to see
his old friend, William Taylor: and great was the
surprise that one who became such a bigot on paper,
in religion and politics, could continue the friend of so
wild a rover in those fields as William Taylor, who
talked more blasphemy, and did more mischief to
young men (through his entire lack of conviction and
earnestness and truth-speaking) than the Hones and
Carliles and others whom Southey abhorred as emis-
saries of Satan.   After reading Southey's Life and
Correspondence, the maintenance of that friendship
appears to me more singular than when we young
people used to catch a glimpse in the street of the
author of ' Thalaba ' and 'Kehama.' The great days of
the Gurneys were not come yet.   The remarkable
family from which issued Mrs. Fry, and Priscilla and
Joseph John Gurney, were then a set of dashing young
people,—dressing in gay riding habits and scarlet
boots, as Mrs. Fry told us afterwards, and riding
about the country to balls and gaieties of all sorts.
Accomplished and charming young ladies they were ;
and we children used to overhear some whispered
gossip about the effects of their charms on heart-
stricken young men : but their final characteristics
were not yet apparent.

There was one occasional apparition which kept
alive in us a sense of what intellectual superiority
ought to be and to produce. Mrs. Barbauld came to
Norwich now and then; and she always made her
appearance presently at our house. In her early
married life, before the happiness of the devoted wife
was broken up by her gentle husband's insanity, she
had helped him in his great school at Palgrave in
Suffolk, by taking charge of the very little boys.
William Taylor and my father had stood at her knee
with their slates; and when they became men, and
my father's children were older than he was when she
first knew him, she retained her interest in him, and
extended it to my mother and us. It was a remarkable day for us when the comely elderly lady in her
black silk cloak and bonnet came and settled herself
for a long morning chat. She used to insist on holding skeins of silk for my mother to wind, or on
winding, while one of us children was the holder:
and well I remember her gentle lively voice, and the
stamp of superiority on all she said. We knew she
was very learned, and we saw she was graceful, and
playful, and kindly and womanly: and we heard with
swelling hearts the anecdotes of her heroism when in
personal danger from her husband's hallucinations, and
when it was scarcely possible to separate her from him,
when her life and his poor chance of restoration required it. I still think her one of the first of writers
in our language, and the best example we have of the
benefits of a sound classical education to a woman.
When I was old enough to pass a few weeks with my
aunt Lee, at Stoke Newington, I went more than once
with my aunt to Mrs. Barbauld's to tea, and was

almost confounded at the honour of being allowed to
make tea.   It was owing to her that I had one literary
acquaintance when I went to London in 1832.   Miss
Aikin, niece of Mrs. Barbauld, came to Norwich now
and then, and was well-known to my mother: and
when I was in the City Road in that memorable
spring of the success of the Prize Essays, my mother
gave me a letter of introduction to Miss Aikin,
then living at Hampstead.   She received me with
kindness at once, and with distinction when the
Prize Essays had come under her eye.   When my
Series was struggling for publication, I sent her my
prospectus.   She returned a bare message of acknowledgment.   This rather surprised me; and it was not
till some years afterwards that I learned how the
matter was.   The anecdote is so creditable to her
candour, that it ought to be told.   Naturally regarding
me as a youngster, as my friendly elderly critics always
did, even when I was long past thirty, she was so
struck with the presumption of the enterprise that she
thought it her duty to rebuke me for it.   She accordingly wrote a letter which she showed to her literary
friends, informing me that I could have no idea how
far beyond any powers of mine was such a scheme;
that large information, an extensive acquaintance with
learned persons and with affairs, &c., &c., were indispensable; and that she counselled me to burn my
prospectus and programme, and confine myself to
humbler tasks, such as a young woman might be competent to.   Those who saw the letter admired it much,
and hoped I should have the grace to thank my stars
that I had so faithful a friend, to interpose between me
and exposure.   She hesitated, however, about sending

it ; and she put off the act till my success was decided
and notorious. She then burned the letter, and herself told the story with capital grace,—felicitating
herself on her having burned the letter, instead of me
on being the object of it. I heard unintelligible references to this letter, from time to time, and did not
know what they meant, till the complete story, as told
by herself, was repeated to me, after the lapse of years.
—She rendered me a real service, about the time of
the burning of the letter. Her friend, Mr. Hallam,
found fault at her house with two statements of mine
about the operation of the law or custom of primo-
geniture ; and she begged of him to make known his
criticisms to me, and told me she had done so,—
being assured that such an authority as Mr. Hallam
would be fitly honoured by me. I was grateful, of
course ; and I presently received a long letter of pretty
sharp criticism from Mr. Hallam. In my reply,
I submitted myself to him about one point, but stood
my ground in regard to the other,—successfully, as
he admitted. He wrote then a very cordial letter,—
partly of apology for the roughness of his method, by
which he had desired to ascertain whether I could bear
criticism, and partly to say that he hoped he might
consider our correspondence a sufficient introduction,
authorising Mrs. Hallam and himself to call on me.
He was from that time forward, and is now, one of the
most valued of my literary friends. One more transaction, however, was to take place before I could make
him and Miss Aikin quite understand what my intentions and views were in indulging myself with the
benefits and pleasures of literary society in London.

Mr. Hallam one day called, when, as it was the first

of the month, my table was spread with new periodicals, sent me by publishers. I was not in the room when Mr. Hallam entered ; and I found him with the 'Monthly Repository' in his hands, turning over the leaves. He pointed to the Editor's name (Mr. Fox) on the cover, and asked me some questions about him. After turning over, and remarking upon a few others, he sat down for a chat. A few days after, I received a note from Miss Aikin, kindly congratulating me on my 'success, thus far, in society,' and on my 'honours' generally; and then admonishing me that the continuance of such 'success' and such 'honours' would depend on my showing due deference to the opinions and standing of persons older and more distinguished than myself; so that she felt it was an act of friendship to warn me against appearing to know of periodicals so low as, for instance, the 'Monthly Repository,' and having any information to give about dissenting ministers, like Mr. Fox.

I replied without loss of time, that there might be no more mistake as to my views in going into society. I thanked her for her kindness and her frankness : told her that I objected to the word 'success,' as she had used it, because success implies endeavour ; and I had nothing to strive for in any such direction. I went into society to learn and to enjoy, and not to obtain suffrages : and I hoped to be as frank and unrestrained with others as I wished them to be with me. I told her how I perceived that Mr. Hallam was her informant, and by what accident it was that he saw the periodical, and heard about its editor ; but I said that I was a dissenter, and acquainted with dissenting ministers, and should certainly never deny it, when

asked, as I was by Mr. Hallam, or object to all the
world knowing it. Once for all, I concluded, I had
no social policy, and no personal aims; no conceal-
ments, nor reasons for compromise. Society was very
pleasant; but it would cease to be so from the moment
that it was any thing but a simple recreation from
work, accepted without the restraint of politic conditions. She took my reply in good part; was somewhat aghast at my not being 'destroyed' by hostile
reviews, when she trembled at the prospect of favourable ones of her own books; but was always gracious
and kind when we met,—which seldom happened,
however, when she grew old and I had left London.

Mr. Hallam's call opened to me a curious glimpse
into some of the devices of this same London literary
society. He told me that if I had not considered our
correspondence a sufficient introduction, we should yet
have become acquainted,—his friend, Dr. ——, having
promised him an introduction. I laughed, and said
there must be some mistake, as Dr. —— was an
entire stranger to me. Mr. Hallam's surprise was
extreme: Dr. —— had told him we were relations,
and had spoken as if we were quite intimate. I replied that there was a very distant connexion by
marriage; but that we were utter strangers; and in
fact, I had never seen Dr. ——. I was less amazed
than Mr. Hallam at the stroke of policy on the part
of a courtier-like London physician, and was amused
when Mr. Hallam said he must learn from him where
the mistake lay. My new friends had not been gone
half an hour, when up drove Dr. — –. In the presence of other visitors, he took my hand in both his,
in true family style, and lavished much affection

upon me,—though he had never recognised my existence during any former visits of mine to London.
The excess of his humility in asking me to dinner
was shocking. He, a physician in immense practice,
entreated me to name my own day and hour, which
I, of course, declined. When I went, on the first
disengaged day, I met a pleasant, small party, and
enjoyed the day,—except its close, when my host, not
only led me through all the servants in the hall, but
leaned into my hackney-coach to thank me for the
honour, &c., &c. This kind of behaviour was very
disagreeable to me ; and I never went to the house
again but once. My mother and I were incessantly
invited ; and we really could not go because the invitations were short, and I was always engaged : but
I was not very sorry, remembering the beginning of
our acquaintance.—The one other time that I visited
Dr. ----- was the occasion of an incident of which it
may be worth while to give a true version, as a false
one was industriously spread. I have said above,
that there were three persons only to whom I have
refused to be introduced; and two of these have been
seen to be Mr. Lockhart and Mr. Sterling. The
third was the poet Moore. One day my mother was
distressed at finding in the 'Times' a ribald song
addressed to me. She folded it in the innermost part
of the paper, and hoped, as I was in the country that
morning, that I should not see it. The event showed
her that it would not do to conceal any thing of the
sort from me, as I could not conduct my own peculiar
case without knowing as much of the circumstances
of it as other people. The song was copied every
where, and ascribed so positively to Moore that I was

compelled to suppose it his, though there was not a
trace of wit to redeem its coarseness.   At Dr. ——'s
party, a few nights after, the host came to me
to say that Mr. Rogers and Mr. Moore had come
for the purpose of making my acquaintance: and
Mr. Moore was standing within earshot, waiting
for his introduction.   I was obliged to decide in
a moment what to do; and I think what I did
was best, under such a difficulty.   I said I should
be happy to be honoured by Mr. Rogers's acquaintance; but that, if Mr. Moore was, as was generally
understood, the author of a recent insult to me in the
'Times' newspaper, I did not see how I could permit
an introduction.   I added that there might be a mistake about the authorship; in which case I should be
happy to know Mr. Moore.   Dr. —— was, of course,
very uncomfortable.   Having seated Mr. Rogers beside me, he and Moore left the room together for a
little while.   When they returned, Moore went to the
piano, and sang several songs.   Then, he screened his
little person behind a lady's harp; and all the time she
was playing, he was studying me through his eye-
glass.   When she finished her piece he went away to
another party, where a friend of mine happened to be;
and there he apologised for being late, on the plea that
he had been 'singing songs to Harriet Martineau.'
The story told was that I had asked Dr. —— to introduce us, and had then declined.   The incident was, in
one sense, a trifle not worth dwelling on: but in another view, it was important to me.   At the outset of
so very new a course of life, it seemed to me necessary
to secure personal respect by the only means in a
woman's power;—refusing the acquaintance of per-

sons who have publicly outraged consideration and propriety. My mother thought me right; and so did the other friends who witnessed the transaction: and it was effectual. I never had any trouble of the sort again.

The first sight of Brougham, then just seated on the wool-sack, and the object of all manner of expectation which he never fulfilled, was an incident to be remembered. I had not previously shared the general expectation of great national benefits from him. I believed that much of his effort for popular objects, even for education, was for party and personal purposes; and that he had no genuine popular sympathy, or real desire that the citizens at large should have any effectual political education. I distrusted his steadiness, and his disinterestedness, and his knowledge of the men and interests of his own time. I believed him too vain and selfish, and too low in morals and unrestrained in temper, to turn out a really great man when his day of action came. Many a time has my mother said to me, 'Harriet, you will have much to answer for for speaking as you do if Brougham turns out what the rest of us expect:' to which my answer was, 'Yes, Mother, indeed I shall.' She was at length very glad that I was not among the disappointed. Yet, there was a strong interest in meeting for the first time, and on the safe ground of substantial business, the man of whom I had heard so much from my childhood, and who now had more power over the popular welfare than perhaps any other man in the world. After two or three interviews, he was so manifestly wild, that the old interest was lost in pity and dislike; but at first I knew nothing of the manifestations of eccentricity which he presently made public enough. Those

were the days when he uttered from the platform his
laments over his folly in accepting a peerage, and
when he made no secret to strangers who called on
him on business, of his being 'the most wretched
man on earth.' But I first met him when nothing of
the sort had taken place so publicly but that his
adorers and toadies could conceal it.

A day or two after my arrival in London, I met
him at dinner at the house of the correspondent of his
through whom he engaged me to help in poor-law
reform. By his desire no one else was asked. The
first thing that struck me was his being not only
nervous, but thin-skinned to excess. Our hostess's
lap-dog brought out the nervousness immediately, by
jumping up at his knee. He pretended to play with
Gyp, but was obviously annoyed that Gyp would not
be called away. He was not accustomed to lap-dogs,
it was clear. Before we went to dinner, I could not
but see how thin-skinned he was. The 'Examiner'
newspaper lay on the table; and it chanced to contain,
that week, an impertinent article, warning me against
being flattered out of my own aims by my host, who
was Brougham's cat's-paw. The situation was sufficiently awkward, it must be owned. Brougham did
not read the article now, because he had seen it at
home : but I saw by glances and pointings that the
gentlemen were talking it over, while my hostess
and I were consulting about her embroidery : and
Brougham looked, not only very black upon it, but
evidently annoyed and stung. He looked black in
another sense, I remember,—not a morsel of his dress
being anything but black, from the ridge of his stock
to the toes of his polished shoes. Not an inch of white-

was there to relieve the combined gloom of his dress and complexion. He was curiously afraid of my trumpet,* and managed generally to make me hear without. He talked excessively fast, and ate fast and prodigiously, stretching out his long arm for any dish he had a mind to, and getting hold of the largest spoons which would dispatch the most work in the shortest time. He watched me intently and incessantly when I was conversing with any body else. For my part, I liked to watch him when he was conversing with gentlemen, and his mind and its manifestations really came out. This was never the case, as far as my observation went, when he talked with ladies. I believe I have never met with more than three men, in the whole course of my experience, who talked with women in a perfectly natural manner; that is, precisely as they talked with men : but the difference in Brougham's case was so great as to be disagreeable. He knew many cultivated and intellectual women ; but this seemed to be of no effect. If not able to assume with them his ordinary manner towards silly women, he was awkward and at a loss. This was by no means agreeable, though the sin of his bad manners must be laid at the door of the vain women who discarded their ladyhood for his sake, went miles to see him, were early on platforms where he was to be, and admitted him to very broad flirtations. He had pretty nearly settled his own business, in regard to conversation with ladies, before two more years were over. His swearing became so incessant, and the occasional indecency

* I then used a caoutchouc tube, with a cup at one end for the speaker to speak into. It was a good exchange when I laid this aside in favour of a trumpet with which the speaker had no concern.

of his talk so insufferable, that I have seen even
coquettes and adorers turn pale, and the lady of the
house tell her husband that she could not undergo another dinner-party with Lord Brougham for a guest.
I, for my part, determined to decline quietly henceforth any small party where he was expected; and this
simply because there was no pleasure in a visit where
every body was on thorns as to what any one guest
might say and do next. My own impression that day
was that he was either drunk or insane. Drunk he
was not; for he had been publicly engaged in business
till the last moment. All manner of protestations
have been made by his friends, to this day, that he is,
with all his eccentricities, ' sane enough :' but my
impression remains that no man who conducted himself as he did that summer day in 1834 could be sane
and sober.

I remember now, with no little emotion, a half hour
of my visit at Lambton Castle, a few months before
that uncomfortable dinner. One evening, when a
guest, Lord H——, had been talking with me about
some matters of popular interest which led us to discuss the Society for the Diffusion of Useful Knowledge,
Lord Durham invited me to the room where music
was going on, and where we could not be overheard.
He asked me whether Lord H—— had understood
me right, that the surest way *not* to reach the people
was to address them through the Society, and by the
agency of the Whig managers. I replied that I had
said so; and I told him why, giving him evidence of
the popular distrust of Lord Brougham and his teaching and preaching clique. Lord Durham heard me
with evident concern, and said at last, in his earnest,

heart-felt way,—' Brougham has done, and will do,
foolish things enough : but it would cut me to the
heart to think that Brougham was false.' The words
and the tone were impressed on my mind by the contrast which they formed with the way in which
Brougham and his toadies were in the habit of speaking of Lord Durham. Brougham's envy and jealousy
of the popular confidence enjoyed by Lord Durham at
that time were notorious. If Lord Durham was unaware of it, he was the only person who was. I need
not continue the story which is remembered by every
body of my own generation, and which the next may
read in the records of the time,—the Grey dinner
at Edinburgh when Lord Durham involuntarily
triumphed,—the attack on him at Salisbury and in a
traitorous article in the Edinburgh Review, which
revealed Cabinet secrets,—the challenge and anticipated encounter of the two noblemen on the floor of
the House of Lords,—and the terror of the feeble
King, who dissolved parliament to preclude the encounter, deprived Brougham of the Seals, and sent Lord
Durham on a foreign mission. I need not tell over
again the terrible story of the triumph of Brougham's
evil passions, in perilling the safety, and overthrow-
ing the government of Canada, and in destroying the
career and breaking the heart of the generous, sensitive,
honest and magnanimous statesman whom he chose to
consider his enemy. It was as much as I could well
bear to contrast the tones of the two men and their
adherents before Lord Durham knew that there was
anything wrong between them ; and when the dismal
story proceeded, my heart swelled, many a time, when
I recalled the moment of Lord Durham's first recep-

tion of a doubt of Brougham's honesty, and the serious countenance and sweet voice of remonstrance in which he said 'It would cut me to the heart to think that Brougham was false.' In seven years from that time he was in his grave,—sent there by Brougham's falseness.

With Brougham, his ancient comrades were naturally associated in the mind of one who knew them only through books and newspapers. I saw much of Jeffrey, and the Murrays, and Sydney Smith. My first sight of Jeffrey was odd enough in its circumstances. It makes me laugh to think of it now. My mother was with me in my second-floor lodgings in my first London winter. It happened to be my landlady's cleaning day; and the stair-carpets were up, and the housemaid on her knees, scouring, when Mrs. Marcet and Lord Jeffrey made their way as they could between the pail and the bannisters. While Mrs. Marcet panted for breath enough to introduce us, Jeffrey stood with his arms by his side and his head depressed,— the drollest spectacle of mock humility :—and then he made some solemn utterance about 'homage,' &c., to which I replied by asking him to sit down. Almost before we had well begun to talk, in burst Mrs. A——, a literary woman whose ways were well known to my mother and me. The moment she saw Lord Jeffrey, she forgot to speak to us, but so thrust herself between Lord Jeffrey and me as actually to push me backwards and sit on my knee. I extricated myself as soon as possible, and left my seat. As she turned her back on me, my mother cast a droll glance at me which I fancy Lord Jeffrey saw; for, though one of the most egregious flatterers of this lady,—as

of vain women in general,—he played her off in a
way which she must have been very complacent not
to understand. He showed that he wanted to talk to
me, and said, when he saw she was determined to go
away with him, that he considered this no visit, and
would, if I pleased, come again on the first practicable day. I am convinced that he discovered in that
short interview what my mother and I felt about the
ways of literary people like Mrs. A——; and, though
he could not easily drop, in any one case, his habit of
flattery, he soon found that I did not like it, did not
believe in it, and thought the worse of him for it. I
never made any secret of my opinion of the levity,
cruelty and unmanliness of literary men who aggravate the follies, and take advantage of the weakness
of vain women; and this was Jeffrey's most conspicuous
and very worst fault. As for my mother and me, we
had a hearty laugh over this little scene, when our visitors were gone ; it was so very like old Norwich, in the
days of the suppers of the ' superior people ! '

Whatever there might be of artificial in Jeffrey's
manners,—of a set ' company state of mind ' and
mode of conversation,—there was a warm heart
underneath, and an ingenuousness which added cap-
tivation to his intellectual graces. He could be absurd enough in his devotion to a clever woman ; and
he could be highly culpable in drawing out the
vanity of a vain one, and then comically making game
of it ; but his better nature was always within call ;
and his generosity was unimpeachable in every other
respect,—as far as I knew him. His bounties to
needy men of letters,—bounties which did not stop
to make ill-timed inquiries about desert,—were so

munificent, that the world, which always knew him to be generous, would be amazed at the extent of the munificence : and it was done with so much of not only delicacy but respect,—in such a hearty love of literature, that I quite understand how easy it would be to accept money from him. If I had needed assistance of that kind, there is no one from whom I could more freely have asked it.—As for his conversation, it appeared to me that he cared more for moralising than any other great converser I have known : but this might be adaptation to my likings; and I heard none of his conversation but what was addressed to myself.   I must say that while I found (or perceived) myself regarded as romantic, high-flown, extravagant, and so forth by good Mr. Empson, and the Jeffrey set generally (even including Sydney Smith), whenever I opened my mouth on matters of morals.—such as the aims of authorship, the rights and duties of opinion, the true spirit of citizenship, &c.,—I never failed to find cordial sympathy in Jeffrey. If at times he was more foolish and idle than most men of his power would choose to appear, he was always higher than them all when his moral sympathies and judgment were appealed to.   I remember a small incident which impressed me, in connexion with this view of him ; and, as it relates to him, it may be worth noting.   At one of Mr. Rogers's breakfasts, I was seated between him and his friend Milman, when the conversation turned on some special case (I forget what) of excessive vanity.   I was pitying the person because, whatever flattery he obtained, there was always some censure ; and the smallest censure, to the vain, outweighs the largest amount of praise. Milman

did not think so, saying that the vain are very
happy ;—' no people more apt at making themselves
happy than the vainest : '—' they feed upon their
own praises, and dismiss the censure ; and, having no
heart, they are out of the way of trouble.' I made
the obvious remark that if they have no heart they
cannot be very happy. Jeffrey's serious assent to this,
and remark that it settled the question, discomposed
Milman extremely. He set to work to batter his
egg and devour it without any reply, and did not
speak for some time after. It was amusing that we
two heretics should be administering instruction on
morals to a Church dignitary of such eminence as a
sacred poet as the Dean of St. Paul's.

I have however seen Milman so act, and so preserve
a passive state, as to be a lesson to all present. One
incident especially which happened at Mr. Hallam's
dinner-table, gave me a hearty respect for his command of a naturally irritable temper. He behaved in-
comparably on that occasion. It was a pleasant party
of eight or ten people,—every one, as it happened, of
considerable celebrity, and therefore not to be despised
in the matter of literary criticism, or verdict on character. I was placed near the top of the table, between
Milman and Mr. Rogers; and the subject of animated
conversation at the bottom presently took its turn
among us. Mrs. Trollope's novel, ' Jonathan Jefferson
Whitlaw,' had just come out, and was pronounced on
by every body present but myself,—I not having read
it. As I had lately returned from the United States,
I was asked what Mrs. Trollope's position was there.
My reply was that I had no scruple in saying that
Mrs. Trollope had no opportunity of knowing what

good society was in America, generally speaking. I added that I intended to say this, as often as I was inquired of; for the simple reason that Mrs. Trollope had thought proper to libel and slander a whole nation. If she had been an ordinary discontented tourist, her adventures in America would not be worth the trouble of discussing; but her slanderous book made such exposures necessary. Every body, except Milman, asked questions, and I answered them. She certainly had no admirers among the party when she was first mentioned; and the account I gave of her unscrupulous method of reporting surprised nobody. At last, Milman put in a word for her. He could not help thinking that she had been illused:—he knew facts indeed of her having been taken in about her bazaar. 'No doubt,' said I. 'Any English traveller who begins the game of diamond cut diamond with Yankee speculators is likely to get the worst of it. No doubt she was abundantly cheated; and hence this form of vengeance,—a vituperative book.' Milman continued that he was aware of what hard usage she had to complain of, by his acquaintance with her. He was proceeding when Rogers broke in with one of his odd tentative speeches,—one of those probings by which he seemed to try how much people could bear. 'O yes,' said he; 'he *is* acquainted with Mrs. Trollope. He had the forming of her mind.' There was a moment of dead pause, and then every body burst into a hearty laugh; every body but Milman. He was beginning with a vehement 'No, no;' but he checked himself and said nothing. He had begun to speak on behalf of Mrs. Trollope, and he would not give it up now that Rogers had so

spoken. His high colour and look of distress showed
what his magnanimous silence cost him; but not a
word more did he say. As I expected and hoped, he
called on me the next morning. He often did so, as
we were neighbours; but that morning he came as
soon as the clock had struck two. His first care was
to disclaim having educated Mrs. Trollope, who was,
in fact, about his own age. His mother and hers, I
think, were friends. At all events, he had known her
nearly all his life. He frankly told me now, in the
proper place and time, why he thought Mrs. Trollope
ill-qualified to write travels and describe a nation:
'but,' he continued, 'the thing is done, and can't
be helped now: so that, unless you feel bound in conscience to expose her,—which might be to ruin her,
—I would intercede for her.' Laying his finger on
a proof-sheet of my American book which lay at his
elbow, he went on, 'Can't you, now, say what *you*
think of the same people, and let that be her answer?'
'Why,' exclaimed I, 'you don't suppose I am going
to occupy any of my book with Mrs. Trollope! I
would not dirty my pages with her stories, even to
refute them. What have I to do with Mrs. Trollope
but to say what I know when inquired of?' 'O,
well, that is all right,' said he. 'I took for granted
you meant to do it in your book: and I don't say that
you could be blamed if you did. But if you mean
in conversation, you are certainly quite right, and
Mrs. Trollope herself could have no title to complain.'
I thought the candour, kindness and generosity shown
in this incident quite remarkable; and I have always
recalled it with pleasure.

With Jeffrey his old Edinburgh comrades were

naturally associated, as far as the influences of time
and chance yet permitted. Brougham had before this
withdrawn himself almost entirely from those friends
of his youth. Horner's Life and Correspondence had
not then been published; but I had gathered up
enough about him to see him, in a spiritual sense,
sitting in the midst of them. ' Did you know Horner?'
inquired Sydney Smith. ' You should have known
Horner ; but I suppose he was gone before you were
invented.' With Horner's name the most closely
associated of all was that of John A. Murray (Lord
Murray, who was Lord Advocate when I first knew
him). Of all my acquaintance, no one was a greater
puzzle to me than Horner's beloved John Murray,
whose share of their published correspondence shows
why there were once splendid expectations from him.
His career as Lord Advocate and Judge was so little
successful that the world could not but wonder how
there could be such an issue from such promise.
Jeffrey's failure in political office and as a parliamentary speaker, was easily accounted for by his uncertain
health, his weak voice, his love of ease and literary
trifling, and his eminence in a totally different function : and he ended by being an admirable Judge.
But in the other case, there was no success in any
other direction to account or atone for the failure of
Lord Murray, when opportunity opened before him in
what should have been the vigour of his years. He
was a kind neighbour, however, and a thoroughly good-
hearted man,—always happy to give pleasure, though
reducing the amount he bestowed by a curious little
pomposity of manner. His agreeable wife joined her
efforts with his to make their guests happy, and en-

joyed society as much as he did. When one could once put away the association of Horner and those old Edinburgh days, the Murrays' parties were really delightful. I had a general invitation to their Thursday evenings at St. Stephen's ; and their carriage usually came for me and took me home. They lived at the Lord Advocate's Chambers, under the same roof with the Houses of Parliament; and there, on Thursday evenings during the session, was a long broad table spread, with a prodigious Scotch cake, iced and adorned, on a vast trencher in the midst. Members of both Houses dropped in and out, when the debates were tiresome ; and there were always a few guests like myself, who went on the way to or from other visits, and gathered up the political news of the night, curiously alternating with political anecdotes or Edinburgh jokes of thirty or forty years before. It was pleasant to see the Jeffreys come in when Sydney Smith was there, and to look on these grey-headed friends as the very men who had made such a noise in the days of my childhood, and who were venerable for what they had done and borne in those days, though they had disappointed expectation when their opportunity came at last. It was at Lord Murray's table that Sydney Smith told me of the fun the Edinburgh reviewers used to make of their work. I taxed him honestly with the mischief they had done by their ferocity and cruel levity at the outset. It was no small mischief to have silenced Mrs. Barbauld ; and how much more utterance they may have prevented, there is no saying. It is all very well to talk sensibly now of the actual importance of reviews, and the real value of reviewers' judgments : but the fact remains that spirits were broken, hearts were sickened, and authorship was cruelly discouraged by the savage and reckless condemnations passed by the Edinburgh Review in its early days. 'We *were* savage,' replied Sydney Smith. 'I remember' (and it was plain that he could not help enjoying the remembrance) 'how Brougham and I sat trying one night how we could exasperate our cruelty to the utmost. We had got hold of a poor nervous little vegetarian, who had put out a poor silly little book; and when we had done our review of it, we sat trying,'—(and here he joined his finger and thumb as if dropping from a phial) 'to find one more chink, one more crevice, through which we might drop in one more drop of verjuice, to eat into his bones.' Very candid always, and sometimes very interesting, were the disclosures about the infant Edinburgh Review. In the midst of his jocose talk, Sydney Smith occasionally became suddenly serious, when some ancient topic was brought up, or some life-enduring sensibility touched; and his voice, eye and manner at such times disposed one to tears almost as much as his ordinary discourse did to laughter. Among the subjects which were thus sacred to him was that of the Anti-slavery cause. One evening, at Lord Murray's, he inquired with earnest solicitude about the truth of some news from America, during the 'reign of terror,' as we used to call the early persecution of the abolitionists. As I had received letters and newspapers just before I left home, I could tell him what he wanted to know. He expressed, with manly concern, his sorrow for the sufferings of my friends in America, and feared it must cause me terrible pain. 'Not unmixed pain,' I told him; and then I

explained how well we knew that that mighty question
could be carried only by the long perseverance of the
highest order of abolitionists; and that an occasional
purgation of the body was necessary, to ascertain how
many of even the well-disposed had soundness of principle and knowledge, as well as strength of nerve, to
go through with the enterprise: so that even this
cruel persecution was not a pure evil. He listened
earnestly, and sympathised in my faith in my personal
friends among the abolitionists; and then a merry
thought came into his head, as I saw by the change
in his eye. 'Now, I am surprised at you, I own,'
said he. 'I am surprised at your taste, for yourself
and your friends. I can fancy you enjoying a feather,
(*one* feather) in your cap; but I cannot imagine you
could like a bushel of them down your back with the
tar.'

My first sight of Sydney Smith was when he called
on me, under cover of a whimsical introduction, as he
considered it. At a great music-party, where the drawing-rooms and staircases were one continuous crowd,
the lady who had conveyed me fought her way to my
seat,—which was, in consideration of my deafness,
next to Malibran, and near the piano. My friend
brought a message which Sydney Smith had passed
up the staircase;—that he understood we desired one
another's acquaintance, and that he was awaiting it
at the bottom of the stairs. He put it to my judgment whether I, being thin, could not more easily
get down to him, than he, being stout, could get up to
me: and he would wait five minutes for my answer.
I really could not go, under the circumstances: and it
was a serious thing to give up my seat and the music;

so Mr. Smith sent me a good-night, and promise to
call on me, claiming this negotiation as a proper introduction. He came, and sat down, broad and comfortable, in the middle of my sofa, with his hands on
his stick, as if to support himself in a vast development of voice ; and then he began, like the great bell
of St. Paul's, making me start at the first stroke. He
looked with shy dislike at my trumpet, for which
there was truly no occasion. I was more likely to
fly to the furthest corner of the room. It was always
his boast that I did not want my trumpet when he
talked with me.

I do not believe that any body ever took amiss his
quizzical descriptions of his friends. I am sure I
never did : and when I now recal his fun of that sort,
it seems to me too innocent to raise an uneasy feeling.
There were none, I believe, whom he did not quizz ;
but I never heard of any hurt feelings. He did not
like precipitate speech ; and among the fastest talkers
in England were certain of his friends and acquaintance ;—Mr. Hallam, Mr. Empson, Dr. Whewell, Mr.
Macaulay and myself. None of us escaped his wit.
His account of Mr. Empson's method of out-pouring
stands, without the name, in Lady Holland's Life of
her father. His praise of Macaulay is well known ;—
' Macaulay is improved! Macaulay improves ! I
have observed in him of late,--flashes of silence ! '
His account of Whewell is something more than wit :
—' Science is his forte : omniscience is his foible.'
As for his friend Hallam, he knew he might make
free with his characteristics, of oppugnancy and haste
among others, without offence. In telling us what a
blunder he himself made in going late to a dinner-

party, and describing how far the dinner had proceeded, and how every body was engaged, he said, 'And there was Hallam, with his mouth full of cabbage and contradiction!' Nothing could be droller than his description of all his friends in influenza, in the winter of 1832–3; and of these, Hallam was the drollest of all that I remember. 'And poor Hallam was tossing and tumbling in his bed when the watchman came by and called "Twelve o'clock and a starlight night." Here was an opportunity for controversy when it seemed most out of the question! Up jumped Hallam, with "I question that,—I question that! Starlight! I see a star, I admit; but I doubt whether that constitutes starlight." Hours more of tossing and tumbling; and then comes the watchman again: "Past two o'clock, and a cloudy morning." "I question that,—I question that," says Hallam. And he rushes to the window, and throws up the sash,—influenza notwithstanding. "Watchman! do you mean to call this a cloudy morning? I see a star. And I question its being past two o'clock:—I question it,—I question it!"' And so on. The story of Jeffrey and the North Pole, as told by Sydney Smith, appears to me strangely spoiled in the Life. The incident happened while the Jeffreys were my near neighbours in London; and Mrs. Sydney Smith related the incident to me at the time. Captain (afterwards Sir John) Ross had just returned from an unsuccessful polar expedition, and was bent upon going again. He used all his interest to get the government stirred up to fit out another expedition: and among others, the Lord Advocate was to be applied to, to bespeak his good offices. The mutual friend who undertook to do Captain Ross's errand to Jeffrey arrived at an unfortunate moment. Jeffrey was in delicate health, at that time, and made a great point of his daily ride ; and when the applicant reached his door, he was putting his foot in the stirrup, and did not want to be detained. So he pished and pshawed, and cared nothing for the North Pole, and at length 'damned' it. The applicant spoke angrily about it to Sydney Smith, wishing that Jeffrey would take care what he was about, and use more civil language. 'What do you think he said to me?' cried the complainant. 'Why, he damned the North Pole!' 'Well, never mind! never mind!' said Sydney Smith, soothingly. 'Never mind his damning the North Pole. *I* have heard him speak disrespectfully of the equator.'

Much as I enjoyed the society of both in London, I cared more for the letters of Sydney Smith and Jeffrey during my long llness at Tynemouth than I ever did for their glorious conversation. The air of the drawing-room had some effect on both ; or I believed that it had : but our intercourse when Jeffrey was ill, and I was hopelessly so, and Sydney Smith old and in failing spirits (as he told me frequently) was thoroughly genuine. Sydney Smith wrote me that he hated the pen, now in his old age, when that love of ease was growing on him, common to aged dogs, asses and clergymen ; and his letters were therefore a valuable gift, and, I am sure, duly prized. There was no drawback on intercourse with him except his being a clergyman. To a dissenter like myself, who had been brought up in strict Nonconformist notions of the sacredness of the clerical office, and the absolute unworldliness which was its first requisite, there was

something very painful in the tone always taken by
Sydney Smith about Church matters. The broad
avowals in his 'Letters to Singleton' of the necessity
of having 'prizes' in the Church, to attract gentlemen into it and keep them there ;—his treatment of
the vocation as a provision, a source of honour,
influence, and money, are so offensive as to be really
wonderful to earnest dissenters. His drawing-room
position and manners were not very clerical; but that
did not matter so much as the lowness of view which
proved that he was not in his right place, to those
who, like me, were unaware that the profession was
not his choice. He discharged his duty admirably,
as far as his conscience was concerned, and his nature
would allow : but he had not the spiritual tendencies
and endowments which alone can justify an entrance
into the pastoral office.

He was not quite the only one of my new friends
who did not use my trumpet in conversation. Of all
people in the world, Malthus was the one whom I
heard quite easily without it ;—Malthus, whose speech
was hopelessly imperfect, from defect in the palate. I
dreaded meeting him when invited by a friend of his
who made my acquaintance on purpose. He had told
this lady that he should be in town on such a day, and
entreated her to get an introduction, and call and
invite me ; his reason being that whereas his friends
had done him all manner of mischief by defending
him injudiciously, my tales had represented his views
precisely as he could have wished. I could not decline
such an invitation as this ; but when I considered my
own deafness, and his inability to pronounce half the
consonants in the alphabet, and his hare-lip which

must prevent my offering him my tube, I feared we should make a terrible business of it. I was delightfully wrong. His first sentence,—slow and gentle, with the vowels sonorous, whatever might become of the consonants,—set me at ease completely. I soon found that the vowels are in fact all that I ever hear. His worst letter was *l*: and when I had no difficulty with his question,—'Would not you like to have a look at the Lakes of Killarney?' I had nothing more to fear. It really gratified him that I heard him better than anybody else; and whenever we met at dinner, I somehow found myself beside him, with my best ear next him; and then I heard all he said to every body at table.

Before we had been long acquainted, Mr. and Mrs. Malthus invited me to spend some of the hot weather with them at Haileybury, promising that every facility should be afforded me for work. It was a delightful visit; and the well planted county of Herts was a welcome change from the pavement of London in August. Mr. Malthus was one of the professors of the now expiring College at Haileybury, and Mr. Empson was another: and the families of the other professors made up a very pleasant society,—to say nothing of the interest of seeing in the students the future administrators of India. On my arrival, I found that every facility was indeed afforded for my work. My room was a large and airy one, with a bay-window and a charming view; and the window side of the room was fitted up with all completeness, with desk, books, and every thing I could possibly want. Something else was provided which showed even more markedly the spirit of hospitality. A habit

and whip lay on the bed. My friends had somehow
discovered from my tales that I was fond of riding;
and horse, habit and whip were prepared for me.
Almost daily we went forth when work was done,—a
pleasant riding-party of five or six, and explored all
the green lanes, and enjoyed all the fine views in the
neighbourhood. We had no idea that it would be my
only visit : but Mr. Malthus died while I was in
America; and when I returned his place was filled,
both in College and home. I have been at Haileybury
since, when Professor Jones was the very able successor
of Mr. Malthus in the Chairs of Political Economy and
History; and Mr. Empson lived in the pleasant house
where I had spent such happy days. Now they are all
gone; and the College itself, abolished by the new Char-
ter of the East India Company, will soon be no more
than a matter of remembrance to the present generation, and of tradition to the next. The subdued jests
and external homage and occasional insurrections of
the young men ; the archery of the young ladies ; the
curious politeness of the Persian professor ; the fine
learning and eager scolarship of Principal Le Bas ;
and the somewhat old-fashioned courtesies of the
summer evening parties, are all over now, except as
pleasant pictures in the interior gallery of those who
knew the place,—of whom I am thankful to have
been one.

Mr. Hallam was one of the coterie of whom I have
said so much : and Mr. Whishaw was another ; and
so were his then young friends,—his wards, the
Romillys. The elder Romillys found themselves in
parliament, after the passage of the Reform Bill ; and
Sir John's career since that time speaks for itself.

They had virtuous projects when they entered political
life, and had every hope of achieving service worthy
of their father's fame : but their aspirations were
speedily tamed down,—as all high aspirations *are*
lowered by Whig influences. They were warned by
prudent counsellors to sit silent for a few years in the
presence of their elders in the legislature : and, when
months and years slid away over their silence, they
found it more and more difficult, and at last impossible
to speak. The lawyer brother got over this, of necessity ; but Edward never did. With poor health and
sensitive nerves, and brought up in the very hot-bed
of Whiggism, they could perhaps be hardly expected
to do more ; but hope in them was strong, in the days
of the Reform Bill, and still alive when I left London.
Good old Mr. Whishaw was still fond and proud of
his ' boys,' and still preaching caution while expecting great things from them, when I last saw him. I
met that respected old man at every turn ; and he did
for me the same kind office as Mr. Rogers,—coming
for me, and carrying me home in his carriage. When
the drive was a long one,—as to Hampstead, or even
to Haileybury, there was time for a string of capital
old stories, even at his slow rate of utterance : and he
made me feel as if I had known the preceding generation of Whig statesmen and men of letters. Mr.
Whishaw was not only lame (from the loss of a leg in
early life), but purblind and growing deaf, when I
knew him : but every body was eager to amuse and
comfort him. He sat in the dining-room before dinner, with host or hostess to converse with him till the
rest came down ; and every body took care that he
carried away plenty of conversation. The attentions

of the Romillys to their old guardian were really a beautiful spectacle.

His attached friend, Mr. Hallam, made abundant amends for the slowness of the Whishaw discourse. It would have been a wonderful spectacle, I have sometimes thought, if Hallam, Macaulay and Empson had been induced to talk for a wager ;—in regard to quantity merely, without stopping to think of quality ; while their friends Rogers, Whishaw, and Malthus would have made good counterparts. Mr. Hallam was in the brightest hour of his life when I first knew him. His son Arthur was living and affording the splendid promise of which all have been made aware by Tennyson, in ' In Memoriam.' In a little while, Arthur was gone,—found dead on the sofa by his father, one afternoon during a continental journey. Supposing him to be asleep, after a slight indisposition, Mr. Hallam sat reading for an hour after returning from a walk, before the extraordinary stillness alarmed him. Alone, and far from home, he was in a passion of grief. Few fathers have had such a son to lose ; and the circumstances were singularly painful. —Then, there was the eldest daughter, on his arm at Carlyle's lectures, and the companion of her delightful mother ; she died in just the same way,—on the sofa, after a slight illness, and while her mother was reading to her. She exclaimed ' Stop !' and was dead within five minutes : and when Dr. Holland had come, and found that there was nothing to be done, he had to go in search of the father, who had gone for his walk, and tell him of the new desolation of his home. Not long after, Mrs. Hallam died with equal suddenness ; and now, in his failing age, the affec-

tionate family-man finds himself bereft of all his large
household,—all his ten children gone, except one
married daughter. His works show that, social as he
has always been, he has enjoyed solitary study. I
remember his once making a ludicrous complaint of
London dinners, and of the sameness of the luxuries
he and I saw every day; and he told me his greatest
longing was for a few days of cold beef and leg of
mutton. He was, like most of the set, a capital gossip. Nothing happened that we ladies did not hear
from Whishaw, Empson, or Hallam : and Mr. Hallam
poured it all out with a child-like glee and innocence
which were very droll in a man who had done such
things, and who spent so much of his time between
passing judicial sentences in literature, and attending
councils on politics and the arts with grave statesmen
and with people of the highest rank, to whom he
showed a most solemn reverence. He was apt to say
rash and heedless things in his out-pourings, which
were as amusing as they were awkward. I remember
his blurting out, when seated on a sofa between Mr.
Whishaw and the remarkably plain and literary Miss
——, a joke on somebody's hobbling with a wooden
leg ; and then an observation on Mrs. —— being the
only handsome authoress. (As there were certainly
two who would answer the description, I put no
initials.) Of Mr. Hallam's works I say nothing, because they are fully discussed in the reviews of the
time, by critics far more competent than myself. I
enjoy them singularly ; and especially his ' History of
Literature.' I had a profound respect for him as an
author, long before I ever dreamed of having him for
a friend : and nothing that I ever observed in him

lessened that respect in any degree, while a cordial regard was, I believe, continually growing stronger between us, from the hour of our first meeting till now.
It does not follow that we agreed on all matters of
conduct, any more than of opinion. I could never
sympathise fully with his reverence for people of rank:
and he could not understand my principle and methods
of self-defence against the dangers and disgusts of
'lionism.' For one instance; I never would go to
Lansdowne House, because I knew that I was invited
there as an authoress, to undergo, as people did at that
house, the most delicate and refined process of being
lionised,—but still, the process. The Marquis and
Marchioness of Lansdowne, and a son and daughter,
caused me to be introduced to them at Sir Augustus
Callcott's; and their not being introduced to my
mother, who was with me, showed the footing on
which I stood. I was then just departing for America.
On my return, I was invited to every kind of party at
Lansdowne House,— a concert, a state dinner, a
friendly dinner party, a small evening party, and a
ball; and I declined them all. I went nowhere but
where my acquaintance was sought, as a lady, by
ladies. Mr. Hallam told me,—what was true
enough,—that Lady Lansdowne, being one of the
Queen's ladies, and Lord Lansdowne, being a Cabinet
Minister, could not make calls. If so, it made no
difference in my disinclination to go, in a blue-stocking way, to a house where I was not really acquainted
with any body. Mr. Hallam, I saw, thought me conceited and saucy: but I felt I must take my own
methods of preserving my social independence. Lord
Lansdowne would not give the matter up. Finding

that General Fox was coming one evening to a soirée of mine, he invited himself to dine with him, in order to accompany him.   I thought this somewhat impertinent, while Mr. Hallam regarded it as an honour. I did not see why a nobleman and Cabinet Minister was more entitled than any other gentleman to present himself uninvited, after his own invitations had been declined.   The incident was a trifle ; but it shows how I acted in regard to this ' lionising.'

Mr. Rogers was my neighbour from the time when I went to live in Fludyer Street ; and many were the parties to which he took me in his carriage.   Many also were the breakfasts to which he invited me ;— those breakfasts, the fame of which has spread over the literary world.   I could not often go ;—indeed, scarcely ever,—so indispensable to my work were my morning hours and strength : and when Mr. Rogers perceived this, he asked me to dinner, or in the evening.   But I did occasionally go to breakfast ; and he made it easy by saving me the street passage.   He desired his gardener to leave the garden gate unlocked ; and I merely crossed the park and stepped in through the breakfast-room window.   It was there that, besides my familiar friends, I met some whom I was glad to see after many years' acquaintance through books.   It was there that I met Southey, when he had almost left off coming to London.   He was then indeed hardly fit for society.   It was in the interval between the death of his first wife and his second marriage. He was gentle, kindly and agreeable ; and well disposed to talk of old Norwich, and many things besides.   But there was a mournful expression of countenance, occasionally verging upon the distress of perplexity :

and he faltered for words at times; and once was painfully annoyed at being unable to recover a name or a date, rubbing his head and covering his eyes long before he would give it up. I told my mother, on coming home, that I feared that he was going the way of so many hard literary workers. We were greatly surprised to hear of his marriage, after what I had seen, and some worse indications of failure of which we had heard. The sequel of the story is known to every body.—I met Lord Mahon there (now Lord Stanhope) when his historical reputation was already established; and my agreeable friend Mr. Harness, whom I liked in all ways but as a dramatist. The Milmans used to extol the ' finish ' of his plays ; and the author of ' Fazio' ought to be a far better judge than I ; but, as I told him, it seems to me that spirit is the first thing in a drama, and matter the next; and that ' finish' comes only third, if so soon ; and I could never see or feel beauty and elevation enough in Mr. Harness's plays to make me think it worth his while to write them. But he was one of my very pleasantest acquaintances, for his goodness at home and abroad,—to his sister and niece, to his parishioners, and to his friends in society. With poor health, and literary tastes craving the gratification which was constantly within his reach, he was a devoted parish priest ; and he made duty pleasure, and endurance an enjoyment, or at worst a matter of indifference,—by his cheerful and disinterested temper. He was a fine example of an accomplished gentleman and poet in the Church, who did his clerical duty to the utmost, and with simplicity, while as agreeable a man of the world as you could meet. I never could fully enter into his dramatic propensities and enthusiasms, any more than into Mr. Dicken's,—in both which cases the drama seems to have drawn to itself an unaccountable amount of thought and interest; but the fault is probably in me,—that I cannot extend my worship of Shakspere so as to take an interest in all forms of dramatic presentment, as these two of my friends do. To me Shakspere is so much of a poet as to be supreme and sole as a dramatist: and they probably appreciate him better than I do, and prove it by loving meaner labours and productions for his sake. Considering that Göthe had the same preponderant taste, I can have no doubt that it is a case of deficiency in me, and not of eccentricity in them.

The Whig dinners of that day were at their highest point of agreeableness. The Queen on her accession found her ministers ' a set of pleasant fellows,' as was well understood at the time;—gentlemen of literary accomplishments, to a moderate extent, which seemed very great to her, accustomed as she had been to such society as her uncles had got about them. The Whigs were in the highest prosperity and briskness of spirits at the time when I first knew them,—in the freshness of power under the declining old King, who had not got out of humour with them, as he did after Brougham's pranks in the autumn of 1834. And then again they were in high feather, after the Queen's accession, before they had arrived at presuming on their position, and while some vestiges of modesty remained among some of them. On returning to London a good many years later, I found a melancholy change which had occurred precisely through their desire that there should be no change at all. I found some who

had formerly been 'pleasant fellows' and agreeable
ladies, now saying the same things in much the same
manner as of old, only with more conceit and contempt
of every body but themselves.   Their pride of station
and office had swelled into vulgarity; and their blind-
ness in regard to public opinion and the progress of
all the world but themselves was more wonderful than
ever.   All that I have seen of late years has shown
me that in those pleasant dinners I saw the then
leading society in literary London to the utmost advantage ;—a privilege which I certainly enjoyed exceedingly.

My place was generally between some one of the
notabilities and some rising barrister.   From the
latter I could seldom gather much,—so bent were
all the rising barristers I met on knowing my views on
'the progress of education and the increase of crime.'
I was so weary of that eternal question that it was a
drawback on the pleasure of many a dinner-party.   In
1838, I went a journey of some weeks into the Lake
district and Scotland, with a party of friends,—some
of whom were over-worked like myself.   We agreed
to banish all topics connected with public affairs and
our own labours, and to give ourselves up to refreshment, without any thought of improvement.   We
arrived at Fort William, where the inn was over-
crowded with passengers for the Loch Ness steamer,
in the evening, so tired that we (and I, especially)
could scarcely keep awake till our room (where all the
ladies of our party were to be lodged somehow,) was
prepared.   Mr. P——, our leader, very properly
brought in a gentleman who could not find a place to
sit down in, to have tea with us.   My companions,

seeing me drooping with sleep, did their utmost to
seat him at the opposite side of the table : but he
seized a stool, forced himself in next me, and instantly
began (rising barrister as he was) to ask my opinion
on the progress of education and the increase of crime
in Scotland. I had no clear idea what I replied : but
my companions told me, with inextinguishable laughter, after our guest was gone, that I had informed him
that I knew nothing of those matters, and had made
no inquiry, because we had all agreed before we left
home that we would not improve our minds. They
said that his stare of astonishment was a sight to be
remembered.—In my London days Lord Campbell
was ' Plain John Campbell : ' but plain John was
wonderfully like the present Lord :—facetious, in and
out of place, politic, flattering to an insulting degree,
and prone to moralising in so trite a way as to be almost as insulting. He was full of knowledge, and
might have been inexhaustibly entertaining if he could
have forgotten his prudence and been natural. When
his wife, Lady Stratheden, was present, there was some
explanation of both the worldly prudence and the behaviour to ladies,—as if they were spoiled children,
—which plain John supposed would please them.
Others were there, Judges then or since,—the Parkes,
the present Lord Chancellor Cranworth, the then Lord
Chancellor Brougham, Coltman, Crompton, Romilly,
Alderson ; (not Talfourd, who was then only a rising
barrister, and not yet seen among the literary Whigs).

There were a few bishops;—Whately, with his odd,
overbearing manners, and his unequal conversation,—
sometimes rude and tiresome, and at other times full
of instruction, and an occasional drollery coming out

amidst a world of effort. Perhaps no person of all my
acquaintance has from the first appeared to me so singularly over-rated as he was then. I believe it is
hardly so now. Those were the days when he said a
candid thing which did him honour. He was quite
a new bishop then; and he said one day, plucking at his
sleeve, as if he had his lawn ones on, 'I don't know
how it is : but when we have got these things on, we
never do any thing more.' Then, there was the
nervous, good-natured, indiscreet rattle,—the Bishop
of Norwich (Stanley), who could never get under weigh
without being presently aground. Timid as a hare,
sensitive as a woman, heedless and flexible as a child,
he was surely the oddest bishop that ever was seen :
and, to make the impression the more strange, he was
as like Dr. Channing as could well be, except that
his hair was perfectly white, and Dr. Channing's dark.
That the solemn, curt, inaccessible, ever-spiritual Dr.
Channing should so resemble the giddy, impressible
Dr. Stanley, who carried his heart upon his sleeve (too
often ' for daws to peck at') was strange enough :
but so it was. Bishop Stanley was, however, admirable in his way. If he had been a rural parish priest
all his life, out of the way of dissenters and of clerical
espionage, he would have lived and died as beloved as
he really was, and much more respected. In Norwich,
his care and furtherance of the schools were admirable;
and in the function of benevolence to the poor and
afflicted, he was exemplary. But censure almost broke
his heart and turned his brain. He had no courage
or dignity at all under the bad manners of his Tory
clergy ; and he repeatedly talked in such a style to
me about it as to compel me to tell him plainly that

dissenters like myself are not only accustomed to ill-
usage for differences of opinion, but are brought up to
regard that trial as one belonging to all honest avowal
of convictions, and to be borne with courage and
patience like other trials. His innocent amazement
and consternation at being ill-used on account of his
liberal opinions were truly instructive to a member of
a despised sect; but they were painful, too. I have
often thought that if Bishop Stanley put himself in
the power of other people as he did in mine he might
expect at any hour the destruction of his peace, if not
of his position,—so grievous were his complaints, and
so desperate his criticisms of people who did not like
his opinions, and teased him accordingly. His lady
and daughters did much good in Norwich ; and, on the
whole, the city, which loved its old Bishop Bathurst,
considered itself well off in his successor.—Then there
was the somewhat shy but agreeable Bishop Lonsdale
(Lichfield); and the gracious, kindly and liberal,—but
not otherwise remarkable,- —Bishop Otter (Chichester).

The common stream of Members of Parliament presented a curious uniformity,—even considering that
they were almost all Whigs. They all had the same
intense conviction that every thing but Whiggism was
bête ; that they could teach ' the people' every thing
that it was good for them to know ; and that the way
to do it was by addressing them in a coaxing and ad-
monitory way. They all had the same intense admiration of Whig measures before they were tried ; and the
same indifference and shamelessness in dropping those
measures when it was found that they would not work.
But among these there were a few who belonged to no
party, and were too good to be confounded with the

rest. There was Charles Buller, the admired and beloved, and now and always the deeply mourned. He was more than a drawing-room acquaintance of mine. He was my friend; and we had real business to discuss occasionally, besides lighter matters. Many an hour he spent by my fireside, both before and after Lord Durham's government of Canada. By means of my American travel and subsequent correspondence, I was able,—or Charles Buller thought I was,—to supply some useful information, and afford some few suggestions; and I was quite as much impressed by his seriousness and fine sense in affairs of business as by his infinite cleverness and drollery in ordinary conversation.—The readers of my ' History of the Peace' must perceive that I had some peculiar opportunities of knowing the true story of that Canada governmental campaign. I feared that it might be taken for granted that Lord Durham or his family gave me the information ; whereas he and they were singularly careful to make no party, and to leave his case in silence till a time should arrive for explanation, without risk of turning out Lord Melbourne's government. They told me nothing of their personal grievances ; and I have said so in a note in the History. But I could not then tell where I did get my information. It was mainly from Charles Buller's Journal of his residence in Canada, which was confided to me on his return by a friend of his and mine. I felt myself bound not to say so while he was living, and with a political career before him which such a disclosure might have injured : but, now that he and his father and mother are gone, and that remarkable household has vanished, and is remembered as a dream, I see no

reason why I should not declare on what high authority I made the statements relating to Lord Durham's
residence in Canada. There was another journal by another of the party, put into my hands at the same time,
from which I have derived some incidents and suggestions: but Charles Buller's narrative, written from day
to day, was the one on which I chiefly relied.—His capacity, and his probable future, could not be adequately
judged of by any thing he had said or done when his
always frail health finally gave way. The Canada
Report is noted for its ability; and the men of his
generation remember how thorough were his Colonization speeches, and how his fine temper and well-
timed wit soothed and brightened the atmosphere of
the House in tempestuous times. But the sound
greatness that lay beneath was known only to his intimates; and they mourned over an untimely arrest of
a glorious career of statesmanship, while the rest of
the world regarded the loss simply as of an effective
and accomplished Member of Parliament.

Another, who stood out from the classification of
Tory and Whig, was my friend R. Monckton Milnes,
whom I know too well, and am too sincerely attached
to, to describe as if he were dead, or on less friendly
terms with me. When I first knew him, it was
amidst the bustle of the discovery of his being a poet;
or, at least, I had seen him, as far as I remember,
only once before that. One evening, at Lady Mary
Shepherd's (where I never went again, for reasons
which I will give presently) my hostess told me that
she was to introduce me, if I pleased, to a young friend
of hers who had just returned from travels in Greece.
I understood his name to be Mills, and did not think

of connecting him with the Yorkshire family whose
name was so well known to me. When the young
friend arrived, he did look young,—with a round face
and a boyish manner, free from all shyness and gravity
whatever. (Sydney Smith had two names for him in
those days: ' Dick Modest Milnes,' and ' the Cool of
the Evening.')   I was just departing, early, when he
first had some conversation with me in the drawing-
room, and then went down to the cloak-room, where he
said something which impressed me much, and made
me distinctly remember the earnest youth, before I
discovered that he was the same with ' the new poet,'
Milnes. He asked me some question about my tales,
—then about half done; and my answer conveyed to
him an impression I did not at all intend,—that I
made light of the work. ' No, now,—don't say that,'
said he, bluntly. ' It is unworthy of you to affect that
you do not take pains with your work. It is work
which cannot be done without pains ; and you should
not pretend to the contrary.' I showed him, in a moment, that he had misapprehended me; and I carried
away a clear impression of his sincerity, and of the
gravity which lay under his *insouciant* manners.
When his poems came out,—wonderfully beautiful in
their way, as they have ever seemed to me,—they
and their author were a capital topic for the literary
gossips,—Empson and Whishaw, and their coterie ;
and I did not wonder at their going from house to
house, to announce the news, and gather and compare
opinions. My pleasure in those poems was greatest
when I read them in my Tynemouth solitude. My
copy is marked all over with hieroglyphics involving
the emotions with which I read them.   He came to

see me there, and did me good by his kindness in
various ways.   He visited me there again on my recovery; and he has been here to see me, lately, in my
present illness.   From time to time, incidents which
he supposes to be absolute secrets have come to my
knowledge which prove him to be as nobly and substantially bountiful to needy merit and ability as he is
kindly in intercourse, and sympathising in suffering.
The most interesting feature of his character, as it
stands before the world, is his catholicity of sentiment
and manner,—his ability to sympathise with all manner of thinkers and speakers, and his superiority to all
appearance of exclusiveness, while, on the one hand,
rather enjoying the reputation of having access to all
houses, and, on the other, being serious and earnest in
the deepest recesses of his character.—This may look
rather like doing what I said I could not;—describing a personal friend : but it is really not so : I have
touched on none but the most patent aspects of an
universally known man.   If I were to describe him as
a personal friend, I should have much more to say.

Another acquaintance who became a friend was Mr.
Grote, then one of the Members for London.   That
was not the period of his life which he relished most.
While doing his duty in parliament in regard to the
Ballot and Colonization, and other great questions of
the time, and exercising hospitality as became his position, he looked back rather mournfully to the happy
quiet years when, before his father suddenly made an
eldest son of him, he was writing his History of
Greece; and earnestly did he long for the time (which
arrived in due course) when he might retire to his
study and renew his labours.   I was always glad to

meet him and his clever wife, who were full, at all times, of capital conversation ;—she with all imaginable freedom ; and he with a curious, formal, old-fashioned deliberate courtesy, with which he strove to cover his constitutional timidity and shyness. The publication of his fine History now precludes all necessity of describing his powers and his tastes. He was best known in those days as the leading member of the Radical section in parliament; and few could suppose then that his claims on that ground would be swallowed up by his reputation as a scholar and author in one of the highest walks of literature. As a good man and a gentleman his reputation was always of the highest. —With him, the remembrance of his and my friend Roebuck is naturally associated. Mr. Roebuck's state of health,—his being subject to a most painful malady, —accounted to those who knew him well for faults of temper which were singularly notorious. I always felt, in regard to both him and Lord Durham, that so much was said about faults of temper because there was nothing else to be fastened upon to their disadvantage. I can only say that, well as I knew them both, I never witnessed any ill temper in either. Mr. Roebuck was full of knowledge, full of energy, full of ability ; with great vanity, certainly, but of so honest a kind that it did not much matter. When in pain, he was an example of wonderful fortitude ; and there was a singular charm in the pathetic voice and countenance with which he discussed subjects that it was wonderful he could take an interest in under the circumstances. When he was well, his lively spirits were delightful ; and a more agreeable guest or host could not be. Since I saw him last, he has undergone the

severest trials of sickness; and it must be almost as
great a surprise to himself as to me and others that he
is now Chairman of the Sebastopol Committee, and
able to take a leading part in the politics of our present serious national crisis. His position now seems to
be a sort of retribution on Lord John Russell and other
Whig politicians, who treated him with outrageous
insolence in public and private, while there was a
Radical section for him to lead. Those who outlive
me may yet see the balance struck between the popular
and colonial tribune and the insolent official liberals,
as they called themselves, who have one and all proved
themselves incompetent to wield the power which they
so greedily clutched, and held with so shameless a
tenacity. I hope Mr. Roebuck may live to retrieve
some mistakes, and to fulfil some of his long baffled
aspirations. His chance seems at least better than
that of his most insolent contemners.

Bulwer and Talfourd were hardly thought of as
Members of Parliament at that time, except in connexion with the international copyright treaty which
authors were endeavouring to procure, and with the
Copyright Act, which was obtained a few years after.
Mr. Macaulay was another Member of Parliament
who associated his name very discreditably at first with
the copyright bill, which was thrown out one session
in consequence of a speech of his which has always remained a puzzle to me. What could have been the
inducement to such a man to talk such nonsense as he
did, and to set at naught every principle of justice in
regard to authors' earnings, it is impossible, to me and
others, to conceive. Nothing that he could propose,
—nothing that he could do, could ever compensate to

him for the forfeiture of good fame and public confidence which he seems to have actually volunteered in
that speech. He changed his mind or his tactics
afterwards ; but he could not change people's feelings
in regard to himself, or make any body believe that
he was a man to be relied upon. He never appeared
to me to be so. When I went to London he was a
new Member of Parliament, and the object of unbounded hope and expectation to the Whig statesmen,
who, according to their curious practice of considering
all of the generation below their own as chicks, spoke
rapturously of this promising young man. They went
on doing so till his return from India, five years afterwards, by which time the world began to inquire when
the promise was to begin to fructify,—this young
fellow being by that time seven-and-thirty. To impartial observers, the true quality of Macaulay's mind
was as clear then as now. In Parliament, he was no
more than a most brilliant speaker; and in his speeches
there was the same fundamental weakness which pervades his writings,—unsoundness in the presentment
of his case. Some one element was sure to be left out,
which falsified his statement, and vitiated his conclusions; and there never was perhaps a speaker or writer of
eminence, so prone to presentments of cases, who so rarely offered one which was complete and true. My own
impression is, and always was, that the cause of the defect is constitutional in Macaulay. The evidence seems
to indicate that he wants heart. He appears to be wholly
unaware of this deficiency ; and the superficial fervour
which suns over his disclosures probably deceives himself, as it deceives a good many other people ; and he
may really believe that he has a heart. To those who

do not hold this key to the interpretation of his career, it must be a very mysterious thing that a man of such imposing and real ability, with every circumstance and influence in his favour, should never have achieved any complete success. As a politician, his failure has been signal, notwithstanding his irresistible power as a speaker, and his possession of every possible facility. As a practical legislator, his failure was unsurpassed, when he brought home his Code from India. I was witness to the amazement and grief of some able lawyers, in studying that Code,—of which they could scarcely lay their finger on a provision through which you could not drive a coach and six. It has long been settled that literature alone remains open to him; and in that he has, with all his brilliancy and captivating accomplishment, destroyed the ground of confidence on which his adorers met him when, in his mature years, he published the first two volumes of his History. His review articles, and especially the one on Bacon, ought to have abolished all confidence in his honesty, as well as in his capacity for philosophy. Not only did he show himself to be disqualified for any appreciation of Bacon's philosophy, but his plagiarisms from the very author (Basil Montagu) whom he was pretending to demolish, (one instance of plagiarism among many) might have shown any conscientious reader how little he was to be trusted in regard to mere integrity of statement. But, as he announced a History, the public received as a *bonâ fide* History the work on which he proposes to build his fame. If it had been announced as an historical romance, it might have been read with almost unmixed delight, though exception might have been taken to his presentment of several characters and facts.   He has been abundantly punished, for instance, for his slanderous exhibition of William Penn.   But he has fatally manifested his loose and unscrupulous method of narrating, and, in his first edition, gave no clue whatever to his authorities, and no information in regard to dates which he could possibly suppress.   Public opinion compelled, in future editions, some appearance of furnishing references to authorities, such as every conscientious historian finds it indispensable to his peace of mind to afford ; but it is done by Macaulay in the most ineffectual and baffling way possible,—by clubbing together the mere names of his authorities at the bottom of the page, so that reference is all but impracticable.   Where it is made, by painstaking readers, the inaccuracies and misrepresentations of the historian are found to multiply as the work of verification proceeds.   In fact, the only way to accept his History is to take it as a brilliant fancypiece,—wanting not only the truth but the repose of history,—but stimulating, and even, to a degree, suggestive.   While I write, announcement is made of two more volumes to appear in the course of the year.   If the radical faults of the former ones are remedied, there may yet be before this gifted man something like the ' career,' so proudly anticipated for him a quarter of a century ago.   If not, all is over ; and his powers, once believed adequate to the construction of eternal monuments of statesmanship and noble edifices for intellectual worship, will be found capable of nothing better than rearing gay kiosks in the flower gardens of literature, to be soon swept away by the caprices of a new taste, as superficial as his own.—I have been led on to say all this by the vivid remembrance of the universal interest there was about Macaulay, when the London world first opened before me. I remember the days when he was met in the streets, looking only at the pavement as he walked, and with his lips moving,—causing those who met him to say that there would be a fine speech from Macaulay that night. Then came the sighs over his loss when he went to India for three years : then the joy at his return, and the congratulations to his venerable father : then the blank disappointment at the way in which he had done his work : and then his appearance in society,—with his strange eyes, which appeared to look nowhere, and his full cheeks and stooping shoulders, which told of dreamy indolence; and then the torrent of words which poured out when he did speak ! It did not do to invite him and Sydney Smith together. They interfered with one another. Sydney Smith's sense of this appears in his remarks on Macaulay's 'improvement,' as shown by 'flashes of silence;' and Macaulay showed his sense of the incompatibility of the two wits by his abstracted silence, or by signs of discomposure.

I had heard all my life of the vanity of women as a subject of pity to men : but when I went to London, lo! I saw vanity in high places which was never transcended by that of women in their lowlier rank. There was Brougham, wincing under a newspaper criticism, and playing the fool among silly women. There was Jeffrey, flirting with clever women, in long succession. There was Bulwer, on a sofa, sparkling and languishing among a set of female votaries,—he and they dizened out, perfumed, and presenting the nearest picture to a seraglio to be seen on British ground,—only the indifference or hauteur of the lord of the harem being absent. There was poor Campbell the poet, obtruding his sentimentalities, amidst a quivering apprehension of making himself ridiculous. He darted out of our house, and never came again, because, after warning, he sat down, in a room full of people (all authors, as it happened) on a low chair of my old aunt's which went very easily on castors, and which carried him back to the wall and rebounded, of course making every body laugh. Off went poor Campbell in a huff; and, well as I had long known him, I never saw him again: and I was not very sorry, for his sentimentality was too soft, and his craving for praise too morbid to let him be an agreeable companion. On occasion of the catastrophe, he came with about forty authors one morning, to sign a petition to parliament for an International copyright law. Then there was Babbage, —less utterly dependent on opinion than some people suppose; but still, harping so much on the subject as to warrant the severe judgment current in regard to his vanity.—There was Edwin Landseer, a friendly and agreeable companion, but holding his cheerfulness at the mercy of great folks' graciousness to him. To see him enter a room, curled and cravatted, and glancing round in anxiety about his reception, could not but make a woman wonder where among her own sex she could find a more palpable vanity; but then, all that was forgotten when one was sitting on a divan with him, seeing him play with the dog.—Then there was Whewell, grasping at praise for universal learning, —(omniscience being his foible, as Sydney Smith said,)—and liking female adoration, rough as was his nature with students, rivals and speculative opponents. —I might instance more : but this is enough. The display was always to me most melancholy; for the detriment was so much greater than in the case of female vanity. The circumstances of women render the vanity of literary women well nigh unavoidable where the literary pursuit and production are of a light kind : and the mischief (serious enough) may end with the deterioration of the individual. Lady Morgan and Lady Davy and Mrs. Austin and Mrs. Jameson may make women blush and men smile and be insolent ; and their gross and palpable vanities may help to lower the position and discredit the pursuits of other women, while starving out their own natural powers : but these mischiefs are far less important than the blighting of promise and the forfeiture of a career, and the intercepting of national blessings, in the case of a Bulwer or a Brougham. A few really able women,—women sanctified by true genius and holy science,—a Joanna Baillie, a Somerville, a Browning,—quickly repair the mischief, as regards the dignity of women ; and the time has not yet arrived when national interests are involved in the moral dignity of individual women of genius. But, as a matter of fact, I conceive that no one can glance round society, as seen in London drawing-rooms, and pretend to consider vanity the appropriate sin of women. The instances I have given are of persons who, for the most part, were estimable and agreeable, apart from their characteristic foible. For Bulwer I always felt a cordial interest, amidst any amount of vexation and pity for his weakness. He seems to me to be a woman of genius enclosed by misadventure in a man's form.

If the life of his affections had been a natural and
fortunate one ; and if (which would have been the consequence) he had not plunged over head and ears in
the metaphysics of morals, I believe he would have
made himself a name which might have lasted as long
as our literature. He has insight, experience, sympathy,
letters, power and grace of expression, and an irrepres-
sible impulse to utterance and industry which should
have produced works of the noblest quality; and these
have been intercepted by mischiefs which may be called
misfortune rather than fault. There is no need to
relate his history or describe his faults. I can only
lament the perversion of one of the most promising
natures, and the intercepting of some of the most
needful literary benefits offered, in the form of one
man, in our time. His friendly temper, his generous
heart, his excellent conversation (at his best) and his
simple manners (when he forgot himself) have many
a time ' left me mourning' that such a being should
allow himself to sport with perdition. Perhaps my
interest in him was deepened by the evident growth
of his deafness, and by seeing that he was not, as yet,
equal to cope with the misfortune of personal infirmity.
He could not bring himself practically to acknowledge
it ; and his ignoring of it occasioned scenes which,
painful to others, must have been exquisitely so to a
vain man like himself. I longed to speak, or get
spoken, to him a word of warning and encouragement
out of my own experience ; but I never met with any
one who dared mention the subject to him ; and I had
no fair opportunity after the infirmity became conspicuous. From the time when, in contradicting in
the newspapers a report of his having lost his hearing

altogether, he professed to think conversation not
worth hearing, I had no hope of his fortitude; for it
is the last resource of weakness to give out that the
grapes are sour.—Campbell was declining when I first
knew him; and I disliked his visits because I was
never quite sure whether he was sober,—his irritable
brain being at the mercy of a single glass of sherry,
or of a paroxysm of enthusiasm about the Poles: but
I adored his poems in my youth; I was aware that domestic misfortune had worn out his affectionate heart;
and it was a pleasure to see that his sympathies were,
to the last, warm on behalf of international morality
and popular liberties.—As for Mr. Babbage, it seemed
to me that few men were more misunderstood,—his
sensitiveness about opinions perverting other people's
impressions of him quite as much as his of them. For
one instance: he was amused, as well as struck, by the
very small reliance to be placed on opinion, public or
private, for and against individuals: and he thought
over some method of bringing his observation to a
sort of demonstration. Thinking that he was likely
to hear most of opinions about himself as a then
popular author, he collected every thing he could
gather in print about himself, and pasted the pieces
into a large book, with the *pros* and *cons* in parallel
columns, from which he obtained a sort of balance,
besides some highly curious observations. Soon after
he told me this, with fun and good humour, I was
told repeatedly that he spent all his days in gloating
and grumbling over what people said of him, having
got it all down in a book, which he was perpetually
poring over. People who so represented him had little
idea what a domestic tenderness is in him,—though

to me his singular face seemed to show it,—nor how much that was really interesting might be found in him by those who viewed him naturally and kindly. All were eager to go to his glorious soirées; and I always thought he appeared to great advantage as a host. His patience in explaining his machine in those days was really exemplary. I felt it so, the first time I saw the miracle, as it appeared to me; but I thought so much more, a year or two after, when a lady, to whom he had sacrificed some very precious time, on the supposition that she understood as much as she assumed to do, finished by saying, 'Now, Mr. Babbage, there is only one thing more that I want to know. If you put the question in wrong, will the answer come out right?' All time and attention devoted to lady examiners of his machine, from that time forward, I regarded as sacrifices of genuine good nature.

In what noble contrast were the eminent men who were not vain! There was the honest and kindly Captain (now Admiral Sir Francis) Beaufort, who was daily at the Admiralty as the clock struck, conveying paper, pen and ink for any private letters he might have to write, for which he refused to use the official stores. There were the friends Lyell and Charles Darwin, after the return of the latter from his four years' voyage round the world;—Lyell with a Scotch prudence which gave way, more and more as years passed on, to his natural geniality, and to an expanding liberality of opinion and freedom of speech; and the simple, childlike, painstaking, effective Charles Darwin, who established himself presently at the head of living English naturalists. These well-employed, earnest-minded, accomplished and genial men bore

their honours without vanity, jealousy, or any apparent
self-regard whatever.   They and their devoted wives
were welcome in the highest degree.   Lady Lyell was
almost as remarkable in society as her husband, though
she evidently considered herself only a part of him.
Having no children, she could devote her life to helping him.   She travelled over half the world with him,
entered fully into his pursuits, and furthered them as
no one else could have done; while there was not a
trace of pedantry in her, but a simple, lively manner,
proceeding from a mind at ease and nobly entertained.
Mr. Rogers used to point out the beauty of her eye,
—'The eye of the stag;' and truly she grew more
charming-looking every year, and was handsomer and
brighter than ever when I saw her not long ago in
London.   If she had no vanity for herself, neither
had she for her husband, of whom her estimate was
too lofty and just to admit the intrusion of so unworthy an emotion.

Many other there were in regard to whom the
imputation of vanity was impossible.   There were Dr.
Dalton and Mrs. Somerville sitting with their heads
close together, on the sofa, talking their own glorious
talk without a thought of what any body in the world
was saying about either of them.   Dr. Dalton was
simple in every way; Mrs. Somerville in all that was
essential.   Her mistakes in taking her daughters to
court, and in a good many conventional matters, were
themselves no worse than a misplaced humility which
made her do as other people did, or as other people
bade her do, instead of choosing her own course.   I
used to wish she had been wise in those matters, and
more self-reliant altogether; but I am sure there was

no ambition or vanity in her mind, all the time. It
was delightful to find her with a letter from her
publisher in her hand, considering it with anxiety;
and to hear what her difficulty was. She was respect-
fully requested to make such alterations in the next
edition of her ' Connexion of the Physical Sciences '
as would render it more popular and intelligible. She
could not at all see her way. The scientific mode of
expression, with its pregnancy, its terseness and
brevity, seemed to her perfectly simple. If she was
to alter it, it could be only by amplifying; and she
feared that would make her diffuse and comparatively
unintelligible. It was delightful to see her always
well-dressed and thoroughly womanly in her conversation and manners, while unconscious of any
peculiarity in her pursuits. It was delightful to go
to tea at her house at Chelsea, and find every thing
in order and beauty;—the walls hung with her fine
drawings; her music in the corner, and her tea table
spread with good things. In the midst of these
household elegancies, Dr. Somerville one evening
pulled open a series of drawers, to find something he
wanted to show me. As he shut one after another, I
ventured to ask what those strange things were which
filled every drawer. ' O! they are only Mrs. Somerville's diplomas,' said he, with a droll look of pride
and amusement. Not long after this the family went
abroad, partly for Dr. Somerville's health : and great
has been the concern of her friends at so losing her,
while it was well known that her longings were for
England. Her husband and her daughters, (turned
Catholics,) have kept her in Italy ever since, to the
privation and sorrow of many who know that scientific

London is the proper place for her, and that, unselfish
as she is, she must long to be there. I own it went
to my heart to hear of one thing that happened soon
after she left England. The great comet of 1843 was
no more seen by her than by any other woman in
Italy. The only good observatory was in a Jesuits'
College, where no woman was allowed to set foot. It
is too bad that she should spend the last third of her
life in a country so unworthy of her.

And there was Joanna Baillie, whose serene and
cheerful life was never troubled by the pains and
penalties of vanity ;—what a charming spectacle was
she ! Mrs. Barbauld's published correspondence tells
of her, in 1800, as ' a young lady of Hampstead, whom
I visited, and who came to Mr. Barbauld's meeting,
all the while, with as innocent a face as if she had
never written a line.' That was two years before I
was born. When I met her, about thirty years afterwards, there she was ' with as innocent a face as if
she had never written a line !' And this was after an
experience which would have been a bitter trial to an
author with a particle of vanity. She had enjoyed a
fame almost without parallel, and had outlived it.
She had been told every day for years, through every
possible channel, that she was second only to Shakspere,
—-if second ; and then she had seen her works drop
out of notice so that, of the generation who grew up
before her eyes, not one in a thousand had read a line
of her plays :—yet was her serenity never disturbed,
nor her merry humour in the least dimmed. I have
never lost the impression of the trying circumstances
of my first interview with her, nor of the grace, simplicity and sweetness with which she bore them. She

was old; and she declined dinner-parties; but she wished to meet me,—having known, I believe, some of my connexions or friends of the past generation;—and therefore she came to Miss Berry's to tea, one day when I was dining there. Miss Berry, her contemporary, put her feelings, it seemed to me, to a most unwarrantable trial, by describing to me, as we three sat together, the celebrity of the ' Plays on the Passions' in their day. She told me how she found on her table, on her return from a ball, a volume of plays; and how she kneeled on a chair to look at it, and how she read on till the servant opened the shutters, and let in the daylight of a winter morning. She told me how all the world raved about the plays; and she held on so long that I was in pain for the noble creature to whom it must have been irksome on the one hand to hear her own praises and fame so dwelt upon, and, on the other, to feel that we all knew how long that had been quite over. But, when I looked up at her sweet face, with its composed smile amidst the becoming mob cap, I saw that she was above pain of either kind. We met frequently afterwards, at her house or ours; and I retained my happy impression, till the last call I made on her. She was then over-affectionate, and uttered a good deal of flattery; and I was uneasy at symptoms so unlike her good taste and sincerity. It was a token of approaching departure. She was declining, and she sank and softened for some months more, and then died, revered and beloved as she deserved. Amidst all pedantry, vanity, coquetry, and manners ruined by celebrity which I have seen, for these twenty years past, I have solaced and strengthened myself with the image of Joanna Baillie, and with remembering the invulnerable justification which she set up for intellectual superiority in women, while we may hope that the injury done to that cause by blue-stockings and coquettes will be scarcely more enduring than their own trumpery notoriety.

I must own that I have known scarcely any political men who were not as vain as women are commonly supposed to be: and if any were not so themselves, their wives were sure to be so for them; and so conspicuously as to do the mischief effectually. Lord Lansdowne was an exception, I believe; and so, I am sure, was his simple-minded, shy lady, with her rural tastes, and benevolent pursuits. The present Lord Grey did not show in private life the sensitiveness which marred his temper and manners in his political function. Lord Morpeth (the present Lord Carlisle) has his weaknesses, which arc cvidcnt enough; but I never saw a trace of vanity in him. His magnanimous, benevolent, affectionate temper, his pure integrity, and devout conscientiousness, are all incompatible with vanity. It seems a pity that his powers are so inadequate to his sensibilities; or that, his abilities being what they are, he has not chosen to remain in that private life which he conspicuously adorns: but it is a benefit, as far as it goes, that his fine spirit and manners should be present in official life, to rebuke the vulgar selfishness, levity, and insolence which have discredited his political comrades, from their accession to power, a quarter of a century since, till now, when their faults have brought on a crisis in the destinies of England. As an order of men, however, politicians are, as far as my experience goes, far inferior in dignity to scientific men, among whom there are, it is true, examples of egregious vanity, but not so striking as the simplicity and earnestness which characterise many whose lives are spent in lofty pursuits which carry them high above personal regards.   And to nearly all, I believe, the pursuit of knowledge for its own sake yields more pleasure than any gain of fame or money. To one Lardner, there is many a Beaufort, Washington, Delabêche, Ehrenberg, Dalton and Gregory.   Some, like Professor Nichol, may not be acquitted of vanity, while uniting with it, as he does, a simplicity, a kindliness, and a genial temper which make them delightful companions.   Others, like Buckland and Murchison, have a love of fun mingling with their genuine worship of science, which makes them highly agreeable, in spite of eccentricities of manner.   Sir Charles Bell was of too tender a nature for the conflicts which await a discoverer ; but his sensitiveness was of too refined and constitutional a kind to be insulted with the name of vanity ; and he was beloved with a tenderness which no grossly vain person could ever win to himself.   While he was grave, quiet and melancholy, men of stouter natures were making fun, if not of their science, of the uses to which they applied it, in that condescension to which their desire of reputation or of something lower led them.   Sir Charles Bell wrote his Bridgewater Treatise, no doubt, with the grave sincerity with which he did every thing, and without any suspicion of the injury he was doing to theology, by attempting to bolster up the Design argument, which he ought to have seen tends directly, as is now widely admitted, to atheism.   Among some of his comrades, the matter was viewed with more levity.   When one of them was writing his

successful treatise, he consigned his manuscript to a
scientific friend for criticism.   It had a good margin
left for notes ; and his critic, after gravely writing his
observations on the scientific portion, scored in pencil
the close of the sections where the Bridgewater application was made, with the words ' Power, wisdom
and goodness as per contract.' There was much covert
laughter about this among the philosophers, while
they presented a duly grave face to the theological
world.

The artists are usually concluded to be the vainest
of all orders of men.   I have not found them so.   A
more dignified, simple-minded and delightful drawing-
room companion I have hardly known than Sir Augustus
Callcott, for one.   His tenderness of heart appeared
in that devotion to his wife which cost him his health
and his life.   She (the Maria Graham of India and
of South America, during Lord Dundonald's achievements there) was a clever woman in her way, with
indomitable spirits, through years of slow consumption:
but, when hearing her gossip and random talk, one
could not, after all allowance for her invalid state and
its seclusion contrasted with former activity, help re-
gretting that her far superior husband should sink
prematurely into melancholy and ill-health, from
his too close attendance upon her, through years of
hot rooms and night watching.   A higher order of
wife would not have permitted it ; and a lower order
of husband would not have done it.—Chantrey was
abundantly aware of his own merits; but there was
an honesty in the avowal which distanced the imputation of vanity.   As I sat next him one day at dinner,
I was rather disturbed at the freedom with which he

criticised and directed the carving of a haunch of
venison, fixing the attention of the whole table on the
process, which the operator bore most gracefully.
Chantrey turned apologetically to me with, ' You
know I have a right. I am the first carver in London.'
He always told every body who he was, and took for
granted that every body knew all his works : but there
was a good-humoured courage and naturalness about
his self-estimate which made it amusing, instead of
disgusting.

Allan Cunningham was, however, far more interesting than his employer and friend. It was quite a sight
to see stalwart Allan and his stalwart wife enter a
drawing-room, and to see how his fine face and head
towered above others in expression as much as in
altitude. His simple sense and cheerful humour rendered his conversation as lively as that of a wit ; and
his literary knowledge and taste gave it refinement
enough to suit any society. I always felt that Allan
Cunningham was precisely the human example that I
had long wished to see ;—of that privileged condition
which I think the very most advantageous that a man
can be placed in ;—the original standing of a workman, with such means of intellectual cultivation as
may open to him the life of books. Allan Cunningham
was one of the hard-handed order, privileged to know
the realities of practical life ; while also a man of letters and a poet, exempt from the deficiencies and
foibles of mere literary life. Thus, while a workman,
a student, and a poet, he was above all a man ; and
thorough manliness was his dominant characteristic.
All this came back upon me, when, in 1849, I met his
son Peter, whose features recalled so much of his

364 AUTOBIOGRAPHY. [1832–1834.

father, and whose industrious and effectual authorship reminds us all of his honourable descent.

Westmacott, again, was seriously full of his art;
and that is the true charm in the manners of an artist.
Phillips was formal and self-complacent, but well read
and communicative : and the friendship between himself and his accomplished family was a pretty spectacle. Macready's sensitiveness shrouded itself within
an artificial manner; but a more delightful companion
could not be,—not only on account of his learning
and accomplishment, but of his uncompromising liberality of opinion, and his noble strain of meditative
thought. He enjoyed playing Jaques,—thinking
that character singularly like himself; and it was so,
in one part of his character : but there was, besides the
moralising tendency, a chivalrous spirit of rare vigilance, and an unsleeping domestic tenderness and social
beneficence which accounted for and justified the idolatry with which he was regarded, through all trials occasioned by the irritable temper with which he manfully
struggled.—The Kembles were of a different sort
altogether; I mean Charles Kemble and his daughters.
They were full of knowledge and accomplishment, of
course, and experienced in all manner of social intercourse : but there seemed to me to be an incurable
vulgarity clinging to them, among all the charms of
their genius, their cultivation, and their social privileges. I think it must have been from their passionate
natures, and from their rather priding themselves on
that characteristic of theirs. I liked Adelaide the best
of the three, because she had herself more under control than the others, and because the womanly nature
did itself more justice in her case than in her sister's.

The admiration and interest which Fanny inspired were as often put to flight as aroused,—so provoking was her self-will, and so vexatious her caprice. And then, there was no relying on any thing she said, while the calmer and more devoted Adelaide was mistress of her own thought and speech, and composedly truthful in a way which ought to have been, and probably was, exemplary in Fanny's eyes. There was a green-room cast of mind about them all, from which Macready was marvellously free. He saw life by daylight, and they by stage lamps; and that was the difference. I am speaking of them as I met them in drawing-rooms, but I have other associations with them. I saw much of Fanny in America, during her early married life, and was present at the christening of her first child. She showed me the proof-sheets of her clever 'Journal,' and, as she chose to require my opinion of it, obtained a less flattering one than from most people. I might be, and probably was, narrow and stiff in my judgment of it; but I was sufficiently shocked at certain passages to induce her to cancel some thirty pages. I really strove hard to like and approve her; and I imposed upon myself for a time, as on others in conversation, the belief that I did so: but I could not carry it on long. There was so radical an unreality about her and her sayings and doings, and so perverse a sporting with her possessions and privileges in life, and with other people's peace, that my interest in her died out completely, in a way which could not have happened if I could have believed her notorious misfortunes to have been other than self-inflicted. By her way of entering upon marriage, and her conduct

in it afterwards, she deprived herself of all title to
wonder at or complain of her domestic miseries, terrible
as they were. She was a finely-gifted creature, wasted
and tortured by want of discipline, principle and self-
knowledge. Adelaide was morally of a far higher
order; and when with her, I desired nothing more
than that she had seen life through other than the
stage medium, and that she had not been a Kemble.
She was charming at their own soirées in London,—
unobtrusively taking care of and amusing every body,
with good nature and simplicity: and she was yet
more charming when she sat beside my couch at Tynemouth, singing ' Auld Robin Gray ' for my pleasure,
and manifesting a true womanly sympathy with me,
of whom she had personally known nothing except
through drawing-room intercourse. It was she who
sent me the chief luxury of my sick-room,—the
' Christus Consolator' of Scheffer, which truly affords
study for as many years as I was ill. If, as I understand, she has found happiness in her domestic life,
after such triumphs as hers on the stage, the genuine
fine quality of her nature is sufficiently proved.

In those days, Eastlake was just home from Italy.
He had already left off landscape painting, with which
he began. I have hanging up in the next room the
engraving which he gave me of his last landscape,—
' Byron's Dream.' He was now producing the early
pictures of that short series which, full of charm at
first, soon proved how *bornés* were his resources.
The mannerism of his colouring, and the sameness of
his female faces, showing that he had but one idea of
beauty, could be made evident only by time; and at
first there was an exquisite charm in the grace, refine-

ment and delicacy of both conception and execution. Since that time, his function has appeared to be the aiding and support of art by other means than himself painting. I always liked to meet him,—ignorant as I was on the subjects which were most important to him. He condescended to talk to me on them; and there was the wide field of literature in which we had a common interest. Kind and conversible as he was, I always felt that there was a certain amount of cynicism in his views, and scepticism in his temper, which must have interfered with his enjoyment of life. It was not very great, and was chiefly noticeable as being the only drawback on the pleasure of conversation with him. I have seen him only once for nearly twenty years; and that was at a distance in Thackeray's lecture-room, in 1851. I should hardly have known the careworn, aged face, if my attention had not been directed to him : and it gave me pain to see how the old tendency to anxiety and distrust seemed to have issued in care or ill-health, which could so alter a man not yet old. He has done so much for art, and given so much pleasure to society, that one wishes he could have enjoyed the strength and spirits which those who love art as he does should, and generally do, derive from its pursuit.—There was Uwins, in those days, with his sunny Italian groups; and, more recently, Rothwell, whose picture (when unfinished) of 'Rich and rare were the gems she wore,' seemed to me wonderfully beautiful : and, among portrait painters, the accomplished and earnest Richmond,—to whom I sat for the only good portrait taken of me.

I seem to have got a long way from the dinner-parties which led me into all these sketches; and I

will not go back to them : but rather tell a little about
the evening engagements which gave variety to my
London life. There were blue-stocking evenings, now
and then ; and I never went twice to any house where
I encountered that sort of reception, except the Miss
Berrys' where there was so much to relieve 'the blue,'
and one was left so freely and pleasantly to be amused,
that one's pride or one's modesty was safe from offence.
By the way, an incident occurred at dinner at Miss
Berry's which I recall with as much astonishment as
paralysed me at the moment, and struck me dumb
when it was of some importance that I should speak.
I have told how a Prime Minister's daughter was for
the first time informed of the Birmingham Church
and King riots, when Dr. Priestley's chapel, house and
library were destroyed. A highborn lady betrayed to
me that evening, at Miss Berry's, what her notion, and
that of her associates, was of the politics of the liberal
party after the passage of the Reform Bill. Lady G.
S. W., whose husband, I think, had been in the United
States, inquired of me about the prospects of Slavery
there. When she seemed surprised at the amount of
persecution the abolitionists were undergoing, I attempted to show her how the vicious institution was
implicated with the whole policy, and many of the
modes, ideas, and interests of society there; so that
the abolitionists were charged with destructiveness,
and regarded by timid persons, whether slaveholders
or other, much as people would be among us who
should be charged with desiring to overthrow every
thing, from the throne to the workhouse. Her reply
completely puzzled me for a moment, and then appeared
so outrageously wide of the mark that I had not

presence of mind to answer it ; and the opportunity
was presently gone. I wonder whether she really
supposed she had given me a check and a set down !
' Come now,' said she ; ' don't let us talk about that.
I want to get this information from you, and we will
talk only about what we agree in. You know we shall
differ about pulling down, and all that.' Why she
talked to me at all if she supposed that I wanted to
pull down every thing, from the throne to the workhouse, I can't imagine. And if she thought so of me,
she must have regarded the then dominant Liberals as
unredeemed destructives. It is a curious state of mind
in the Tory aristocracy that such incidents reveal. She
seemed otherwise sensible enough ; yet she had read
my Series without finding out that I am for ' pulling
down ' nothing, and quietly superseding what can no
longer be endured.

The ancient ladies themselves, the Miss Berrys and
their inseparable friend, Lady Charlotte Lindsay (the
youngest daughter of Lord North), whose presence
seemed to carry one back almost a century, were the
main attraction of those parties. While up to all
modern interests, the old-fashioned rouge and pearl-
powder, and false hair, and the use of the feminine
oaths of a hundred years ago were odd and striking.
E.g. : a footman tells his mistress that Lady So-and-
so begs she will not wait dinner, as she is drying her
shoes which got wet between the carriage and the door.
The response is ' O ! Christ ! if she should catch cold !
Tell her she is a dear soul, and we would not have her
hurry herself for the world,' &c., &c. My mother
heard an exclamation at our door, when the carriage
door would not open, ' My God ! I can't get out ! '

And so forth, continually. But they were all three so cheerful, so full of knowledge and of sympathy for good ideas, and so evidently fit for higher pursuits than the social pleasures amidst which one met them, that, though their parties *were* ' rather blue,' they were exceedingly agreeable. I had a general invitation to go there, whenever, in passing their house in Mayfair from a dinner-party, I saw light over the lower shutters ; and they also invited me to spend summer days with them at their Petersham house. I never did this for want of time; and I went seldom to their evening parties, for the same reason that I seemed to neglect other invitations of the same general kind,—that I was always engaged three or four weeks in advance, by express invitation. When my aged friends perceived this, they gave me express invitations too, and made me fix my own day. The last of the trio, the elder Miss Berry, died in November, 1852. The announcement impelled me to record the associations it excited ; and I did so in an obituary memoir of her in the ' Daily News.'* My friend Milnes offered his tribute in the form of some charming lines in the ' Times,' which show how strong was the natural feeling of concern, on such an occasion, at letting go our hold on the traditions of the last century.

How different were those parties from the express ' blue' assemblies of such pedants as Lady Mary Shepherd ! She went about accompanied by the fame given her by Mr. Tierney, when he said that there was not another head in England which could encounter hers on the subject of Cause and Effect, and some

* Appendix A.

kindred topics: and it did indeed appear that she was, in relation to the subtlest metaphysical topics, what Mrs. Somerville was to mathematical astronomy. The difference was,—and a bottomless chasm separated the two,—that Mrs. Somerville was occupied with real science,—with the knowable; whereas, Lady Mary Shepherd never dreamed of looking out first for a sound point of view, and therefore wasted her fine analytical powers on things unknowable or purely imaginary. It was a story against her that when in a country house, one fine day, she took her seat in a window, saying in a business-like manner (to David Ricardo, if I remember rightly,)—'Come, now; let us have a little discussion about Space.' I never went to her house but once. Though I there first made Mr. Milnes's acquaintance, I never would go again; and I then made my escape as soon as I could. First, I was set down beside Lady Charlotte Bury, and made to undergo, for her satisfaction, a ludicrous examination by Lady Mary, about how I wrote my Series, and what I thought of it. Escaping from this, to an opposite sofa, I was boarded by Lady Stepney, who was then, as she boasted, receiving seven hundred pounds apiece for her novels. She paraded a pair of diamond earrings, costing that sum, which she had so earned. She began talking to me on the ground of our mutual acquaintance with Mrs. Opie, who had once been an intimate friend and correspondent of hers. She complained of the inconvenience of Mrs. Opie's quakerism; and insisted on having my suffrage whether it was not very wrong in people to change their opinions, on account of the inconvenience to their friends. The difficulty in conversing with this extraordinary personage was that she stopped at intervals, to demand an unqualified assent to what she said, while saying things impossible to assent to   She insisted on my believing that ' that dreadful Reform in Parliament took place entirely because the dear Duke' of Wellington had not my 'moral courage,' and would not carry a trumpet. She told me that the dear Duke assured her himself that if he had heard what had been said from the Treasury-benches, he should never have made that declaration against parliamentary reform which brought it on : and thence it followed, Lady Stepney concluded, that if he had heard what was said behind him,—that is, if he had carried a trumpet, he would have suppressed his declaration ; and the rest followed of course. I was so amused at this that I told Lady Durham of it ; and she repeated it to her father, then Prime Minister ; and then ensued the most amusing part of all. Lord Grey did not apparently take it as a joke on my part, but sent me word, in all seriousness, that there would have been parliamentary reform, sooner or later, if the Duke of Wellington *had* carried a trumpet ! Lady Stepney pointed to a large easy chair at my elbow, and said she supposed I knew for whom that was intended. She was surprised that I did not, and told me that it was for Captain Ross ; and that the company assembled were longing for him to come, that they might see the meeting between him and me, and hear what we should say to each other. This determined me to be off ; and I kept my eye on the doors, in order to slip away on the entrance of the newest ' lion.' It was too early yet to go with any decency. Lady Stepney told me meantime that the Arctic voyagers had gone

through hardships such as could never be told : but it
only proved (and to this in particular she required my
assent) 'that the Deity is everywhere, and more particularly in barren places.' She went on to say how
very wrong she thought it to send men into such places,
without any better reason than she had ever heard of.
'They say it is to discover the North Pole,' she proceeded ; ' and, by the bye, it is curious that Newton
should have come within thirty miles of the North
Pole in his discoveries. They *say*, you know,' and
here she looked exceedingly sagacious and amused ;
'they *say* that they have found the magnetic pole.
But you and I know what a magnet is, very well.
We know that a little thing like that would be pulled
out of its place in the middle of the sea.' When I
reported this conversation to my mother, we determined to get one of this lady's novels immediately,
and see what she could write that would sell for seven
hundred pounds. If she was to be believed as to this,
it really was a curious sign of the times. I never saw
any of her books, after all. I can hardly expect to be
believed about the anecdote of the magnet (which I
imagine she took to be a little red horse-shoe ;) and I
had some difficulty in believing it myself, at the moment : but I have given her very words. And they
were no joke. She shook her head-dress of marabout
feathers and black bugles with her excitement as she
talked. I got away before Captain Ross appeared,
and never went to the house again, except to drop a
card before I left London.

Some people may be disposed to turn round upon
me with the charge of giving blue-stocking parties.
I believe that to blue-stocking people my soirées might

have that appearance, because they looked through
blue spectacles: but I can confidently say that, not
only were my parties as diverse in quality as I could
make them,—always including many who were not
literary; but I took particular care that no one was in
any way shown off, but all treated with equal respect
as guests. My rooms were too small for personages
who required space for display: and such were not
therefore invited. A gentleman who expected a sofa
all to himself, while a crowd of adorers simpered in his
face, was no guest for a simple evening party in a
small house: nor a lady who needed a corner in which
to confide her troubles with her husband; nor for
another who hung her white hand over the arm of her
chair, and lectured metaphysically and sentimentally
about art, to the annoyance of true connoisseurs who
felt that while she was exposing herself, she was mis-
leading others who knew no more about the real thing
than she did. Nor had I a place for rouged and made-
up old ladies who paraded literary flirtations in the style
of half a century ago. Such were not therefore invited.
I was too nervous about having parties at all to introduce any persons who might be disagreeable to people
of better manners. All I ventured upon was to invite
those who knew what to expect, and could stay away
if they liked. What they had to expect was tea below
stairs, and ices, cake and wine during the evening,
with a very choice assembly of guests who did not
mind a little crowding, for the sake of the conversation
they afforded each other. I became more at ease when
I found that all whom I invited always came: a test
which satisfied me that they liked to come.

I have particularised only well-known persons: but

it must be understood that these were not my intimates,
or most valued acquaintances. If they had been intimate
friends, I could not have characterised them. There
were three or four houses where I went freely for rest
and recreation ; families too near and dear to me to be
described in detail. There were country houses where
I went every week or two, to meet pleasant little dinner-parties, and to sleep, for the enjoyment of country
air and quiet. Such as these were the H. Béllenden
Kers', whose Swiss Cottage at Cheshunt was a sort
of home to me : and the Porters', first at Norwood,
and then on Putney Heath : and then the Huttons'
at Putney Park : and the Fishers' at Highbury : and
the Potters' at Notting Hill : and the Marshes' at
Kilburn: and the Hensleigh Wedgwoods'; in their
Clapham home first, and then in Regent's Park :
and my old friend, Mrs. Reid's, in Regent's Park :
besides my own relations. All these were home
houses to me ;—each a refuge from the wear and tear
of my busy life, and from the incessant siege of lion-
hunting strangers. One yearly holiday was especially
refreshing to me. With the first fine weather in May,
Mr. and Mrs. Fisher and I used to go, for a few days,
or a week, to Boxhill, or Godstone, or some other
pretty place not too far off, and carry a book or two,
and lie on the grass, or ramble among hills, commons,
or lanes, as if we had nothing to do ; and I never
came home without fresh spirits for my work, and
valuable suggestions about new efforts. With them
I planned or thought of some of my tales : with
them I discussed 'Deerbrook,' the week before I
began it, though Mrs. Ker was my great confidante
during its progress. I spent a month or more of every

summer with her at her Swiss Cottage : and a month
of luxury it always was,—well as my work proceeded
in my own ' den ' there.

I was spending a couple of days at Mrs. Marsh's,
when she asked me whether I would let her read to
me ' one or two little stories ' which she had written.
From her way of speaking of them, and from her
devotion to her children, who were then for the most
part very young, I concluded these to be children's
tales. She ordered a fire in her room, and there we
shut ourselves up for the reading. What she read
was no child's story, but ' The Admiral's Daughter.'
My amazement may be conceived. We were going
to dine at the Wedgwoods' : and a strange figure we
must have cut there; for we had been crying so
desperately that there was no concealing the marks
of it.   Mrs. Marsh asked me what I thought of
getting her tales published. I offered to try if, on
reading the manuscript at home, I thought as well of
it as after her own most moving delivery of it.   A
second reading left no doubt on my mind ; and I had
the pleasure of introducing the ' Two Old Men's
Tales ' to the world through Messrs. Saunders and
Otley, from whom, as from the rest of the world, the
author's name was withheld as long as possible. Mr.
Marsh made this the condition of our attempt : a condition which we thought perfectly reasonable in the
father of many daughters, who did not wish their
mother to be known as the author of what the world
might consider second-rate novels. That the world
did not consider them second-rate was immediately
apparent ; and the reason for secrecy existed no longer.
But no one ever knew or guessed the authorship

through my mother or me, who were for a considerable time the only possessors of the secret. From that time Mrs. Marsh managed her own affairs; and I never again saw her works till they were published. I mention this because, as I never concealed from her, I think her subsequent works very inferior to the first: and I think it a pity that she did not rest on the high and well-deserved fame which she immediately obtained. The singular magnificence of that tale was not likely to be surpassed: but I have always wished that she had either stopped entirely, or had given herself time to do justice to her genius. From the time of the publication of the 'Two Old Men's Tales' to the present hour, I have never once as far as I remember succeeded in getting another manuscript published for any body. This has been a matter of great concern to me: but such is the fact. I have never had to make any proposal of the kind for myself,—having always had a choice of publishers before my works were ready; but I have striven hard on behalf of others, and without the slightest success.

No kind of evening was more delightful to me than those which were spent with the Carlyles. About once a fortnight, a mutual friend of theirs and mine drove me over to Chelsea, to the early tea table at number five, Cheyne Row,— the house which Carlyle was perpetually complaining of and threatening to leave, but where he is still to be found. I never believed that, considering the delicate health of both, they could ever flourish on that Chelsea clay, close to the river; and I rejoiced when the term of lease had nearly expired, and my friends were looking out for another house. If they were living in a 'cauldron' and a

' Babel,' it seemed desirable that they should find an airy quiet home in the country,—near enough to London to enjoy its society at pleasure. Carlyle went forth, on the fine black horse which a friend had sent him with sanitary views, and looked about him. Forth he went, his wife told me, with three maps of Great Britain and two of the World in his pocket, to explore the area within twenty miles of London. All their friends were on the look-out; and I, from my sick chamber at Tynemouth, sent them earnest entreaties to settle on a gravelly soil : but old habit prevailed, and the philosopher renewed the lease, and set to work to make for himself a noise-proof chamber, where his fretted nerves might possibly obtain rest amidst the London ' Babel.' I like the house for no other reason than that I spent many very pleasant evenings in it: but it has now become completely associated with the marvellous talk of both husband and wife. There we met Mazzini, when he was exerting himself for the education of the Italians in London, and before he entered openly on the career of insurrection by which he has since become the most notorious man in Europe. I entirely believe in all that his adorers say of the noble qualities of his heart and temper. I can quite understand how it is that some of those who know him best believe him to be the best man in existence. There is no doubt whatever of his devotedness, his magnanimity, his absolute disinterestedness. But the more, and not the less, for all this does his career seem to me almost the saddest spectacle of our time. He is an ideologist who will preach for ever in a mood of exaltation and a style of fustian, without being listened to by any but those who do not need his incitements.

Insurrection is too serious a matter to be stirred up by
turgid appeals like his, vague and irreducible to the
concrete. Accordingly, here are twenty years since I
knew him gone by without success or the prospect of
it. His beacon fire blazed longer at Rome than any
where: but it went out; and it left in ashes many a
glorious relic from ancient times, and the peace of
many households. The slaughter of patriots from
abortive insurrections has gone on through a long
course of years, till, if Mazzini's heart is not broken,
many others are; and the day of an Italian republic
seems further off than ever. To Mazzini it seems
always at hand, as the Millennium seems to Robert
Owen; but I cannot find that any one else who knows
the Italians has the least belief that, as a people, they
desire a republic, or that the small minority who do
could ever agree to the terms of any republican constitution, or maintain it if established. His career
will be, I fear, as it has hitherto been, one of failure;
and of failure so disastrous as to set it above every
other *vie manquée*. When I knew him, face to face,
these purposes of his were growing in silence. His
still, patient, grave countenance was that of a man
who had suffered much, and could endure to any ex-
tremity: but I could not have supposed that experience
and experiment could have been so lost on him as they
appear to have been. His self-will was not the less
strong for his disinterestedness, it appears; and it has
taken possession of his intellect, causing him to believe, with a fatal confidence, what he wishes. When
we consider how Sardinia has advanced, during the
whole period of Mazzini's bloody and fruitless struggles, and how that State is now a striking spectacle

of growing civil and religious liberty, while Mazzini, with his perfect plots, his occult armies, his buried arms and ammunition, his own sufferings and dangers, and his holocaust of victims, has aggravated the tyranny of Austria, and rendered desperate the cause of his countrymen, we can hardly help wishing that his own devotedness had met with acceptance, and that the early sacrifice of his life had spared that of hundreds of his followers who are wept by thousands more.

Another *vie manquée* was before my eyes at the Carlyles'. John Sterling was then in the midst of his conflicts of all sorts,—with bad health, with the solemn pity and covert reprobation of orthodox friends and patrons, and with his own restless excitement about authorship. I cannot say that I knew him at all; for I never heard the sound of his voice. When we met at the tea table, he treated me like a chair; and so pointed was his rude ignoring of me that there was nothing to be done but for Carlyle to draw off apart with him after tea, while the rest of us talked on the other side of the room. When our meetings were over,—when I was on my couch at Tynemouth, and he was trying to breathe in Devonshire, he suddenly changed his mind, on meeting with 'Deerbrook,' and was as anxious to obtain my acquaintance as he had been to avoid it. Supposing me to be at Teignmouth, and therefore within reach, he wrote to Mrs. Carlyle to ask whether it was too late, or whether she would sanction his going to Teignmouth to ask my friendship. I should have been very happy to hear the voice belonging to the striking face and head I knew so well : but it *was* too late. The length

of the kingdom lay between us ; and before I emerged
from my sick-room, he was in his grave. I am glad
I saw him, whatever he might have been thinking of
me ; (and what it was I have not the remotest idea :)
for I retain a strong impression of his noble head and
vital countenance.

Another memorable head was there, now and then.
Leigh Hunt was there, with his cheery face, bright,
acute, and full of sensibility ; and his thick grizzled
hair combed down smooth, and his homely figure ;—
black handkerchief, grey stockings and stout shoes,
while he was full of gratitude to ladies who dress in
winter in velvet, and in rich colours ; and to old dames
in the streets or the country who still wear scarlet
cloaks. His conversation was lively, rapid, highly
illustrative, and perfectly natural. I remember one
evening when Horne was there (the author of
' Orion,' &c.) wishing that the three heads,—
Hunt's, Horne's and Carlyle's,—could be sketched
in a group. Horne's perfectly white complexion, and
somewhat coxcombical curling whiskers and determined picturesqueness contrasted curiously with the
homely manliness of Hunt's fine countenance, and the
rugged face, steeped in genius, of Carlyle. I have
seen Carlyle's face under all aspects, from the deepest
gloom to the most reckless or most genial mirth ; and
it seemed to me that each mood would make a totally
different portrait. The sympathetic is by far the
finest, in my eyes. His excess of sympathy has been,
I believe, the master-pain of his life. He does not
know what to do with it, and with its bitterness, seeing that human life is full of pain to those who look
out for it : and the savageness which has come to be a

main characteristic of this singular man is, in my opinion, a mere expression of his intolerable sympathy with the suffering. He cannot express his love and pity in natural acts, like other people; and it shows itself too often in unnatural speech. But to those who understand his eyes, his shy manner, his changing colour, his sigh, and the constitutional *pudeur* which renders him silent about every thing that he feels the most deeply, his wild speech and abrupt manner are perfectly intelligible. I have felt to the depths of my heart what his sympathy was in my days of success and prosperity and apparent happiness without drawback; and again in sickness, pain, and hopelessness of being ever at ease again: I have observed the same strength of feeling towards all manner of sufferers; and I am confident that Carlyle's affections are too much for him, and the real cause of the 'ferocity' with which he charges himself, and astonishes others. It must be such a strong love and honour as his friends feel for him that can compensate for the pain of witnessing his suffering life. When I knew him familiarly, he rarely slept, was wofully dyspeptic, and as variable as possible in mood. When my friend and I entered the little parlour at Cheyne Row, our host was usually miserable. Till he got his coffee, he asked a list of questions, without waiting for answers, and looked as if he was on the rack. After tea, he brightened and softened, and sent us home full of admiration and friendship, and sometimes with a hope that he would some day be happy. It was our doing, —that friend's and mine,—that he gave lectures for three or four seasons. He had matter to utter; and there were many who wished to hear him; and in

those days, before his works had reached their re-
munerative point of sale, the earnings by his lectures
could not be unacceptable. So we confidently proceeded, taking the management of the arrangements,
and leaving Carlyle nothing to do but to meet his
audience, and say what he had to say. Whenever I
went, my pleasure was a good deal spoiled by his un-
concealable nervousness. Yellow as a guinea, with
downcast eyes, broken speech at the beginning, and
fingers which nervously picked at the desk before
him, he could not for a moment be supposed to enjoy
his own effort; and the lecturer's own enjoyment is a
prime element of success. The merits of Carlyle's
discourses were however so great that he might probably have gone on year after year till this time, with
improving success, and perhaps ease : but the struggle
was too severe. From the time that his course was
announced till it was finished, he scarcely slept, and
he grew more dyspeptic and nervous every day ; and
we were at length entreated to say no more about his
lecturing, as no fame and no money or other advantage could counterbalance the misery which the
engagement caused him.—I remember being puzzled
for a long time as to whether Carlyle did or did not
care for fame. He was for ever scoffing at it ; and he
seemed to me just the man to write because he needed
to utter himself, without ulterior considerations. One
day I was dining there alone. I had brought over
from America twenty-five copies of his ' Sartor
Resartus,' as reprinted there ; and, having sold them
at the English price, I had some money to put into
his hand. I did put it into his hand the first time :
but it made him uncomfortable, and he spent it in a

pair of signet rings, for his wife and me (her motto being 'Point de faiblesse,' and mine 'Frisch zu!') This would never do; so, having imported and sold a second parcel, the difficulty was what to do with the money. My friend and I found that Carlyle was ordered weak brandy and water instead of wine; and we spent our few sovereigns in French brandy of the best quality, which we carried over one evening, when going to tea. Carlyle's amusement and delight at first, and all the evening after, whenever he turned his eyes towards the long-necked bottles, showed us that we had made a good choice. He declared that he had got a reward for his labours at last: and his wife asked me to dinner, all by myself, to taste the brandy. We three sat round the fire after dinner, and Carlyle mixed the toddy while Mrs. Carlyle and I discussed some literary matters, and speculated on fame and the love of it. Then Carlyle held out a glass of his mixture to me with, ' Here,—take this. It is worth all the fame in England.' Yet Allan Cunningham, who knew and loved him well, told me one evening, to my amazement, that Carlyle would be very well, and happy enough, if he got a little more fame. I asked him whether he was in earnest ; and he said he was, and moreover sure that he was right—I should see that he was. Carlyle's fame has grown from that day ; and on the whole his health and spirits seem to be improved, so that his friend Allan was partly right. But I am certain that there are constitutional sources of pain (aggravated, no doubt, by excess in study in his youth) which have nothing to do with love of fame, or any other self-regards.

In 1837, he came to me to ask how he should

manage, if he accepted a proposal from Fraser to publish his pieces as a collection of ' Miscellanies.' After discussing the money part of the business, I begged him to let me undertake the proof-correcting,—supposing of course that the pieces were to be simply reprinted. He nearly agreed to let me do this, but afterwards changed his mind. The reason for my offer was that the sight of his proofs had more than once really alarmed me,—so irresolute, as well as fastidious, did he seem to be as to the expression of his plainest thoughts. Almost every other word was altered; and revise followed upon revise. I saw at once that this way of proceeding must be very harassing to him; and also that profit must be cut off to a most serious degree by this absurdly expensive method of printing. I told him that it would turn out just so if he would not allow his ' Miscellanies ' to be reprinted just as they stood, in the form in which people had admired, and now desired to possess them. As might be expected, the printing went on very slowly, and there seemed every probability that this simple reprint would stand over to another season. One day, while in my study, I heard a prodigious sound of laughter on the stairs; and in came Carlyle, laughing loud. He had been laughing in that manner all the way from the printing-office in Charing Cross. As soon as he could, he told me what it was about. He had been to the office to urge on the printer : and the man said, ' Why, Sir, you really are so very hard upon us with your corrections ! They take so much time, you see !' After some remonstrance, Carlyle observed that he had been accustomed to this sort of thing,— that he had got works printed in Scotland, and . . .

' Yes, indeed, Sir,' interrupted the printer. ' We
are aware of that. We have a man here from Edinburgh; and when he took up a bit of your copy, he
dropped it as if it had burnt his fingers, and cried out,
" Lord have mercy; have you got that man to print
for? Lord knows when we shall get done,—with
all his corrections ! " ' Carlyle could not reply for
laughing, and he came to tell me that I was not singular in my opinion about his method of revising.

He has now been very long about his ' Frederick
the Great,' which I must, therefore, like a good many
more, die without seeing. I could never grow tired
of his biographies. From the time when I first knew
him, I am not aware that he has advanced in any
views, or grown riper in his conclusions; and his
mind has always seemed to me as inaccessible as
Wordsworth's, or any other constitutionally isolated
like theirs: and therefore it is that I prefer to an out-
pouring of his own notions, which we have heard as
often as he has written didactically, and which were
best conveyed in his ' Sartor Resartus,' a commentary on a character, as in biography, or on events, as in
a history. For many reasons, I prefer his biographies.
I do not think that he can do any more effectual work
in the field of philosophy or morals : but I enjoy an
occasional addition to the fine gallery of portraits
which he has given us. I am now too much out of
the world to know what is the real condition of his
fame and influence : but, for my own part, I could not
read his Latter Day Pamphlets, while heartily enjoying his Life of his friend Sterling, and, in the main,
his ' Cromwell.' No one can read his ' Cromwell '
without longing for his ' Frederick the Great : ' and

I hope he will achieve that portrait, and others after
it. However much or little he may yet do, he certainly ought to be recognised as one of the chief influences of his time. Bad as is our political morality,
and grievous as are our social short-comings, we are at
least awakened to a sense of our sins : and I cannot
but ascribe this awakening mainly to Carlyle. What
Wordsworth did for poetry, in bringing us out of a
conventional idea and method to a true and simple
one, Carlyle has done for morality. He may be himself the most curious opposition to himself,—he may
be the greatest mannerist of his age while denouncing
conventionàlism,—the greatest talker while eulogis-
ing silence,—the most woeful complainer while glori-
fying fortitude,—the most uncertain and stormy in
mood, while holding forth serenity as the greatest good
within the reach of Man : but he has nevertheless in-
fused into the mind of the English nation a sincerity,
earnestness, healthfulness and courage which can be
appreciated only by those who are old enough to tell
what was our morbid state when Byron was the representative of our temper, the Clapham Church of our
religion, and the rotten-borough system of our political morality. If I am warranted in believing that the
society I am bidding farewell to is a vast improvement
upon that which I was born into, I am confident that
the ' sed change is attributable to Carlyle more
than to any single influence besides.

My mornings were, as   have said, reserved for
work ; and the occasions were very rare when I allowed any encroachment on the hours before two
o'clock. Now and then, however, it was necessary ;
as when the Royal Academy Exhibition opened, and

I really could not go, except at the early hour when
scarcely any body else was there. The plain truth is
that I was so stared at and followed in those days that
I had not courage to go (indicated by my trumpet)
to public places at their fullest time. Even at the
Somerset House Exhibition, in the early morning,
when the floors were still wet with watering, I was
sure to be discovered and followed. There was a party,
I remember, who so pushed upon me, and smiled at
me under my bonnet (having recognised me by Evans's
portrait on the wall) that my mother exercised her
sarcastic spirit with some effect. She said to me,
after many vain attempts to get away from the grin-
ning group,—' Harriet, these ladies seem to have
some business with us. Shall we ask them how we
can be of any service to them ?' By Mr. Macready's
kindness, we escaped this annoyance at the theatre,
where we spent many a pleasant evening. He gave
us the stage box, whenever we chose to ask for it ;
and there my mother, whose sight was failing, could
see, and I, deaf as I was, could hear ; and nobody saw
us behind our curtain, so that we could go in our
warm morning dress, and be as free and easy as if we
were at home. This was one of my very greatest
pleasures,—Macready's interpretation of Shakspere
being as high an intellectual treat as I know of.

I have mentioned Evans's portrait of me,—of
which Sir A. Callcott said to me, ' What are your
friends about to allow that atrocity to hang there ?'
We could not help it. Mr. Evans was introduced to
me by a mutual acquaintance, on the ground that he
was painting portraits for a forthcoming work, and
wanted mine. I could not have refused without down-

right surliness; but it appeared afterwards that the
artist had other views. I sat to him as often as he
wished, though I heartily disliked the attitude, which
was one in which I certainly was never seen. The
worst misfortune, however, was that he went on painting and painting at the portrait, long after I had
ceased to sit,—the result of which was that the
picture came out the 'atrocity' that Callcott called
it. The artist hawked it about for sale, some years
after, and I hope nobody bought it; for my family
would be sorry that it should be taken for a representation of me. While on this subject, I must say that
I have been not very well used in this matter of portraits. It signifies little now that Mr. Richmond's
admirable portrait and the engraving from it exist to
show what I really look like: but before that, my
family were rather disturbed at the 'atrocities' issued, without warrant, as likenesses of me; and especially by Miss Gillies, who covered the land for a
course of years with supposed likenesses of me, in
which there was (as introduced strangers always exclaimed) 'not the remotest resemblance.' I sat to
Miss Gillies for (I think) a miniature, at her own request, in 1832; and from a short time after that, she
never saw me again. Yet she continued, almost every
year, to put out new portraits of me,—each bigger,
more vulgar and more monstrous than the last, till
some of my relations, having seen those of the
'People's Journal,' and the 'New Spirit of the Age,'
wrote to me to ask whether the process could not be
put a stop to, as certainly no person had any business
to issue so-called portraits without the sanction of
myself or my family, and without even applying to see

me after the lapse of a dozen years. The drollest
thing was to see the Editor of the ' People's Journal,'
when we first met. He had been complacent and gratified, as he told me, about presenting a likeness of me
in the Journal; on which I had made no observation,
as it could answer no purpose to object when the thing
was done. When we did meet, his first words were,
as he sank back on the sofa,—' Ma'am, the portrait!
There is not the remotest resemblance!'

I think there were fourteen or fifteen bad portraits
before Mr. Richmond's good one was obtained. I
need not say that their fabrication was a disagreeable
process to me. That is of course: but I could not
prevent them. For some I did not sit: in other cases,
I really could not help myself. I refused to sit; but
the artists came, with easel and implements, and
established themselves in a corner of my study, requesting me to go on with my work, and forget that
they were there. The only one besides Richmond's,
and Miss Gillies's first, that has been liked by any
body, as far as I know, is Osgood's, taken in America.
I do not myself think it good. It is too good-looking
by far; and the attitude is melodramatic. But it is
like some of my relations, and therefore probably more
or less like me. All the rest are, we think, good for
less than nothing.—Two casts have been taken of my
head; one in 1833, and one in 1853. They were
taken purely for phrenological purposes. As I have
bequeathed my skull and brain, for the same objects,
I should not have thought it necessary to have a
second cast taken (to verify the changes made by
time) but for the danger of accident which might
frustrate my arrangements. I might die by drown-

ing at sea; or by a railway smash, which would
destroy the head: so I made all sure by having a cast
taken, not long before my last illness began.

It may be as well to explain here some transactions
which might appear strange, if their reasons and their
course were not understood. At the time of my removal to London, the special horror of the day was
the Burke and Hare murders; and all wits were set
to work to devise a remedy for the scarcity of bodies
for dissection which bred such phenomena as the
Burkes and Hares. The mischief was that the only
authorised supply was from the gallows; and disgrace
was added to the natural dislike of the idea of dissection. Good citizens set to work in various ways to
dissolve the association of disgrace with *post mortem*
dissection. Some sold the reversion of their bodies;
and others followed Bentham's example of leaving his
body for dissection, by an express provision of his will.
I, being likely to outlive my only remaining parent,
and to have no nearer connexion, did this, when my
new earnings obliged me to make a new will in 1832.
The passage of Mr. Warburton's bill, and its success,
relieved the necessity of the case; and in my next
will, the arrangement was omitted. This was one of
the transactions I referred to. The next was much
later in date. When I found that, easy as it is to
procure brains and skulls, it is not easy to obtain those
of persons whose minds are well known, so that it is
rather a rare thing to be able to compare manifestations with structure, I determined to do what I could
to remedy the difficulty by bequeathing my skull and
brain to the ablest phrenologist I knew of; and this I
did in the will rendered necessary by the acquisition of

my Ambleside property. Soon after that will was
made, I received a letter from Mr. Toynbee, the well-
known benevolent surgeon, enclosing a note of introduction from a mutual friend, and going straight to
the point on which he wished to address me. He laid
before me the same consideration in regard to cases of
deafness that I have set down above in connexion
with phrenology generally, saying that it is easy
enough to obtain the skulls of deaf persons, in order
to study the structure of the ear ; and it is very easy
to meet with deaf people in life ; but it is very difficult
to obtain the defunct ears of persons whose deafness
has been a subject of observation during life. He
therefore requested me to leave him a legacy of my
ears. He added a few words, in explanation of his
plain speaking, about the amount of mischief and
misery caused by the ignorance of surgeons in regard
to the ear ; an ignorance which can be removed only
by such means as he proposed. I was rather amused
when I caught myself in a feeling of shame, as it
were, at having only one pair of ears ;—at having
no duplicate for Mr. Toynbee after having disposed
otherwise of my skull. I told him how the matter
stood ; and my legatee and he met, to ascertain
whether one head could in any way be made to
answer both their objects. It could not be, and Mr.
Toynbee could not be gratified. I called on him in
London afterwards, and showed him as much as he
could see while I was alive : and he showed me his
wonderful collection of preparations, by which mal-
formation and impaired structure of the ear are already
largely illustrated. This is the other transaction which
I referred to, and which may as well be distinctly

understood, as I do not at all pride myself on doing odd things which may jar upon people's natural feelings.

Two or three times during my residence in London, I was requested to allow my head to be pronounced upon by professional phrenologists, under precautions against their knowing who I was. I entirely disapprove, and always did, that summary way of deciding on the characters of utter strangers, whose very curiosity is a kind of evidence of their not being in a state to hear the sober truth; while the imperfect knowledge of the structure of the brain at that time, and our present certainty of the complexity of its action, must obviate all probability of an accurate judgment being formed. At the time I speak of, every body was going to Deville, to see his collection of bronzes, and to sit down under his hands, and hear their own characters,—for which they paid down their half-sovereigns, and came away, elated or amused. Among those who so went was a remarkable trio,— of whom Lord Lansdowne and Sydney Smith were two; and I think, but am not sure, that Jeffrey was the third. They went on foot, and avoided naming each other, and passed for ordinary visitors. Lord Lansdowne, to whom was consigned at that time, on account of his aptitude for detail, all the small troublesome business of the Cabinet which every body else was glad to escape, was pronounced by Deville to be liable to practical failure at every turn by his tendency to lose himself in the abstract, and neglect particulars. What he said to Jeffrey (if Jeffrey it was) I forget; but it was something which amused his companions excessively. ‘ This gentleman's case,' said Deville of

Sydney Smith, 'is clear enough. His faculties are those of a naturalist, and I see that he gratifies them. This gentleman is always happy, among his collections of birds and of fishes.' 'Sir,' said Sydney Smith, turning round upon him solemnly, with wide open eyes, 'I don't know a fish from a bird.' Of about the same accuracy was Deville's judgment of me. We were a large party,—seven or eight,—of whom my mother was one, and three others were acquaintances of Deville's. It was agreed that his friends should take the rest of us, as if to see the bronzes; that I should hide my trumpet in a bag, and that nobody should name me (or my mother) or speak to me as to a deaf person. We were certain to be invited by Deville, they said, to hear a little address on Phrenology; and he would then propose to pronounce on the character of any one of the company. I was instructed to take my seat at the end of the group, nearest Deville's right hand, and to take off my bonnet at a certain signal. All went exactly as foreseen. For some time the party listened gravely enough to the oracle which I heard mumbling above my head; but at length all burst into a roar of laughter. Mr. Deville pronounced that my life must be one of great suffering, because it was a life of constant failure through timidity. I could never accomplish any thing, through my remarkable deficiency in both physical and moral courage. My mother then observed that it was so far true that I was the most timid child she had ever known. Satisfied with this, Deville proceeded. Amidst some truer things, he said I had wit. Some very properly denied this: but one exclaimed, 'Well, I say that any one who has read

Miss Martineau's poor-law tale. . . . . . .' And now
the murder was out. Deville was much discomposed,
—said it was not fair,—desired to do it all over
again,—to come to our house and try, and so forth:
but we told him that the whole proceeding was spontaneous on his own part, and that he had better leave
the matter where it was. An amended judgment
could not be worth anything.—Another time, I went
with my friends, Mr. and Mrs. F., to call on Mr.
Holm the Phrenologist. They had some acquaintance
with him, and had an appointment with him, to have
him pronounce on Mrs. F.'s head. Mrs. F. thought
this a good opportunity to obtain an opinion of my
case; and I therefore accompanied her,—no trumpet
visible, and no particular notice being taken of me.
Mr. Holm pronounced my genius to be for millinery.
He said that it was clear, by such and such tokens,
that I was always on the look-out for tasteful bonnets
and caps; and that my attention being fixed on one
at a shop window, I should go home and attempt to
make one like it: and should succeed. Such was the
sum and substance of his judgment. I afterwards,
at his request, attended a few private lectures of his,
in a class of three members, the other two being the
Duke of Somerset and Rammohun Roy. I really
used to pity the lecturer when, from the brain or cast
which he held in his hand, he glanced at the heads of
his pupils; for the Duke of Somerset had a brown
wig, coming down low on his forehead: Rammohun
Roy had his turban just above his eyebrows; and I,
of course, had my bonnet. No one who knows me
will suppose that in thus speaking of so-called phrenologists and their empirical practices, I am in the

slightest degree reflecting on that department of physiological science. It is because such empirical practice is insulting and injurious to true science that I record my own experience of it. The proceedings of the fortune-telling oracles, which pronounce for fees, are no more like those of true and philosophical students of the brain than the shows of itinerant chemical lecturers, who burned blue lights, and made explosions, and electrified people half a century ago are like the achievements of a Davy or a Faraday.

One of my rare morning expeditions was to see Coleridge at his Highgate residence. I cannot remember on what introduction I went, nor whether I went alone : but I remember a kind reception by Mr. and Mrs. Gilman, and by Coleridge himself. I was a great admirer of him as a poet then, as I am, to a more limited extent, now. If I had thought of the man then as I have been compelled by Cottle's Life to think of him since, I should not have enacted the hypocrisy of going to see him, in the mode practised by his worshippers. In these days, when it is a sort of fashion among wise men of all opinions to insist upon the disconnexion of religion and morals, one may have a strong sympathy with a man or a writer of eloquent religious sensibilities, even if his moral views or conduct may be unsatisfactory. But then, the religious eloquence must be of a sounder intellectual quality than Coleridge's appears to me to be. In truth, I do not know how to escape the persuasion that Coleridge was laughing in his sleeve while writing some of the characteristic pieces which his adorers go into raptures about. A great deal of cloud-beauty there is in the climate and atmosphere of his religious writings; and if his disciples would not attempt to make this charm, and his marvellous subtlety, go for more than they are worth, one could have no objection to any amount of admiration they could enjoy from such a source. But those who feel as strongly as I do the irreverence and vanity of making the most solemn and sacred subjects an opportunity for intellectual self-indulgence, for paradox, and word-play and cloud-painting, and cocoon-spinning out of one's own interior, will feel certain that the prophesied immortality of Coleridge will be not so much that of his writings as of himself, as an extreme specimen of the tendencies of our metaphysical period, which, being itself but a state of transition, can permit no immortality to its special products but as historical types of its characteristics and tendencies. If Coleridge should be remembered, it will be as a warning,—as much in his philosophical as his moral character.—Such is my view of him now. Twenty years ago I regarded him as poet,—in his ' Friend ' as much as his verse. He was, to be sure, a most remarkable-looking personage, as he entered the room, and slowly approached and greeted me. He looked very old, with his rounded shoulders and drooping head, and excessively thin limbs. His eyes were as wonderful as they were ever represented to be;—light grey, extremely prominent, and actually glittering : an appearance I am told common among opium eaters. His onset amused me not a little. He told me that he (the last person whom I should have suspected) read my tales as they came out on the first of the month ; and, after paying some compliments, he avowed that there were points on which we differed : (I was full of wonder that there

were any on which we agreed :) 'for instance,' said
he, 'you appear to consider that society is an aggregate of individuals!' I replied that I certainly did :
whereupon he went off on one of the several metaphysical interpretations which may be put upon the
many-sided fact of an organised human society, subject
to natural laws in virtue of its aggregate character
and organisation together. After a long flight in
survey of society from his own balloon in his own
current, he came down again to some considerations
of individuals, and at length to some special biographical topics, ending with criticisms on old biographers,
whose venerable works he brought down from the
shelf. No one else spoke, of course, except when I
once or twice put a question ; and when his monologue
came to what seemed a natural stop, I rose to go. I
am glad to have seen his weird face, and heard his
dreamy voice ; and my notion of possession, prophecy,
—of involuntary speech from involuntary brain action,
has been clearer since. Taking the facts of his life
together with his utterance, I believe the philosophy
and moralising of Coleridge to be much like the action
of Babbage's machine ; and his utterance to be about
equal in wonder to the numerical results given out by
the mechanician's instrument. Some may think that
the philosophical and theological expression has more
beauty than the numerical, and some may not : but
all will agree that the latter issues from sound premises,
while few will venture to say that the other has any
reliable basis at all. Coleridge appears to me to have
been constitutionally defective in will, in conscientiousness and in apprehension of the real and true, while
gifted or cursed with inordinate reflective and analogi-

cal faculties, as well as prodigious word power. Hence
his success as an instigator of thought in others,
and as a talker and writer; while utterly failing in
his apprehension of truth, and in the conduct of his
life.

The mention of Coleridge reminds me, I hardly
know why, of Godwin, who was an occasional morning visitor of mine. I looked upon him as a curious
monument of a bygone state of society; and there
was still a good deal that was interesting about him.
His fine head was striking, and his countenance remarkable. It must not be judged of by the pretended
likeness put forth in Fraser's Magazine about that
time, and attributed, with the whole set, to Maclise,
then a young man, and, one would think, in great
need of one sort or another, if he could lend himself
to the base method of caricaturing shown in those
sketches. The high Tory favourites of the Magazine
were exhibited to the best advantage; while Liberals
were represented as Godwin was. Because the finest
thing about him was his noble head, they put on a
hat; and they presented him in profile because he had
lost his teeth, and his lips fell in. No notion of
Godwin's face could be formed from that caricature:
and I fear there was no other portrait, after the one
corresponding to the well-known portrait of Mary
Wollstonecraft. It was not for her sake that I desired to know Godwin; for, with all the aid from the
admiration with which her memory was regarded in
my childhood, and from my own disposition to honour
all promoters of the welfare and improvement of
Woman, I never could reconcile my mind to Mary
Wollstonecraft's writings, or to whatever I heard of

her. It seemed to me, from the earliest time when I
could think on the subject of Woman's Rights and
condition, that the first requisite to advancement is
the self-reliance which results from self-discipline.
Women who would improve the condition and chances
of their sex must, I am certain, be not only affectionate and devoted, but rational and dispassionate, with
the devotedness of benevolence, and not merely of
personal love. But Mary Wollstonecraft was, with all
her powers, a poor victim of passion, with no control
over her own peace, and no calmness or content except
when the needs of her individual nature were satisfied.
I felt, forty years ago, in regard to her, just what I
feel now in regard to some of the most conspicuous
denouncers of the wrongs of women at this day;—
that their advocacy of Woman's cause becomes mere
detriment, precisely in proportion to their personal
reasons for unhappiness, unless they have fortitude
enough (which loud complainants usually have not)
to get their own troubles under their feet, and leave
them wholly out of the account in stating the state of
their sex. Nobody can be further than I am from
being satisfied with the condition of my own sex,
under the law and custom of my own country; but I
decline all fellowship and co-operation with women
of genius or otherwise favourable position, who injure
the cause by their personal tendencies. When I see
an eloquent writer insinuating to every body who
comes across her that she is the victim of her
husband's carelessness and cruelty, while he never spoke
in his own defence : when I see her violating all good
taste by her obtrusiveness in society, and oppressing
every body about her by her epicurean selfishness every

day, while raising in print an eloquent cry on behalf
of the oppressed ; I feel, to the bottom of my heart,
that she is the worst enemy of the cause she professes
to plead. The best friends of that cause are women
who are morally as well as intellectually competent
to the most serious business of life, and who must be
clearly seen to speak from conviction of the truth, and
not from personal unhappiness. The best friends of
the cause are the happy wives and the busy, cheerful,
satisfied single women, who have no injuries of their
own to avenge, and no painful vacuity or mortification
to relieve. The best advocates are yet to come,—in
the persons of women who are obtaining access to real
social business,—the female physicians and other professors in America, the women of business and the
female artists of France ; and the hospital administrators, the nurses, the educators and substantially
successful authors of our own country. Often as I am
appealed to to speak, or otherwise assist in the pro-
motion of the cause of Woman, my answer is always the
same :—that women, like men, can obtain whatever
they show themselves fit for. Let them be educated,—
let their powers be cultivated to the extent for which
the means are already provided, and all that is wanted
or ought to be desired will follow of course. Whatever
a woman proves herself able to do, society will be
thankful to see her do,—just as if she were a man.
If she is scientific, science will welcome her, as it has
welcomed every woman so qualified. I believe no
scientific woman complains of wrongs. If capable of
political thought and action, women will obtain even
that. I judge by my own case. The time has not come
which certainly will come when women who are prac-

tically concerned in political life will have a voice in making the laws which they have to obey; but every woman who can think and speak wisely, and bring up her children soundly, in regard to the rights and duties of society, is advancing the time when the interests of women will be represented, as well as those of men. I have no vote at elections, though I am a tax-paying housekeeper and responsible citizen; and I regard the disability as an absurdity, seeing that I have for a long course of years influenced public affairs to an extent not professed or attempted by many men. But I do not see that I could do much good by personal complaints, which always have some suspicion or reality of passion in them. I think the better way is for us all to learn and to try to the utmost what we can do, and thus to win for ourselves the consideration which alone can secure us rational treatment. The Wollstonecraft order set to work at the other end, and, as I think, do infinite mischief; and, for my part, I do not wish to have anything to do with them. Every allowance must be made for Mary Wollstonecraft herself, from the constitution and singular environment which determined her course : but I have never regarded her as a safe example, nor as a successful champion of Woman and her Rights.

Nothing struck me more in Godwin than an order of attributes which were about the last I should have expected to find in him. I found him cautious, and even timid. I believe this is often the case, towards the close of life, with reformers who have suffered in their prime for their opinions : but in Godwin's case, it was not about matters of opinion only that he was timid. My mother and I went, with a mutual friend,

to tea at the Godwins' little dwelling under the roof
of the Houses of Parliament, just before I went to
America. Godwin had a small office there, with a
salary, a dwelling, and coals and candle; and very
comfortable he seemed there, with his old wife to take
care of him. He was so comfortable that he had
evidently no mind to die. Three times in the course of
that evening, he asked questions or made a remark on
the intended length of my absence, ending with 'When
you come back, I shall be dead:' or 'When you come
back, you will visit my grave,'—evidently in the
hope that I should say ' No, you will see me return.'
I was much amused at the issue of a sudden impulse
of complaisance towards me, under which he offered
me letters of introduction to various friends and
correspondents of his in America. I accepted the
offer exactly as I accepted every offer of the kind,—
with thanks, and an explanation that my friends must
not take it amiss if their letters should chance not to
be delivered, as I could not at all tell beforehand what
would be the extent or the circumstances of my
American travel: and I observed to my mother that
this precaution might be particularly necessary in the
case of Mr. Godwin's introductions, if they should
chance to be addressed to persons whose views bore no
relation to the politics of their time and their republic.
On the next Sunday in came Godwin, in evident uneasiness and awkwardness. He threw his gloves into
his hat, as if preparing for some great effort; and then
he told me, with reluctance and confusion, that he
wished to recal his offer of letters to his American
correspondents; for this reason:—that I should be
known there as a political economist; and, if he intro-

duced me, it might be supposed that he had changed
his views in his old age, and become one of the order of
men against whom he had written in his earlier years.
I told him I thought he was quite right; and his spirits
rose immediately when he saw I was not offended. —I
liked best getting him to speak of his novels; and at
times he was ready enough to gratify me. He told me,
among other things, that he wrote the first half of
' Caleb Williams' in three months, and then stopped
for six,—finishing it in three more. This pause in
the middle of a work so intense seems to me a remarkable incident. I have often intended to read ' Caleb
Williams' again, to try whether I could find the
stopping place : but it has never fallen in my way,
and I have not seen the book since my youth.

That last evening at Godwin's was a memorable
one to me. The place is gone, and all who were there
are dead except myself. Before it grew too dusk (it
was in July) Godwin took us through the passages of
that old Parliament House, and showed us the Star
Chamber, and brought the old tallies for us to ex-
amine, that we might finger the notches made by the
tax-collectors before accounts were kept as now.
Within three months those tallies burnt down that
Star Chamber, and both Houses of Parliament. They
burned old Godwin's dwelling too. His good wife
saved him from a fright and anxiety which might
have destroyed him at once. He was at the theatre ;
and she would not have him called, but packed and
removed his goods, and so managed as that he was
met and told the story like any body else. He was,
however, dead before my return, as he had said he
should be. When I returned, he was in his grave,

and faithful friends were taking kind care of the wife who had done so much for him.

Another old man, of a very different order, was a pretty frequent visitor of mine, and always a kind one, —Mr. Basil Montagu. He, with his venerable head, and his majestic-looking lady were occasionally the ornaments of my evening parties : and I was well acquainted with the Procters, Mrs. Montagu's daughter and son-in-law. I was always glad to see Mr. Procter in any drawing-room I entered. It was delightful to know the ' Barry Cornwall ' who won his first fame when I was living on poetry, down at Norwich, and when his exquisite metres were on my tongue or in my head day and night : but all I found in him supported and deepened the interest with which I met him. He was always so kind and courteous, so simple and modest, so honest and agreeable that I valued his acquaintance highly, and have continued to do so, to this day.—As for Mr. Montagu, his benevolence was the first attraction ; and the use of the gallows had not then been so long restricted as to permit the efforts of our Romillys and our Montagus to be forgotten. No one man perhaps did so much for the restriction of the punishment of death as Mr. Montagu ; and none based the cause on so deep a ground. I was not aware of Mr. Montagu's philosophy till the latest period of my acquaintance with him. I wish I had been ; but he was timid in the avowal of it to a wholly unnecessary, and, I think, faulty degree. Before his death, he distinctly declared in a message to me his approbation of the avowal which his friend Mr. Atkinson and I had made of opinions like his own : and, if he could have lived to see how little harm, and how much good, the

avowal has done us, he would have regretted his own
caution,—though it was more justifiable in his time
than it would have been in ours. I imagine that his
curious strain of sentimentality was,—(as far as it was
his at all, but I have always believed his lady to have
intervened in that case)—to cover up to himself and
others the differences between himself and others;—
an attempt to find a ground of sympathy, when the
broadest and firmest did not exist.

The rising up of his countenance before me as I
write reminds me of an occasion when he drew me
away from my morning work, to occupy an odd place,
and witness a remarkable scene. I found a note from
him on the breakfast table, one morning, to say that
he would call at ten o'clock, and take me down to
Westminster, to witness the trial of the Canadian
prisoners, on whose behalf Mr. Roebuck was to plead
that day. So early an hour was named, that I might
be well placed for hearing. All London was in excitement about this trial, which followed the Canadian
rebellion, and the Court was daily crowded. My
sister Rachel was with us at the time, and she was
glad to accompany Mr. Montagu and me. Early as
we were, the Court was full;—completely crowded to
the back of the galleries. Mr. Montagu looked in at
every door, and then committed us to the charge of
one of the ushers while he disappeared for five minutes.
He returned, threw his cloak over the arm of the
usher, gave us each an arm, in perfect silence, and led
us through a long succession of passages till we arrived
at a door which he opened, lifting up a red curtain,
and pushing us in. To our amazement and consternation, we found ourselves on the Bench, facing the

sea of heads in the Court. It was dreadful; and at first, I crouched behind a bulwark: but we agreed that there was nothing to be done. There we were: Mr. Montagu had disappeared; and we could not help ourselves. The only vacant bench in the Court below was presently filled. In came the Canadian prisoners, and seated themselves there. We could hardly believe our eyes, but the men wore hand-cuffs, and we saw the gleam of the steel as they moved. Our consultation about this, and our observation of the prisoners while talking about it, made us the subject of the hoax of the day.—We saw the prisoners lay their heads together, and make inquiries of their attendants; and then there was some bustle about handing paper, pen and ink to them. Presently a letter appeared, travelling over the heads of the crowd, and handed from counsel to counsel till it was presented to me by the one nearest the bench. It was a note of compliment and gratitude from the *chef* of the prisoners. Plenty of lawyers were in a minute pressing pen, ink and paper on me; and I again crouched down and wrote a civil line of reply, which was handed to my new correspondent. We found ourselves particularly stared at till we could bear it no longer, and slipped away,—meeting Mr. Montagu in time to save us from losing ourselves in the labyrinth of passages. We did not know till some time afterwards what pathos there was in the stare which followed the notes. A waggish acquaintance of ours was among the lawyers in the Court. He put on a grave look during the transmission of the notes; and then, hearing speculation all round as to who we were, he whispered to one and another,—'Don't you know? They are the wives of the Canadian prisoners.'

As he intended, the news spread through the Court, and our countenances were watched with all due compassion. I am afraid we were pronounced to be very unfeeling wives, if we might be judged by our dress and demeanour.

When my morning work was done, there was usually a curious variety of visitors, such as it bewilders me more to think of now than it did to receive at the time. More than once, my study door was thrown open, and a Frenchman, Italian or German stood on the threshold, with one hand on his heart and the other almost touching the top of the door, clearing his throat to recite an ode, of which he wanted my opinion. Sometimes it was a lady from the country, who desired to pour her sorrows into my bosom, and swear eternal friendship. This kind of visitor could never be made to understand that it takes two to make a friendship; and that there was no particular reason why I should enter into it with a perfect stranger. By such as these I was favoured with the information that they had inquired my character before coming,—whether I was amiable and so forth; but they seemed to forget that I knew nothing of them. Sometimes some slight acquaintance or another would enter with a companion and engage me in conversation while the companion took possession of a sheet of my writing paper, or even asked me for a pencil, sketched me, and put the sketch into her reticule; by which time the ostensible visitor was ready to go away. Sometimes my pen was filched from the inkstand, still wet, and taken away to be framed or laid up in lavender. Sometimes ambitious poets, or aspirants to poetic honours, obtained an introduction, on purpose to consult me as to how they

should do their work. One young clergyman I remember who felt that he was made for immortality
in the line of Shaksperian tragedy ; but he wanted my
opinion as to whether he should begin in that way at
once, or try something else ; and especially, whether or
not I should advise him to drink beer. Amidst such
absurd people, whose names I have long forgotten,
there were many agreeable visitors, beside the multitude whom I have sketched above, who made that
time of the day exceedingly pleasant. It was then
that I saw Dr. Chalmers on his visits to town. His
topics were pauperism and (in those antediluvian days
before the ark of the Free Church was dreamed of)
the virtues of religious establishments : and fervid and
striking was his talk on these and every other subject.
Mr. Chadwick, then engaged on the Poor-law, was a
frequent visitor,—desiring to fix my attention on the
virtues of centralisation,—the vices of which in continental countries were not then so apparent as they
have since become. One always knew what was coming when he entered the room ; and indeed, so busy
a man could not make morning calls, but for the pro-
motion of business. I regarded his visit, therefore, as
a lesson ; and I never failed to learn much from the
master,—the first of our citizens, I believe, who
fairly penetrated the foul region of our sanitary dis-
orders, and set us to work to reform them. It might be
that his mind was an isolated one ; and his faculty narrow and engrossed with detail, so that it was necessary
at length to remove him from the administrative position to which his services seemed to entitle him : but
there is no question of his social usefulness in instituting
the set of objects which he was found unequal to carry

out. Twenty years ago, he was just discovered by the Whig Ministers, and he was himself discovering his own department of action. He was a substantial aid to me while I was writing about social evils and reforms; and he has gone on to supply me with valuable information from that day to this,—from his first exposition of the way in which country justices aggravated pauperism under the old law, to the latest improvement in hollow bricks and diameter of drains.— Judging by the reforms then discussed in my study, that period of my life seems to be prodigiously long ago. Several of the beneficent family of the Hills came on their respective errands,—penny postage, prison administration, juvenile crime reformation, and industrial and national education. Mr. Rowland Hill was then pondering his scheme, and ascertaining the facts which he was to present with so remarkable an accuracy. His manner in those days,—his slowness, and hesitating speech,—were not recommendatory of his doctrine to those who would not trouble themselves to discern its excellence and urgent need. If he had been prepossessing in manner and fluent and lively in speech, it might have saved him half his difficulties, and the nation some delay : but he was so accurate, so earnest, so irrefragable in his facts, so wise and benevolent in his intentions, and so well timed with his scheme, that success was, in my opinion, certain from the beginning ; and so I used to tell some conceited and shallow members and adherents of the Whig government, whose flippancy, haughtiness and ignorance about a matter of such transcendent importance tried my temper exceedingly. Rowland Hill might and did bear it ; but I own I could not always. Even

Sydney Smith was so unlike himself on this occasion
as to talk and write of ' this nonsense of a penny postage :' as if the domestic influences fostered by it were
not more promotive of moral good than all his preaching, or that of any number of his brethren of the
cloth! Lord Monteagle got the nickname of ' the
footman's friend,' on that occasion,—the ' Examiner'
being a firm and effective friend of Rowland Hill and
his scheme. Lord Monteagle, who is agreeable enough
in society to those who are not very particular in regard to sincerity, was, as Chancellor of the Exchequer
or any thing else, as good a representative as could be
found of the flippancy, conceit, and official helplessness and ignorance of the Whig administrations. He
actually took up Rowland Hill's great scheme, to
botch and alter and restrict it. With entire complacency he used to smile it down at evening parties, and
lift his eyebrows at the credulity of the world, which
could suppose that a scheme so wild could ever be tried:
but he condescended to propose that it should super-
sede the London twopenny post. The ' Examiner'
immediately showed that the operation would be to
save flunkeys the fatigue of carrying ladies' notes;
and Lord Monteagle was forthwith dubbed ' the footman's friend,'—a title which has perversely rushed
into my memory, every time I have seen him since.
The alteration in Rowland Hill himself, since he won
his tardy victory, is an interesting spectacle to those
who knew him twenty years ago. He always was full
of domestic tenderness and social amiability; and these
qualities now shine out, and his whole mind and manners are quickened by the removal of the cold obstruction he encountered at the beginning of his career.

Grateful as I feel to him, as the most signal social
benefactor of our time, it has been a great pleasure to
me to see the happy influence of success on the man
himself. I really should like to ask the surviving
Whig leaders, all round, what they think now of 'the
nonsense of the penny postage.'

Good Mr. Porter, of the Board of Trade,—amiable
and friendly, industrious and devoted to his business,
—but sadly weak and inaccurate, prejudiced and *borné*
in ability,—was a frequent and kindly visitor. His
office was at hand, when we lived in Fludyer Street;
and he found time to look in very often, and to bring
me information, sometimes valuable, and sometimes
not. His labours, industrious and sincere, were a
complete illustration of Carlyle's doctrine about statistics. Nothing could be apparently more square and
determinate ; while nothing could be in fact more un-
trustworthy and delusive. Some exposures of his mistakes have been made in parliament ; and plenty more
could be pointed out by parties qualified to criticise
his statements; as, for instance, the Birmingham manufacturers, who find that the spirits of wine used in
vast quantities for the burnishing of their goods are set
down by Mr. Porter as alcoholic liquor drunk by the
English people : and, again, the ship-owners, who find
the tonnage of the kingdom estimated by him by the
number of ships going to sea or returning in the course
of the year,—no allowance being made for ships going
more voyages than one. It is a serious injury to the
nation that the Whig administrations have employed,
to obtain and publish information, such unfortunate
agents as Bowring, Macgregor and Porter, whose
errors and incompetence any sensible man of business

could have informed them of. Many thousands of
pounds, much valuable time, and no little exertion,
have been spent in actually misinforming the people,
on the supposition of procuring valuable facts for them.
Bowring and Macgregor were obviously unfitted for
such work from the outset, by their vanity, incompetence and unscrupulousness. Mr. Porter was of a
far higher order. His innocent vanity, which was far
from immoderate, never interfered with his steady
labour ; and he was honourable, disinterested and
generous : but his deficiency in sense and intellectual
range, together with his confidence in himself and his
want of confidence in all public men, was an insuper-
able disqualification for his sound discharge of an
office requiring a wholly different order of mind from
his. His intimate friend, his guide and crammer, was
David Urquhart, whose accounts of royal, diplomatic
and administrative personages he reverently accepted :
and this accounts for a good deal of prejudice and
perversion of judgment. It was at his table that I
saw Mr. Urquhart for the only time that I ever met
him. Once was enough ; and that once was too like
a pantomime to leave the impression of a rational dinner-party. Mr. Urquhart had arrived from Turkey
with mighty expectations from what he called the
friendship of William IV. But the King was dead, and
Victoria reigned in his stead : and the oracle's abuse of
the Queen,—a young girl entering upon the most difficult position in the world,—was something wonderful.
He railed at her every where and perpetually,—with a
vehemence which luckily prevented any harm, such as
might have resulted from moderate censure. On the
day that I met him, he engrossed the whole conver-

sation, as he sat between our hostess and me. What he
gave us, besides abuse of the Queen, was a series of
oracular utterances on political doctrine, which he
assured me from time to time I was incapable of
comprehending; and an intense eulogium on Turkish
life, which owed its excellence, political and moral, to
the Turkish women being not allowed to learn to
read and write. He addressed this to Mrs. Porter (the
sister of David Ricardo, and the author of certain
books), on the one hand, and to me on the other. His
odd ape-like gestures, his insane egotism, his frail
figure and pale countenance, and the ferocious discontent which seemed to be consuming his life, left a
strange and painful impression on my mind. His
mother soon after died happy in the belief that he
would be the saviour of his country: and now, after
half a lifetime, he seems, by newspaper accounts, to be
just the same man, talking in the same mood and
style, with no other change than that he has been
tried in parliament and has failed, and that he has
been constantly moulting his tail, all these years. His
adherents have fallen off and been replaced in constant succession. He has never retained any body's
confidence long (he lost Mr. Porter's at last) and he
has never failed to find impressible, half-informed
and credulous people ready to shut their eyes and
open their mouths, and swallow what doctrine he
should please to give.

With Mr. Porter came Mr. Duppa, the devoted and
indefatigable friend of popular education, and the
organiser and support of the Central Society of Education, which diffused some useful knowledge and good
views in its day. Some foreigner or another, dis-

tinguished by eminence in some department within Mr. Porter's range, often gave me a call, and taught me something, or offered inducements to foreign travel, which I never was able to avail myself of, till the failure of my health made it too late. Mr. Senior used to come and talk about the poor-law, or Ireland. The Combes came and talked about phrenology and educational improvement. Mr. Robertson came to talk of the 'Westminster Review,' of which he was editor, under the direction of Mr. J. S. Mill. He had prodigious expectations from his own genius, and an undoubting certainty of fulfilling a grand career : but he has long sunk out of sight. For fifteen years past he seems to have been forgotten. I fear he has suffered much, and caused much suffering since the days when I knew him. I never understood him at all, and was duly surprised to find that he represented himself to be my most intimate friend,—philosopher, and guide! but the delusions of his vanity were so many and so gross that one may easily be let pass among the rest.—An even more unintelligible claim to my friendship has been advanced in print by the Howitts. I can only say that I do not remember having seen Mrs. Howitt more than twice in my life, and that I should not know her by sight : and that I have seen Mr. Howitt about four or five times :—three or four times in London, and once at Tynemouth, when he came with a cousin of mine to cool himself after a walk on the sands, and beg for a cup of tea. This he and Mrs. Howitt have represented in print as visiting me in my illness. Such service as they asked of me in London (to obtain a favourable review of a book of Mr. Howitt's in which he had grossly abused me) I endeavoured to render ; but I really was barely acquainted with them; and I was glad the intercourse had gone no further when I witnessed their conduct to their partner in the ' People's Journal,' and in some other affairs. I so greatly admire some of their writings, in which their fine love of nature and their close knowledge of children are unmingled with passion and personal discontent, that I am thankful to enjoy the good their genius provides without disturbance from their unreasonable and turbulent tempers.

One of the most striking of my occasional visitors was Capel Lofft the younger, the author of that wonderful book, the merits of which were discovered by Charles Knight ;—' Self-formation,' which should be read by every parent of boys. Those who know the work do not need to be told that the author was a remarkable man : and if they happen to have met with his agrarian epic, ' Ernest,' a poem of prodigious power, but too seditious for publication, they will feel yet more desire to have seen him. When he called on me to ask my advice what to do with his poem, his card revived all I had heard about his eccentric father, the patron of the poet Bloomfield. He was neat and spruce in his dress and appearance, —with his glossy olive coat, and his glossy brown hair, parted down the middle, and his comely and thoughtful face. He was as nervous as his father; and by degrees I came to consider him as eccentric; especially when I found what was his opinion of the feminine intellect, and that his wife, to whom he appeared duly attached did not know of the existence of his poem. (The Quarterly Review put an end to the secrecy, some time afterwards.) He died early; but not before he had left a name in the world, by his 'Self-formation,' and an impression of power and originality by his formidable epic.—Another poet whose face I was always glad to see was Browning It was in the days when he had not yet seen the Barretts. I did not know them, either. When I was ill at Tynemouth, a correspondence grew up between the then bedridden Elizabeth Barrett and myself; and a very intimate correspondence it became. In one of the later letters, in telling me how much better she was, and how grievously disappointed at being prevented going to Italy, she wrote of going out, of basking in the open sunshine, of doing this and that; 'in short,' said she, finally, 'there is no saying what foolish thing I may do.' The 'foolish thing' evidently in view in this passage was marrying Robert Browning: and a truly wise act did the 'foolish thing' turn out to be. I have never seen my correspondent, for she had gone to Italy before I left Tynemouth; but I knew her husband well, about twenty years ago. It was a wonderful event to me,—my first acquaintance with his poetry.—Mr. Macready put 'Paracelsus' into my hand, when I was staying at his house; and I read a canto before going to bed. For the first time in my life, I passed a whole night without sleeping a wink. The unbounded expectation I formed from that poem was sadly disappointed when 'Sordello' came out. I was so wholly unable to understand it that I supposed myself ill. But in conversation no speaker could be more absolutely clear and purpose-like. He was full of good sense and fine feeling, amidst occasional irritability;—full also of fun and harmless

satire; with some little affectations which were as
droll as any thing he said. A real genius was Robert
Browning, assuredly; and how good a man, how wise
and morally strong, is proved by the successful issue of
the perilous experiment of the marriage of two poets.
Her poems were to me, in my sick-room, marvellously
beautiful: and, now that from the atmosphere of the
sick-room, my life has been transferred to the free open
air of real, practical existence, I still think her poetry
wonderfully beautiful in its way, while wishing that
she was more familiar with the external realities which
are needed to balance her ideal conceptions. They are
a remarkable pair, whom society may well honour and
cherish.

Their friend Miss Mitford came up to town occasionally, and found her way to Fludyer Street. I was
early fond of her tales and descriptions, and have always regarded her as the originator of that new style
of 'graphic description' to which literature owes a
great deal, however weary we may sometimes have felt
of the excess into which the practice of detail has run.
In my childhood, there was no such thing known, in
the works of the day, as 'graphic description:' and
most people delighted as much as I did in Mrs.
Ratcliffe's gorgeous or luscious generalities,—just as
we admired in picture galleries landscapes all misty
and glowing indefinitely with bright colours,—yellow
sunrises and purple and crimson sunsets,—because we
had no conception of detail like Miss Austen's in manners, and Miss Mitford's in scenery, or of Millais' and
Wilkie's analogous life pictures, or Rosa Bonheur's
adventurous Hayfield at noon-tide. Miss Austen had
claims to other and greater honours; but she and Miss

Mitford deserve no small gratitude for rescuing us from the folly and bad taste of slovenly indefiniteness in delineation. School-girls are now taught to draw from objects: but in my time they merely copied their masters' vague and slovenly drawings: and the case was the same with writers and readers. Miss Mitford's tales appealed to a new sense, as it were, in a multitude of minds,—greatly to the amazement of the whole circle of publishers, who had rejected, in her works, as good a bargain as is often offered to publishers. Miss Mitford showed me at once that she undervalued her tales, and rested her claims on her plays. I suppose every body who writes a tragedy, and certainly every body who writes a successful tragedy, must inevitably do this. Miss Mitford must have possessed some dramatic requisites, or her success could not have been so decided as it was; but my own opinion always was that her mind wanted the breadth, and her character the depth, necessary for genuine achievement in the highest enterprise of literature. I must say that personally I did not like her so well as I liked her works. The charming *bonhommie* of her writings appeared at first in her conversation and manners; but there were other things which presently sadly impaired its charm. It is no part of my business to pass judgment on her views and modes of life. What concerned me was her habit of flattery, and the twin habit of disparagement of others. I never knew her respond to any act or course of conduct which was morally lofty. She could not believe in it, nor, of course, enjoy it: and she seldom failed to ' see through ' it, and to delight in her superiority to admiration. She was a devoted daughter, where the duty was none

of the easiest ; and servants and neighbours were sincerely attached to her. The little intercourse I had
with her was spoiled by her habit of flattery; but I
always fell back on my old admiration of her as soon
as she was out of sight, and her ' Village' rose up in
my memory. The portrait of her which appeared in
(I think) 1854 in the ' Illustrated London News' is
one of the most remarkable likenesses I have ever seen :
and it recals a truly pleasant trait of her conduct.
Some years ago, Lady Morgan published a furious
comment on some unfavourable report of her beauty,
at the very same time that Miss Mitford happened to
be addressing a sonnet to an artist friend who had
taken her portrait ;—a morsel of such moral beauty
that I was grateful to the friend (whoever it might
be) who took the responsibility of publishing it. The
absence of personal vanity, the *bonhommie*, and the
thoughtful grace of that sonnet contrasted singularly,
(and quite undesignedly) with the pettish wrath of the
sister author.—When I knew Miss Mitford, she was
very intimate with the Talfourds. Mr. Talfourd (as
he was then) was one of my occasional visitors; and
he was also exulting in his dramatic success as the
author of ' Ion.' To see Macready's representation
of ' Ion' was a treat which so enraptured London as
to swell Talfourd's reputation beyond all rational
bounds. I shared the general enthusiasm; and I told
Talfourd so; for which I was sorry when I knew
better, and learned that the beauty of the play is actually in spite of its undramatic quality. During my
absence in America, Talfourd's sudden rise in reputation and success,—professional, parliamentary and
literary, was something extraordinary : but the inevit-

able collapse was not long in coming. His nature
was a kindly but not a lofty one; and his powers
were prodigiously over-rated. He, of whom I had
heard in my youth as a sentimental writer in the
' Monthly Repository,' died a judge ; but he had outlived his once high reputation, which was a curious
accident of the times, and might well mislead him
when it misled society in general, for months, if not
years. His most intimate friends loved him. By
those who knew him less he was less liked, – his
habits and manners being inferior to his social pre-
tensions and position.

The most complete specimen of the literary adventurer of our time whom I knew was one who avowed
his position and efforts with a most respectable frankness. Mr. Chorley, who early went to town, to throw
himself upon it, and see what he could make of it,
was still about the same business as long as I knew
him. He had a really kind heart, and helpful hands
to needy brethren, and a small sort of generosity
which was perfectly genuine, I am confident. But his
best qualities were neutralised by those which belonged
to his unfortunate position,—conceit and tuft-hunt-
ing, and morbid dread of unusual opinions, and an
unscrupulous hostility to new knowledge. The faults
of the ' Athenæum ' are well known :—Mr. Chorley
assumed to be the sub-editor of the ' Athenæum ' at the
time I knew him ; and I suppose he is so still ; and
by a reference to it, his qualities, good and bad, may be
best conveyed. For a considerable time, I over-rated
him, trusting, from his real goodness of heart when
his nature had fair play, that he would improve. But
I fear,—by what I recently saw of his singular

affectations in dress and manners in public places, and
by the deteriorating quality of the ' Athenæum,' that
the bad influences of his position have prevailed.
From him alone,—unless it were also from Mr.
Robertson,—I obtained a conception of the life of
the literary adventurer as a vocation. Every author
is in a manner an adventurer; and no one was ever
more decidedly so than myself : but the difference
between one kind of adventurer and another is, I
believe, simply this ;—that the one has something
to say which presses for utterance, and is uttered at
length without a view to future fortunes ; while the
other has a sort of general inclination toward literature, without any specific need of utterance, and a
very definite desire for the honours and rewards of the
literary career.   Mr. Henry F. Chorley is, at least, an
average specimen of the latter class ; and perhaps
something more.   But the position is not a favourable one, intellectually or morally, to the individual,
while it is decidedly injurious to the sincerity and
earnestness of literature.

I twice saw Miss Landon, —the well-known
' L.E.L.' of twenty years ago.   Both times it was
in our own house that I saw her ;—once, when she
was accompanying Mrs. A. T. Thomson in her round
of calls, and a second time when she came to me for
information about her needful preparations for living
at Cape Coast Castle,—a cousin of mine having
recently undergone an experience of that kind as the
wife of the Chief Justice of Sierra Leone.   I was at
first agreeably surprised by Miss Landon's countenance, voice and manners.   I thought her very pretty,
kind, simple and agreeable.   The second time, it was

all so sad that my mother and I communicated to
each other our sense of dismay, as soon as the ladies
were gone.   Miss Landon was listless, absent, melancholy to a striking degree.   She found she was all
wrong in her provision of clothes and comforts,—
was going to take out all muslins and no flannels,
and divers pet presents which would go to ruin at
once in the climate of Cape Coast.   We promised,
that day, to go to Dr. Thomson's, and hear her new
play before she went : and I could not but observe
the countenance of listless gloom with which she
heard the arrangement made.   Before the day of our
visit came round, it was discovered that she had been
secretly married, and I saw her no more.   The shock
of her mysterious death soon followed the uncomfortable impression of that visit.

Miss Edgeworth happened never to be in London
during my residence there ; but she sought some correspondence with me, both before and after my American travel.   Her kindly spirit shone out in her letters,
as in all she did ; but her vigour of mind and accuracy
of judgment had clearly given way, under years and
her secluded life.   Her epistles,—three or four sheets
to my one,—confirmed in me a resolution I had
pondered before ; to relax my habit of writing in
good time ; and to make to myself such friends, among
my nephews and nieces, as that I might rely on some
of them for a check, whenever the quality of my
writing should seem to deteriorate.   A family connexion of Miss Edgeworth's had told me, long before,
that there was a garret at Edgeworth's-town full of
boxes of manuscript tales of Maria's which would
certainly never see the light.   This was before the

appearance of 'Helen;' and the appearance of 'Helen,' notwithstanding the high ability shown in the first volume, confirmed my dread of going to press too often, and returning to it too late. An infamous hoax, in which Miss Edgeworth was betrayed to ridicule, in company with the whole multitude of eminent living authors, deepened the warning to me. That was a remarkable hoax. I was the only one of the whole order who escaped the toils. This happened through no sagacity of my own, but by my mother's acuteness in detecting a plot.

One day in 1838, when my mother and I were standing by the fire, waiting for the appearance of dinner, a note arrived for me, which I went up to my study to answer,—requesting that my mother and aunt would not wait dinner for me. The note was this :—

'82, Seymour Street, Somer's Town :
'October 4th, 1833.

'Madam,
        'A Frenchman named Adolphe Berthier, who says he acted as Courier to you during one of your visits to France, has applied for a situation in my establishment. He says that you will give him a character. May I request the favour of an answer to this note, stating what you know of him.
                ' I have the honour to be, Madam,
                        'Your obedient Servant,
                                'GEORGE MILLAR.
'To Miss Martineau.'

My reply was easy and short. There must be some mistake, as I had never been in France. As I came down with the note, my mother beckoned me into her room, and told me she suspected some trick. There had been some frauds lately by means of signatures fraudulently obtained. She could not see what any body

could do to me in that way; but she fancied somebody
wanted my autograph. The messenger was a dirty
little boy, who could hardly have come from a gentleman's house; and he would not say where he had come
from.—I objected that I could not, in courtesy, refuse
an answer; and my only idea was that I was mistaken
for some other of the many Miss Martineaus of the
clan. My mother said she would write the answer in
the character of a secretary or deputy: and so she
fortunately did. We never thought of the matter
again till the great Fraser Hoax burst upon the town,
—-to the ruin of the moral reputation of the Magazine,
though to the intense amusement of all but the sufferers from the plot. Among these, I was not one.
My mother's note was there, signed ' E. M. ;' and the
comment on it was fair enough. After a remark on
their failure to get my autograph, the hoaxers observed
that my story ' French Wines and Politics' might have
saved me the trouble of assuring them that I had never
travelled in France. Miss Edgeworth suffered most,—
and it really was suffering to her modest and ingenuous
nature. She sent a long letter about her lady's-maids,
—sadly garrulous in her desire not to injure a servant
whom she might have forgotten. The heartless traitors
sent a reply, which drew forth, as they intended, a mass
of twaddle; and having obtained this from her very
goodness, they made game of her.—Many of the
other replies were characteristic enough. Scott's
puzzles me most. I cannot see how there could be
one from him, as he died in 1832, and was incapable
of writing for long before : and the hoax could hardly
have been whole years in preparation. Yet I distinctly
remember the universal remark that Scott's was, of

all, the most unlike the writer. He called the ficti-
tious applicant a scoundrel, or a rascal, or something
of that sort. Coleridge's was good,—'Should be
happy to do anything within my knowledge or power.'
But I need say no more, as the whole may be seen by
a reference to Fraser's Magazine. All who may look
back to it will be of the same mind with every gentleman whom I heard speak of the trick ;—that plotter
and publisher deserved to be whipped from one end
of London to the other.

Among the eminent women who sought my acquaintance by letter, and whom I have never seen, are
Fredrika Bremer, and Miss Kelty, the author of the
first successful 'religious novel,' 'the Favourite of
Nature,' which I remember reading with much pleasure in my youth. Miss Kelty wrote to me when I
was ill at Tynemouth, under the notion that I had
been her school-fellow some years before I was born.
She then sent me her little volume, 'Fireside
Philosophy ;' and I have lately received from her her
autobiography, published under the title of 'Remi-
niscences of Thought and Feeling.' It is a painfully
impressive biography ; but its tendency is to indispose
me to intercourse with the writer,—sincere and frank
and interesting as she appears to be. Systems of religion and philosophy are evidently something very
different to her from what they are to me : and I cannot lay open, or submit to controversy, the most
solemn and severe subjects of all, when they can be
made a means of excitement, and a theme of mere
spiritual curiosity. But I am glad to have read the
Memoir ; and glad that it exists,—painful as it is :
for it is a striking emanation of the spirit of the time,

and illustration of its experiences. Of the ability, courage and candour of the writer there can be no question.

If Miss Kelty desired correspondence with me on the ground of the Atkinson Letters, Miss Bremer, I believe, dropped it for the same reason. Miss Bremer also accosted me when I was ill at Tynemouth, in a letter of pretty broken English. Her style is so well known now that I need not describe the mingled sentimentality, fun and flattery of her letters. The flattery, and the want of what we call common sense, rather annoyed me till I was made sure, by her American experiences, that those were her weak points, and quite irremediable. I was a good deal startled, before she went to America, at a little incident which filled me with wonder. A neighbour lent me her novel, 'Brothers and Sisters,' the first volume of which we thought admirable : but the latter part about Socialism, Mesmerism, and all manner of *isms* which she did not at all understand, made us blush as we read. Presently a letter arrived for me from her announcing the approach of a copy of this book, which she hoped I should more or less enjoy, as I had in fact, by my recovery and some other incidents and supposed views of mine, suggested and instigated the book. I mention this, because Miss Bremer may probably have explained the origin of her book in a similar manner elsewhere ; and I am really bound to explain that, in that book, she does not represent any views and opinions that I ever had. I fear I did not answer that letter ; for, if I remember right, I could not find any thing to say that she would like to hear ; for she could not be satisfied with what I can truly say to others, that I enjoy and admire her books exceedingly, after throwing out the 'views' and the romance. The sketches of home life in Sweden are exquisitely done ; and their coarseness of morals and manners is evidently merely Swedish, and not attributable to Miss Bremer,—unconscious as she evidently is of any unlikeness to the women around her. Her sentimental pietism is naturally offended by the accounts which have been given her of the Atkinson Letters, as I dare say it would be by the book itself ; for philosophical research with a view to truth, is quite out of her way. As she thinks every woman's influence springs from a hot-bed of sentiment, she naturally supposes that my influence must be destroyed by my having taken root on an opposite ground. But she is not aware how much further sound reason and appeals to science go with the best of our people than a floating religiosity which she proposes through the 'Times' newspaper as the means of reforming the world through the influence of women. Much more than she has lost in England through that singular obtrusion have I, as it proves, gained by a directly opposite method of proceeding. But I dare say it would be difficult to convince her of this, and painful to her, in her life of dreams, to be so convinced. I hoped to have enjoyed more of her exquisite pictures of Swedish homes ; and I yet trust that others may. It would be a world-wide benefit if this gifted woman could be induced to leave social reforms and published criticism to other hands, and to discharge while she lives the special function by which she scatters a rare delight broadcast over whole nations.

A frequent topic of conversation between my

morning guests and myself was the various methods of
doing our work. Sooner or later, almost every author
asked me about my procedure, and told me his or hers.
The point on which I was at issue with almost every
body was the time of beginning in the morning. I
doubt whether I was acquainted with any body who
went to work during the fresh morning hours which
have always been delightful to me,—before the post
came in, and interruption was abroad. I found my
friends differ much as to the necessity of revision,
re-writing and delay,—on which I have already given
my opinion and experience. The point on which perhaps they were most extensively agreed was that our
occupation changes our relation to books very remarkably. I remember Miss Aikin complaining of the
difficulty of reading for amusement, after some years'
experience of reading for purposes of historical or other
authorship. I found this for a time when stopped in
my career by illness : but, though I have never since
read so fast or so efficiently as in my youth, I have
experienced some return of the youthful pleasure and
interest, though in regard to a different order of books.
I could not now read ' Lalla Rookh' through before
breakfast, as I did when it appeared. I cannot read
new novels. It is an actual incapacity; while I can
read with more pleasure than ever the old favourites,
—Miss Austen's and Scott's. My pleasure in Voyages
and Travels is almost an insanity; and History and
philosophical disquisition are more attractive than
ever. Still, I can sympathise heartily with those who
declare that the privilege of being authors has deprived
them of that of being amateur readers. The state of
mind in which books are approached by those who are

always, and those who have never been, in print is no
doubt essentially different.—I believe Miss Aikin's
methòd of writing is painstaking ; and she has so high
an opinion of revision by friends, that I have no doubt
she copies very conscientiously. Her enjoyment of
her work is very great. I remember her saying, at a
time when her physician forbade her fatiguing herself
with writing, that if ever she saw a proof-sheet again,
she thought she should dance.

Mrs. Opie wrote slowly, and amidst a strenuous
excitement of her sensibilities. She liked trying the
effect of her tales on hearers before they went to press.
I remember my mother and sister coming home with
swollen eyes and tender spirits after spending an
evening with Mrs. Opie, to hear ' Temper,' which
she read in a most overpowering way. When they
saw it in print, they could hardly believe it was the
same story. Her handwriting was execrable, for
smallness and irregularity. Miss Aikin's is formal,
but very legible. Miss Edgeworth's, an ordinary
' lady's hand.' Mrs. Somerville's the same. Miss
Brontë's was exceedingly small, nervous and poor,
but quite legible. Miss Edgeworth's method of composition has been described already, on her own published authority. Mrs. Somerville, being extremely
short-sighted, brings her paper close to her eyes,
supported on a square piece of pasteboard. Miss
Brontë did the same ; but her first manuscript was a
very small square book, or folding of paper, from
which she copied, with extreme care. She was as
much surprised to find that I never copy at all as I
was at her imposing on herself so much toil which
seems to me unnecessary.—Mr. Rogers used to give

me friendly admonition, now and then, to do every thing in my practice of composition in an exactly opposite method to my own :—to write a very little, and seldom ; to put it by, and read it from time to time, and copy it pretty often, and show it to good judges; all which was much like advising me to change my hair and eyes to blonde and blue, and to add a cubit to my stature. It was a curious commentary on his counsel to hear Sydney Smith's account of Mr. Rogers's method of composition. The story is in print, but imperfectly given, and evidently without any consciousness that 'the brooding dove' of Shakspere is concerned in it,—'the brooding dove, ere yet her golden couplets are disclosed.' The conversation took place soon after Rogers had given forth his epigram on Lord Dudley :

> 'Ward has no heart, they say: but I deny it.
> Ward *has* a heart ;—and gets his speeches by it.'

'Has Rogers written any thing lately?' asked some body ; to which another replied,—'No, I believe not. Nothing but a couplet.'

'Nothing but a couplet!' exclaimed Sydney Smith. 'Why, what would you have? When Rogers produces a couplet, he goes to bed :

And the caudle is made :

And the knocker is tied :

And straw is laid down :

And when his friends send to inquire,—" Mr. Rogers is as well as can be expected." '

Mr. Rogers's rate of advance would not suit a really earnest writer ; and, granting that poetry is under wholly different conditions from prose, it will still

occur to every body that the world may be thankful
that Milton and Shakspere did not require so much
time.   Lope de Vega, with his eighteen hundred plays,
may have been in excess of speed ; but literature would
have no chance if the elaboration and expression of
thought and feeling were so sophisticated as they must
be by extreme timidity or excessive polish.

Mr. Hallam, taking up a proof-sheet from my table,
one day, while I was at work on the second volume of
the same book, expressed his surprise at my venturing
to press before the whole was finished and tied up ; and
said that he should not have nerve to do this.   I think
he agreed with me that much depends on whether the
work is or is not composed of complete sections,—of
distinct parts,—each of which is absolutely finished
in its own place.   He was industrious when at work ;
but he did it for pleasure, and took as much time as
he pleased about it.   When I first knew him, his hand-
writing was one of the finest I ever saw; and there
was a remarkable elegance about the whole aspect of
his authorship.—Mr. Rogers's hand was old-fashioned
and formal, but so clear that you might teach a child
to read from it.—I have mentioned the appearance of
Carlyle's proof-sheets.   His manuscript is beautifully
neat, when finished ; and a page holds a vast quantity
of his small upright writing.   But his own account of
his toil in authorship is melancholy.   He cannot sleep
for the sense of the burden on his mind of what he has
to say ; rises weary, and is wretched till he has had his
coffee.   No mode of expression pleases him ; and, by
the time his work is out, his faculties are over-wearied.
It is a great object in his case to have the evenings
amused, that his work may not take possession of his

mind before bedtime. His excessive slowness is a perfect mystery to me,—considering that the work is burdensome. If he dwelt lovingly on its details, and on his researches, I could understand it. But perhaps he does, more than he is aware of. If not, his noble vocation is indeed a hard one.

Almost every one of these is late in sitting down; and I believe few write every day. Mrs. Somerville's family did not breakfast early; and she ordered her household affairs before sitting down to work. She worked till two only; but then, it was such work! Dr. Somerville told me that he once laid a wager with a friend that he would abuse Mrs. Somerville in a loud voice to her face, and she would take no notice; and he did so. Sitting close to her, he confided to his friend the most injurious things,—that she rouged, that she wore a wig, and other such nonsense, uttered in a very loud voice; her daughters were in a roar of laughter, while the slandered wife sat placidly writing. At last, her husband made a dead pause after her name, on which she looked up with an innocent, 'Did you speak to me?'

Sir Charles Lyell sits down late, and says he is satisfied with a very few pages: but then, his work is of a kind which requires research as he proceeds; and pages are no measure of work in that case. In writing my 'History of the Peace,' I was satisfied with seven manuscript pages per day; whereas, in general, I do not like to fall short of ten or twelve.—Dr. Chalmers was another mystery to me. He told me that it was a heavy sin to write (for press) longer than two hours per day;—that two hours out of the twenty-four are as much of that severest labour as the human brain is

L

fitted to endure. Yet he must have written faster
than that, to produce his works. Dr. Channing entirely agreed with Dr. Chalmers, and was apt to tax
people with rashness who wrote faster. His practice
was, when in Rhode Island, to saunter round the garden once every hour, and then come back to the desk:
and when in Boston, he went to the drawing-room instead, or walked about in his library. No person can
judge for another; but we used to compare notes. I
wondered how he could ever get or keep his ideas in
train, under such frequent interruption : and he was
no less surprised at my experience;—that every hour
is worth double the last for six hours, and that eight
are not injurious when one's subject naturally occupies
them : but then, it is an indispensable condition that
there shall be no interruptions. The dissipation of
mind caused by interruption is a worse fatigue than
that of continuous attention.—Southey and Miss
Edgeworth wrote in the common sitting-room, in
the midst of the family. This I cannot understand,
though I am writing this Memoir under circumstances
which compel me to surrender my solitude. Under a
heart-disease, I cannot expect or ask to be left alone :
and I really find no *gêne* from the presence of one person, while writing this simple and plain account of my
life. I can imagine that Miss Edgeworth's stories
would not require very much concentration; but how
a man can write epics in the midst of the family circle
is inconceivable, even to some of Southey's warmest
admirers. The comment is inevitable;—that his
poems might have been a good deal better, if he had
placed himself under the ordinary conditions of good
authorship.—Wordsworth was accustomed to compose

his verses in his solitary walks, carry them in his memory, and get wife or daughter to write them down on his return.—The varieties of method are indeed great. One acquaintance of mine takes a fit of writing,—a review or a pamphlet,—and sends his wife to an evening party without him. He scribbles, as fast as his pen will go, on half sheets of paper, which he lets fly to the floor when finished ;—i.e., when a dozen or a score of lines run awry, so as to cover the greater part of the expanse. His wife, returning after midnight, finds him sitting amidst a litter of paper, some inches deep,—unless he has previously summoned the butler to sweep them up in his arms and put them somewhere. By five in the morning the pamphlet is done. How it is ever got into order for press I cannot imagine.—But enough ! I have met with almost every variety of method among living authors; and almost every variety of view as to the seriousness of their vocation. But I believe the whole fraternity are convinced that the act of authorship is the most laborious effort that men have to make : and in this they are probably right : for I have never met with a physician who did not confirm their conviction by his ready testimony.

APPENDIX A.

MISS BERRY.

From the 'Daily News' of November 29, 1852.

AN event occurred last Saturday night which makes us ask ourselves whether we have really passed the middle of our century. In the course of Saturday night, the twentieth of November, one died who could and did tell so much of what happened early in the reign of George the Third, that hearers felt as if they were in personal relations with the men of that time. Miss Berry was remarkable enough in herself to have excited a good deal of emotion by dying any time within the last seventy years. Dying now, she leaves as strong as ever the impression of her admirable faculties, her generous and affectionate nature, and her high accomplishments, while awaken · ing us to a retrospect of the changes and fashions of our English in tellect, as expressed by literature. She was not only the woman of letters of the last century carried forward into our own—she was not only the woman of fashion who was familiar with the gaieties of life before the fair daughters of George the Third were seen abroad, and who had her own will and way with society up to last Saturday night: she was the repository of the whole literary history of fourscore years ; and when she was pleased to throw open the folding-doors of her memory, they were found to be mirrors, and in them was seen the whole procession of literature, from the mournful Cowper to Tennyson the laureate.

It was a curious sight—visible till recently, though now all are gone—the chatting of three ladies on the same sofa—the two Miss

Berrys and their intimate friend, Lady Charlotte Lindsay. Lady Charlotte Lindsay was the daughter of Lord North; and the Miss Berrys had both received, as was never any secret, the offer of the hand of Horace Walpole. It is true he was old, and knew himself to be declining, and made this offer as an act of friendship and gratitude; but still, the fact remains that she, who died last Saturday night, might have been the wife of him who had the poet Gray for his tutor. These ladies brought into our time a good deal of the manners, the conversation and the dress of the last century; but not at all in a way to cast any restraint on the youngest of their visitors, or to check the inclination to inquire into the thoughts and ways of men long dead and the influence of modes long passed away. It was said that Miss Berry's parties were rather blue; and perhaps they were so; but she was not aware of it: and all thought of contemporary pedantry dissolved under her stories of how she once found on the table, on her return from a ball, a volume of 'Plays on the Passions,' and how she kneeled on a chair at the table to see what the book was like, and was found there—feathers and satin shoes and all—by the servant who came to let in the winter morning light; or of how the world of literature was perplexed and distressed—as a swarm of bees that have lost their queen—when Dr. Johnson died; or of how Charles Fox used to wonder that people could make such a fuss about that dullest of new books—Adam Smith's 'Wealth of Nations.' He was an Eton boy, just promised a trip to Paris by his father, when Miss Berry was born; and Pitt was a child in the nursery, probably applauded by his maid for success in learning to speak plain. Burns was then toddling in and out, over the threshold of his father's cottage. Just when she was entering on the novel-reading age, Evelina came out; and Fanny Burney's series of novels were to that generation of young people what Scott's were to the next but one. If the youths and maidens of that time had bad fiction, they had good history; for the learned Mr. Gibbon gave them volume after volume which made them proud of their age. They talked about their poets, and, no doubt, each had an idol in that day as in ours and every body's. The earnestness, sense, feeling and point of Cowper delighted some; and they reverently told of the sorrows of his secluded life, as glimpses were caught of him in his walks with Mrs. Unwin.   Others stood on tiptoe to peep into Dr. Darwin's 'chaise' as he went his professional round, writing and polishing his verses as he went; and his admirers insisted that nothing so brilliant had ever been written before.   Miss Berry must have well remembered the first exhibition of this brilliancy before the careless eyes of the world : and she must have remembered the strangeness of the impression when Crabbe tried the contrast of his homely pathos, encouraged to do so by Burke. And then came something which it is scarcely credible that the world should have received during the period of Johnson's old age, and the maturity of Gibbon, and Sir William Jones, and Burns—the wretched rhyming of the Batheaston set of sentimental pedants.   In rebuke of them, the now mature woman saw the theory of Wordsworth arise; and in rebuke of him, she saw the young and confident Jeffrey and his comrades arise ; and in rebuke of them, saw the 'Quarterly Review' arise, when she was beginning to be elderly. She saw Joanna Baillie's great fame rise and decline, without either the rise or decline changing in the least the countenance or the mood of the happy being whose sunshine came from quite another luminary than fame. She saw the rise of Wordsworth's fame, growing as it did out of the reaction against the pomps and vanities of the Johnsonian and Darwinian schools ; and she lived to see its decline when the great purpose was fulfilled, of inducing poets to say what they mean, in words which will answer that purpose. She saw the beginning and the end of Moore's popularity ; and the rise and establishment of Campbell's.   The short career of Byron passed before her eyes like a summer storm : and that of Scott constituted a great interest of her life for many years. What an experience—to have studied the period of horrors—represented by Monk Lewis—of conventionalism in Fanny Burney—of metaphysical fiction in Godwin—of historical romance in Scott—and of a new order of fiction in Dickens, which it is yet too soon to characterise by a phrase.

We might go on for hours, and not exhaust the history of what she saw on the side of literature alone. If we attempted to number the scientific men who have crossed her threshold—the foreigners who found within her doors the best of London and the cream of society, we should never have done. And what a series of political changes she saw—the continental wars, the establishment of American independence—the long series of French revolutions—the career of Washington, of Napoleon, of Nelson, of Wellington, with that of all the statesmen from Lord Chatham to Peel—from Franklin to Webster! But it is too much. It is bewildering to us, though it never overpowered her. She seemed to forget nothing, and to notice every thing, and to be able to bear so long a life in such times; but she might well be glad to sink to sleep, as she did last Saturday night after so long-drawn a pageant of the world's pomps and vanities, and transient idolatries and eternal passions.

Reviewing the spectacle, it appears to us, as it probably did to her, that there is no prevalent taste, at least in literature, without a counteraction on the spot, preparing society for a reaction. Miss Berry used to say that she published the later volumes of Walpole's correspondence to prove that the world was wrong in thinking him heartless; she believing the appearance of heartlessness in him to be ascribable to the influence of his time. She did not succeed in changing the world's judgment of her friend; and this was partly because the influences of the time did not prevent other men from showing heart. Charles James Fox had a heart; and so had Burke and a good many more. While Johnson and then Darwin were corrupting men's taste in diction, Cowper was keeping it pure enough to enjoy the three rising poets, alike only in their plainness of speech—Crabbe, Burns, and Wordsworth. Before Miss Burney had exhausted our patience, the practical Maria Edgeworth was growing up. While Godwin would have engaged us wholly with the interior scenery of man's nature, Scott was fitting up his theatre for his mighty procession of costumes, with men in them to set them moving; and Jane Austen, whose name and works will outlive many that were supposed immortal, was stealthily putting forth her unmatched delineations of domestic life in the middle classes of our aristocratic England. And against the somewhat feeble elegance of Sir William Jones's learning there was the safeguard of Gibbon's marvellous combination of strength and richness in his erudition. The vigour of Campbell's lyrics was a set-off against the prettiness of Moore's. The subtlety of Coleridge meets its match, and a good deal more, in the development of science; and the morose complainings of Byron are less and less echoed now that the peace has opened the world to gentry whose energies would be self-corroding if they were under blockade at home, through an universal continental war. Byron is read at sea now, on the way to the North Pole, or to California, or to Borneo; and in that way his woes can do no harm. To every thing there is a season; and to every fashion of a season there is an antagonism preparing. Thus all things have their turn; all human faculties have their stimulus, sooner or later, supposing them to be put in the way of the influences of social life.

It was eminently so in the case of the aged lady who is gone from us; and well did her mind respond to the discipline offered by her long and favourable life of ninety years. One would like to know how she herself summed up such an experience as hers,—the spectacle of so many everlasting things dissolved—so many engrossing things forgotten—so many settled things set afloat again, and floated out of sight. Perhaps those true words wandered once more into her mind as her eyes were closing :--

> 'We are such stuff
> As dreams are made of; and our little life
> Is rounded with a sleep.'

END OF THE FIRST VOLUME.

If you would like to know more about Virago books, write to us at Ely House, 37 Dover Street, London W1X 4HS for a full catalogue.

Please send a stamped addressed envelope

VIRAGO
Advisory Group

Andrea Adam
Carol Adams
Sally Alexander
Rosalyn Baxandall (USA)
Anita Bennett
Liz Calder
Beatrix Campbell
Angela Carter
Mary Chamberlain
Anna Coote
Jane Cousins
Jill Craigie
Anna Davin
Rosalind Delmar
Christine Downer (Australia)

Zoë Fairbairns
Carolyn Faulder
Germaine Greer
Jane Gregory
Suzanne Lowry
Jean McCrindle
Cathy Porter
Alison Rimmer
Elaine Showalter (USA)
Spare Rib Collective
Mary Stott
Rosalie Swedlin
Margaret Walters
Elizabeth Wilson
Barbara Wynn

Book Tokens

Give them
the pleasure of choosing
Book Tokens can be bought
and exchanged at most
bookshops